F-35

F-35

The Inside Story of the Lightning II

TOM BURBAGE
BETSY CLARK
ADRIAN PITMAN

with DAVID POYER

Skyhorse Publishing

Skyhorse Publishing books may be purchased in bulk at special discounts for sales promotion, corporate gifts, fund-raising, or educational purposes. Special editions can also be created to specifications. For details, contact the Special Sales Department, Skyhorse Publishing, 307 West 36th Street, 11th Floor, New York, NY 10018 or info@skyhorsepublishing.com.

Skyhorse® and Skyhorse Publishing® are registered trademarks of Skyhorse Publishing, Inc.®, a Delaware corporation.

Visit our website at www.skyhorsepublishing.com.

10 9 8 7 6 5 4 3 2

Library of Congress Cataloging-in-Publication Data is available on file.

Cover design by David Ter-Avanesyan
Cover image courtesy of Lockheed Martin

ISBN: 978-1-5107-7757-6
Ebook ISBN: 978-1-5107-7767-5

Printed in the United States of America

CONTENTS

LIST OF PHOTOS AND FIGURES

PREFACE

The F-35's journey through time has been unlike any other in the annals of aerospace and defense history. It was devised under the gospel of acquisition reform, it undertook the unprecedented challenge of unifying three very different US armed services in a common platform to replace ten existing and aging aircraft, it involved eight other allied nations in the development and production phases, and it was charged with delivering transformational military capability across the joint allied partnership.

The F-35 has been vilified by critics from multiple corners. A barrage of headlines over the last two decades has focused on its cost and delays and has highlighted every problem and bump in the road. It is a program of near-unfathomable complexity along multiple dimensions that include the integration of transformational new technologies.

The design, development, and production have proceeded against a backdrop of international stakeholders and a supply chain spanning all eight partner countries and thousands of companies, within an environment of interservice rivalries and competition for dollars. Somehow, amid a roar of criticism, some deserved but much ill-informed and driven by competing interests, the program continued on.

This book captures that journey through the accumulation of over one hundred interviews with the people that made it happen. The program challenges, trials, setbacks, and successes are documented through their eyes. The idea for the book came about from discussions between Adrian Pitman, who led a series of six reviews for the Australian Government Department of Defence, and Betsy Clark, who participated in those reviews. Betsy's first introduction to the program was as part of a mandatory US Department of Defense F-35 review team following the Nunn-McCurdy breach in early 2010. Over the initial series of reviews, Pitman and Clark had a growing and shared sense that the program, while far from perfect, was unfairly maligned in the press and that the program's accomplishments were not well appreciated outside of the people intimately involved in the program. Their original idea was to write a case study for future program managers in the government and contractor communities. They approached Steve Over, who at that time was Lockheed's lead for Australia. Steve enthusiastically endorsed the idea and approached Lockheed Martin to obtain support in allowing Pitman and Clark to interview specific individuals to gain the benefit of their experience and advice. Permission was also granted by the F-35 Joint Program Office and the Australian Government Department of Defence. This book would have never gotten off the ground without Steve Over's assistance.

One of the people interviewed was Tom Burbage, who had retired, but who, as the former general manager of the F-35 program over a thirteen-year period, had unmatched knowledge about the program's history and its many twists and turns. Burbage offered to help and joined forces with Pitman and Clark. At this point, the book transformed from a case study to a book for a more general audience encompassing the human journey of the F-35 from its very beginnings. The journey moves from the research programs in the 1980s and 1990s to the competition between the X-32 and X-35 concept demonstrators and the contract award in 2001 that changed the course of history in several ways. It recounts the multitude of challenges, some technical, many human, to the ultimate delivery of the F-35 to the warfighters of the US services and their international allies.

The F-35 program is unlike any previous program. Hundreds of thousands of people have been involved around the world in its challenges and in its success. The real storytellers of this book are the more than one hundred people who participated in the interviews and the many hundreds of thousands of other people both in the government and contractor communities around the world who have been involved in the program over its more-than-twenty-five-year history and who continue to make the F-35 a reality. This is their story.

Chapter 1

A DARK AND STORMY NIGHT

Contemplate this:

You're standing on the deck of a rather small ship, far out on a sky-tented sea. A chill rain drizzles down as the cold creeps through your flight suit. The steel deck, only a few yards wide, rises and falls with a booming roar. An icy wind slaps your cheeks, ruffling your hair and stinging your eyes until tears run.

Beside you, towering over you, rises an aircraft. Assembled, it seems, of angular, slanted surfaces, with abrupt juts to the broad wings and canted twin tail fins. It's painted—or is that actually paint?—in strange, muted hues of light and dark gray. Its insignia are a paler fog on the dark slate of a shark's back. And it does resemble a shark, with aggressive fins and forward-jutting, sharp-edged intakes. Its flattened fuselage blends smoothly into a thick wing, giving it a husky, broad-shouldered appearance. Yet everything is smoothly faired. Not even a bomb pylon mars the sleek lines. Its lethality is hidden from sight in internal weapon bays.

A warplane, obviously. Yet there's no runway here. Not even a catapult. Just a not-so-large patch of American steel, far out on a stormy, whitecapped sea.

This futuristic-looking machine is the end product of the most expensive defense program in history, one more costly than the Manhattan Project, Polaris, or Trident. More than the B-2 stealth bomber. But those sound bites are deceptive and often misunderstood. The F-35 program replaces fourteen different aircraft in the flying services of the United States and our closest allies. A true accounting of final costs would have to factor in major savings in training expenses, combined operations, and sustainment over the course of this massive upgrade from a miscellany of aging, less-capable air fleets.

But this isn't the fastest plane ever built, though it's fast. Or the most maneuverable, though it's a bitter opponent in a dogfight. Nor the most heavily armed, or possessing the longest range, or carrying the heaviest bomb load, or reaching the highest operational ceiling.

None of these traditional attributes of a successful warplane even hints at the most revolutionary aspect of this implausible aircraft.

Modern war is still, in the end, taken to the enemy with bombs and missiles. Yet that's only the final link in what the military calls the "kill chain." Long before that point, a network of human intelligence assets, satellites, sensors, and computers has detected, classified, and localized those targets.

But, of course, the enemy operates sensors, radars, and computers too, many of them just as advanced as ours. To keep us from scoring our goals.

So, to survive in the face of modern defenses, an aircraft must become . . . nonexistent. Invisible. Transparent, not just to radar, but to infrared vision, and to other, passive detectors, which listen for an attacker's communications and radars, as well.

The aircraft standing beside you on this rain-swept deck can eradicate any trace of itself. Not only that. It can mislead and disorder those advanced enemy sensors. Presenting false targets, or none at all. Confusing, sabotaging, and crippling enemy missiles and radar from a distance, without ever dropping an explosive or triggering a gun.

Until it, or accompanying, less-stealthy aircraft, goes in for the kill.

This warplane of the future is being built in three versions. The A variant is the "conventional" model, designed for takeoff and landing on land-based military airstrips or civilian airfields. Destined for the U.S. Air Force and foreign air forces, it is the "Swiss Army Knife" of coalition future fighter forces. The B version—your plane, here on the slanting deck, today—adds a short takeoff capability, and can land vertically, like a helicopter. It's tailored for the U.S. Marines and for deployment from small ships and secondary or expeditionary airfields, or even sections of civilian highways. The C version is designed to absorb the much higher structural loads of catapult launches and arrested landings aboard the U.S. Navy's big deck aircraft carriers. Its slightly larger wing allows it to fly its approaches at lower speeds, making it much safer in the shipboard landing phase. That larger wing, and additional volume available from not carrying an internally mounted gun, also allows it to carry additional fuel, thereby extending the carrier battle group's striking range.

The aircraft on the rain-swept deck next to you is the F-35B Lightning II. And you're about to fly it on a combat mission.

"Lieutenant?" Your crew chief beckons. In coveralls, boots, a helmet, and ear protectors, she hoists a thumb. "You're good to go."

After a quick walkaround you climb in, mounting via an internal ladder that drops down, allowing the pilot to scale one smooth side of the craft. Following you up, the crew chief buckles you in snugly. Your "brick," a combination of your physical stature, your mission requirements, and your cyber protection code, is inserted and marries you with your aircraft. In front of you, instead of multiple dials, switches and indicators, is one panoramic touch screen. You activate an umbilical cord, connecting you to the life-support systems of the mother ship, welding human and machine into one integrated fighting element. And lastly, don your helmet, connecting you to the real-world video arcade.

You start the engine. Its turbine spools upward with a whine, quickly growing into a deafening roar that seeps through your helmet's sound protection and vibrates through your soul.

And just like that, you're superhuman. Like Argus, the farsighted, many-eyed watchman of Greek myth. The helmet-mounted display lets you see the contours of the land, far to the west. Every ship and plane and terrain feature for hundreds of miles around. The helmet feeds you warmed oxygen, maintains pressure even if the cockpit's shattered by enemy fire, and scrubs the carbon dioxide from your breath. Essentially, you're wearing a space suit. The helmet of this one, however, also has a media room built in. High-definition cameras surface mounted within the aircraft's fuselage feed live video to a mission computer. The computer stitches the entire 360-degree surround into a single scene that seamlessly follows your head movement. You don't see the aircraft you're sitting in. Instead, you're suspended in space. When you look down now, you see the ship's deck beneath you.

The aircraft you're warming up for combat is the first true fifth-generation multi-role, multiservice coalition fighter.

But even that term is a misnomer. A "fighter" isn't all the Lightning is, by a long shot. The F-35's talent at instantaneously collecting, analyzing, then sharing information across a whole theater of war—day and night, in any weather, while remaining hidden from enemy defenses or countermeasures—makes it far more.

During World War II, it took weeks of research, planning, rehearsal, and thousands of men and women—spies, radar operators, SIGINT interpreters, observers, plotters, high-altitude reconnaissance, photo analysts, then the pilots, navigators, gunners, and bombardiers of hundreds of bomber aircraft and escorting fighters—to destroy one high-value enemy target . . . such as a ball-bearing factory.

This single aircraft you're sitting in could have destroyed the entire plant complex at Schweinfurt, Germany, on its own. In minutes. And never have been spotted.

It could have detected, localized, and shattered the tanks of the 21st Panzer Division as they clanked toward the beach at Normandy. All on its own.

It could have evaded the Nazi radar and early warning systems, detected the buried bunker in Berlin, and killed the genocidal dictator in his subterranean lair with one concrete-penetrating bomb.

A flight of four Lightning IIs could have done all these things, and ended that war, on the same mission.

While you were belting in, the plane's internal diagnostics have been busy. Nearly 1,200 hardware components share software handshakes in seconds to ensure mission readiness. You don't need to compare dozens of dials to a checklist, or cycle rudder or ailerons. Any flaw or fault will be presented automatically on your screen. A glance is all you need to reassure yourself all systems are go.

Out on the deck, you spot the Fly 1 Petty Officer responsible for the silent-launch process. You turn on your wingtip lights, signaling you're ready to go. He touches the deck with his covert night wand, clearing you to launch.

You check the screen one last time and advance the throttle to full power.

Heavier-than-air flight has always depended on engines. The Wright brothers' four-cylinder aluminum-block engine, more powerful for its weight than any before, allowed them to finally lurch a few yards into the air. That pitifully primitive power plant generated a whopping twelve horsepower.

But behind you now, a Pratt & Whitney F135 radar and infrared stealthy afterburning jet engine is spooling up to generate 43,000 pounds of thrust. Thirty thousand horsepower, 2,500 times more muscle than the Wrights had. The most powerful fighter engine ever built, and the most complex.

You'll need every erg to get aloft. Almost half of the aircraft around you is fabricated of advanced structural composites, including lighter-weight epoxies in which carbon nanotubes are embedded. But it still weighs sixty thousand pounds. About a quarter of that is fuel.[1] Your internal weapon bays are loaded with two tons of air-to-ground and air-to-air weapons. Once enemy air defenses are mitigated, you can also carry weapons externally, on pylons, at the sacrifice of some stealth.

A large rear-opening door lifts behind the cockpit, exposing a ducted fan. The noise builds to a roar, only partially masked by the helmet and cockpit soundproofing. You begin your takeoff roll to generate early lift over the wings. The engine nozzle swings down, adding its thrust to that of the counterrotating lift fan. They both strain to bench-press thirty tons of fuel, electronics, weapons, airframe, and pilot.

As the deck quickly recedes, you're airborne and accelerating. The lift fan disengages, and the lift-fan door slowly closes. Your F-35B is now nearly identical to any other advanced enemy fighter in the up-and-away flight regime.

The ship shrinks to a gray dot in a black, wind-whipped sea.

Aloft, your sensors sharpen. Your view reaches out literally hundreds of miles. Your consciousness expands in a vast sphere. Multi-spectrum sensors on wings and fuselage stream data into your computers, interpreting infinitesimally minute pulses of radar and visible and infrared light into actionable intelligence. Even far from the approaching coast, you can peer deep inland. You can make out individual tanks parked in a dense forest. You can distinguish actual missile batteries from inflated dummies. Or identify and track aircraft or drones, even those flying at treetop level.

And you're not alone. Every allied ship, plane, and ground force in the entire battlespace is an information-sharing node, and you know and see everything they do.

A warning tone sounds in your earphones, and a scarlet symbol winks to life on your helmet visor. The plane's calling your attention to a possible threat. You zoom in with electro-optics. A patrol boat's lurking in a mangrove swamp off the coast you're approaching. Your systems identify it as enemy. You agree, tag it for destruction, and hand off the info to a British carrier far to seaward of you, maintaining a combat air patrol. Within minutes, a British F-35B, acting on your targeting information, releases a smart bomb. A massive blast strews fire, fragments, and torn-apart bodies across the hidden stream and into the jungle. Moments later a secondary explosion rips the foliage, as a stockpile of shells hidden nearby goes off as well.

There's only one pilot in your plane, but two intellects. The "back seat driver," your sensor manager, is continuously scanning the environment for threats and targets of opportunity. This artificial intelligence can work autonomously, or you can direct the system's attention to a specific area or type of target. You're the final decision-maker. Once you notice a point of interest, or the sensors call your attention to it, you can zoom in optically and identify it—even in complete darkness—to prevent targeting friendly forces and minimize civilian casualties. But you're getting information from other sources as well: other aircraft, ships, antimissile radars, even satellites passing high above. It's all one picture, as if you had a thousand eyes and ears, senses far beyond human, and a superhumanly fast analyst with you in the cockpit.[2]

It's as if you're one with the Lightning II. A melding of mind and computer. Your own consciousness is ultimately in charge, but with your senses and intelligence augmented and multiplied thousands of times.

Besides being a fighter, the F-35 is also a reconnaissance aircraft, an electronic warfare jamming platform, a warning and control platform, a massively capable data fusion center, a precision night bomber, and a control node for pilotless aircraft. Seven aircraft in one.

Far below, the coast pushes up over the horizon. But what you see in your helmet is "denied battlespace." A hemisphere of air and near-space that an adversary intends to bar against you. An enemy who'll quickly kill you if he can see you. His radars have been searching for you since you left the deck, many miles back. His radar pulses are even now groping to detect your presence, so he can target you.

But those hostile impulses die within your fuselage and wings, trapped and muffled. They're twisted by your computers, and sent back attenuated, altered, until nothing at all registers on the enemy's screens. You're not even a phantom. You are invisible.

But you're still known to the three other aircraft in today's mission. You launched from widely separate locations, so there's no formation, no concentration to vector interceptors against. Two Lightning IIs cruise far ahead of you, scanning and sanitizing the battlespace ahead of your strike mission. And another strike plane, forty miles off your starboard wing, disguises the attack vectors, but is in constant communication with the flight lead. Only one of these escorts is American, a U.S. Air Force F-35A; the others are Australian and Japanese. From time to time, hostile radars flicker, then are extinguished, as your sweepers dispense radar-homing missiles to obliterate surface-to-air batteries, clearing your path.

Then you glimpse something far ahead, pushing up over the blue curve of the earth. A symbol winks on and off: the primary target. Perhaps a command bunker. A transporter-erector-launcher, carrying a road-portable ICBM with a thermonuclear warhead. Or a transport plane, speeding toward a war-torn, savagely tormented country to deliver a load of prohibited weapons to ruthless terrorists.

But new symbols light on your visor. Fast-moving aircraft! To your three o'clock, high! They haven't seen you. Not yet. With a terse voice command, heard only within your mask, you put markers on them. Enemy. Possible target. The symbols illuminate on your binocular view inside the helmet, along with a pulsing green line showing the direction to the primary target. You fly the line but keep a watch on the enemy fighters as your plane keeps you constantly updated on where they are, how fast they're going, and what aircraft type they are. You have that information on your tactical display screen, too.[3]

Engage them? Hmmm . . . you decide not to. When you can see and the other guy can't, you can pick and choose your battles. Why risk a knife fight on the way to a bank heist? But though you're invisible to their radar, you can still be glimpsed with the naked eyeball if they get close enough. If that should happen, you'll pickle off defensive missiles. If those fail, you'll dogfight with cannon, a four-barreled 25mm with 186 rounds. But the good news is, yours is a very maneuverable plane. It's forgiving, easy to fly, and almost impossible to stall or spin.[4]

Pulling an incredibly abrupt maneuver, you slow, roll hard right, and dive for the forest, skimming the treetops at a hundred feet. The enemy fighters, the latest in their inventory, flash overhead without detecting you. Then, suddenly, they begin to dodge, evade, and finally explode and fall. One of your sweep planes, also invisible, has cut down their ranks with supersonic missiles that seem to suddenly assemble themselves out of empty space.

Altering course again, you set up for the final leg of the mission. The smart bombs you carry don't depend on GPS. They derive their positioning from your computers, updated instant by instant with inertial guidance. If the target's on the move, its position is fed to those same computers by the network of sensors. They knit the sky with invisible beams from overhead, from far over the horizon, from your own aircraft, and from a deep-cover team of special forces operators thirty miles away.

As weapon door clamshells open in the smoothly faired belly the plane gives the bomb its last instructions. You don't need to worry about flying the right approach. You've pushed a button. Locking the plane into the attack pattern. You could almost go to sleep. Except of course you can't! The enemy may still offer a surprise. So, you stay alert, continually scanning. Managing your battle space. You issue a final permission, and a moment later the weapon drops away. It will guide itself from here, correcting course, then detonating at last above the surface, at ground level, or far beneath, depending on its target. Meanwhile you've banked smoothly away, heading for the next objective.

Half an hour later you're headed back. Not for the ship, but to land on a captured island. It pushes up over the horizon, a dreadfully short strip of asphalted road that would take the pilot of any other aircraft hundreds of flight hours to dare tackling. All you need to do is line up, press a button on your throttle, and the plane holds approach landing speed and the proper angle of attack. You nudge it a bit to correct for wind. You've used up most of your fuel and expended most of your ordnance, putting the jet in the envelope for a vertical landing. You touch down exactly on the designated point and as the wheels thump to the ground, the engine drops to idle.

Time to clamber out for a short break while the crew swarms over the plane, refueling and rearming. Then you climb in again for the next sortie.

★ ★ ★

You've just flown a sample mission in the F-35.

Now you understand why the "Lightning II," also known as the Joint Strike Fighter, is the most advanced aircraft ever built. The most capable single plane that flies in the world today.

Also, the most complex. It's been called "the costliest and most technically challenging weapons program the Pentagon has ever attempted."[5] Running the mission you just returned from required nearly 9 million lines of computer code and thousands of person-years of coding and debugging. To put that in perspective, the Apollo 11 Lander required only 145,000 lines of code, and NASA's Mars Curiosity Rover about 2.5 million.[6]

The cost for developing, producing, operating, and sustaining the fleet over the lifetime of the jet, is by some estimates pushing a trillion and a half dollars . . . but no program has ever tried to estimate those costs. The same estimators say that the cost of the family of airplanes the F-35 is replacing, under the same set of assumptions, may be three to four times more expensive.

This flying marvel has its detractors. In development for over fifteen years before the first declaration of initial operational capability, with two significant cost overruns, one of which resulted from a redesign, it's been called a "scandal," a "global wrecking ball," and a "fiasco" by critical journalists. It's been attacked for problems in its oxygen supply systems, landing gear, ejection seat, and helmet and for its weight, mission reliability, maintenance expenses, software glitches, aeronautic design, logistics footprint, exhaust temperature, low sortie rate, limited range, stall recovery, testing delays, and dozens of other alleged or real shortfalls or compromises.[7] Not all of these issues were significant. Many were corrected before the reporting agencies even released their negative evaluations. But as early costs increased and delivery dates were pushed further into the future, initially enthusiastic partner nations reevaluated their participation. In some cases, partners reduced their buys.

Today, it's the future of both air defense and offensive operations for all of the original partners, with the exception of Turkey, which was kicked out of the program in 2019 after buying Russian's S-400 missile defense system. That makes a dozen nations: the United States, Britain, the Netherlands, Italy, Israel, Australia, Denmark, Japan, Norway, South Korea, Canada, and Singapore. In addition, following the Russian invasion of Ukraine, Poland, Belgium, Finland, Switzerland, Germany, and others are now lining up to be part of the F-35 alliance. To date, the F-35 has not lost a competitive evaluation by any allied air force.

The Lightning II has also become famous as the most heavily spied-upon program since the Manhattan Project. The most aggressive cyberattacks in history have targeted it. These cyberattacks have been launched by China, but also by Russia, North Korea, and possibly other state and nonstate actors. They salivate for the smallest detail: design specifics, maintenance procedures, performance statistics, diagnostics, sensor spectra. Complicating security, production has been spread among eight NATO allies and hundreds of contractors, with each having access to different tranches of data. Thus, penetration of a less rigorously cyber-defended ally or small contractor may provide access to secrets that are more closely guarded in the United States or Britain. Chinese cyber penetrations by the Technical Reconnaissance Bureau, were passed to the state-run aviation industry. They are being used to build a new fighter that attempts to mimic the capabilities of the F-35.

Widely derided first as too futuristic and ambitious, then as too expensive and complicated, the Lightning has retraced the developmental history of every breakthrough weapons system, from the *Monitor* to the Garand rifle. It was called impossible, then derided, and finally recognized as indispensable. The fighter will fly until the middle of this century—and if history is any guide, far longer. It's already seen action in the skies of Syria with the Israeli Defense Forces and is forward deployed with the U.S. Marines and U.S. Air Force in the Pacific. Like its namesake predecessors, the twin-boom Lockheed P-38 Lightning and the English Electric Lightning supersonic interceptor, our leaders expect it to penetrate the skies of our enemies at will and wreak havoc on aggressors while holding them at arm's length from our homeland and those of our allies.

But history's also replete with "wonder weapons" that never worked. Along with *Monitor*s and Spitfires came hydrogen-filled battle dirigibles, Brewster Buffalos, and the Puckle Gun. Not to mention others that were simply so expensive that although effective in a limited way, they exhausted a nation's treasury and ultimately weakened it—think the V-2, or the Maginot Line.

Which will the F-35 Lightning ultimately be? Only time will tell. But for better or for worse, in a very real sense the West has pushed in all its chips to bet on this one plane. The evidence to date, based on limited operational experience and exercises, says it's a winning wager.

In the pages to come, you'll read about the F-35's four precursor programs and how they were rolled into an overarching vision of one fighter to rule them all.[8] You'll witness its development and growing pains, its challenges and setbacks. You'll see how heroic men and women, engineers and test pilots, military and civilian, managers and technicians, labored to break through the iron gates of politics and the more arcane yet even more robust barriers of advanced technology. They pioneered new accomplishments in high angle of attack and low-speed flight. They integrated and built on the forty other vertical takeoff and landing (VTOL) aircraft that preceded this one but with the sole exception of the Harrier and the V-22 Osprey, never attained operational status. They overcame skepticism, criticism, and doom-laden jeremiads from the Congressional Research Service and the GAO and from multiple participating nations.

"Expanding the envelope," as test pilots say, became an everyday occurrence. Engineers advanced the state of the art in aerodynamics, cybersecurity, computer engineering, and defense analysis to forge an invisible sword of awesome, nearly godlike power. As the program dodged potholes and icebergs, managers negotiated and horse-traded with political and military leaders in six languages and four continents. This complex sarabande of dramatic reversals and near-disasters at times left the program nearly dead, and the alliance nearly defenseless against hostile and quickly advancing peer competitors overseas. Security experts, programmers, and counterespionage operatives had to wage a whole new campaign of shadowy battle to keep these hard-won secrets from a cunning and deceitful adversary and secure the Holy Grail of advanced technology against those who would steal it from the Holy of Holies.

It's a compelling drama, packed with more twists and turns than the fictions of Tom Clancy or Alan Furst. And that's where this book will take you.

The settings will be the design teams at Lockheed Martin and Pratt & Whitney, the testing grounds at Edwards and Eglin and Pax River and at sea. The cabinet offices of Canberra and Ottawa and London. The halls of Congress and the Pentagon and their partner equivalents. And, most importantly, the shop floors where workers around the world toiled to build a weapon system like none before it, with materials new to aircraft fabrication.

The cast of characters will include pilots, politicians, managers, engineers, and workers, all the way from the guys and gals who "bend metal" to the "green eyeshades" who fight to keep the program on budget and on schedule.

This book is the epic chronicle of a dream conceived in vaunting ambition and pushed resolutely ahead despite enormous technical and political obstacles. An idea that was attacked, derided, and set back . . . yet whose proponents still persisted. They were spied on, defunded, defended, and debugged. But at long last their incredible warbird rose screaming into the sky, with grace and power and maneuverability and deadliness that has astonished the planet and dismayed those who consider themselves our adversaries.

This will be the story of that aircraft, and of those men and women.

The amazing true story of the Lightning II.

Reference

1. Rick Attaway, "F-35." International Powered Conference presentation, 2010.

2. LtGen David Deptula, "Airpower Evolution: Moving into the Information Age," Headquarters USAF briefing, April 14, 2010.

3. Interview with Lockheed Martin chief test pilot Al Norman, by Betsy Clark and Adrian Pitman on November 17, 2017. Held in F-35 Interview Archive.

4. Ibid.

5. Siobham Gorman et al. "Computer Spies Breach Fighter-Jet Project," *Wall Street Journal*, April 21, 2009.

6. Johnson, Phil, "Curiosity about Lines of Code," *Computerworld*, August 8, 2012.

7. GAO Report, "F-35 JOINT STRIKE FIGHTER: DOD Needs to Complete Developmental Testing Before Making Significant New Investments," April 24, 2017.

8. Attaway, op. cit.

Chapter 2

HISTORY OF FIGHTER AIRCRAFT

The development of heavier-than-air fighting craft paralleled the rapid evolution of modern warfare in the twentieth and twenty-first centuries. The very earliest days, roughly 1900–1914, produced wood, wire, and fabric airplanes based on early observations of avian flight by Otto Lilienthal, the Wrights, Octave Chanute, and others.

The first necessity of powered flight is lift: the upward force necessary to counteract gravity and hoist the weight of an earthbound object into the air. Generating lift depends on a deep understanding of wing camber and other elements of basic aerodynamic engineering. For sustained flight it must be artificially generated, not a secondary effect of thermal updrafts or wind. Thus: Thrust, to overcome the entropic influence of drag, or put more simply, enough forward force to overcome air resistance and generate lift via a pressure differential over a moving wing. The final necessity is control, the fine balance of stability and instability that permits a pilot to manage the velocity and direction of a craft in flight.

These basic demands, limited by the available power, materials, and techniques, defined the early challenges of aircraft design. Of course, things quickly become exponentially more complicated.

Although the first combat aircraft were intended for observation, they quickly diversified into subtypes: reconnaissance, transport, bomber, ground attack, and pursuit (fighter). During World War I the single-engine, single-pilot fighter inherited the panache and glamour of the cavalryman. Fighter pilots battled man against man, machine against machine, dueling high above the trenches in the central blue.

The fighter's subsequent evolution has been highlighted by several significant technological innovations.

Consider the fact that the early battles in the clouds were fought with pistols and rifles. The first real advance was mounting a machine gun. Unfortunately, the optimal line of sight, between the pilot's eye and the target, was interrupted by a rapidly rotating propeller, which could quickly be shot away. This required guns to be positioned on top of the upper wing. But this yielded poor accuracy and few lethal results.

The French were the first to come up with an answer, though not a great one. Roland Garros equipped the propeller of his Morane-Saulnier L with steel wedges. As the gun fired, any bullets encountering the propeller would deflect off the plates, one hopes in some other direction than toward the cockpit. He shot down three Germans with the arrangement, but the bullets' impacts delaminated his wooden props.

★ ★ ★

Anthony Fokker, a Dutchman, owned Fokker Aeroplanbau in Johannisthal, Germany. At the outbreak of World War I, the German government took over his factory. Fokker built a line of bi-wing, tri-wing, and finally monoplane fighters, made famous by legendary pilots like the Red Baron, Manfred von Richthofen. Fokker was the largest manufacturer of aircraft in the world at one time. They would also be a key partner many years later on the F-35.

Fokker came up with the Stangensteuerung mechanism. This cam-and-rod arrangement prevented the gun from firing when the prop blade was in the way. Now the gun could be mounted on the forward fuselage just ahead of the pilot, greatly improving his aim. The synchronization-equipped Fokker Eindecker (a monoplane) is considered by many to mark the real beginning of fighter aviation.

The Germans kept their technological lead in this area until mid-1916, when the French and British designers were able to match, then exceed, the German advantage with the excellent SPAD and Sopwith designs, faster, more agile, better-performing platforms for aerial combat.

In the two decades between the end of World War I and just before World War II, military aviation, and particularly fighters, progressed more gradually. Wood and fabric construction reached the limits of speed, maneuverability, and endurance. Only a few aero engines could develop as much as 250 horsepower, and top speeds of 120 miles per hour were exceptional.

The replacement of wood by metal was the next step, but this would be a significant cultural change for an industry dependent on artisanal skill. Although the first all-metal airplane flew as early as 1915, widespread use did not occur until the 1930s. Over the next decade, every major power fielded all-metal monoplanes with closed cockpits and retractable landing gear. Gyroscopically driven flight instruments and electrical cockpit lighting permitted night flying as well as sorties in adverse weather. Pilots were provided with oxygen masks. They could converse with other aircraft and ground stations by voice radio, and parachutes had become standard equipment.

Each of these advances provided incremental advantages to fighter performance but the critical edge still remained the skill of the pilot flying the machine.

One of the most distinctive and influential fighters in the latter stages of World War II was the Lockheed P-38 Lightning, namesake for the F-35. Designed for the Army Air Corps, the P-38 had a distinctive twin-boom design flanking a central nacelle containing the cockpit and armament. Dual turbo-superchargers gave it a significant performance advantage at higher altitudes. The placement of the Lightning's machine guns on the nose was unusual among American fighters of World War II, which usually relied on wing-mounted guns. While wing-mounted guns were calibrated to shoot at converging trajectories of between 100 to 250 yards, the Lightning's straight-ahead arrangement gave its armament a significantly longer useful range. P-38s could reliably deliver concentrated machine gun fire at up to one thousand yards. In addition, the P-38 was the first American fighter to make extensive use of stainless steel and smooth, flush-riveted, butt-jointed aluminum skin panels. These drag reduction techniques made it the first military airplane to fly faster than 400 mph in level flight.[1] (**See Figure 1: Lockheed P-38 Lightning**)

The Republic P-47 Thunderbolt was huge by the standards of World War II and the heaviest fighter of the conflict. Ironically, the "Jug" had initially been conceived as a light interceptor, but between proposal and prototype, the Army raised concerns about the engine, resulting in the substitution of a more powerful one. This in turn meant the plane no longer needed to be small or short-ranged. Two important lessons came out of the Thunderbolt. First, the effect of "requirements creep" on the development of a high-performance fighter requires careful management of critical trade-offs. Second, the eventual operator may change war-fighting tactics to take full advantage of the product he or she is given. Both lessons were hard-learned over the history of fighters and remained key factors in the Joint Strike Fighter program, especially the Short Takeoff and Vertical Landing (STOVL) variant.

The Japanese Mitsubishi A6M "Zero" was the first carrier-based fighter capable of besting land-based opponents. American naval aviators were dismayed to discover their Brewster F2As and Grumman F4F Wildcats were outclassed by the faster, more maneuverable, longer-ranged Zero. It was clear an improved shipboard fighter was needed. Grumman had been working on a successor to the F4F prior to America's entry into the war. Its foldable wings, for easier storage in narrower spaces, allowed aircraft carriers and transports to carry a greater number of fighters. The F6F was faster, more powerful, more maneuverable, and had a longer range than its predecessor. It outclassed the Zero in every way, except maneuverability at low speed.

In parallel with the move to metal construction was the widespread realization by aero designers and engineers that a new propulsion concept was essential. It was physically impossible to design much more speed into an aircraft with a propeller whirling in front of it. The jet engine was independently invented at about the same time in two countries that would soon be at war once more. In Germany, Hans Joachim Pabst von Ohain developed a working gas turbine to power the Heinkel HE 178. In Britain, Royal Air Force officer Frank Whittle received a patent for his concept in 1930. He developed the first jet engine to fly, in the Gloster E 28.

With the jet engine, the limitations of the propeller-driven planes fell away, introducing dramatic new performance regimes and began the elusive chase for the next great fighter. The evolution of future fighter aircraft would pick up the moniker of "Generations."

Each generation of aircraft would be defined by a functional compromise between threat definition and scientific and engineering innovation. A "generational shift" occurs when new technology can no longer be incorporated into existing planes through life-cycle upgrades or retrofits. This presents a challenge. Any new design must overcome current performance limitations, while at the same time the military and industry must accurately specify requirements, usually quickly, to anticipate a possible opponent. These requirements must reach far enough in the future to accommodate the lengthy design, development and fielding time element, while resulting in a plane that will still have combat value years later. Then, designers must use the latest technology, or even develop new technologies, to meet those requirements.

"First generation" jet fighters were the Meteors, Me 262s, and Bell Airacomets coming out of World War II. Aerodynamic designers were providing dramatically increased speeds and altitudes, as well as a dawning understanding of the dynamics of transonic and supersonic flight. Wing shapes were developing from straight wing to swept wing for controllability in these new flight regimes. In terms of sensors, first-generation fighters were limited to visual engagements. Their armament consisted of machine guns, cannon, and unguided bombs and rockets.

There's no clear line between first and second generation, but the experience gained in the Korean War, plus breakthroughs in materials and avionics, drove significant changes for the next iteration of fighters. Onboard radar and guided antiair missiles, like the AIM-7 Sparrow, the AIM-9 Sidewinder, and the K-5 Alkali, coupled with the advent of afterburning turbojet engines, dramatically increased the operating envelope.

Third-generation fighters continued the modernization, but their designers increased the emphasis on aerial maneuvering and ground attack. Experience in Korea and Vietnam emphasized the ability to win close-in dogfights. Aerodynamic enhancements introduced new flight control surfaces, such as canards and variable sweep wings, as well as complex flow-control devices like slats and blown flaps. Early thrust vectoring techniques triggered development of several innovative concepts with STOVL capabilities. Only one would progress to full production, the AV-8 Harrier "jump jet." Air-to-air missiles became the primary weapons, and sophisticated electronic countermeasures increased mission complexity. Finally, rising costs and research difficulties resulted in a new focus on multi-role aircraft. The McDonnell F-4 Phantom became the first fighter in history to be used by every branch of the United States Armed Services.

While the capabilities of airplanes continued to improve, the threat had also evolved. Surface-to-air radars and missile batteries neutralized many of the advances in speed and maneuverability and led to heavy US losses in Vietnam.

Fourth generation fighter jets, such as the F-16 and F-18, MiG-35, Rafale, and Grifon, were almost all multi-role aircraft. Advanced "fly-by-wire" systems—with flight surfaces controlled by computers rather than by hydraulics—allowed designers to relax earlier stability and control constraints. This increased complexity and cost, but dramatically improved maneuverability. Other sophisticated electronics included head-up and multifunction displays, long-range frequency-shifting radars, and more capable missiles. Again, this expanded the tactical capabilities of the fighter. Breakthroughs in advanced composite structures and early stealth applications revolutionized the construction processes. But at the same time, the threat continued to keep pace.

★ ★ ★

In December 1964, three days before Christmas, a revolutionary aircraft took flight for the first time. Legendary aerospace engineer Clarence "Kelly" Johnson based the shape of the SR-71 on the A-12, one of the first aircraft designed with a reduced radar cross section. The Blackbird could operate at speeds above Mach 3 and above 80,000 feet. Even today, its capabilities have not been equaled. Its canted tails and Johnson's application of new materials to withstand the blazing heat of near-hypersonic flight foreshadowed developments that would radically change fighter aviation.

As we've said, during the Vietnam War Soviet- and Chinese-supplied air defenses damaged and shot down a significant number of Allied aircraft. Consequently, the Defense Advanced Research Projects Agency (DARPA) launched an effort to find a way to defeat the very effective radar systems that were defining this new generation of threats. Adding fuel to the fire was a study analyzing Israeli losses in the Yom Kippur War. According to this study, a potential Warsaw Pact invasion across the central European plain would have seen NATO forces "out of airplanes" in a fortnight.[2]

In 1975, Ben Rich became the head of Lockheed's famed Skunk Works in Burbank, California. Under the leadership of Kelly Johnson, the Skunks had concentrated on changing the rules of pure performance with the invention of the P-38, U-2, and SR-71 and others. Ben recognized the emerging new threat to survivability and moved the research toward the advent of stealth. Surprisingly, Lockheed was not invited, in the beginning to participate in the DARPA project. Lockheed had always done their work with CIA money, not Department of Defense. Ben would need CIA backing to jump into this fray. Stealth was much more of an art than a science in the early days with the heavy concentration on becoming "nearly invisible" to radar but also reducing other forms of detectability like the visual, infrared, electromagnetics, and acoustics spectra. Combining these new technologies into an airplane that could actually fly was a challenge, but first, they had to address the vulnerability to radar. They found an unlikely ally.

★   ★   ★

A Soviet physicist and mathematician named Pyotr Ufimtsev became interested in describing the reflection of electromagnetic waves. His theory was that angled surfaces could deflect radar pulses away from radar sites. He gained permission to publish his research results internationally because they were considered to be of no significant military or economic value. In retrospect, his work was foundational to the development of stealth.[3]

Denys Overholser, a stealth engineer at the Skunk Works, was famous for his technical acumen and his reverence of John Wayne. As Tom Burbage recalled, "when I first met Dennys, I felt like I was in a shrine for John Wayne. He had a number of pictures of 'the Duke' on his office walls and I thought he may have resonated with his tough-guy image in his battle with the so-called 'skeptical experts.'" Dennys had read the publication and felt that Ufimtsev had created the mathematical theory and tools to allow finite analysis of radar reflection. Overholser discovered a set of formulas in Ufimtsey's work that could apply. The formulas had been derived by a Scottish physicist and refined by a German electromagnetics expert. "As Denys admitted," Rich later wrote in his memoir, "the paper was so obtuse and impenetrable that only a nerd's nerd would have waded through it all."[4]

Overholser's idea was to compute the radar cross section of an airplane by dividing it into a series of angled flat panels that would divert or scatter radar beams.[5] He thought he would need six months to create the software at a time when computers were in their infancy. Rich gave him three months. He delivered his revolutionary software program, called "Echo 1" in five weeks, validating Lockheed's decision to hire him because he was an engineer who could write computer code.

The key to Lockheed's project would hinge on the accuracy of radar cross section calculations, which denote how detectable an object is with radar. The smaller the radar cross section, the more difficult it is to detect. The engineers built a model they named the Hopeless Diamond for testing in their secret facility. The prototype completely evaded radar detection. "That's when they decided instead of the village idiot, I was the village genius," Overholser said.[6]

The USAF awarded Lockheed a contract to design and build two demonstrators under the Code name Have Blue with the option for a full contract if the military was interested in the project. The project was labeled black, or highly classified, which meant it was not acknowledged publicly by the government, military personnel or defense contractors.

The Have Blue demonstrator, a complex-shaped design, owed a lot to electrical engineers' efforts to implement Denys Overholser's new ideas on dissipating radar energy. Once the electrical experts had calculated the shapes, the design was turned over to the aerodynamic engineers to try to make it fly. Unfortunately, on its first flight, the Have Blue demonstrator crashed in 1977, highlighting the challenge of merging a stealthy design with traditional flight controls. Bill Park, the Lockheed pilot on that flight, was badly injured in ejection.

On August 22, 1980, Secretary of Defense Harold Brown, in a Pentagon press conference, announced the existence of a "stealth" program. The announcement caused some concern about releasing this news. But by then the program was already three years old. The circle of knowledgeable people had widened and there had already been leaks in the media. Frank Reynolds on ABC reported the announcement, and NBC shortly followed. Even as the Air Force acknowledged its existence, they were creating a new security category to protect information about it. The most important revelation in SecDef Brown's speech was that "stealth technology does not involve a single technical approach but is a complex synthesis of many." In June 1981, Lockheed test pilot Hal Farley flew the first flight on the F-117. (**See Figure 2: F-117 Nighthawk**)

The slowly-building, top secret F-117 force was based in the Nevada desert, at Tonapah, far from any prying eyes. The weird-looking jets would fly only at night on training missions in Northern California. In the early 1980s, well before its existence was acknowledged, one crashed in the mountains. The crash was only covered on local California TV stations but there was a real risk that, even though the crash site was remote, the community of stealth conspiracy zealots would try to find the crash site and could compromise the technology. A quick mission was set up to load a C-130 from Point Mugu with a jumble of smashed-up parts from an F-101 crash years earlier. It flew over the site and dumped them to create confusion.

The F-117 had some unique features. Its "stealth switch" would retract all antennas below the skin to go covert. The Nighthawk drivers were essentially flying with no communications, alone, in the dark. Technology advances would later incorporate conformal antennas embedded in the skin. In the end, about 70 percent of the Nighthawk stealth was derived from its shape, and the rest was from a complex set of radar absorbing materials.

Harken back to the origins of the famous "Skunk Works" name. It originated from the old Al Capp cartoon series where a mysterious "moonshine still" emitted strange odors. In the cartoon strip Al called it the "Skonk Works," and the strange Lockheed operation across the runway in Burbank in the early days emitted similar noxious odors as scientists developed those stealth coatings. The Skonk Works became the now-famous Skunk Works, picked up a friendly skunk logo, and changed history.

The Nighthawk's baptism by fire was the "Trip to Downtown Bagdad" on the first night of the Gulf War. On 22 June 2001, at the gala celebration of the twentieth anniversary of the F-117's first flight, Major General Dave Deptula recounted "I see some of those combat pilots out there tonight who, in the run up to the Gulf War, said to themselves, 'I sure hope this stealth stuff really works.' By the January 16, 1991, there was a certain degree of confidence. Everybody waited that first night, trying to look confident, but since you flew 'stealthed up', once you left the tankers, nobody would have contact for the next couple of hours until the antennae came back out to contact the tanker for the trip back home."[7]

The pilots that night deserve a huge thanks for having the stones to take an untried aircraft over one of the most heavily defended cities in the world. They penetrated Saddam's Soviet-supplied and very dense air defenses with no losses, and placed a very high percentage of their ordnance right on target. Though only fifty-nine were ever built, the F-117 was proven to be a very effective combat system. Stealth technology suddenly became highly desirable.

The F-117 traded off aerodynamic performance for the geometric shapes called for by early stealth theory, and it required sophisticated treatments and coatings.

★ ★ ★

After the Gulf War, technology quickly evolved from the Nighthawk's flat-tish, faceted surfaces and sophisticated microwave-absorbing coatings to curved surfaces and tailless flight control technology. This can be seen in the Northrop Grumman B-2 Spirit bomber. (**See Figure 3: B-2 Spirit**)

Tails present a particularly difficult challenge for stealth designers, due to the laws of physics. As most sailors know, the intersection of horizontal and vertical surfaces creates a corner reflector for radar. (One often sees corner reflectors on sailboat masts.) The B-2 is a very effective, covert, subsonic, high weapon capacity delivery system, but it too was a compromise. Like the F-117, it's black, and operates most effectively at night, since the trade-off for stealth in this tailless design was lack of maneuverability. If the plane's detected visually, by a high-performance fighter or ground-launched missile system, sluggish maneuverability was a clear weakness.

★　★　★

Any discussion of the history of high-performance airplanes would be remiss without attention to the power plant that drives them. While the public conception of the lethality of any new weapon is generally an image of its exterior, the major design driver for a fighter has traditionally resided in its propulsion system. In 1903 the Wright Brothers were trying to fly the first heavier-than-air, self-propelled, maneuverable piloted aircraft. They needed a power plant that could drive two counterrotating propellers behind the wings. That early engine had no fuel pump, carburetor, or spark plugs. Nor did it have a throttle. It did, however, use aluminum for the first time in aircraft construction.[8] Yet this simple, light motor produced twelve horsepower, an acceptable margin above the Wrights' minimum requirement of eight.

Demands for more power with less weight have driven engine technology ever since. At no time was this more critical than during the two world wars. The evolution from airscrew propulsion to the jet engine, occurring in the early 1940s, provided a distinct combat edge to early adopters. In the following decades, jet technology continued to advance in dependability, altitude, and pure power, often under classified cover. This evolved into revolutionary machines such as the U-2 (the highest-flying single-engine craft) and SR-71 (the only one so far capable of flying three times the speed of sound). But these capabilities were limited to unique, small-quantity missions.[9]

Government investments in the Joint Advanced Fighter Engine Program in 1983 boosted reliability, fuel efficiency, and efficient production for a new generation of turbines. Breakthroughs included high-temperature composite structures, which could reduce weight and improve the fatigue life of critical components. While military buyers still focused on higher thrust, often driven by weight growth over the life of a tactical fighter as weapons and sensor payloads increased over time, fuel efficiency also became essential to the next generation of engines.

Pratt & Whitney and General Electric had faced off for the contract that would power the Advanced Tactical Fighter (later the F-22). Each of the airframe contractors would build two prototypes, one using the Pratt & Whitney and the second using the GE engine. In a sense, it was a competition within a competition. The government would evaluate the engine manufacturers and the airframe competitors separately. On 3 August 1991, Pratt & Whitney was awarded the contract for the ATF engine, and the Lockheed/Boeing/General Dynamics team won the airframe contract.

P&W's winner, the YF119, was an afterburning turbofan evolved from the earlier F-100, but with over 20 percent more thrust and 40 percent fewer parts. It was rated at 35,000 foot-pounds of thrust at supercruise, and could sustain speeds up to Mach 1.8 without the afterburners. It also had thrust vectoring; the exhaust could swivel twenty degrees up or down to enhance maneuverability.[10] Despite all this, it was a more conventional design compared to General Electric's YF120. During the competition, Pratt & Whitney accrued far more test hours, and their proposal emphasized the lower risk of their design.

Interestingly, the Lockheed Martin winning bid for the airframe, designated the YF-22, offered a higher-risk design. The evaluators chose the higher-risk airframe and the lower-risk engine alternative.

In the Pentagon press room on April 23, 1991, the Honorable Don Rice, the Secretary of the Air Force and source selection authority, said, "There were other considerations, including the potential need for a Naval Variant which also had some unique engine and airframe considerations. It was clear the Lockheed and Pratt Whitney combination was a better solution for that requirement."[11]

On September 7, 1997, the F-22 Raptor completed its first flight at the Lockheed Martin production facility in Marietta, Georgia. The test pilot on that flight was Paul Metz, and the F-22 Executive Vice President and general manager observing that flight (and providing moral support to a very nervous

Mrs. Metz), was Tom Burbage. Both men would later play major roles on the Joint Strike Fighter.

★ ★ ★

Speed and maneuverability are the ultimate measures of fighter performance. Stealth technology had continued to advance and, when coupled with the very high, very fast performance of the Raptor, could allow some relaxation of traditional stealth design to allow increased maneuverability.

But you had to be very fast and very agile. In the words of one of the Raptor's test pilots, "hitting Mach 2 at high altitude in an F-15 is very uncomfortable, as the engines start to struggle and the controls battle with the thin atmosphere. Meanwhile, the F-22 remains as smooth as riding in a limousine"[12] Agility is another revolutionary Raptor capability with the integration of software algorithms connecting thrust vectoring engines with flight control surfaces. So where is the relaxation?

The best example of "some relaxation" is the use of large, canted vertical tails, which are needed to ensure stability in high supersonic flight, compared to the tailless design of the B-2 bomber. The unique combination of high altitude, non-afterburning supersonic flight, fully integrated engine and flight controls and very low observable radar signature, is why, at the time of publication of this book, the Raptor remains the dominant air-to-air fighter design in the modern world. (See **Figure 4: F-22 Raptor**)

One of the more interesting criteria for the F-22 was a carryover from the F-117. Early stealth theory essentially eliminated any electronic emissions, such as radio, radar, or data transmission, to further reduce risk of detection. The initial Raptor model could receive information from a variety of sources passively, but its designers rigorously limited any transmissions. Thus, it had little ability to covertly share information.

★ ★ ★

The design freeze between the F-22 and the F-35 was over ten years. That decade saw many technology evolutions, both in electronics and in materials that would change the design strategy for the Joint Strike Fighter. The evolution of digital design tools would now enable a truly integrated three-dimensional design. This drove the implementation of the F-35 "Digital Thread," which became a major enabler of the multinational partnership.

The use of advanced composite manufacturing was also in its infancy but evolving quickly during that ten-year gap. This meant major structural segments that still had to be metal in complex areas on F-22 and earlier stealth airplanes could move to composite structures for F-35. Aluminum, titanium, and stainless steel required sophisticated surface treatments, not only in their initial manufacturing, but throughout their lives, to maintain low observable features. These treatments needed temperature- and humidity-controlled environments. While this isn't a problem for the Air Force, with their huge, environmentally controlled hangars, it would be a big challenge for any aircraft designed to serve with the Navy and Marine Corps that would be housed and maintained in dusty, rainy environments and at sea.

In the late 1990s, high-level decision-makers at the Secretary of Defense and senior Air Force levels faced the question: What next? A program of gradual improvements for the F-22? Or an entirely new aircraft? And if the latter, what should it look like? Revolutionary design changes cannot be retrofitted into existing designs without prohibitive costs. Replacing metal parts with composite parts changes the fundamental structural characteristics of an airplane requiring significant structural and operational testing.

In the end, they decided to look far ahead and seek a transformational design. Clearly, current generation combat aircraft, a huge inventory of older aircraft, were not survivable in the projected threat environment of more sophisticated enemy radars. The opportunity to implement a common training and tactics environment across all three US services and their allies could, for the first time, enable reduction in expensive training and support infrastructure. It could also allow much greater burden sharing across all partners as none would be left behind due to inferior configurations. Remember transformations? New inventions and procedures aren't just technological advances, they alter how the community feels, acts, and interacts, and shakes up the national and even global balance of power.

But that decision immediately presented two major challenges. First, the United States and its allies hadn't flown and fought as a single service or a single country for the last several decades. A transformational air combat system had to weld the Navy, Air Force, and Marines, and maybe the Army and space assets too into an integrated joint fighting machine, while recognizing the unique operational environments of each. Additionally, it had to include the closest allies of the United States as a truly interoperable force. And, presumably, also ensure something like equitable burden sharing in long-term war-fighting and peacekeeping operations.

Introducing a transformational plane would depend on an ability to manufacture and deliver the new aircraft on a reasonable time line. Two competing forces had to be kept in mind. The first was Moore's law: Digital technology doubled its power every two years or so, making previous technology quickly obsolete. The second was the long acquisition and test time lines typical of complex, expensive defense programs. When these two factors butt heads, large-scale programs tend to be starved or even killed off. Another critical piece would be the ability to develop, scale up, and transform a global supply chain to meet the tight tolerances required for stealth component manufacturing.

There would also be political and bureaucratic obstacles. Ever-changing governments, on top of fluid and sometimes contradictory environmental and investment concerns, would continually threaten to deep-six any such program. Considering the internal politics of three US services, eight international partners, four special-category nations, and additional countries considering joining the program, this dimension might prove to be the most frustrating Rubik's Cube of all.

If all these challenges could be managed, coordinated, and integrated, a transformational air combat system might succeed.

Perhaps the largest cultural issue—we're speaking about the early to mid 1990s—was the fact that each of the US services were starting development programs to replace their aging frontline fighters.

The Marine Corps was farthest along. It was developing prototypes for an advanced short takeoff and vertical landing (ASTOVL) replacement for the venerable AV-8 Harrier, a Hawker Siddeley design that had been improved by McDonnell Douglas into the successful and versatile AV-8B.

Along with the Marines, the United Kingdom was a partner in codeveloping the concept. Both countries had signed a document that defined the requirements. Three major prime contractor teams were competing. Boeing was proposing a "direct lift" concept—channeling main engine exhaust to rocket-like nozzles at the fuselage and wingtips—generally like the Harrier layout. McDonnell Douglas, teamed with Northrop Grumman and BAE Systems, envisioned a second gas turbine, for augmented lift during the short-takeoff and vertical-landing stages of flight. They called this the "gas-driven lift fan" concept. The third competitor, Lockheed, stayed with a single engine, but added a disengageable lift fan driven through a gearbox, the "shaft-driven lift-fan concept." Lockheed was convinced that only this last concept could achieve the exigent combination of supersonic flight, internal weapon carriage, and STOVL performance.

The U.S. Air Force was also in the early stages of developing the operational requirements for a multi-role fighter (MRF). They needed to replace several aging fleets, including the F-16, A-10, and potentially the F-117.

The U.S. Navy had been through several attempts to replace their 1960s-vintage F-14/A-6/A-7 carrier-operated inventory, including the A-12 Avenger II stealth attack plane (overweight, over budget, and finally canceled by Secretary of Defense Richard Cheney in 1991) and a derivative of the F-22 called the Naval Advanced Tactical Fighter (NATF) succeeded by the AX/AFX. All had been abandoned in favor of a less-risky approach, upgrading and modernizing the F-18 into the F/A-18 E/F Super Hornet.

In 1992, Cheney was faced with severe pressures on the defense budget. He decided to change the historical, individual service acquisition paradigm to one of joint acquisition. He based this decision on the reality that for the last several decades, both our combat and our peacekeeping efforts had depended on joint and allied cooperative engagement—not on going it alone.

The two largest drawbacks to this new model were the lack of interoperability (communication and shared situational awareness) among participants, and the technology gap between US platforms and those of the other participants. Many of our allies were flying frontline American planes, procured through foreign military sales channels, but often with lesser capabilities. Both problems decreased operational effectiveness and made burden-sharing harder.

On 23 February 1993 the Department of Defense initiated a formal bottom-up review (BUR) of US military forces and modernization plans. The purpose of the BUR was to develop a strategy for defense planning in the post–Cold War era. The review assumed that the United States should be able to fight and win two near simultaneous major regional conflicts. In September 1993, the results of the BUR were formally announced. The F-22 and F/A-18 E/F program would continue while the Air Force's MRF and the Navy's A/F-X would be canceled. A new Joint Advanced Strike Technologies, or JAST, program would be started. The program would develop a Joint Strike Fighter intended to replace the Air

Force F-16 and F-111 and F-117 and the Navy's A-6 and F-14 as well as a few other allied frontline fighters. The objective was to introduce, for the first time in history, a true tri-service, multinational-coalition force. The plane would be able to operate in the very different environments of the USAF (land-based runways), the Navy (catapult launches, arrested landings, and cramped hangars) and the USMC (STOL/VSTOL ops from expeditionary fields and ships without catapults and arresting gear). This would demand three variants, with significant structural differences, that would "look" identical to the pilot and share many parts in common. Such standardization would, for the first time, enable true interoperability . . . in short, they could all fight shoulder to shoulder.

The second element of Cheney's vision was to make the JAST an example of acquisition reform. This included rapid development, with a heavy dependence on modeling and simulation for proof of concept and test and evaluation. Designing for rapid manufacturing and assembly would be critical to drive down production time. If successful, this could allow procurement in larger quantities, capturing economies of commonality and scale.

The third element of the grand vision was to form a true partnership with our closest allies. They would participate in funding the system development and demonstration (SDD) Phase. They would be represented by National Deputies in the Joint Program Office and participate in critical decisions. They would buy their planes in common production lots with the US government, helping everyone achieve economies of scale. An additional incentive, and one of the most challenging aspects of the program, was the invitation from the US government for all allies joining the program to help build the plane. Industrial participation would be based on a concept referred to as "best value" rather than offset.

("Offset" meant that if an ally bought a given US weapon system, we would incorporate some of their technology or subsystems if feasible or would establish unrelated procurements of their goods and services to "offset" their costs of procurement. Italy buys F-16s for their air force; we buy Beretta pistols for our army.) No one really liked that system, but foreign leaders had to justify "buying American" somehow. The JAST would be different. Companies from Allied countries would secure high-technology work directly related to the development and production of the new fighter. Participation would be on a competitive basis, and would be for the entire production run, not just for those planes being bought by the individual country.

The rewards for participating would be great. A small participating partner, like Denmark, could buy a small quantity of F-35s but provide parts and components for thousands of F-35s if they could remain competitive and provide best value to the F-35 supply chain. No partner wants to pay more for their F-35. The risks, relative to traditional "offset," were also huge. No longer would industrial benefits be considered a gift to an ally. Everyone would have to pull their weight, or the whole program would crash and burn.

The plan to build three variants was not without its critics. Vice Admiral (ret.) Joe Dyer, who was the chief engineer for the Naval Air Systems Command (NAVAIR) and later served as its commander, argued that the STOVL variant for the Marine Corps added significant risk.

Dyer said, "I'm a big supporter of Marine aviation, but I counseled strongly and unsuccessfully against including the Marine Corps version because it was a technical challenge in and of itself and one that was going to drive three airframes and that brought significant cost and technical risk. STOVL is just harder than conventional fixed wing. When it was apparent that the Office of the Secretary of Defense was hell-bent on a common airplane, I went over to talk with—we'll call him a senior executive—and said, 'Look, it's going to take longer than you're talking about. It's going to cost more than you're talking about. . . . If you really want to de-risk the program and reduce the cost, then do STOVL as a separate program.'"[13] In retrospect, VAdm Dyer's assessment was valid, as the STOVL variant was a very significant challenge to the program. But the need for the STOVL variant was more critical than for the other US services and pressurized the time line for the program. In the end, the ability to close the technology challenge of maintaining all three variants proved the original vision of the F-35 founding fathers. Years later, VADM Dyer would say, "I'm glad the program proceeded with the three variants. My point to OSD was 'You'll have to take the heat on cost and schedule.'"

But, as aerospace and defense expert Bill Sweetman said in his book *The Ultimate Fighter: Lockheed Martin F-35 Joint Strike Fighter*, "We know how to build a stealth fighter. We know how to build a long-range agile fighter. We may even have a good way of building a fighter that can land and take off vertically. But trying to build a fighter that can do all three is very, very difficult."[14]

As it turned out, Sweetman was wrong. It wouldn't be very, very difficult.

It would prove to be damn near impossible.

Reference

1. Warbirdsflying.com, Lockheed P-38 Lightning, https://www.warbirdsflying.com/lockeed-p-38-lightning/ accessed January 12, 2020.

2. Nedwick, Thomas, F-22 Test Pilot Details the Raptor's Incredible Speed, The War Zone Wire, published December 21, 2022.

3. Musa, Larry, "Physicist of the Week: Pyotr Ufimtsev," January 15, 2009, http://www.larrymusa.com/Physicists/ufimtsev.aspx, accessed January 20, 2020.

4. Rich, Ben. *Skunk Works: A Personal Memoir of My Years at Lockheed* www.avalonlibrary.net, accessed January 10, 2020.

5. Lynn, Capi. *Statesman Journal*, "Secret Weapon for Stealth Tech Is from Dallas" April 16, 2016, https://www.statesmanjournal.com/story/news/2016/04/16/secret-weapon-stealth-tech-dallas/82678480/.

6. Ibid.

7. Waldo, Anna Maria. Platinum Nighthawk Speech: Commemoration of the First Flight of the F-117A, June 21, 2021, www.mitchellaerospacepower.org.

8. Smithsonian National Air and Space Museum, "Inventing a Flying Machine," accessed Dec. 7, 2021.

9. Rich, Ben. *Skunk Works: A Personal Memoir of My Years at Lockheed.*

10. Wikipedia. "Pratt & Whitney F-119," accessed December 16, 2021.

11. Wikipedia. Advanced Tactical Fighter Selection, F-2 Announcement, April 23, 1991.

12. Nedwick, Thomas. F-22 Test Pilot Details the Raptor's Incredible Speed, The War Zone Wire, published Dec 21, 2022.

13. Interview with VADM Dyer, USN (Ret.), by Betsy Clark and Adrian Pitman on February 18, 2017. Held in F-35 interview archive.

14. Sweetman, Bill, "The Ultimate Fighter" from his interview for the *NOVA* (PBS) production "The Battle of the X-Planes," www.pbs.org/wgbh/nova/x-planes.

Chapter 3

THE TENSION BUILDS

By 1994, the Joint Advanced Strike Technologies (JAST) program was rolling. This tri-service, multinational-coalition plane had to be able to fly from land-based runways, large Navy nuclear carriers, smaller L-Class ships, and expeditionary fields. It would be developed quickly, with close attention to manufacturability to restrain costs and speed up final assembly. Finally, the plane would be both designed and built in a close partnership with our allies. But a lot had to happen before metal could be pressed.

In the United States, major defense acquisition programs typically move from advanced concept studies to a concept demonstration phase, system development and demonstration, and low-rate initial production, and—eventually—full-rate production. At each stage, certain requirements must be met. This process takes a long time, and managers and Congress are always trying to speed it up and save money. The JAST program was no exception. It included cost sharing between the US government and the competing contractors for the concept demonstration phase. Also, there was extensive use of high-fidelity simulations to develop sensors and subsystems, and also to replace some of the traditional (and expensive) flight tests.

When the services finally okayed the draft requirements—while stipulating they could revisit them later—the concept development phase launched. The request for proposals outlined an aircraft that would replace several "legacy" fighters in the current inventory, and be stealthier and cheaper. It could also be sold to our allies. As discussed in chapter 2, three variants would be needed to meet the unique operating environments of the Air Force, Navy, and Marine Corps. While there would be differences among the variants, such as a heavier undercarriage needed by the Navy for catapult launches and wire-arrested landings on carriers, it did seem possible to design variants using the same basic "air vehicle" design, vehicle management systems, engines, and mission systems. This would enable level of interoperability and force multiplication never before possible. This could also save on both production and maintenance costs and simplify the logistical and training tails as well. It promised to dramatically reduce the cost of sustaining long-term peacekeeping or combat air operations.

The government team for the concept demonstration phase was led by Major General Mike Hough, call sign "Hog." He began as an enlisted sailor who received an appointment to the Naval Academy in 1965. He would retire as a lieutenant general responsible for all Marine Corps aviation, holding the record as the longest-serving graduate of his USNA class.

Lieutenant General Jon "Dog" Davis USMC was a protégé of Mike Hough and later rose to the same position in the Corps. Jon recalls, "Hog Hough was not only forward thinking but he had the work ethic and common sense of a blue-collar guy. He had a solid reputation as a fair but demanding leader. He focused on execution. In DC, he looked at future capabilities from the perspective of a warfighter, but also from the eyes of a mechanic that would have to sustain a platform in harm's way."

"General Hough was well versed, experienced and had mastered what he called 'Beltway 101' and tutored us in how to successfully fight the enduring battle in DC to garner and protect resources to bring USMC requirements to life and sustain them once we had them. His sense of humor was legend, as was his invective if you acted in a way that hurt our Corps or our cause. As majors, he taught us that you could be a flag officer that got hard stuff done, have fun doing it, not take yourself overly seriously, and be a normal human. There would be no F-35 without Mike Hough."[1]

★ ★ ★

One "paper" proposal was from McDonnell Douglas, builder of the F-18 and many other Navy and Air Force fighters over the decades. Another came from Boeing, which hadn't built a fighter since the 1930s, but was a leader in commercial aviation and bombers. The final entry was from Lockheed, fresh off a major win with the F-22 Raptor.

Hough, and his widely distributed team at the Naval Air Test Center in Patuxent River, Maryland, and the Air Force Systems Command in Dayton, Ohio, evaluated the proposals in sections. The proposals were so detailed and extensive that no individual could review the entire set of documents. The sections were evaluated separately and then assigned a grade. The section grades were then weighted and totaled to determine a final evaluation assessment. The team finished their evaluations in 1996.

The biggest shocker was the quick elimination of McDonnell Douglas, which had partnered with British Aerospace and Northrop Grumman, from further competition. Their entry was futuristic-looking, with twin inlets and a shallow V tail. An exhaust gas-driven fan mounted behind the cockpit provided lift to the front during vertical takeoff and landing. This complex concept was a "calculated gamble," and seemed to be a higher-risk system. The loss, along with their previous withdrawal from commercial airliner building, doomed McDonnell Douglas as an aircraft prime manufacturer. It led to intense soul-searching as to what future remained for one of the most successful aircraft design organizations in history, and in 1997 the company merged with Boeing.

Now there were two left standing.

The stakes were immense. As originally announced, the production runs envisioned were 3,000 for the US military, 250 for the United Kingdom, and probably many more thousands to allies throughout the world, if the sales record of the F-16 was any guide. It was billed as the "largest acquisition program in the history of the Department of Defense" and "the last manned fighter." Executives and engineers at both corporations realized this would be the most important competition of their lives.

The final bout would take place high over the desert, far from prying eyes. But a lot had to happen before then.

★ ★ ★

Why was this new fighter so necessary? As the clock ticked down toward the end of the twentieth century, the combat planes that made up the bulk of the US inventory dated back to the 1980s and even the 1960s. Primarily intended to fly beneath enemy radars and mix it up in dogfights, they had great performance at low altitudes, but weren't designed for stealth, either in the radar or infrared spectra. They operated independently, or communicated by voice radio, rather than being able to pass data to ground stations, ships, or other aircraft.

Worst of all, they were wearing out. The Navy was experiencing problems with wing cracking, since carrier landings imposed heavy stresses on F-18 airframes. The Air Force's aging F-15 Strike Eagle was showing structural fatigue too, leading to safety stand-downs. The A-10, a close air support plane designed specifically to kill tanks, dated to 1975. Though excellent for its time, it was fast becoming a billboard flashing "Shoot Me" over a modern battlefield.

The Marine Corps was desperate for a replacement for the Harrier, which operated from short runways and landed vertically. But the AV-8B was slow, carried a limited bomb load, and suffered a high accident rate.

Vertical and/or short takeoff and landing technology was a tough nut to crack. For more than forty years, US, Soviet, and European aerospace enterprises had pursued V/STOL, yielding only the subsonic Harrier as a truly operational fighter. Only three research vehicles had demonstrated both hovering and supersonic capability: the German VJ-101C, French Mirage III-V, and the Soviet Yak-141. However, none were operational weapons platforms, and their limited performance had prevented them from accomplishing hover and supersonic flight in a single mission.

The whole concept of the original JAST program had been to replace all these legacy aircraft with a single design that could operate far into the twenty-first century. It would be "fifth-generation" from the start, with stealth, advanced sensor fusion, and unprecedented connectivity across a wide variety of other combat aircraft and weapon systems. It would have to penetrate the defenses of advanced adversaries and support operations across a multi-domain battlespace including air, land, sea, cyberspace, and space. It also had to pull out of the costly "death spiral" experienced by the F-22 where increasing costs resulted in fewer planes being bought by the Air Force. As a result, the cost per plane became even higher, resulting in even fewer being bought. Thus, this new plane would need to be affordable and produced in large quantities.

Pretty much a perfect storm of high expectations. Supersonic, vertical takeoff, stealthy, carrier capable, and cheap? History was against it. The last tri-service aircraft had been Robert McNamara's F-111 Aardvark. Overweight, over budget, and terrifically complicated, it had ended up rejected by the Navy and the British. The Royal Australian Air Force were fond of its long-range features, which were a match for their unique operational environment, and performed a midlife avionics systems upgrade in the 1990s.

Not a great example for the Joint Strike Fighter to follow.

★ ★ ★

Since historically great aircraft have resulted from great engines, and underper-forming ones from lousy engines, it's worth looking more closely at how both companies intended to power their designs.

Pratt & Whitney dated back to 1860, when it made guns for the Union Army. Their aircraft subsidiary, established in 1925, had built the Wasp and Hornet air-cooled piston engines that powered early Navy and Air Corps fight-ers in the 1930s. In World War II, their engines lofted half the combat aircraft America fielded. They entered the jet age in 1952 with the revolutionary J57 turbojet, which powered the F-100 Super Sabre, the F-102 Delta Dart, the Navy F8U-1, the U-2, and other famous planes and missiles.[2]

P&W had developed the F119 for the F-22 Raptor program. This impressive engine combined low-observable technologies with high thrust-to-weight per-formance. Its two-dimensional pitch-vectoring exhaust nozzle provided extreme maneuverability when coupled through software with the flight control systems. While the F119 had the potential to adapt to short takeoffs, it was not adapt-able for vertical takeoff and landing. The Raptor's two F119s gave the Raptor "supercruise"—the ability to fly supersonically without turning on fuel-gulping afterburners, reducing the infrared signature for high-speed flight.

One of the challenges of adapting the F119 to the JSF Navy mission was the extremely high temperatures such power outputs demanded. The heart of the engine, the turbine, featured single-crystal superalloy blades and complicated cooling technologies. But questions remained as to whether it would be reliable enough, especially over water. This was the reason so many famous Navy jets—the Banshee, Phantom, and Tomcat—had been twin-engined. Pratt's winning argument was that there were many redundant safety features built into a single-engine fighter that were not included in a multi-engine configuration because of the redundancy of the second engine in the event of an emergency. Eliminating a second engine would significantly reduce the acquisition and life-cycle costs of a fleet of new fighters. P&W's reliability tests, coupled with historical statistics, proved that there were no significant safety or reliability differences between single or dual engine fighters.

Bennett Croswell was a charismatic PW partner and had worked closely with Burbage as the engine lead on the F-22 program. He moved from there to the JSF as the X-plane F119 program manager, cementing a long-term rela-tionship that went through many years developing fifth-generation fighters F-22 and F-35. Bennett and the Pratt & Whitney team had the responsibility for delivering all of the engine combinations to both Boeing and, with their Rolls-Royce lift-fan partner, to the Lockheed Martin team. Bennett said, "PW contributed a lot to make the lift fan work. It was apparent that the STOVL version was critical to winning this program, and we were committed to make it succeed."[3]

Previous American fighter programs had always considered the engine a subsystem . . . a part that could be swapped out more or less at will. This fostered competition among contractors, both to force innovation and drive down prices. But the daunting performance requirements of the JSF meant only one existing engine had the capability to power both challengers in this early competitive phase. That was the 119. Both Boeing and Lockheed Martin would use it in their concept demonstrators.

This essentially preselected P&W as the engine provider for the F-35, without competition.[4] One essential program objective thus became to develop a second engine that could compete with the P&W engine when the program got into full production. This opportunity for a second engine would become a significant flashpoint later.

But integrating the F119 into the two X-airplanes would prove unexpectedly difficult. Bob Cea was the Pratt & Whitney VP for the JSF concept demonstration program. A New Yorker, he was a straightforward "what you see is what you get" engineer. Bob recalled, "Our biggest challenge was software. We had to develop new engine modifications around the F119 core engine to power the competing X-32 and X-35 concepts, which had some very significant differences. We had twenty months to get both engines into test. The Lockheed engine was ready first, but we had to run both before we could make a public announcement. We also had the requirement to integrate the Rolls-Royce lift fan engine into the Lockheed X-35. The lift fan was having development issues with dissimilar metals, oil leaks, and clutch dynamics, which made our job much more difficult."[5]

Frank Gillette, Pratt & Whitney's chief engineer on the F119, was drafted to bring that capability to the JSF. "We had to modify the most advanced fighter engine in the world to meet two different X-airplane development designs and integrate another version of the engine into the unique Lockheed STOVL Lift Fan integration design. While all that was going on, we were simultaneously developing a preferred system concept for the eventual production designs that both Lockheed and Boeing were proposing. I'm not sure anyone really appreciated the magnitude of that task."[6]

★ ★ ★

DoD acquisition programs typically move from phase to phase at the pace of a snoozing snail. This is regularly reviled by Congress and the media as "wasteful," "slow," and "bureaucratic," but it's intended to reduce cost by defining and solving problems before major investments are made. (On the other hand, if a plane crashes, the program suddenly becomes "too risky" "too hasty" and "inadequately managed.")

The concept demonstration phase falls between paper concept and production aircraft. It's a "fly before you buy" approach, to make sure designs perform to specifications. In the JSF's case, since a family of commonly and concurrently derived airplanes was envisioned, the concept demonstration phase would test their aerodynamic concepts and generate credible flight sciences data. Not only would the planes fly, the mission systems and the planes' observables (how visible they were to radar and infrared) would be demonstrated in laboratory tests.

Congress appropriated $3 billion for the concept development process. A relatively small portion of that would go to the flight demonstration phase with the remainder going to the many other development activities in wind tunnels, laboratories and simulation facilities. Four aircraft would be built, two from Boeing and two from Lockheed Martin. Having two aircraft afforded some redundancy in case of a crash, and let the competitors respond to the challenges of the three variants.

Both for the companies involved, and for the United States, the stakes were huge: the survival of the allies against rapidly evolving defenses—not just fighters, but also missile systems—by peer competitors such as Russia and China.

But, although the two remaining companies used the same engine, their proposals envisioned radically different aircraft. The battle would take place in the air over the Chesapeake Bay and the Mojave Desert and in arcane software labs. Other campaigns would rage in the press and in national and local political arenas. Both companies were among the heaviest hitters in American politics, always working to sway decision-makers to their side.

The battle would rage over half a decade. The victor would sweep the board; winner take all. The loser might well go out of business forever.

★ ★ ★

The Boeing design was now designated the X-32, the Lockheed plane the X-35. But why those numbers? And what happened to X-33 and X-34?

The "X" planes, beginning with the famous X-1, were "experimental" aircraft. From various manufacturers, each plane incorporated such new technologies as supersonic flight, new engine designs, flight controls, and stealth. Over the years, some had been judged successful, and others failures. But all had been radical departures in one way or another, and each contributed to pushing the envelope of aircraft design.

The X-32 had been the original designation of McDonnell Douglas's ASTOVL demonstrator, mentioned in the previous chapter. When Boeing bought McDonnell Douglas in 1996, announced exactly one month after the latter company had been eliminated from the JSF competition, that designator rolled over into the JSF requirement.

The 1999-ish X-33 was Lockheed's unmanned "space plane," a single-stage-to-orbit experimental vehicle. After technical problems developed, it was canceled. The X-34, Orbital Sciences' attempt at the same type of reusable spaceplane, was also canceled. That left "X-35" as the next designator available, so it was assigned to the Lockheed Martin version of the JSF.

As outlined above, the two designs shared an engine, but little else. This was because they descended from different evolutionary streams, complicated by Boeing's purchase of McDonnell Douglas, which brought back some of the design team and concepts that had worked on the "McAir" entry for the JSF. (That erased one of the black marks against Boeing, that they supposedly didn't understand how to design a successful fighter). The two competing teams worked less than a mile apart. The Boeing Phantom Works is in Palmdale, California. So is Lockheed's famed Skunk Works.

Both teams began with restraints, but also with some "gimmes" from the JSF Office. The tight budget and close deadlines were the most significant restraints. The most important relaxations were that the prototypes had only to meet a very limited structural life, would not be expected to be stealthy, and would not include mission systems or weapons bays, though they'd include weight and space reservations for their later incorporation. Some systems, such as landing gear, could be borrowed from current aircraft. Each of the four planes would be hand built, but supply chains from prospective subcontractors would have to be set up at the same time.

But each would be designed differently from any such craft before. Carl Hoffman, writing for *Wired*, put it well: "Until now even high-performance fighters were designed largely on paper. To make sure the thousands of parts and systems matched up, full-scale wooden and cardboard mock-ups were built. A single change required hundreds of pieces of paper, and the addition of new pieces to the mock-up. When it came time to assemble parts, they were so imprecise that holes couldn't be drilled until the pieces were jigged and shimmed together. The first planes off the assembly line often differed in size by inches. Boeing and Lockheed both made major commitments to using design and modeling software in every phase of the JSF's creation."[7]

The test pilots would be flying the first fighters designed entirely by computer-aided software.

★ ★ ★

The Boeing design team was led by legendary engineer Frank Statkus. By then Statkus had worked on the defense side of the aviation business for nearly thirty years. Prior to this assignment, he'd been the program manager for the portion of the F-22 Raptor that Boeing was responsible for. "Frank was the epitome of a partner and an inspirational leader" said Tom Burbage, program general manager for the Lockheed Martin F-22 program at the time. "His commitment to deliver a quality product, on time, was critical to our F-22 program success."

The Joint Strike Fighter would be Statkus's first assignment as the lead for a prime contractor for a new fighter, though.

Statkus emphasized affordability from his first day in charge. He was laser-focused on minimizing design costs, fabrication costs, and especially, assembly costs.

Boeing had immense experience in these areas. They'd honed lean design and manufacturing in the 777 and 737 jetliner programs. Though they weren't lead on the F/A-18 fighter and T-45 trainer, Boeing had participated as a subcontractor and learned from them, as well as from participation in the F-15 Strike Eagle and F-22 programs. The recently added McDonnell Douglas engineers had redesigned the VTOL Hawker Siddeley Harrier, the first operational vertical takeoff fighter, to produce the AV-8B for the U.S. Marines. In CTOL fighters, they'd designed the F-15 Strike Eagle and the Navy F/A-18 Hornet and had recently had a near miss with the canceled A-12 Avenger stealth bomber. Finally, Boeing had been studying direct lift under a previous government contract.

In short, the Phantom Works was a serious competitor with deep resources from a multitude of secret projects and advanced technology, both military and commercial. However, perhaps their most significant advantage, as Statkus saw it, was Boeing's unmatched ability to streamline production. They were a pioneer in composite wing structures and unitized construction where previously assembled parts requiring multiple pieces and fasteners could be manufactured as a single part, eliminating complexity and reducing both weight and assembly time. They were clearly recognized as experts in advanced 3D modeling and deep flight-simulation techniques. No one argued with Boeing quality, either. Their strength in the competition would be the promise of cheaper development and significantly reduced manufacturing and maintenance costs.

Here's how Boeing intended to win. First, affordability was key. But they would also unveil a radical innovation, a high-tech, graphite composite "box" delta wing. The first variant, the X-32A, would be beefed up for catapult and arresting gear operations. The second, the X-32B, would be optimized for short takeoff and vertical landing.

But the riskiest part of their entry was that startlingly massive, monolithic (single-piece) delta wing.

Tailless, delta-winged aircraft offer certain advantages over tailed designs. That huge wing can hold additional fuel. It also imposes less drag at high speeds than a conventional swept wing and tail. More fuel *plus* less drag means extended range, or a weight saving that can be applied as a trade-off elsewhere, say bomb load. Deltas had included the very first flying-wing jet fighter, the Horten Ho 229, as well as the YF-12 Blackbird and Northrop Grumman's stealth bomber, the B-2 Spirit.

But deltas tend not to be stellar in the maneuverability department. Their control surfaces are on the trailing edge of the wing, so using them lifts the nose and increases drag. Thus, they can have trouble negotiating fast turns . . . such as in a dogfight. Some recent deltas, like the Eurofighter Typhoon and French Rafale, use canards (smaller control surfaces forward of the main wing). There are two problems with canards, though. First, you have to have a long enough fuselage to set them forward of that big wing. Second, they're really tough to incorporate into a stealth design. The X-32 didn't have a long fuselage . . . for reasons we'll get to in a moment . . . and it *had* to meet that stealth requirement. So, canards were out.

Boeing envisioned the "box" or "one piece" wing as a monolithic unit built separately from the rest of the aircraft. The fuselage would be 'bolted' up onto the high-mounted wing, rather than the wings being attached to the fuselage from the sides. This promised both great strength and cheaper production. Again, Statkus was concentrating on reducing cost down the road, just as the JSF Project Office had requested.

For their VTOL variant, Boeing decided to adapt the "direct lift" system originally employed on the Hawker Siddeley Harrier, which had in turn been derived from earlier French, British, and German efforts. McDonnell Douglas had reengineered the original design into the AV-8B, so the blended Boeing/ McDonnell Douglas teams could draw on a lot of experience.

In direct lift aircraft, the main engine nozzle rotates downward. This supports the rear of the plane. Engine exhaust is also piped to rocketlike nozzles up front and outboard near the wingtips. It's a balancing act. Films of the early Harriers show how hard they were to control. But modern computers made it easier. This approach allowed the relatively simple addition of nozzles and valves to produce the X-32B. The fewer the differences between the versions, of course, the more commonality, and thus lower cost, a strength of Boeing's approach.

But such systems have downsides. To balance the aircraft when hovering, the engine has to be fairly close to the center of gravity. This places it farther forward than in conventional designs, leading to a short, stubby-appearing plane.

Direct lift had also proven troublesome in another way. Since the descending (or ascending) plane was balanced on exhaust gas, it ran the danger, when near the ground, of sucking hot, oxygen-depleted "used" air into the engine. When the turbine lost power, the plane would drop, entering the exhaust plume even more deeply. This vicious spiral of "exhaust ingestion" had led to crashes with the Harrier. Akin to this was the "pop stall," when the engine would choke or lose power entirely if it sucked in too much gas. The Harrier has long been regarded as a hazardous aircraft to fly, both by the U.S. Marine Corps and by the UK and Indian navies.

Boeing would have to demonstrate these problems were things of the past, to build confidence in their design.

★ ★ ★

Meanwhile, the Lockheed Martin entry, the X-35, was under development at the famed Skunk Works. Under hard-driving director Kelly Johnson, the Skunk Works had built, in total secrecy, such paradigm-shattering planes as the P-80, the U-2, the F-104, SR-71, and the Stealth F-117, which had brought low observables to the world of fighter aircraft.

Lockheed started with two advantages. First, its team, now chaired by lead engineer Rick Rezabek, had been working on supersonic STOL and VTOL aircraft since the 1980s, in "black" programs largely funded by DARPA.

Second, they were fresh off the design of the F-22 Raptor, which had some of what the JSF specifications wanted—stealth and speed—but which had two engines, was expensive, and had no vertical capability.

Nevertheless, Rezabek had begun with concepts derived from that aircraft, and his design's looks reflected that, though in a smaller package and with a single engine. The X-35 demonstrator would have twin vertical tails and two engine inlets on either side of the cockpit. The wing and horizontal tail were conventional. So far, so good.

But to add VTOL to this design for the Marines and the Royal Navy, direct lift just wouldn't work. The engine was too far aft. And anyway, there were the exhaust ingestion and pop stall problems. Maybe it would be best to avoid direct lift altogether?

In 1985 Paul Bevilaqua joined the Skunk Works as the chief engineer of Advanced Development Projects. During the brief post-Gorbachev period, when it looked as if Russia was on a glide path to democracy, Lockheed had contacted the Yakovlev design bureau in Moscow with the offer of a partnership. Four hundred million dollars of Lockheed cash had enabled Yakovlev, designer of the YAK-38 Forger—a VTOL fighter that had operated from Soviet carriers—to build a demonstration model of the YAK-141M, a supersonic-capable version. Both the Yak-38 and Yak-141 had supplemented down-vectored thrust from the rear-mounted engines with two smaller, separate jet engines mounted forward, angled out and down just behind the pilot. These were used only during the vertical takeoff and landing. Two prototypes were built before the partnership ended, but it proved there may be a workable alternative to direct lift.

The Lockheed team, led by Bevilaqua, worked diligently to develop the concept of a shaft-driven lift fan. The concept was a radical change from the traditional thinking of short takeoff and vertical landing engineering design.

It centered on a conviction that adding more engines up front wasn't the way to get either cost or weight down. Instead, they envisioned a "lift fan" behind the cockpit.

Imagine the aircraft balancing on two points of thrust. One is the exhaust from the main engine, directed downward with a rotatable thrust vectoring nozzle. The second point, farther forward, is a jet of cool, dense outside air blown downward by a fan. But not a fan like the one in the local diner! This unit generates enormous thrust in a small package, is lightweight, and is guaranteed not to fail.

This was a radical departure from both the Harrier and the Yakovlev designs. How should this fan be driven? The Pratt & Whitney engineers had planned ahead. A hefty driveshaft emerged from the front of the J119 engine, connected to the rear turbine. This was a well-known design feature for turbine-powered propeller engines as the propeller would attach to the shaft and thrust would be governed by changing the pitch of the propeller blades. This dynamic dramatically increased the thrust potential of propeller driven airplanes like the C130J Hercules and E2D Hawkeye.

But the JSF application would introduce an additional very challenging technical innovation. The challenge was to translate the energy from a rotating shaft to a counterrotating lift fan operating in a different plane. In addition, the fan would only be engaged during STOVL operations. Then, the energy of the rapidly spinning shaft would have to translate to the counterrotating fan when transitioning to the hover mode. Balancing the total thrust across the STOVL variant was an additional complication. Smaller "roll post" nozzles outboard on the wings would divert cool bypass air to provide balance during landing and takeoff and allow a balanced landing in the event of combat damage, hung ordnance on one side, or some other emergency.

All engineering involves a series of more or less unsatisfactory trade-offs. The advantage of the lift fan was that it permitted the engine to be mounted farther aft and lessened the risk of exhaust ingestion. It also made the forward aspect of the plane stealthier, since the engine face could be hidden with curved ducting. The downside was that it added mechanical complexity, weight, and risk. The only moving parts for a direct lift system were butterfly valves to control the flow of exhaust to the nozzles. But the lift fan, driven at up to 26,000 RPM through a long shaft and complicated gears, added multiple points of possible failure.

The unit would have to deliver ten tons of cold thrust with a fifty-inch-diameter, two-stage counterrotating fan. (The gyroscopic effects of a single-rotation fan would degrade flying qualities.) Also, it had to be *utterly dependable*. If it failed during takeoff or landing, and especially in the hovering mode, the X-35 would jam itself into the ground nose-first. Even with a zero-zero ejection seat (zero forward speed, zero altitude), it was anybody's guess whether a pilot could escape such a near-ground nosedive. Because of their long tradition of precision engineering, Lockheed decided to contract Rolls-Royce to build the lift fan. (**See Figure 5: The Lift-Fan Concept for the X-35B STOVL Variant**)

But that new lift fan would need to be fully integrated with new variants of the F119 engine. Bennett said, "PW contributed a lot to make the lift fan work. It was apparent that the STOVL version was critical to winning this program and we were committed to make it succeed."[8]

★ ★ ★

In contrast to Boeing, the Lockheed team would package CTOL and STOVL in the same airframe, the X-35A/B. The "C" variant would have a larger wing and vertical tail to allow slower landing speeds and be strengthened to meet Navy catapult and arresting gear stresses. The variants would share as many parts as possible, but the different requirements would drive significant challenges in design.

Both teams set to work to build their prototypes, with a tight schedule and even tighter budget, and the "winner take all" threat looming over them. For the two companies involved, as for the United States and its closest allies, both the stakes and the risks were sobering. The defense of the West against rapidly evolving threats, both sophisticated air defenses and next-generation enemy fighters, could depend on the outcome.

Yet both teams quickly ran into problems. Boeing, attempting to apply their expertise in new materials, failed in fabricating a graphite-reinforced plastic skin for their huge unitary wing. Lockheed found it wasn't easy making huge titanium machinings and getting the required parts in on time.

But the most glaring error was Lockheed's, and it wasn't even the fault of the shop floor or the engineers.

Instead, it came from the accounting department.

★ ★ ★

Lockheed Martin had been battling an internal conflict between the Skunk Works and the new Aeronautics Headquarters in Fort Worth. That friction was a cause for angst among the government observers but was rooted in the new challenge of merging the Skunk Works culture of Lockheed with the "in-house" culture of General Dynamics. The integration of large corporate entities is always a very significant challenge. It traditionally takes years to accomplish and, when inserted into a major strategic program challenge, can derail the best intentions of all involved. The X-35 management team at the Skunk Works acknowledged a supplier accounting error that identified a $30 million overrun against the fixed price development contract. On a competitive, cost-sharing contract with the US government, that could be a death knell.

To settle the dispute, Lockheed Martin leadership developed an agreement dubbed the "Magna Carta." The document stipulated that the Skunk Works would take charge of the prototype, but that Fort Worth would lead the program. Some in the Pentagon wanted to just award the contract to Boeing, but that would have generated long-running protest activities.

The Navy was the least supportive service based on years of trying to develop "carrier-suitable" airplanes from designs that started for other service applications.

But the Marines were not in that camp. JSF PEO BGen Mike Hough met with then Secretary of Defense Donald Rumsfeld to argue the need to continue the competition. Rumsfeld agreed.

Hough then met with Frank Cappuccio, vice president and the JSF program manager for Lockheed Martin. He told Cappuccio that the competition could continue, but that Lockheed had to invest their own dollars over and above what the government had provided. Accordingly, Lockheed paid for the overrun, but stockholders registered their displeasure by asking for a leadership change. Finally, Hough went to Congress and was directed to keep the competition going. The flying prototype phase of the CD phase was only a part of the total funding appropriated for the government program manager; there were many other nonflying technology, subsystem, and system development activities.

At this point, Lockheed Martin brought in Charles T. "Tom" Burbage from the F-22 program, which was now running smoothly.

Burbage had a unique background for this assignment. A rangy, laconic Naval Academy graduate, class of 1969, he'd survived the Navy test pilot school and had more than three thousand hours under his belt in thirty-eight types of military aircraft. He'd also held a "side job" as an A-7 Corsair pilot in the Naval Reserve, retiring with the rank of captain. He also understood the aircraft carrier operating environment as a Navy test pilot on the carrier trials of the E-2C and S-3A and a subsequent assignment as the catapult and arresting gear officer aboard USS *Eisenhower*.

Within Lockheed, which he joined in 1980, he'd progressed through several demanding assignments, including managing the Washington operations for the Lockheed Aeronautical Companies, leading their Navy aircraft programs and then the F-22 Raptor program. He had a short assignment as the President of the Lockheed Martin Aeronautical Systems Company in Marietta, Georgia. The following year the decision was made to consolidate the three Lockheed Martin airplane companies into a single company with headquarters in Fort Worth, Texas.

In mid-2000, Burbage was asked by Dain Hancock, the new president of the consolidated companies, to take over the JSF Program. His initial reaction was "no." He'd already been the lead on a major acquisition program and president of a company; this seemed like a step backward. But Vance Coffman, CEO of Lockheed Martin, followed up on the request by underscoring the fact that this program would likely change the face of the aerospace industry. In August 2000, Burbage agreed to the task.

★ ★ ★

Now, though, in mid-2000, both competing JSF programs were falling behind schedule. To make matters worse, the Navy suddenly exercised its option to update its requirements for the carrier-capable version. The sea service wanted more maneuverability and more weapon-carrying capacity. Neither of these requirements were in line with fifth-generation fighter design. To some, this was a move to kill the Navy variant. This was predictable based on historical participation in joint programs where the Navy felt they were not in full control of their carrier-capable designs. Despite the fact that the Joint Program

Office was only a short drive up the road from the Naval Air Test Center at Patuxent River, Maryland, and that the JPO was staffed with engineers from Naval Air Systems Command, the sovereign rights of the Navy as the final authority for any airplane entering the fleet seemed compromised to some in Navy leadership.

This requirements change stunned the Boeing team, who were forced to abandon their original delta design. They were too far into production, though, to alter their radical new wing. They would have to fly their original design; the prototypes rolled out on December 14, 1999, two weeks shy of the new millennium.

Meanwhile, both teams had hundreds of engineers and coders hard at work developing the flight control software.

Modern planes are inherently unstable. Pilots can't react fast enough to keep them aloft. The answer is software. The pilot inputs a command, and the computer calculates how to angle the control surfaces and vary engine throttle to accomplish the maneuver. This is called "fly by wire." To accomplish it, both Boeing and Lockheed were running thousands of aerodynamic simulations.

For the X-35, control software was being developed for a limited envelope, but this was still a challenge. The X-35A would fly first and demonstrate basic aerodynamic qualities. Later it would be converted to an X-35B by installing the lift fan, adding the ability to hover, transition to forward flight, transition back to STOVL flight and still perform at supersonic speeds. The X-35C would have to demonstrate exceptional flying qualities in the carrier approach or shipboard landing configuration. History had shown that Navy accident rates were directly correlated to the ability to land at slow but controllable speeds.

Once again, this related to one of the most significant differences in the two companies' design strategies. For Boeing, the decision to employ a "direct lift" concept drove their STOVL variant to be the least common one, and the CTOL and CV variants to share the most commonality. For Lockheed Martin, the lift fan system allowed the CTOL and STOVL variants to retain high degrees of commonality, primarily because of the ability to move the main engine toward the back of the airplane. The CV variant, however, had unique structural and aerodynamic requirements. This meant less commonality than the other two variants.

This would become a significant discriminator between the two offerings.

★ ★ ★

One of the people with a long and critical role in both the X-35 and F-35 design and development was Santiago "Santi" Bulnes. A tall beanpole of an engineer, then in his early thirties, with an inquisitive and coaching leadership style, Santi was a major force in developing a design team that could deal with the stress of a program of the scale and complexity of JSF. Santi started with General Dynamics designing microprocessors on the flight controls hardware team for the F-16. In early 1995, he came to Palmdale to consult on the flight controls for the X-35. From the first day, Santi was concerned with the flight control system hardware components for the X-35.

As he explains, "When you're building a prototype like this, you're trying to do it as fast and as cheaply as possible. So, we used off-the-shelf hardware whenever possible. They had picked an off-the-shelf computer for processing and another computer for data input and output. I was very concerned about the processing portion of that computer because it didn't have the throughput that was required to manage the aircraft."[9]

Shortly after Santi arrived in Palmdale, Cappuccio asked him to lead the flight controls hardware team . . . a big responsibility for a young hardware engineer. As time went on, Bulnes became increasingly concerned about the off-the-shelf computer selected as a baseline. "Things kept going in the wrong direction with insufficient throughput and memory for the demands we knew were coming. We made a decision about two years into that effort to cancel the processor part of that computer."

Computers can be overwhelmed if the demand exceeds the capability of their processors. In the JSF case, the baseline requirement was constantly increasing as the technical solution matured. "That, for me, was a significant red flag," said Santi. "I was in a meeting with the Aeronautics Division President, Dain Hancock, who had just heard an explanation of the situation. To my surprise, he said, 'Okay Santi. I've seen the charts. I've heard people talk about it. I want to hear it from you.' I told him, 'If we don't swap out this processor, I'm going to be looking for another job, because I'm convinced that this is either going to fail, or worse yet, we're going to kill somebody, and I don't want to be part of that.' To management's credit, they said okay and let me select the replacement. I selected two possible suppliers as having the ability to quickly develop a new processor that could meet our computing needs in the aggressive time frame required. Both had been working with me on research and development to design what the final production computer would look like. I selected one of them and was told to go build that computer.

"Frank Cappuccio asked me how well the computer was doing flying and I said, 'Sir, it's not flying on anything.' He then asked "How's it working in the lab?' and I looked at him and I hated giving him this answer. I said, 'Sir, we haven't built one yet.' And he said, 'You mean we canceled a perfectly good computer for a young kid's idea of what a better computer is?' and I said, 'No Sir, you canceled a computer that wouldn't work for one that I know how to make work.' To his credit, he supported me and asked me to give him daily updates. We canceled the baseline computer in July. We had a working prototype in October, and we had it fully integrated with the rest of the computer and the test beds by January. I don't know anybody who's ever put a computer together that fast from scratch. I had a very small team, and we worked really long hours with our suppliers. During that time, I was working till one and two in the morning and I did that for two years of my life. People would look at me and say, 'You look really beat up and tired.' It was a testimony to a prime contractor and supplier team willing to work hand in hand with a very unique requirement."

During the X-plane period, Santi's team also did a number of trade studies, to look at alternatives for the vehicle management and flight controls, should Lockheed win. Santi recalls. "These trades would evaluate performance and cost and risk to try to select the best option for the jet. While we were doing the X-35, all the teams were also running future production tradeoffs for credibility in our proposal for the final F-35 configuration. We were redirected by our manager, who said, 'We want you to focus on getting X-35 to work' and I told him 'I really want to do both. I don't care if I work crazy hours, because I don't want to live this pain ever again. I want to be the lead of the production trade studies for the processing infrastructure being proposed for all the vehicle systems portion of the F-35.' So, we prepared ourselves so that if we won the F-35, we had a computing architecture ready to go on day one."

Both teams strained every sinew as they neared the finish line. Work on the software, trade studies, and production studies kept going at a furious pace, since as soon as a contract was awarded, the government would expect rapid progress.

But one last hurdle, and the most demanding one of all, still remained.

As the old century ended and the new millennium dawned, it was time for the ultimate face-off. And there would be no second-place winner.

Reference

1. Interview with LtGen Jon Davis on February 12, 2018, by Tom Burbage, Betsy Clark, and Adrian Pitman, held in F-35 interview archive

2. https://www.company-histories.com/Pratt-Whitney-Company-History.html, accessed November 8, 2022.

3. Tom Burbage Interview with PW Executives on 24 October 2019: Bennett Croswell, President PW Military Engines.

4. "F-35 Aircraft Program," Interview with Michael Hough. *Washington Journal*, August 23, 2010. https://www.c-span.org/video/?295139-6/35-aircraft-program, accessed October 26, 2022.

5. Interview with Pratt-Whitney Executives by Tom Burbage on October 24, 2019: Bob Cea, PW VP JSF CDP.

6. Interview with PW Executives by Tom Burbage on October 24, 2019: Frank Gillette, PW JSF F-119 Chief Engineer

7. Hoffman, Carl, The X Wars, July 1, 2001, *Wired,* https://www.wired.com/2001/07/fighter/, accessed November 8, 2022.

8. Interview with PW Executives with Tom Burbage on 24 October 2019: Bennett Croswell, President PW Military Engines. Held in F-35 interview archive.

9. Interview with Santi Bulnes on January 11, 2022 by Tom Burbage, Betsy Clark, and Adrian Pitman. Held in F-35 interview archive.

Chapter 4

A BATTLE IN THE SKY

America's first jet fighters, the P-59 and P-80, had first flown at Edwards Air Force Base. Southern California's clear skies and empty desert offered secrecy, as well as safety. There, in 1947, Chuck Yeager had become the first to fly supersonically, in the X-1 rocket plane *Glamorous Glennis*. Edwards' long concrete runways debouched onto a dry lake bed that provided all the room one could want if things went south. As they often did; many of the base's streets are named for pilots who died testing experimental aircraft.

Late in 2000, both planes flew there from Palmdale. For the first time, two X prototypes would face off nose to nose, in what would come to be called the "Battle of the X planes."

As they land, let's look at each in turn. First, from the viewpoint of aesthetics.

Looks weren't a factor mentioned in the JSF requirements, but something about these two planes struck everyone, pilot or not, who viewed them together for the first time. There was an old pilot's cliché: "If it looks right, it will fly right." Or as Kelly Johnson used to put it, at the Skunk Works, "If it looks ugly, it'll fly the same."

The Lockheed plane sat low to the ground, with wings low as well. With twin intakes to either side of a slim cockpit, it came across as sleek, sharklike, and dangerous. It just . . . *looked like* a twenty-first-century fighter.

In contrast, the Boeing X-32 tended to rock viewers back on their heels. Its wing was set high, not low, with the fuselage whale-bellied beneath it. That high wing made the landing gear long and thin, turning the plane gawky on the ground and stork-like on takeoff and landing. (**See Figure 6: X-32 and X-35 side by side**)

The single, gaping front air intake, set just below the bubble cockpit, enhanced the whale shark impression. The aircraft seemed to grin malevolently, like Batman's Joker, yet its stubby fuselage and swollen belly hardly made it look either threatening or fast. Perhaps the pending wing-and-tail redesign would ameliorate its appearance. But it was one of those weapons, like the M-16 or F-117, that looked so different from their predecessors that tastes would have change to accommodate new ideas of "looking right."

Looks aside, the X-32 flew first. Test pilot Fred Knox ferried it to Edwards. He and Navy pilot Phil "Rowdy" Yates would take the plane through its various test points, including simulated carrier landings. Fred and Rowdy were both former Navy carrier pilots who cut their teeth on the F-14 Tomcat and then the F-18 Hornet. Both brought an extensive operational perspective to the JSF program and were experienced test pilots. Both recognized the "once in a life-time" opportunity to be the first to fly a new-generation jet. Like the Lockheed Martin early test pilots, they would wear multiple hats as test pilots, engineering troubleshooters, and salesmen during the intense flight phase of the battle.

Six weeks later, Tom "Squid" Morgenfeld, Lockheed's lead test pilot, took the X-35 to Edwards. Squid had been one of the early test pilots to fly the YF-22 during the Advanced Tactical Fighter fly off against the Northrop Grumman YF-23. Like the Boeing test pilots, Squid was a Tomcat pilot with carrier opera-tional experience. He also had extensive test pilot experience with the F-117 Nighthawk and the YF-22 Raptor. He and USAF LCol Paul Smith would put the Lockheed entry through its paces. "Tall Paul" or "TP" Smith was a very experienced F-16 pilot and brought the Air Force dimension to the team.

Radio call signs are used to identify specific unit aircraft. Each must be of two syllables and one or two words. Bob Burton, Lockheed Martin's X-35 Flight Test Director and his team chose "Hat Trick" for the X-35's call sign. In the United States, the term's used in hockey or soccer to mark three goals in one game by the same player. In cricket, it means three wickets by the same bowler with successive balls. In this case, the name was perfect for the JSF US-UK partnership, with the connection to both soccer and cricket. The three cards in the cocked hat on the airplane's logo represented their goal to "Win X-35A, Win X-35B, Win X-35C . . . Hat Trick!" When the team later decided to take the risk of performing Mission X, a second call for a Hat Trick was informally tagged to the objective of making a short takeoff, a supersonic dash, and a vertical landing on the same flight.

If the X-35—or the Boeing X-32 entry, for that matter—could complete all three, it would indeed be the ultimate hat trick.

The trials would take less than a year to complete and would be the most aggressive flight test accomplishment in history. They would include a daunting array of milestones. Among them were aerial refueling, supersonic flight, simulated carrier catapult launches and arrested landings, short takeoff and vertical landing operations, and early indicators of systems reliability.

★ ★ ★

High-performance jet engines gulp fuel at an astonishing rate. The P&W F119 is no exception, leading to a range in the neighborhood of 1,500 miles, or perhaps three hours aloft. (Exact numbers are confidential, and in any case actual consumption rates vary with bomb load, temperature, altitude, etc.). But over and over, air campaigns—like that of the Battle of Britain,[1] or the Mighty Eighth's bomber offensive over Germany[2]—have been largely decided by the effective radii of action, and combat endurance over the target, of the aircraft involved. That demand hasn't abated in the twenty-first century. Aerial refueling is essential for fighters in long-range strike missions, and the JSF was designed above all to suppress the air defenses of a peer or near-peer enemy in a major campaign.

Aerial refueling had another specific benefit for the X-planes in that it would make flight testing much more efficient, especially when the long transits to the sea ranges became involved. Cross-country flights would also be required when Navy testing began in earnest at the Naval Air Test Center at Patuxent River, Maryland.

Both teams decided to attempt in-flight refueling early in the program. On December 19, 2000, the X-32 was first, behind a KC-10 tanker. The Boeing prototype was equipped with a Navy standard refueling probe, which extends from the forward fuselage. But during that flight, air turbulence edged the drogue trailing the tanker dangerously close to the pitot probes on the nose of the X-32A. Rowdy Yates did connect the probe into the drogue, but the fuel transfer was not successful, with excessive spillage. After evaluation of the flight data and video images, the Boeing team and the Joint Program Office decided that it would be too dangerous to resume air-to-air refueling . . . an initial black mark for the Boeing plane.

On January 23, 2001, the X-35C completed its in-flight refueling certification behind a KC-10. It was also the first flight for USAF Test pilot TPSmith in the X-35C. (The X-35 airplanes used the Air Force–style refueling receptacle, not the Navy probe system.) The certification was quickly completed, which provided a significant advantage to the LM team in terms of flight testing efficiency.

On February 9, the X-35C completed a 2,500-mile transcontinental flight from Edwards to Patuxent River Naval Air Station, south of Washington, D.C. The flight had a single stop in Fort Worth so the rest of the LM JSF team could see the airplane and completed the flight the following day.

In sharp contrast, the X-32 ferry to Patuxent River took several days and multiple stops without aerial refueling.

★ ★ ★

Supersonic flight was also a contract stipulation. But at the century's end, only one operational combat aircraft in the world was both fully stealthy and supersonic. Neither the F-117 Nighthawk nor the Northrop B-2 was capable of supersonic flight,[3] and the Harrier had never been either stealthy or supersonic. The Lockheed Martin F-22 Raptor, which first flew in 1997, was the only one. Its top speed is classified, but it incorporated supercruise, enabling Mach 1.5 or better without the use of afterburners.

Indeed, high speed, good aerodynamics, VTOL, and stealth imposed mutually conflicting requirements. (Remember our earlier discussion about tradeoffs in delta-winged versus tailed designs.) For example, supersonic flight emits a lot of energy, both from skin heating and the hot-burning engines. This can be fatal when an adversary has infrared sensors on its satellites and air-to-air missiles that home on emissions. Other observables had to be minimized, too, including radar, visual, contrails, engine smoke, acoustic, and electromagnetic signatures.[4]

These tradeoffs had required many hours and a lot of experiments and had generated some infrared-emitting arguments at both Seattle and Palmdale. But going faster than sound was a sine qua non.

Lockheed Martin was first. On November 21, 2000, less than one month after first flight, Tom Morganfeld achieved supersonic flight in the X-35A. Rick Rezabeck, the LM X-35 Program Director, recalls: "Tom taxied the X-35A away from the hangar and took off with a gut-thumping roar, quickly disappearing over the desert. A few minutes later, I heard his voice crackle through my radio: 'Ready to go. Ready. Ready. Now.' Then there was silence—he was twenty miles out, too far for us to hear the sonic boom when he broke the sound barrier. A few seconds later I hear 'I'm at one-oh-five at 24,000. It's a good day at the office!'"

Boeing went supersonic three months later in the X-32A. LtCol Ed Cabrera, the USAF test pilot assigned to that team, broke the sound barrier and matched the X-35 milestone, but with a difference.

Due to its original delta wing, Boeing had intended to demonstrate STOVL flight with the X-32B, and go supersonic with the A/C variant only. Not only that, but some parts (notably the front intake cowling) were removed from the B variant in order to hover. The idea was that both designs would be blended later, along with the redesigned wing and tail. This was an awkward position for Boeing to defend, but the Navy had put it in a tight spot.

The early achievement of supersonic flight showed how hard the program was being pushed. The X-35C was validating its Navy performance objectives at Edwards. As part of those tests, the X-35C went supersonic for the first time on January 31, about six weeks after its first flight.

The X-35B first flew on June 23, 2001. Less than a month later, on 20 July, the F-35B became the third X-35 variant to go supersonic.

Although Boeing had originally planned to go supersonic only with the X-32A/C prototype, they also flew their X-32B prototype faster than sound on its last two flights of their STOVL test program on July 17, 2001. So, though supersonic flight was a tough test, all four prototypes had met it.

They were still neck and neck.

★ ★ ★

Reliability and its cousin, ease of maintenance, were two other issues that would be subjected to microscopic scrutiny at Edwards.

Unfortunately, previous stealth designs had poor reputations in these quarters. The F-117, the first low-observable combat aircraft, was really hard to keep in flying condition. "In the early days of the F-117, the aircraft's Radar Absorbent Materials had to be applied by hand, by maintenance personnel who described their work as 'more an art than a science,'" said one program official. Gaps in the RA and access panels that needed to be opened on a regular basis, had to be meticulously smoothed over with a special putty and then left to cure for many hours before a mission."[5]

The B-2 also sucked down expensive maintenance. For each hour in the air, the bomber needed fifty to sixty hours in a hangar, being worked on.[6]

Again, maintaining the stealth coatings seemed to be the most difficult and time-consuming task, requiring specialized and scarce skills and materials.

The F-22 was still too new by then to have accumulated much of a record, but the problems with the earlier designs meant leading indicators of either good or poor reliability would be examined very closely.

But there's a lot more to maintenance and stealth than coatings!

Historically, about 70 percent of a stealthy design is due to shaping of the air vehicle. This includes alignment of planform edges (making sure the forward and aft facing edges were exactly aligned to minimize radar returns.) Secondarily, the ability to hide the engine was also critical.

The choice of a propulsion concept was the key driver that separated the X-32 and X-35 designs. Recall that the X-32's "direct lift" concept used a single engine to generate total thrust. This required the massive weight of engine and nozzles to be located over the plane's center of gravity, for weight and balance reasons. Direct lift was a simpler and less risky option for STOVL flight, but it introduced significant downsides from the stealth and maintainability perspectives.

The X-35 propulsion design, with the lift fan behind the cockpit, allowed the designers to move the engine aft, a more traditional location for jet fighters. It also made possible bifurcated air inlet ducts, hiding the air path to the engine face with its rotating turbine blades. This was hard to do with the X-32 due to the forward placement of the engine, but easier with the X-35's curved engine inlet ducting.

Internal weapon carriage, also essential to covert operation, was integrally tied to the ability to remove and replace an engine, a common and time-consuming requirement for maintenance. The shorter, stubbier design of the X-32 required "slenderizing" the aft fuselage to reduce drag and enable supersonic flight, but this also restricted the maintenance crews' ability to pull an engine out the back of the airplane. Internal weapon bays would have had to be specially constructed and moved up onto the sides of the airplane to allow the engine to "drop out the bottom." The longer fuselage of the X-35 allowed this routine procedure to be accomplished "out the back," making the internal weapon bays easier to build and the plane far easier to service. This would be especially vital in the austere operational environments being considered by the Navy and the Marine Corps.

Not that these issues were officially part of the flight program. The test airplanes did not have weapon bays or any stealth requirements other than basic shaping, but both considerations would translate forward to the final JSF concepts being proposed.

The lift fan concept had one other major advantage as noted in the previous chapter. The flow of air through the lift fan was cool, dense air, as opposed to hot exhaust air from the direct lift propulsion. This would turn out to be a major benefit for the LM design over the X-32. The historical Achilles' heel of direct-lift concepts was susceptibility to loss of lift in the landing phase if the hot exhaust gases were ingested by the main engine. The shaft-driven lift fan completely avoided that risk.

But all that aside, both planes hit all required test points, flying several times a day, which attested to reliability. Speaking to the general press before contract award, General Hough said, "Did they fly it twice a week, like most experimental airplanes? Noooo, they flew it three times a day. They flew it five times a day! I had to take the keys away from them. . . . Ordinarily it would take four or five months to get the test points. We had them in twenty days each, Boeing and Lockheed alike."[7]

★ ★ ★

Low observability was another indispensable requirement. In today's battlespace, a plane that can be detected will quickly be destroyed. The shootdown of a F-117 over Kosovo in 1999 substantiated this. The Nighthawk was stealthy in flight, except when the bomb bay doors were open. It was apparently at this moment that a Serbian air defense battery was able to get a missile off.[8]

Unfortunately, LO is also the most sensitive area of technology. Even a general discussion of how stealth is achieved was classified until lately. But let's discuss this in depth in a later chapter, since it wasn't really part of the Battle of the X-Planes.

★ ★ ★

As spring turned to summer, both designs still seemed to be running more or less neck and neck. Which is what one might expect, given that both contractors were experienced, savvy, and utterly determined to win.

What, then, would constitute the final proof test? The breaker of an all-too-close tie?

The competition seemed to come down to meeting the toughest requirement of all: demonstrating that the design could take off vertically, hover, transition to level flight, then land again in the same way.

Both aircraft hovered on the same day, but in different places, and with quite different results.

The Boeing craft demonstrated hovering at Patuxent River Naval Air Station, on the Chesapeake Bay. The air's denser there than at the 2,300-foot elevation at Edwards. This increased engine thrust, while also being realistic, considering the Marine variant would usually be operating at or near sea level.

Dennis "Irish" O'Donoghue had logged over five thousand hours in fifty different planes. He'd been a Marine test pilot for the AV-8B Harrier and F-14 Tomcat, then flown for NASA before hiring on at Boeing as the lead pilot for the X-32B.

A Navy reporter wrote, "According to Boeing Flight Test Manager Paul Martin, the coming weeks will see the X-32B complete its first transition from wing-borne flight to fully jet-borne hover flight. The next step will be vertical landings, beginning at Pax River's custom Hover Pit facility. Martin explained that the pit 'emulates the out-of-ground-effect environment,' meaning that it allows an aircraft to touch down without suffering the complications of near-ground hover flight. Those complications include a suck-down effect that increases sink rate toward the end of the landing sequence, and potential inges-tion of hot exhaust gases into the engine intake."[9]

Over the weeks preceding the X-32 VTOL trial, Irish and LtCdr Paul Stone RN had flown several STOVL flight tests. They gradually reduced landing speed from 180 knots down to 125, rotating the engine nozzles to touch down at well below conventional stall speeds. O'Donoghue was confident about the plane. "You'll see a lot of smiling faces around here this afternoon," he said. And, "One of the nice things about this aircraft is that it compensates for (ground effect) automatically." He said the X-32 was designed to have "level one" flying quali-ties, meaning that the pilot does not have to work as hard to control the plane. "This is by far the lowest workload cockpit I've ever flown in."[10]

Unfortunately, the smiling faces turned out to be few. As O'Donoghue tran-sitioned from horizontal flight to vertical landing, he experienced that dreaded hot gas ingestion over the hover pit.

He recovered and got down safely, but it was evident that without a good crosswind, an X-32 pilot might suffer the same dangers Harrier pilots had long endured. As testing continued, the design also suffered a pop stall, an engine blip due to hot gas ingestion.

Meanwhile, back at the Skunk Works . . .

As the reader will recall, Lockheed had installed the Rolls-Royce lift fan in the A variant, along with the three-bearing swiveling aft nozzle and wing "roll post" wingtip ducts, turning it into the X-35B. Its first hovering tests would be carried out over a steel-gridded pit.

On June 23, 2001, Simon Hargreaves, a jockey-sized test pilot with the bravado of a Kentucky Derby winner, a former British Harrier pilot and Falklands combat veteran who was now the chief STOVL test pilot for the X-35 test program, taxied to the pit to attempt the first "press up" flight.

Hargreaves, though, wasn't a Lockheed employee. He worked for BAE.

Historically, aerospace programs had a prime contractor leading all the major elements, with partners assuming a supplier or secondary role. The JSF program would be different. The Lockheed Martin management team, led by Frank Cappuccio and Harry Blot, recognized early on that every partner brought expertise that would be critical to program success. They introduced what they called the "best athlete" concept: Whoever could do the job the best would get that job. As Simon would later say, "I couldn't believe another prime contractor was going to allow me to be a chief pilot on their premier program." But so it was, and it would prove a smart choice.

The tests of the X-35A and X-35C had proven that the up-and-away flight envelope of the X-35B should be predictable, with possible small differences on the margins. Testing in the jet-borne (flying on engine power only) regime and the transition between that and wing-borne flight would be the proof of the pudding. Equally hairy would be the reverse transition, back into hover and vertical landing.

The flight test team considered several options. They could get comfortable in hover mode first, then accelerate out to wing-borne flight. Alternatively, they could demonstrate wing-borne flight dynamics and slowly "back into" the hover. After quite a few arguments, the team concluded that since the X-35A and B were essentially the same in wing-borne aerodynamics, the starting point should be in the hover- and jet-borne regime.

The government oversight folks, on the other hand, liked the more traditional path of backing slowly into the hover. Also, they were superconservative in estimating the total lift capability of the X-35B. Anticipating this disagreement, the LM team had bolted the airplane to the hover pit and installed gauges to measure the true lifting capability. They knew exactly how much thrust could be generated. But the government engineers still insisted on lightening the plane to ensure successful "press up." They reduced the fuel load. Although viewed as a "risk reduction" by the government, this actually *increased* the difficulty: The pilot would have to control the thrust much more carefully due to the lighter weight of the airplane as the throttle advanced toward full power.

The plan was to slowly give it gas, "pressing" the airplane up to 1–2 feet. A photo of daylight under the wheels would confirm success.

In the cockpit, though, it was a different story. As Hargreaves later said, "The pilot was the proverbial 'one-armed paperhanger' trying to control many different dynamics in a first-ever event. He had to balance main engine thrust, lift fan thrust, roll post thrust, and center of gravity impacts. This wouldn't be a problem for the eventual F-35, but in the X-35B, because of the requirement to demonstrate two variants in one prototype, he had to raise the nose 7 degrees off the ground prior to liftoff. This position introduced small lateral wing oscillations at the start of the press up." Simon was aware of this and had rehearsed it in the simulator. But because it was divergent (kept getting worse), he had to move swiftly through that regime or risk a "stop test" due to the oscillations.

The upshot was that as he advanced the throttle to move past the fiddly bit, the lightened airplane jumped into the air. Thinking quickly, Simon stabilized the hover at forty feet, then slowly brought the airplane back down onto the pit. Then he very coolly taxied around and repeated the maneuver, just as if it had always been planned that way.

Watching, program manager Tom Burbage muttered to his project leaders, Rick Rezabek and Scott Winship, "I think we just changed the future of military aviation." (**See Figure 7: Simon Hargreaves performs first hover in X-35B. Note Hat Trick logo on tail.**)

The reaction from the government engineers was the opposite of the elation felt by Lockheed leadership. The Program Office rep on-site accused Simon of violating the test card and "showboating," since he'd exceeded the altitude point. But Burbage aggressively rebutted: "Once a procedure starts, the pilot's in charge, not the engineers." In the end, Burbage carried the day. Simon Hargreaves's inspired response, taxiing around and repeating the feat, was an exclamation point on the confidence of the LM team.

Actually, the Lockheed design turned out not even to need a hover pit. The cold air driven downward from the fan blew the oxygen-depleted exhaust backward, away from the front intakes. Unless there was a very stiff tailwind indeed, an easy contingency to guard against, it appeared gas ingestion wouldn't be an issue. The final tests were run with the pit fully plated over, to resemble a ship's deck during vertical landings and takeoffs.[11]

"STOVL temperature and velocity measurements were even better than predicted, and we achieved sustained, full operational thrust," said Harry Blot, deputy program manager and a former Harrier pilot himself. "This not only positions the X-35B for STOVL flight this summer, but also means that no further engine development is needed to meet JSF STOVL requirements. The Pratt & Whitney engine and Rolls-Royce fan performed beautifully. . . . Everything worked as advertised. It was totally reliable."

"All lift-fan engagements worked exactly as expected," Hargreaves said. "The propulsion system responded predictably to pilot inputs, and thrust and thrust-vector commands were crisp. Noise and vibration at full power with the thrust vector at the hover setting were comfortable."

Over a hundred tests had demonstrated "abundant" vertical lift and relatively low exhaust temperatures, resulting in a safer environment for the ground crew than direct-lift systems. The X-35B repeatedly operated at maximum thrust for periods of up to ninety seconds. Individual test series were regularly run with a full fuel load for as much as an hour.

The lift-fan system worked. Though, again, at the cost of increased complexity and weight over the direct lift setup on the X-32.

But would it be enough to seal the deal at Edwards?

That remained to be seen.

★　★　★

Remember the lobbying effort? After all, this was a head-to-head slugfest between two of the most experienced defense heavyweights in the world. In parallel with the technical tests, a much more shadowy, but nonetheless real, contest was going on in Washington and elsewhere, aiming at the hearts and minds of senior senators of both parties and many states.

Burbage recalls: "During this phase of the program, the industrial base was not established, and the major objective was keeping the program sold within

Congress. We often had to deal with a phenomenon we referred to as 'the 1,500-mile screwdriver' where congressional staffers who knew little about engineering would question why we were having some challenge on the program and offer their solution. Many times they were reacting to 'old news' that had been corrected, or to competing lobbyists' misinformation. That's how the game is played in Washington." The promise of jobs in districts was promising but not a reality until the program was decided. Tom added, "Much of our activity on the Hill was fully coordinated with the Joint Program Office and the Services. In many cases, our access to deliver factual information to key staffers was greater than the Pentagon's. Our main objective then was to keep the program funded in the authorization and appropriations processes. One new dimension was the involvement of international partners in this early phase. This became an important part of the support for the program and information flow to Hill staffers."

★ ★ ★

But still, the outcome wasn't predetermined. The race was still on; and as Ecclesiastes observed, it goeth not always to the swift, nor the battle to the strong. As the final demonstration flights drew near, Lockheed huddled. It was time for a Hail Mary pass.

As mentioned in the previous chapter, only three research vehicles had previously demonstrated both hovering and supersonic capability: the German VJ-101C, French Mirage III-V, and Russian Yak-141. But none had managed it in the same flight. A test consisting of a short takeoff, a supersonic dash, then a vertical landing would conclusively demonstrate a design that had overcome the fundamental incompatibilities of supersonic and STOVL flight. Doing this, while maintaining true fifth-generation stealth—yeah, that could be the closer.

With that in mind, the X-35B team planned what they called "Mission X." If it worked, that would blow the competition out of the water. But it would be risky. An accident could cost them the plane, the contract, even the life of the pilot.

Lockheed Martin decided to push all its chips into the pot.

On July 20, 2001, at Edwards, Marine Corps test pilot Major Art "Turbo" Tomassetti took the X-35B up in its final demonstration flight.

Here's Tomassetti's after-action report:

The sortie was to consist of a short takeoff, climbing to 25,000 feet, making a supersonic dash, and returning to the field for a vertical landing. Each event . . . had been accomplished on a previous X-35B sortie, but putting them all together on one flight would be an aviation first. Previous STOVL aircraft achieved supersonic speeds when they had been put in a steep dive, but today we would up the ante by making a level supersonic dash.

The day started with a pre-sunrise flight brief. The early start allowed our team to complete testing before other units at Edwards started flight operations. Additionally, today the field was to close from 10 to 11:30 a.m. for a memorial service. We planned to be done with our test by 9, so there was little time to spare

Until now, I had flown the aircraft for only three brief vertical takeoffs and landings, which gave me a total flight time of about three minutes. The first flight of the day would basically familiarize me with STOVL flight, allowing me to get a feel for the airplane while completing just a few test points. After landing, the ground crew would hot-refuel the jet (load fuel with the engine running), and I would take off again. The second flight would be Mission X.

With all the buildup we had given Mission X over the past three years, I suppose I should have been more excited. Actually, I was more focused on completing all the test events and, more importantly, not making a mistake. Although Mission X consisted of only the three basic events, there were several other test events planned to fill the rest of the sortie. As I was gathering my flight cards . . . the lead military flight test engineer shook my hand and said, "Good luck, and don't forget to have fun out there." I guess I must have looked more worried than excited. . . . After suiting up and completing my preflight, I gave the airplane my traditional pat on the nose. I wouldn't say I'm superstitious, but that day I wasn't taking any chances.

The first flight went very well, and I was able to get a good feel for the airplane while it was in the STOVL mode. Perhaps the most surprising thing about the flight was that there were no surprises. All that time in the simulator had paid off. In fact, the previous night, the simulator team stuck around late so I could practice the mission profile a few times. Another reason the flight had gone well was that the airplane was very easy to fly. Although the Harrier is a remarkable airplane and an amazing achievement in its own right, it is difficult to fly. It takes a long time to train a Harrier pilot, and he must practice a lot to stay proficient. If the first flight in the X-35B was any indication, we were on the right track to making STOVL flight much easier.

During the few minutes it took to refuel, I went over the sequence of events for the Mission X flight. When the test conductor called on the radio to talk about prioritizing the events in the test cards, I realized that we were going to cut it close to the field closing time. There wasn't any room for mistakes or repeats. . . .

I was finally ready to go. Once in position for takeoff, I moved the Thrust Vector Lever back about an inch, initiating the process of converting the aircraft from CTOL mode to STOVL. Behind the cockpit, four sets of doors were opening. This would allow air to flow through the lift fan and enable the vectoring rear nozzle to move through its full range of travel. While the doors were opening, the clutch was engaging, transferring power from the engine to the lift fan. The only noticeable change in the cockpit was an increase in noise as the lift fan spooled up.

A "good conversion" call came from the control room, which confirmed the indications in the cockpit. I radioed the chase aircraft that I was ready and slowly advanced the throttle and released the brakes. The aircraft quickly accelerated down the runway, and at 80 knots, after only 200 feet, I vectored the thrust to 60 degrees and the aircraft leapt off the ground. I completed the post-takeoff checks, climbed through 5,000 feet, and converted the aircraft from STOVL mode back to CTOL by moving the TVL (*thrust vector lever—Au.*) fully forward.

Climbing to test altitude, I turned toward the supersonic corridor, the airspace designated for supersonic flight tests. Upon reaching 25,000 feet, I stabilized briefly, then advanced the throttle to full afterburner. As the afterburner engaged and the aircraft rapidly accelerated, I was pressed back in the seat. I watched the head-up display on the windscreen to make sure that I was maintaining level flight, but mostly I focused on the airspeed indicator. As the airspeed passed Mach 1.0, I adjusted the throttle for Mach 1.05, the target speed for the test. In the cockpit, the transition through the sound barrier was barely noticeable.

Now two of three Mission X events were complete—just one more to go. As I started slowing down for the next test point, I checked fuel and time. It was getting close, but there was still enough time to get everything done before the field closed. I set up for the next event, a set of slow-speed flying-qualities tests. . . . It took about 10 minutes to complete the set. Checking fuel and time again, I realized that we probably didn't have enough of either to complete the last set of tests. After a quick discussion with the test conductor, we decided to head back to the field to set up for the vertical landing.

I began the descent and turned the airplane back toward the runway. Passing through 5,000 feet I slowed below 200 knots, converted the aircraft back to STOVL mode, and began my final approach. Once over the runway, I started the deceleration to the hover. . . . I set up to come to a stop just short of the landing pad, which was just off the runway at about midfield. I brought the aircraft to a hover over the runway, stabilized for a few seconds, and began to cross over to a position above the landing pad. Once the aircraft was centered over the landing site, I reduced the throttle slightly to begin the descent. Out of the corner of my eye, I caught a glimpse of the many spectators in the observation area. No one was running away from the airplane—a good sign.

The aircraft firmly touched down and I quickly chopped the throttle to idle. "Touchdown," I called over the radio. Mission X was complete.

During the taxi back to the ramp, I completed the after-landing checklist and had a few minutes to let the events of the past hour sink in. . . . I glanced at my watch before getting out of the cockpit: just before 10 a.m. All things considered, not bad for a morning's work.[12]

"Not bad"? *The X-35B had become the first aircraft in history to achieve both supersonic and hovering flight in a single sortie.* In 2001, the lift-fan team was awarded the Collier Trophy by the National Aeronautic Association "for the greatest achievement in aeronautics or astronautics in America, with respect to improving the performance, efficiency, and safety of air or space vehicles, the value of which has been thoroughly demonstrated by actual use during the preceding year."[13]

Simon Hargreaves repeated Mission X on July 26, proving it was no fluke.

Boeing attempted a riposte on July 28. Their B variant broke the sound barrier again with a short takeoff, transition to conventional flight, and a burst at supersonic speed. However, that flight did not end with a vertical descent, but another short landing. A second sortie that day included more supersonic runs.

Jerry Daniels, president and CEO of Boeing Military Aircraft, crowed, "Few, if any, flight-test programs have been more successful than the X-32. It is a testament to the dedicated people on the Boeing JSF One Team that the X-32's demonstrated performance so precisely matched predictions."

But "matching predictions" isn't really what competition's about. It's about beating the other guy, which Boeing clearly hadn't, at least that day.

But the final results still weren't in. Both entrants had met the requirements, although Lockheed had established something of a lead in performance, while Boeing still held out the promise of lower production costs.

★ ★ ★

The contest now moved behind closed doors. A government team, chaired by MajGen Mike Hough, the program executive officer, carried out the evaluation. The Lockheed Martin proposal was approximately 25,000 pages, with Boeing's equally thick. No single person read either entire proposal, but each one evaluated specific elements.

Three factors were critical: affordability, the system development and demonstration plan, and past performance. "Affordability" included subfactors for the air vehicle, the sustainment system, and life-cycle costs. The SDD factor addressed the proposed program, including technical plans, management, and SDD cost. The evaluation team assigned each component both proposal ratings and risk ratings and calculated a final ranking via a multi-attribute utility function.

Behind the evaluation process, though, was a concomitant wrestling match: the internal politics of major DoD programs. Funding priorities are always a challenge, but nowhere more bitterly fought out than in joint service acquisitions. For the JSF, the individual services were required to contribute significant resources to the DoD funding profiles. These funding dollars were subject to the tribal wars within the individual services, who often would rather divert those resources to their other priorities. As the final steps of the JSF competition neared, the reality of funding the future stages of a very expensive program seemed to dawn on everyone.

There would be two funding lines: the research and development costs and, separately, the production costs.

As time went on and the development phase stretched out, funding was gradually moved over from the production account to fund shortfalls in development. All the services have competing priorities, but none may be more intense and deeply felt than the Navy's, with multiple procurement challenges in submarines, surface ships, and aircraft. From the beginning, the Navy tended to take a back seat in the F-35 program, despite its aging inventory of Harriers and Hornets. Any delay opened the door to the "more of the same, but cheaper" alternative. The argument to keep buying equipment already familiar to frontline operators, perhaps with a few new bells and whistles added, has long been a tactic of incumbent contractors. Strategically, however, for the Navy to abandon the move to fifth-generation aircraft would eventually erode the capability of their enormous investment in nuclear supercarriers. Over time, these conflicting priorities would become a factor with every stakeholder in the program.

★ ★ ★

After their proposal was submitted, LM management shifted to wait-and-see mode. While prudent and definitely economical, this failed to recognize the need to start investing in the elements that would be critical to starting up, should they be the winner. Little did anyone know how decisive this would become within a very few weeks.

Think about the challenge that would be handed to the winner. Design, develop, test, field, and sustain a family of first-line fighters that could carry out conventional air operations, operate off small ships and unprepared fields, and project power from large deck carriers. Embed the most sophisticated suite of multispectral sensors ever employed. Make sure US allies could participate, with the goal of interoperability and burden sharing. In addition, revitalize a global industrial base that had atrophied over the post–Cold War years. Implement a revolutionary manufacturing capability based on high-precision automation and motion-based production systems. Transfer technology that would enable US allied partner nations to compete on a global stage. And do it all during a generational change in the workforce, with the media watching like hungry hawks.

Equally challenging would be the incorporation of the partner countries into the design and development. Currently, each contractor team used a different set of 3D computer-aided design tools, and converting to a common one wouldn't be quick or easy. Strict control of access to technical data would also complicate things, to guard against spying.

In short, this is what management should have been doing. Yet they weren't.

And then, the whole game suddenly changed. Overnight.

★ ★ ★

September 11, 2001, dawned as a beautiful fall day. The skies were clear. Hurricane Erin was sidling past a few hundred miles off the Atlantic coast, but it wasn't expected to strike New York or Washington.

Instead, another catastrophe unfolded. Islamic terrorists from Saudi Arabia, masterminded by a dark figure ensconced in the mountains of Afghanistan, hijacked four fully fueled airliners after they took off for California from airfields on the East Coast. Osama bin Laden hit the country with an unexpected weapon, with astonishing effect. Two planes demolished the twin towers of the World Trade Center, in Manhattan, while the third struck the west facade of the Pentagon. The fourth, United Airlines Flight 93, was brought down by its passengers when they stormed the cockpit. It crashed near Shanksville, Pennsylvania. Its target was probably the US Capitol.

The attack triggered shock and horror across the world. The Cold War had ended with what felt like an American victory. Now that Pax Americana was suddenly shattered. President George W. Bush announced, "Our responsibility to history is already clear: to answer these attacks and rid the world of evil. . . . This conflict was begun on the timing and terms of others. It will end in a way and at an hour of our choosing."

On that very day, the executive management team of Lockheed Martin, Northrop Grumman, and BAE Systems were meeting in LM's Fort Worth facility to review the program's status as they awaited contract award. They'd just started the review when Linda Brightwell, the president's long-serving administrative assistant, came in. She whispered to Dain Hancock that an airplane had just hit the World Trade Center.

Burbage says, "Our first reaction was one of deep discounting, assuming an errant pilot in a small plane. But Linda came in again a few minutes later and said a second airplane had hit the second tower. We suspended the meeting and watched in horror with the rest of the world as the events of September 11, 2001 unfolded." With the cessation of air traffic, the executives were stuck in Fort Worth until the chaos was sorted out.

The Defense Acquisition Board met as planned on October 24, 2001, to "downselect" the winner of the JSF competition. "Downselect" is acquisition-speak for naming the winner, and certifying that the design was ready to enter the next phase.

The dramatic public announcement was made on Friday, October 26, 2001, in the press room at the Pentagon. Present were the Under Secretary of Defense for Acquisition, Technology, and Logistics, Edward C. "Pete" Aldridge; the Source Selection Authority, Secretary of the Air Force James Roche; Gordon England, Secretary of the Navy; Lord William Bach, UK Parliamentary Under-Secretary for Defence; Sir Robert Walmsley, UK Chief of Defense Procurement; and VADM Jeremy Blackham, RN, Deputy Chief of Defense Staff (Equipment Capability). Also there were MajGen Mike Hough, the JSF PEO, and BGen Jack Hudson, USAF, JSF Deputy PEO. (**See Figure 8: "The Winner Is . . . Lockheed Martin" at the Pentagon Press Room, and Figure 9: "The Winner Is . . . Lockheed Martin" in the Fort Worth Conference Center**)

Secretary Roche stated that both competitors' proposals were "very strong," but that the Lockheed Martin team "emerged continuously as the clear winner" on a best-value basis, considering strengths, weaknesses, and relative risks.

Oddly, the "F-35" designation seemed to be assigned off the cuff. Questions from the press are always challenging, but when a reporter asked Secretary Aldridge what the airplane would be called, he looked down the row of principals and asked General Hough, "What are we going to call this?" Hough's answer was, "Let's call it the F-35, since the X-35 was the winning competitor." (In fact, the USAF has naming responsibility for fighter aircraft and the sequential designation should have been the F-23.) But henceforth, the CTOL variant would be designated the F-35A, the STOVL variant the F-35B, and the carrier variant the F-35C.

Lockheed's shares jumped to $52.70 after hours, after finishing the regular session up $1.02 at $49.92. Boeing slipped to $35.05 in after-hours trading.[14]

The jubilation at Lockheed was matched by silence and disconsolate faces at Boeing.

Spurred on by 9/11, the government wasted no time sealing the deal. The model contract submitted with Lockheed Martin's proposal was signed without further negotiation, the same day. This was a surprise, and would become an issue later, as program requirements continued to evolve, as costs rose, as new tugs-of-war emerged between the government, Lockheed, and suppliers, not to mention the often hostile oversight of the press.

The clash of corporate titans, grimly fought out for years in the design departments, the software labs, the halls of Congress and the Pentagon, and finally in the cloudless skies above the Mojave and Chesapeake, was over.

But the struggles and controversies over the Joint Strike Fighter had only begun, and the starting gun was about to go off.

Reference

1. Deighton, Len, et al. *Battle of Britain*. Penguin Group, London, 1990, 214.

2. Hogan, Eric, "Mighty Eighth was decisive force against Nazi Germany," *Augusta Chronicle*, May 2, 2020.

3. Correll, John T. "History of Stealth: From Out of the Shadows," *Air Force Magazine*, Sept. 1, 2019.

4. Correll, John T. "History of Stealth: From Out of the Shadows," *Air Force Magazine*, Sept. 1, 2019.

5. Tirpak, John A. "Two Decades of Stealth." *Air Force Magazine*, June 1, 2001.

6. Hennigan, W. J. "Costly B-2 bombers both tech marvels, 'hangar queens,'" *Los Angeles Times*, June 13, 2010.

7. Interview LtGen Mike Hough with Tom Burbage, Betsy Clark, held in F-35 Interview Archive

8. Tirpak, John A. "Two Decades of Stealth." *Air Force Magazine*, June 1, 2001.

9. Darcy, James, "X-32B Takes First Flight Tests at PAX," NAS Patuxent River Public Affairs Department release, June 21, 2001.

10. Darcy, James, "X-32B Takes First Flight Tests at PAX," NAS Patuxent River Public Affairs Department release, June 21, 200.

11. "X-35B Completes Hover Pit Testing," Lockheed Martin News Release, undated (this and previous three paragraphs).

12. Tomassetti, Arthur, "Above & Beyond: Mission X," *Air & Space Magazine*, May 2002. By Permission.

13. Regele, Nicole, "Integrated Lift Fan Gets Nod for Collier Trophy." *NAA News*, February 25, 2002. Accessed October 7, 2021.

14. CNN Money, "Lockheed Awarded Contract: Defense Dept taps Lockheed Martin for $200B Joint Strike Fighter," October 26, 2001.

Chapter 5

THE RUBIK'S CUBE OF PARTNERING

Most people are familiar with the multicolored three-dimensional plastic puzzle invented by Ernő Rubik. Each surface can be rotated independently to line up so that eventually, if you're really good, each of the six formerly multicolored facets of the cube ends up as a single color. Rotation along one plane changes every alignment on the other planes. Though a toy, it could also be seen as a training aid for managing complex situations with many frequently changing interactions.

Similarly, the F-35 program was thought of by many as "just another airplane." But its many critical relationships meant a variation in one would subtly or overtly ripple over into and transform all the others.

Like a Rubik's Cube? Yeah, maybe . . . but imagine trying to solve such a puzzle in six dimensions, rather than three.

The X-35 had been prototyped by a company only recently soldered together in the merger of former competitors. To produce the F-35, that company, in turn, had to manage a partnership of formerly independent aerospace companies that historically had been dagger-wielding rivals. Getting them to work together without murdering each other was akin to solving one level of the cube. But then, international dimensions had to be added *on top of that*.

Each level had to snap precisely into place to solve the puzzle and create a coherent, effective organization.

★ ★ ★

The Lockheed Martin company had already been through one gut-wrenching near-death experience. At the "Last Supper" at the Pentagon in July 1993, Deputy Defense Secretary William Perry had presided over a meeting with industry executives. He pulled no punches: the new "peace dividend" would not support the current defense industrial base. Companies with historic names—Grumman, Boeing, Lockheed, Rockwell, McDonnell Douglas, Martin Marietta, and others—would have to either merge or exit the business.[1] The meeting led to a wave of consolidation to shrink the industry rationally before *everyone* went screaming down the tubes together.

In 1993 Lockheed bought the Fort Worth Division of General Dynamics. This acquisition gave the company "two thirds" of the F-22, since GD was one of the partners along with Boeing and Lockheed. It also acquired a long-running cash cow: the F-16 Fighting Falcon, a lightweight warplane but a heavyweight champ in the international fighter arena. But GD's company culture was quite different from Lockheed's traditional mindset of rapid prototyping and advanced technology development in a sister company, the Skunk Works. Rather, in the General Dynamics culture, everything was done at the parent company.

On March 15, 1995, Lockheed and Martin Marietta officially merged to become Lockheed Martin. That same year, Tom Burbage became the executive VP and general manager for the F-22 Raptor. In 1999 he was appointed president of the Lockheed Martin Aeronautical Systems Company in Marietta, Georgia.

The next twist of the cube began internally, in the year 2000. The Lockheed Martin Corporation was engaged in a major downsizing and consolidation itself, after a strategic review the previous year. LM was divesting noncore businesses and buying others that promised synergy going forward. As part of this, Chairman Vance Coffman was merging three previously independent aeronautical companies—the Lockheed Martin Aeronautical Systems Company in Marietta, Georgia, the Lockheed Martin Fort Worth Company, and the Lockheed Martin Advanced Development Company in Palmdale California—into a single operating enterprise. The new Lockheed Martin Aeronautics, the corporation's single aircraft company, would be headquartered in Fort Worth, Texas, with secondary operating sites in Marietta and Palmdale.

★ ★ ★

The Lockheed Martin Aeronautical Systems Company in Marietta, Georgia, had a rich aviation history. It got its start as the Bell bomber plant supporting the war effort in the 1940s. A government-owned, contractor-operated facility known as Air Force Plant 6, it began by building the Boeing B-29 Superfortress, producing more than 650. Lockheed took over operation of the facility in 1951 and began overhauling B-29s there.

Meanwhile, at the Skunk Works facility in Burbank, California, Lockheed was developing the C-130A Hercules under a classified contract for the U.S. Air Force. After development, the transport would later be transferred to Marietta for production.

The inaugural flight of the first C-130A Hercules in the spring of 1955 was the opening chapter of a story legendary in aviation annals. A prototype being tested at the Skunk Works caught fire, burning one of the wings completely off. Few could have imagined that that same airframe would still be on active duty thirty-seven years later and would fly in to be parked next to the 2,000th C-130 (the C-130J) for its delivery in May 1992! The C-130 has been in continuous production for nearly half of the time since the Wright Brothers showed the world that powered flight was possible—the longest-running aircraft production line in history. Later known as "the airlifter capital of the world," Marietta also built the C-141 Starlifter and the C-5 Galaxy, both famous in their own rights.

★　★　★

For a long time, aviation enthusiasts had considered McDonnell Douglas and General Dynamics the major players in the Air Force fighter community and Grumman the same for the Navy. Despite that, the two companies locked in the final flight demonstration phase of the Air Force's Advanced Tactical Fighter competition in the 1980s were Lockheed and Northrop.

However, although Lockheed was mainly known for its "big airplane" family of airlifters and anti-submarine warfare airplanes, it also had a history of innovative fighter designs. The P-38 Lightning first flew in 1939. More than 10,000 P-38 "fork-tailed devils" were churned out, and it was operated by twelve nations. The P-80 Shooting Star first flew in 1945. Lockheed built two thousand, and six nations flew it. The F-104 became the first real allied fighter, flying first in 1958. Fifteen nations flew 2,500 Starfighters. The company also built fifty-nine F-117 Nighthawk stealth fighters, which began operation in 1983.[2]

In 1990, the Air Force awarded Lockheed the Advanced Tactical Fighter program. In traditional company style, the YF-22 prototype development and flight testing had been done by the Skunk Works in Palmdale, California. Initially, production was planned for the Lockheed Burbank facility.

But those decisions changed dramatically as the "Last Supper" kickstarted the restructuring of the defense industry. With the Lockheed Martin merger, the Burbank operation was closed, relocating the Skunk Works to a facility in Palmdale that had formerly hosted L-1011 Tri-Star production. F-22 production, if Lockheed Martin won the ATF competition against the Northrop YF-23, would relocate to Marietta, Georgia.

★ ★ ★

All this corporate reshuffling presented significant stumbling blocks for management, especially since it was happening simultaneously with the JSF development. Boeing was a mean competitor; LM had to focus not just on designing the best plane, but also writing the winning proposal and making a convincing case the company could design, produce, and maintain such an advanced weapon system.

By the 1999–2000 time frame, the JSF maturation and analysis work and the extensive proposal effort were all taking place in Fort Worth.

Meanwhile, two thousand miles away in the high desert of Palmdale, the build of the X-35 concept demonstrators and the flight testing to gather data supporting the proposal was led by the Skunk Works in Palmdale, following their rapid prototyping model.

Integrating legacy individual company and corporate cultures into a consolidated operating model is always demanding and time consuming, even more so when the organizations are technically and geographically complex. Most critical was the need to establish trust across the new company boundaries. It wasn't as easy as just reassigning desks and uploading a new logo. While each piece of the new Lockheed Martin Aero puzzle depended on every other piece for success, it would be a long time before it became a seamless operation.

And it was about to get a lot more complex.

★ ★ ★

The third twist of the cube required forming a winning *industry* team. When the final competition on major programs moves from three to two competitors a second tectonic plate shift often occurs. And it did.

Realigning the industry had a huge impact on the shape of the US aeronautics business. When the McDonnell Douglas-Northrop Grumman-BAE team's design was ruled out, almost immediately Boeing acquired McDonnell Douglas, giving them a lock on the commercial airplane market and adding current fighter expertise with the addition of the F-18 program. Northrop Grumman and BAE Systems joined Lockheed Martin, bringing deep stealth technology and STOVL experience.

The job of building the new world-class Lockheed Martin organization was daunting enough; trying to do it again with three global prime contractors made it even gnarlier. Incorporating two potential engine manufacturers under associate partner agreements as well, drove LM management to recognize they had to develop a "JSF Culture" that could transcend the traditional prime/subcontractor relationship. But more on this in the next chapter!

A subdimension of this was the need to forge a good working relationship with a new government program office. Traditionally, the individual services had developed their own aircraft. Their program offices were located at their individual acquisition and test centers. Major USAF programs like the F-22 had been managed by system program offices (SPOs) at Wright-Patterson Air Force Base, under the Air Force Materiel Command. Navy programs like the F-18 Hornet were managed out of Naval Air Systems Command in Patuxent River, Maryland.

The Joint Strike Fighter arrangement was quite different. It was managed by a joint program office (JPO) headed up by the JSF program executive officer (PEO) in Arlington, Virginia. That close-to-Washington, D.C., location was important, since a multiservice program required much more intimate liaison with Pentagon and Congress than single-service efforts. The JPO drew on the best engineers from the Air Force and Naval Air Systems Commands.

The PEO position rotated among the Air Force, the Navy, and the Marine Corps. When the PEO leads changed service, their immediate reporting responsibility also shifted, so Air Force commanders would report to the Secretary of the Navy, and the Navy and Marine Corps commanders would report to the Secretary of the Air Force. The intent of this square dance was to ensure "fair treatment" among the services, but it also added new opportunities for friction and buck-passing.

Aligning the contractor team and the government team was thus essential to prevent confusion. This task fell to the first PEO, USAF Maj Gen Jack Hudson, who assumed his position at the Pentagon announcement of the winner.

Hudson was an acquisition professional and had previously worked with Burbage on the F-22. His style came out in two questions he'd ask in nearly any situation. The first was a simple "How're you doing?" . . . usually easy to answer, especially to a general. The second would always generate long pauses and often very interesting discussion: "How do you know?" Very few could answer that one without extensive probing and discussion.

Hudson described those early days: "On October 26th, 2001, Lockheed Martin was awarded the contract, and I became PEO the next day. My charter was to spend the taxpayer and partner country monies carefully in the SDD phase. We needed to get the program underway, keep the services together, and keep the allied partnership intact. We had a lot of big challenges. We had to staff the program office with all three services and membership from all partner countries." Eventually this would also include Israel, Japan, and Singapore joining in a more traditional foreign military sales category.

"Aligning organizations was a challenge but we worked hard to match up our government and industry organizations, element by element. This provided clear JPO-contractor counterparts. It was a massive effort and big challenge to keep communications and energy focused across the government/industry teams. If we could do it right, we knew the airplane would be a beast, and would be with us for a long time."

The cube became even more complex with the addition of a fourth and fifth dimension. The fourth involved establishing the government-to-government agreements; the fifth meant involving the industrial base of each partner country.

Let's start with the government-to-government agreements.

★ ★ ★

Over the years, the technological lead in aviation had shifted back and forth across the Atlantic. The Wrights began as the front-runners, of course, but the French quickly overtook them. The United States lagged through the 1930s, but by the end of World War II had drawn even with the British and Germans. Ever since, the United States has held the lead throughout the Jet Age and into the Space Age.

For the past few decades, many allies had purchased American warplanes, both fighters and transports (though our bombers don't seem to be a popular product line overseas). Typically, they placed orders once development was complete.

Once airplanes were ordered, they expected what's called an "offset"—a quid pro quo. The US government agreed to purchase certain of that country's goods, in exchange. This helped with balance-of-payment issues and could make a heavy expenditure more politically palatable.

The JSF program would be structured differently from the start. The Department of Defense wanted a new model of cooperation. The UK was the prime partner, but other allies were also invited to join the program up front, *as equals.*

The announcement of the F-35 winner was undoubtedly influenced by the events of 9/11 and the need to develop a "coalition of the willing" to prosecute the War on Terror. Although a partnership on JSF would not actually add significant war-fighting capability for many years to come, it was a real enabler of future coalition war fighting. It was clear to Pentagon planners that a war in the desert against jihadist ideology could easily escalate to a wider conflict, possibly with a more technologically advanced nation. To be unprepared to deal with that would be a strategic blunder. The recognition that participation would significantly elevate the role of smaller, allied air forces in any bigger conflict was also critical in winning support.

The government-to-government invitation to participate would be codified in a series of bilateral agreements enacted by the George W. Bush administration over the year after the F-35 contract award. Secretary Aldridge tasked Al Volkman, a very experienced Department of Defense negotiator, to lead the JSF concept demonstration phase (CDP) international cooperative agreement strategy. Frank Kenlon from the Navy's International Programs Office was his principal deputy, supported by Jon Schreiber from the JSF Program Office. Together, they negotiated the government-to-government partnerships that would define the future for allied airpower.

Frank Kenlon recalled,

In mid-1994, while the program was still named JAST, DoD's international cooperation experts were asked to develop a strategy that would allow select allied nations to join the JSF concept demonstration phase as cooperative partners. To say this was a precedent-setting decision would be a huge understatement. DoD had *never* encouraged partner nations to join a major tactical aircraft program this early before, let alone one designed with stealth characteristics from its inception. After some dialogue within the Pentagon, top DoD leadership decided that the UK would be offered a significant role as the primary partner, including participation in the source selection process for the winning contractor. This meant the UK would be a 10 percent partner, with the objective of replacing their AV-8B Harriers with JSF STOVLs. Fortunately, the DoD and JSF leadership gave us performance objectives, rather than try to tell us how to do it, an all-too-common problem in the Pentagon.

The framework had three major phases. First, the concept demonstration phase would have four levels. The UK would be a collaborative partner; others could be associate partners for a contribution of about $50 million or an informed partner for about $10 million. Others could be considered later for traditional foreign military sales. Second, the system development and demonstration phase would have three partner levels based on contributions and would be by DoD invitation only. Third would be the production phase, which would be based on an international agreement for cooperative production.

From a US and partner nation perspective, the approach was a radical departure from all previous cooperative development agreements, and it provided each nation with minimal partnership risks. The United States was able to run CDP efforts without "partner interference," a major DoD concern based on previous experience in other cooperative agreements. Except for the UK, the other partner nations were able to join based on a scope and schedule of their choosing at minimal expense. DoD used the $250 million contributed by the various partner nations to expand the scope of the CDP effort in areas of mutual interest. The web of government-to-government cooperation encouraged the partner nations' industries to establish "best value" teaming arrangements at the inception of the program that would provide mutual benefits. All partner nations had the choice of either continuing JSF cooperation after the SDD prime contractor selection through some type of follow-on agreement or departing the program without penalty.[3]

This framework led the international agreement team to devise a two-tiered negotiation concept. They nicknamed it the "pepperoni pizza" approach, because it "divided the pie" among the allied participants. The United States and UK got the largest pieces because of their involvement in the ASTOVL and investment in JSF. The remainder of the pie would be proportional to the level of investment of other participants. The heftier the investment, the tastier the benefits.

The DoD team negotiated the first "pepperoni slice" with the Northern European "F-16 Falcon Community" Ministries of Defense of the Netherlands, Norway and Denmark. The Royal Netherlands Air Force was the largest fleet operator of the European Participating Air Forces (EPAF) F-16 Fighting Falcon. The EPAF countries (Netherlands, Norway, Denmark, Belgium) had long operated as a unified group and often deployed as an integrated force. As the Dutch went, so would go the EPAF group. Thus, it was crucial to get the Royal Netherlands Air Force on board.

The Dutch decided to join as a Level 2 partner with an investment of approximately $1 billion. As one of only two Level 2 partners, the Netherlands would have the opportunity to purchase operational test planes and participate in the US-based operational test and evaluation program (OT&E).

General Ben Droste, then chief of the Royal Dutch Air Force, said, "The JSF would be the first time that all three US services and allied air forces would use one base program designed against a cost criterion. It would not be just an industrial project like the F-16 production line, but Dutch industry would have to compete with the global aerospace industry. Additionally, the Dutch F-16 had always been kept modernized to the USAF standards which meant the Dutch were the only European air force allowed to fly frontline missions including combat at night." But committing to procure two test planes as a Level 2 partner would be an interesting political decision, since it would happen several years before the politicians would be asked to buy operational F-35s.

Droste added, "If you ask me how did European industry view US dominating the global fighter market? The German Luftwaffe commander was fired (retired early) because he said the only real successor to the F-16 was the F-35. Germany's tie to Airbus and Eurofighter politically was a very tough obstacle."

Norway and Denmark were also important but operated much smaller fighter fleets. They joined in a cooperative investment as Level 3 partners with a combined contribution of about $250 million. Denmark also contributed a F-16 to be part of the F-35 test program at Edwards as a "contribution in kind." (**See Figure 10: Danish F-16 Chase Plane with JSF Program Tail Flash**)

The third slice of the pizza was negotiated with the Italian Ministry of Defense. Italy, a strong US ally during the Cold War era and after, would be the first partner to procure both the F-35A and the F-35B. The Air Force had operated US fighters from the days of the P-47 Thunderbolt and P-51 Mustang. They would replace their F-104s, Tornados, and leased F-16s with sixty F-35As. The Italian Navy's Air Arm would also replace its AV-8B Harrier II Plus fleet with thirty F-35B STOVL jets. Those jets would fly from the new flagship of the Marina Militare (Italian Navy), the aircraft carrier *Cavour*. *Cavour* was launched in 2004 and entering service in 2009. These ninety F-35s would make Italy one of the largest F-35 operators in the F-35 international partnership. Italy joined in the summer of 2002 as a Level 2 partner with the same privileges as the Netherlands.

Turkey, historically one of the largest operators of the F-16, had built that fighter in the Turkish Aircraft Industries facility in Ankara. They joined as a Tier 3 partner. Their investment was $175 million, with the intent of making the biggest buy of the new fighter after the United States. Turkey had an exceptional industrial capability and eventually made components on every F-35 from the very beginning of the program. (The Turkish F-35 program would later become the victim of global politics, but more on that later.)

The last country to join was Australia, in October 2002, one year after the contract was awarded. Australia would join as a Tier 3 partner. Their investment was $125 million. Australia, a Boeing F-18 Hornet operator for many years, had a strong Boeing presence that factored into the decision-making structure. Boeing had several thousand Australian employees and a very effective lobbying organization and was anxious to supplant the F-35 program with additional buys of the F-18. Australia possessed a skilled but not very large aerospace industry, mostly based on an automotive production capability. They had strong engineering resources, excellent technology in robotics, and advanced tooling capability. They also had an innovative culture of customer service that facilitated the advance of their global specialties despite their geographical challenges.

In late August 2001, Burbage got an unofficial call to meet with AVM Ray Conroy and BRIG Dave Hurley, from Australia. (Tom had worked with AVM Conroy in a previous assignment on the C-130J.) They met up at the Capital Grille, a restaurant that historically has kept many secrets, in downtown Washington, D.C. The conversation centered on the upcoming decision to join or not. According to Conroy, the Australian Government Department of Defence was worried Australia's late arrival at the party might kneecap their ability to secure manufacturing contracts. Would the last country to sign on find enough left on the pizza platter to justify joining?

Burbage, as Lockheed Martin's F-35 program manager, couldn't make commitments for the US government, of course. But he assured the Australians that no hard-and-fast decisions or commitments had been made yet. Their industry would be given ample opportunity to compete. His assurances probably helped firm up Australia's 2002 decision to join.

Strategy aside, in February 2002, Canada was the first country to officially join the SDD phase. Canada's proximity to the United States, alliance in the NorthCom Military Command, and broad-scale aerospace and defense industrial base offered them a great chance to capture some of the initial contracts. Ottawa joined as a Level 3 partner with a commitment of $125 million over ten years.

★ ★ ★

The fifth dimension, industrial participation, was complicated too. Sort of like having the squares on that twisty cube suddenly switch colors.

Several partner countries had specialized "boutique" industries, competitive in the automotive industry but not qualified in aerospace. Some had no experience in advanced complex composite manufacturing but wanted to get into that next-generation manufacturing capability. All would need to step up their game to get a spot on the team. As always, their ability to participate was critical to sustaining political support. A future chapter will take a closer look at Australia, where industry advocacy provided critical backing during a firestorm of criticism in the early 2010s. But the United States has strict rules governing international trade agreements, especially in defense technologies. Even though participation was a tasty lure for the partners, State Department rules were cumbersome. State and multiple U.S. Department of Defense offices had to agree somehow to make that work.

The sixth dimension was to integrate all the US multiservice test organizations into a coherent operation. The agreements for the UK and the Netherlands granted those two partners the right to participate in OT&E as well. Their investment in the test aircraft was offset by the need to conduct their individual test and evaluation after delivery. The test program would involve the U.S. Air

Force, the U.S. Marine Corps, and the U.S. Navy, along with the two international partner countries in a flying role. The six other international partners would be observers in a nonflying role. There were three primary test sites, ten secondary test sites, five formal test organizations, fifteen instrumented test aircraft, and more than 15,000 flight test hours.

No program had ever successfully navigated such labyrinthine shoals before.

★ ★ ★

These multiple and often conflicting dimensions of the F-35 Rubik's Cube introduced complexity over and above any previous program. To many, solving the puzzle seemed well-nigh insurmountable. The onset and growth of social media and the hair-trigger judgments of its users, the relentless personnel turnover across stakeholders and leaders every couple of years, and the changing and often frosty political and economic winds only increased the peril.

This unprecedented international alliance, with its dimensions of politics, economics, engineering, production, and even questions of military force structure and changing strategic circumstances, was to quickly become even more convoluted, frustrating, expensive, and occasionally argumentative than anyone expected at first.

So . . . could *anyone* snap this six-dimensional cube into alignment? Could such a program survive at all?

A major reorientation, not just in contracts, but in the way each participant thought, would have to be engineered.

The very culture had to be rebuilt, and a new, worldwide way of working, feeling, and speaking would be necessary.

If not, the F-35 would crash and burn before it ever had a chance to take to the air.

Reference

1. "A Merger of Equals," Lockheed Martin website, accessed 8 Oct 2021.
2. https://www.Lockheedmartin.com/our history.
3. Interview with Frank Kenyon by Tom Burbage, Betsy Clark, and Adrian Pitman on July 13, 2021, plus extensive email exchanges. Held in the F-35 interview archive.

Chapter 6

BUILDING THE GLOBAL SECURITY PARTNERSHIP— EUROPEAN AND PACIFIC ALLIANCES

B y the late 1980s and early 1990s, fighter inventories around the world were aging. Though most US allies had at least tentative replacement programs underway, their reduced perception of menace after the collapse of the Soviet Union tightened defense budgets.

In 1990, the Joint Advanced Strike Technology (JAST) program launched into the teeth of this headwind. JAST would develop the technologies essential to developing the next-generation fighter referred to as the Joint Strike Fighter (JSF). To make matters worse, European industry was taking an increasingly dim view of the United States dominating the fighter market. They were cheering on their own contenders (notably Eurofighter, Gripen, and Rafale). To persuade other nations to sign up with the F-35 team, the promise of a revolutionary new aircraft would not be enough. Many people, at the highest levels of the military and government, would have to make strenuous and sustained efforts to bring a cohesive, effective global partnership into being.

★ ★ ★

As explored in previous chapters, US planes had always been developed to operate within the distinctive environments (and cultures) of the Air Force, the Navy, and the Marines. International allies tended to buy their frontline fighters based on the US service most aligned with their own operating environment. Shipboard operators, such as the UK and Italy, aligned with the Marines and the AV-8 Harrier. Land-based operators tended to follow the Air Force, often sharing training and doctrine development as well. In some cases, allied air forces procured designs originally developed for the U.S. Navy, usually because of the safety factor of twin engines. The Royal Canadian Air Force, Finland, and Switzerland operated over austere, frozen, and mountainous geography. The Royal Australian Air Force also operated over a vast, largely unpopulated countryside. All were Navy F-18 operators.

The strategic environment was also changing. Most war-fighting and peacekeeping actions had become joint and combined (allied) operations. Unfortunately, the actual combat effectiveness of multinational forces had often proved disappointing. Export control restrictions and many nations' insistence on installing locally manufactured systems and modifications meant allied air forces found it hard to play as part of a team. Not only that, sustaining and maintaining such a diverse inventory was increasingly expensive.

In stark contrast to this legacy way of thinking, the Joint Strike Fighter was developed around a far more expansive vision. If all three US services and major allied air forces and navies could operate the same airplane, global security would be significantly enhanced, and at a lower cost to all concerned.

But there were huge obstacles to achieving that goal.

★ ★ ★

The F-35 "global map," or long-range plan, began with the long-standing USAFE/NATO alliance in Europe, and largely followed in the footsteps of the F-16 European Participating Air Forces (EPAF) program. The Netherlands, Norway, and Denmark were all original partners in the development of the F-35. In later years, Belgium, Finland, and Switzerland also later joined the F-35 alliance. Belgium had been one of the original F-16 EPAF air forces, and both Finland and Switzerland had operated the twin-engine Boeing F-18. Most surprisingly, Germany, a founding partner on the Eurofighter, also joined the F-35 consortium following the Russian invasion of Ukraine.

★ ★ ★

Few people advanced the global program in as many ways as General Philip Breedlove, USAF. One of the most experienced USAF F-16 pilots, he was an architect of the night precision attack capability of that fighter. His deep knowledge about air combat was invaluable as the new fighter took shape. He also had a unique theater perspective; his first connection was as the Vice Commander of the 16th Air Force, and then of the 3rd Air Force, both in Europe. After a requirements tour in the Pentagon, he was appointed overall commander, U.S. Air Forces Europe.

Breedlove said, "I saw partners as a positive influence throughout the process as most wanted our Air Force capabilities. Even those buying the B variant wanted the same basic requirement as the Air Force.

"The European allies needed to replace their F-16 fleet to compete with the Russian threat to the North. They needed stealth to compete with Russia. We needed to maintain the F-35 production rate. We needed intelligence gathering, we needed precision targeting and attack, we needed all the F-35 capabilities for our theater commanders in Europe and Africa."[1]

His final assignment was as Supreme Allied Commander Europe and Commander of NATO. That position was unique since most entities under his command were critical elements of any future coalition. "We needed to hold the line on capabilities. We needed penetrating stealth that can deliver long-range precision strike. As a general officer, I could not recommend airplanes to sovereign nations, but I could emphasize the unique requirements . . . and the reality that there was only one out there that could meet the needs of the alliance."

Europe has a unique perspective due to its assemblage of small countries, each with a modest air force, and their proximity to a very real and increasingly aggressive threat. In particular, the northern nations of the Netherlands, Norway, and Denmark valued their relationship with the USAF. These countries often formed composite squadrons, each contributing pilots and airplanes into a single deployable fighting unit.

Among the EPAF air forces, the Netherlands had been the largest F-16 fleet operator. Lockheed Martin strategists were convinced that, as the Dutch went, the other F-16 operators would go also. But to everyone's astonishment, the smallest of the Nordic countries, Denmark, was the first to join.

Though it was not without a lot of effort, and what one commentator called "A surprisingly catty but unsurprisingly bureaucratic process."[2]

★ ★ ★

Lockheed Martin and the Danes have enjoyed a long and successful relationship for over a half century, with the T-33 Shooting Star, the F-104 Starfighter, the C-130 Hercules, and the F-16 Fighting Falcon. Royal Danish Air Force Maj Gen Lars Fynbo, the Chief of the Materiel Command; BGen E. T. Pedersen, at that time a LtCol and head of the MOD Materiel Procurement Office; and Kai Poulsen, chief engineer for the F-16 program, were the leads on the JSF.

Fynbo explained, "Denmark is a small country of about five million people. Our experience on F-16 was very important background for the F-35 program, particularly in how to work with other countries. Our participation as part of the European Participating Air Forces was very important since our timing was too early for F-16 replacement in the beginning. Industrial participation was very important. Peace was breaking out in the world, so politically we had to address 'why do you need fighters?' Some politicians even questioned 'Why do you even need the F-16?' Danish industry being involved was very important to maintaining political support."[3]

Danish businesses had always been guaranteed work associated with any military procurement, but not necessarily as part of that specific program. Suddenly, they were facing a program that didn't include any offsets at all. Its aerospace manufacturers would have to compete against all the other partners, and the opportunities would be technically demanding direct F-35 content. This created tension. Everyone wanted work on the program for their industry, but no one wanted to pay a premium for another country's noncompetitive work.

LtCol Pedersen said, "In the early days we had problems convincing politicians it would be a great opportunity for Danish industry even without guaranteed industrial participation. I went on an industry tour, with the help of Tom Burbage, to try to convince Danish industry to co-fund the early participation to prove they were interested. This would really help gain the political support we needed. Four of our major companies became contributors in an agreement with the Ministry of Defense to help fund the Danish contribution to join the system development and demonstration phase of the program."

Kai Paulsen added, "The SDD program lasted a long time and was coincidental with the birth of the internet, and negative publicity became a much bigger issue. Newspapers had been very negative. The Swedish SAAB Gripen and Boeing F-18 Super Hornet had good communicators and often spoke about things they knew nothing about. They did not influence the RDAF or the MoD, but they were influential on public opinion. In the final evaluations, the government provided all the real data to the decision-makers about the competitors."

Fynbo added, "Denmark's opposition parties were outspoken about the cost, estimated at over DKK 56 billion (about $8.6 billion). The entire annual Danish defense budget is about $4 billion, so the F-35 would dominate the expenditures for a number of years. Marie Krarup, a member of Parliament and former reserve officer said at the time, 'There will be an intense debate on this. There are varying views on cost, affordability and the number of fighter aircraft that Denmark needs. It will be up to the national parliament to decide the direction and outcome of this project.'"[4]

★ ★ ★

This aspect of the competition warrants a closer look. Being open societies, every European country needed to be able to show, or at least credibly assert, that they were getting the best value for their money. Within NATO, every contest seemed to include the Eurofighter, the SAAB Gripen, the Boeing F-18, and sometimes the Rafale.

Each plane was an excellent design, focused on a primary mission and then modified to be effective in other missions. The need for a multi-mission airplane was also important politically. The F-18, as an example, started as the F-18, then later became the F/A-18. Similarly, the F-22 went through a phase where its designation was modified from F-22 to F/A 22 when additional support as a multi-mission platform was needed in the budget battles.

Each competitor brought certain strengths to the table. And each was backed by determined and savvy industry teams, with significant political support and the ability to generate positive media coverage.

The Boeing F-18 Hornet was a robust and dependable supersonic twin-engine fighter/attack plane that grew out of the Air Force Light Weight Fighter competition. The two front-runners in that contest had been the YF-16, a General Dynamics design that grew into the F-16, and the YF-17, a Northrop design that became the F-18, the U.S. Navy's replacement for the A-7 Corsair and F-4 Phantom. Most friendly air forces aligned with the USAF and bought the single-engine F-16.

The Eurofighter Typhoon was a twin-engine fighter based on shared work across Britain, Germany, Spain, and Italy. Its delta wing and canards made it effective against other fourth generation adversaries from a maneuverability per-spective, but it was less competitive in scenarios that required lower cost, low observability, and highly interoperable systems.

The Swedish SAAB JAS-39 Gripen presented itself as the most ostensibly similar plane to the F-35A. A light, delta-winged, single-engine canard design, its later iterations were advertised as being more interoperable with NATO forces than certain of the other competitors.

The Dassault Rafale was another twin-engine, canard-configured French design. Essentially it could be seen as a more compact version of the Eurofighter, with the additional structure needed to operate off French aircraft carriers.

Understandably, none of these could really compete with a new fighter developed from a generation of investment in stealth and advanced engine technology, not to mention new-generation, interoperable mission systems. But their advocates tried to make the case that they offered more bang for the buck. Inevitably, this carried some sway with media and political actors who preferred either to reduce taxes or spend the resources on social programs but had little technical knowledge of the real differences.

But the facts didn't support that conclusion. Non-stealthy designs were increasingly unsurvivable against the proliferation of sophisticated threats. They also weren't interoperable with other allied air, ground, and naval forces. In addition, the JSF also offered the immense advantage of economies of scale. A small power like Denmark could buy their thirty-five planes as part of a much higher-rate production run, which included all three US services and seven other nations.

Entirely aside from its technical advantages, the Lightning II has never lost a competition based on cost.

★ ★ ★

As the ball neared LM's end zone, Boeing in particular fought very hard, initiat-ing what amounted to a legal challenge to the internal decision-making process of a friendly foreign government. A Boeing executive challenged the accuracy of the cost analysis and even met with the Danish parliament's defense committee.[5]

Lockheed Martin's strategy was quite different. Tom Burbage was the lead for the international partnership. Each country had a dedicated program man-ager in Fort Worth and, in key locations, a local program lead. Interactions with local media and with government officials were generally limited to that group. When senior corporate executives visited, they were fully briefed on any issues and accompanied by the same team. The intent was to have a unified messaging and build close personal relationships with key decision-makers. Strong encouragement to visit Fort Worth and experience the production line and the larger execution team were also important in building trust and confidence.

The importance of this personal relationship strategy is illustrated by an early visit to Fort Worth by the Danish Defense Committee. While touring the facility, the delegation observed an F-35, and one of the Danish politicians remarked "Oh, so there really is a F-35? We were told by the other candidates that F-35 was a PowerPoint airplane." Dana Pierce, the Danish F-35 program manager at the time, asked her to go over to the airplane and kick the tire. "We took a great picture of her doing that and the next visit to Denmark presented it to her to hang in her office. On every visit over the next few years, she proudly pointed out that picture hanging over her desk."

This strategy fit well with the widespread perception that lobbying doesn't pay off with the practical, straight-shooting Danes. Bottom-line cost and the amount of industrial payback were the pivotal issues. Since industrial participation was based on direct work on the plane, commitments for payback had to be based on "guesstimates" of future production rates over many years, even decades. As such, they depended on a lot of other countries buying in as well, which naturally meant risk. This made it subject to challenge and skepticism by Danish critics, but it also supported the personal relationship dimension with key decision-makers.

But the Danish advocates had one more card to play to gain support. The Royal Danish Air Force provided a contribution in kind against the dollar figure required to join up as a Tier 3 partner. They sent one of their F-16 test aircraft to Edwards to provide chase services.

"This became very important politically," Poulsen said, "because the cost of participation as a full JSF partner in the system development and demonstration phase was credited for about twelve million US dollars with the addition of this asset. With this move, we were able to get the total bill for participation below a hundred million. For politicians, this was a real win for the program. Our aircraft and pilots flew chase for about two thousand hours. In addition to the financial benefit, this also provided firsthand knowledge of the program."

The Danish evaluation of the three finalists—F-35, F-18, and the Eurofighter—was the most detailed assessment done by any partner country, and they shared it with other nations. The following excerpt is taken from that evaluation:[6]

The three candidates have been evaluated within four specific areas:

1. *Strategic aspects: the ability of the candidates to support or fulfill overarching Danish defense and security policy objectives, including the potential for cooperation with other countries.*

2. *Military aspects: the ability of the candidates to successfully conduct fighter missions (mission effectiveness), the candidates' survivability, opportunities for keeping the aircraft operational and technically relevant within its expected life span (future development) as well as the risks associated with each candidate that cannot be economically quantified (candidate risk).*

3. *Economic aspects: the estimated life-cycle costs of the candidates, including costs associated with procurement, ongoing operations and sustainment as well as quantifiable risks.*

4. *Industrial aspects: the ability of the candidates to support significant Danish security interests through industrial cooperation with the Danish defense industry. The evaluations are based on an operational period of thirty years for the new fighter aircraft (2020–2049). Additionally, the evaluations have assumed a continuation of the current tasks and level of ambition of the Danish F-16 fighter capability to conduct national and international tasks within NATO collective defense tasks.*

The F-35 was judged superior in all four categories.[7]

In April 2021, the first Royal Danish Air Force F-35 rolled out of the factory in a ceremony at Lockheed Martin Fort Worth.

Lt Gen Ben Droste was one of the first international pilots to fly the F-16. Fifteen years later he would lead the Royal Netherlands Air Force in the early stages of deciding the follow-on to that jet. He faced pressure to consider the Eurofighter, Gripen, and Rafale, but knew that the only real new generation airplane would be the JSF. The Dassault Rafale was a late entry, attempting to capitalize on the close industry relationships between the French and the Dutch.

Droste recalls,

> At that time, the JSF attraction was the terms being used like "system of systems," "internet of the skies" and "stealth." It was clear we needed a different state of mind than our traditional F-16 dogfighters had. Today, only the Dutch F-16 is completely up to speed with the latest USAF F-16. That makes us fully interoperable with the USAF when we operate in allied operations. Other operators fly less compatible and interoperable versions.
>
> My air force had two major arguments. The first was that it was based on affordability. This would be the first real Joint Strike Fighter in the sense that all US services and major allies would have a single base airplane configuration and that airplane would be designed against cost criteria. That was also important from the standpoint that achieving that cost objective would require Dutch industry to be competitive on a global basis. The program also had complicated political reactions. Questions like, "Why do we need such an advanced fighter? And why not the Gripen?" were often heard in political circles. These debates delayed our entrance into the JSF partnership. Every day there were articles about the F-35. Our navy was buying four submarines for about the same cost as all thirty-seven F-35s.

The Netherlands finally joined as a Level 2 partner with an initial investment equivalent to about a billion US dollars. This would allow them the opportunity to procure two OT&E aircraft and participate in the full USAF test and evaluation process. The requirement to purchase the test airframes took place about three years prior to parliament having to decide to buy production aircraft. In the view of the Air Force, the two decisions were independent but, if they could get political support, would allow a very strong potential for longer term commitment. For the parliamentarians, it was a program commitment made many years earlier but was not a commitment to buy the airplane as a replacement for their F-16s.

The Dutch Air Force has a long-standing tradition to mark significant victories. Officers sit at a piano and toast the future as someone douses the instrument with lighter fluid and sets it on fire. As it burns, they play it, singing patriotic songs. In Operation Allied Force over Yugoslavia in 1999, a Dutch F-16 flown by Major Peter Tankink shot down a Yugoslavian MiG 29, which qualified for a "piano." The decision to buy the OT&E test F-35s, signaling a new future for the Royal Netherlands Air Force, also rated torching a piano. The Lockheed team somehow found an old piano they donated to the Officers' Club in Leeuwarden, and the ceremony was completed in fine fashion. (See **Figure 11: Dutch piano burning celebration**)

Droste went on, "The German Luftwaffe commander was retired early because he said the only real successor for NATO Air Forces was the F-35. Germany was very tied to Airbus and Eurofighter politically. While everyone felt that the Dutch would lead the Northern European F-16 community in pursuit of the F-35, we needed to compete with Eurofighter. Politically, it would be very helpful to have an F-35 production facility in Europe." This would become a major strategic objective for the F-35 program.

In early 2010, LtCol Bert de Smit, another very experienced F-16 pilot with an earlier tour in the F-35 JPO, was tapped to lead the Dutch OT&E team. De Smit: "We had learned the hard way that OT&E is a real requirement. It was critical to understanding tactics, especially in coalition operations, as we learned from the EPAF program. Initially the plan was for F-35 OT&E to be US only but the UK worked hard to become a full OT&E partner. We also needed to figure out how to also get involved with OT&E. Early on the response was 'not no, but hell no.'"[8]

Before this, even joint service OT&E, where more than one US service was involved, was anathema. Every service had its own requirements, and they were fiercely defended. To move to involve all three services *plus international participants* was, to some, a bridge too far. But the government-to-government agreements eventually specified that the Tier 1 partner, the UK, and the Tier 2 partners, the Netherlands and Italy, would all be welcomed aboard.

But the welcome mat from the OT&E community took a little more convincing. De Smit and his Dutch team would have to operate out of Eglin Air Force Base in Florida, some two thousand miles away from the test center at Edwards Air Force Base in California. Fortunately, cooler heads prevailed.

De Smit said,

We had four pilots plus our maintainers. In January 2015, we finally took our airplanes from Eglin to Edwards. We went to a system of broad skill trades for our maintainers vice the narrow skill trades of the F-16. We wanted to use our team with many fewer people. It was risky because it was a new airplane and telling enlisted maintainers that they needed to have multi skills was new to them. But it quickly began to pay off. Our team was a quarter the size of the USAF and half the size of the UK maintainer force. Our sortie rate began increasing—and we were flying two to three times as many sorties per airplane than the other test squadrons could do. That is what OT&E is all about.

Burbage recalls, "From an initial decree that the Dutch OT&E team would have to operate out of the Eglin Air Force Base F-35 training center to becoming the most efficient OT&E team at Edwards, was a real testimony to Bert's leadership."

There was one other risky but high-payoff move in May 2016. The Dutch minister of defense went to parliament to discuss the F-35 noise issue, which opponents were characterizing as extremely loud and environmentally unacceptable. The minister offered to bring the two test jets over and "you can see for yourself that it's not a problem."

While a stroke of public relations genius, this was a real operational challenge. No F-35 had crossed the Atlantic before. Even worse, these were test beds, without the internal electronics (including a full suite of navigational gear) of operational fighters. As De Smit recalled, "It was high risk and could backfire big time. But it could also be a huge step forward for the program."

In the end, the crossings were seamless, and provided real evidence supporting the reliability of a modern single-engine design. (De Smit modestly fails to mention he was one of the two pilots on the flight.) The two planes also took part in the Netherlands' biggest air show, the Netherlands Open Days.[9]

He goes on, "We had planned to be there at a certain time; we did arrive within hours which was impressive given the maturity of the F-35 program. We performed a few environmental flights over the next two weeks. The general reaction was 'it's not as bad as we thought.' We found there were a lot of people in country that were very proud to be owners of these two airplanes that suddenly showed up from the other side of the world. We planned a tour to a few cities with pictures over well-known Dutch landmarks and put them out on social media. Before we knew it, people were asking, 'Why are you going to that city and not to our city?' . . . It was a tipping point for the F-35 program in the Netherlands."

★ ★ ★

Switching our focus from northern Europe to Italy: General Giovanni Fantuzzi began his flying career in the F-104, a 1960s-era Lockheed design. He attended test pilot school at Edwards and later commanded the Italian school. He was Italy's first JSF program manager. Fantuzzi recalled, "Our relationship with the USAF was extremely important as was our need for meaningful industrial participation. Italian engineers assigned to the tiger team for the B model weight reduction issues was a highlight as that airplane was essential for our future."

Italy had an opportunity to procure two test airplanes and participate in the US OT&E program, along with the Netherlands. They chose instead to invest in a final assembly and checkout facility. The FACO would be a clone of the Lockheed Martin Fort Worth production facility, but designed for a much lower rate of about four planes per month. It would be located at the Italian Air Base in Cameri, in Northern Italy. Starting in July 2022, it became the maintenance depot for European F-35s with the induction of the first Norwegian F-35.

"This was a difficult decision. I may be biased, as a test pilot, to buy the OT&E airplanes, but it was more critical to gain the political support through the industry participation. From the OT&E perspective, F-35 is a complex weapons system we had to understand to be able to exploit its full capabilities. Our question was, do we want to invest in FACO or the OT&E jets? History taught us that the FACO stabilized the Italian political commitment. We are proud of the fact that we are the only partner buying both the A model and the B model of the F-35."[10]

The Dutch-Italian partnership is unique. F-35s coming off the Cameri line are officially delivered to the US government, though physically they remain in Italy, for further transfer to the final customer country. The Italian and Dutch buys formed the early basis of Cameri's production plan. The strategy was to provide a European production face to the new plane, a critical factor in Dutch participation.

Fantuzzi said, "The FACO success has led to that facility being designated as the maintenance hub for European aircraft. For me, as a logistics commander, this is important. We think we have the expertise and the willingness to build upon the JSF future. We would like to be the European center for maintenance and rebuilding of jets, including US jets that are deployed in this part of the world."

Admiral Cavo Dragone received his U.S. Navy wings in 1990 and went to Marine Corps Base Cherry Point for joint training in the Harrier, which the Italian Navy would fly from their light carrier, ITS *Giuseppe Garibaldi,* and the three other ships of its class. He graduated from the Navy test pilot school at Patuxent River and was involved with the F-35 program during the early requirements definition and negotiation phases. In 2005 he was promoted to command the Italian Naval Air Fleet.

Dragone said, "Soon only three European countries will have shipboard strike capability: the UK, France, and Italy. But France has only fourth-generation airplanes. . . . It is mandatory that our F-35B capability comes online quickly and are ready. There are twenty-two spots on *Cavour,* so seven spots are available for allies. We are hoping the USMC will join us. Our pilots are very excited about the airplane. We have technicians in training, and the *Cavour* will go to Beaufort [Marine Corps Air Station in South Carolina] and pick up pilots, maintainers and airplanes."[11]

On 30 April 2021, the *Cavour* completed a three-month Ready for Operations campaign that ended with the full achievement of all the objectives initially proposed. During the sea trials, two American F-35B aircraft were embarked on the *Cavour.* The F-35B completed all the planned tests, carrying out over fifty flight missions, in different weather conditions and sea conditions, including night activities. About 120 vertical landings and as many short take-offs with the help of the ski jump, as well as vertical take-off tests were conducted. This was the formal authorization to use the F-35B on board the *Cavour* aircraft carrier by the US Naval Air Systems Command, the certifying authority.

In the fall of 2021, two Italian Navy F-35B aircraft flew aboard HMS *Queen Elizabeth II* and joined a composite squadron of British and U.S. Marine F-35Bs for operations in the Mediterranean Sea. This was the first true demonstration of a combined striking force from a sea-based platform.

★ ★ ★

Across the Mediterranean, another collaboration began promisingly, but eventually ran aground.

Turkey had long been a major F-16 partner with a production line at Turkish Aircraft Industries in Ankara. General Dynamics (later Lockheed Martin) had built that factory as a "green field" facility many years earlier. Straddling two continents and controlling the shipping lane between the Mediterranean and the Black Sea, Turkey was very important to NATO as well. In the original F-35 partnership, it would be the largest potential operator, with an initial estimate of 175 airplanes.

Murad Bayar was the Undersecretary for Defense Industries and the most influential Turkish representative on the F-35 program. He did his graduate studies at North Carolina State and earned his MBA at Yale. He was responsible for managing all acquisitions for the armed forces.

Bayar said, "The Turkish Air Force had been flying American fighters for a half century with the F-105, the F-16 and now looking at the F-35. We had caught up with the top air forces. F-35 was very different with the challenge to join the program early rather than buy a mature airplane. We had built up a top tier industrial capability with the implication of free trade zones, and joint ventures with companies like Pratt & Whitney and Fokker Elmo for the F-35."[12]

The US Government Accountability Office (GAO) came out with a series of reports that were critical of the F-35 program during the late 2000s[13] and early 2010s.[14] These reports eroded confidence in the F-35 program and public support in several partner countries.

"It was difficult to maintain momentum with the critical assessments of the GAO but Tom's (Burbage's) work with the Turkish press helped negate that influence. His ability to form friendships with historically negative reporters and to forge relationships with opinion makers were critical to maintaining support. My opinion on the program is that Turkey has remained steadfast to the program and is one of the only partners that has stayed fully committed to the program. We have had no changes to our quantities or our time line. Unfortunately, our country has much turbulence politically. It may take decades to recover."

"Much turbulence" may be the understatement of the decade. After surviving a coup attempt in 2016, president Recep Erdoğan conducted a ruthless purge of his senior military. One Turkish analyst estimated a 38 percent reduction in the number of generals and an 8 percent shrinkage in the officer cadres.[15]

Following the elimination of many US-trained generals, as well as crushing opposition parties, Erdogan increasingly turned to Moscow for support.

The U.S. Department of Defense officially ejected Turkey from the program in 2019, after that government decided to procure the Russian S-400 air defense system. Turkey had been offered a reduced-capability version of the US Patriot but rejected that proposal. The fear was that the S-400 could potentially learn to exploit weak spots in the F-35, undermining NATO security. When the Turks went ahead with the buy, the State Department sent their student pilots and program office representatives home.

Further complicating matters, Turkish industry had a large industrial package supporting the F-35 supply chain. That participation was also set to end, but it was harder to do quickly since their suppliers were very cost competitive. Companies like Kale Aero, Turkish Aircraft Industries, and Turkish Engines Industry had been dependable partners in US aerospace for decades. As of this writing, the country is still a member of NATO. Thus, there might still be a slim chance Turkey could rejoin the program at some point.

★ ★ ★

The US Indo-Pacific Command's area of responsibility encompasses about half the earth's surface, stretching from California to the western border of India, and from Antarctica to the North Pole. More than half the world's population lives there, speaking three thousand different languages. Five nations, Australia, Japan, The Republic of Korea, Singapore, and India are allied with the United States through mutual defense treaties, and four (the exception being India) are committed to the F-35.

General Gary North commanded the Pacific Air Forces from 2009 to 2012. Air Chief Marshal Sir Angus Houston was Chief of the Australian Air Force and then Chief of the Australian Defense Force from 2001 to 2011. These two were instrumental in growing the Pacific allies' involvement. (The Australian relationship will be covered in detail in a later chapter.)

The Republic of Korea, Japan, and Singapore are very important allies, but do not traditionally fly and fight as allied commands. They're part of the security partnership and often stand behind US interests in their corners of the world. Singapore joined the F-35 program, along with Israel, in a separate category, referred to as "security cooperative participants." The difference was that those countries would not share in the requirements definition or have industrial participation. Rather, they would simply buy the plane through traditional foreign military sales channels.

Once these air forces mature, the Pacific theater has the potential to parallel the European alliance, with the strength of an interoperable force based on the F-35.

★ ★ ★

The final piece in the global partnership is located on the edge of the Arctic. The far North is growing in strategic importance as melting ice opens sea-lanes and provides access to new sources of ores and energy. New coastlines are forming as the Arctic melts. Sovereign nations bordering the Arctic Circle include the United States (Alaska), Canada, Denmark (Greenland), Norway, Finland, Sweden, Iceland, and finally Russia, with the latter nation possessing by far the longest stretch of relevant coastline.

By mid 2022, the United States had operated both F-35s and F-22s in significant numbers out of Eielson AFB in Alaska. Additionally, Denmark, Norway, and new entries Finland and Switzerland will be F-35 operators, potentially forming a joint, combined fifth-generation-based fighting alliance.

But two decades later there was still a missing partner. Despite being the first to join the partnership, Canada had yet to commit to procure the F-35. They were absent from the table. But with the Russian invasion of Ukraine, the reality of conflict may have finally trumped politics and the Canadians began a commitment process to procure the F-35. So how do politics play in this puzzling picture? That deserves a deeper dive later. Eh, Canada?

Reference

1. Interview Gen Phil Breedlove with Tom Burbage, Betsy Clark, and Adrian Pitman on July 29, 2019, held in F-35 interview archive.

2. Bennett, Jay, "Boeing Petitions Denmark to Please Buy Some Super Hornets Instead of the F-35," *Popular Mechanics*, Sept. 16, 2016. Accessed January 18, 2022.

3. Interview with Danish team, Lt Gen Lars Fynbo, E.T. Pederson, Kai Paulsen with Tom Burbage, Betsy Clark and Adrian Pitman on July 25, 2020, held in F-35 interview archive.

4. Interview with Danish team, Lt Gen Lars Fynbo, E.T. Pederson, Kai Paulsen with Tom Burbage, Betsy Clark and Adrian Pitman on July 25, 2020, held in F-35 interview archive.

5. Bennett, Jay, "Boeing Petitions Denmark to Please Buy Some Super Hornets Instead of the F-35," *Popular Mechanics*, September 16, 2016. Accessed January 18, 2022.

6. Executive Summary: Type Selection of Denmark's New Fighter Aircraft—Evaluations of Eurofighter, Joint Strike Fighter and Super Hornet, Danish Ministry of Defense. Available online https://www.globalsecurity.org/military/library/report/2016/denmark-new-fighter-type-selection.pdf, accessed January 11, 2023.

7. Pocock, Chris, AIN Online, "Denmark Confirms F-35 After Evaluating Fighter Alternatives," May 12, 2016. Accessed January 22, 2022.

8. Interview Bert de Smit, the Netherlands, with Tom Burbage, Betsy Clark, and Adrian Pitman on May 10, 2019. Held in F-35 interview archive.

9. Sigman, Lara, "Dutch F-35s land in the Netherlands," *Defense News*, May 25, 2016. Accessed January 29, 2022.

10. Interview Giovanni Fantuzzi, Italian Air Force, with Tom Burbage, Betsy Clark, and Adrian Pitman on December 3, 2019. Held in F-35 interview archive.

11. Interview Cavo Dragone, CNO Italian Navy, with Tom Burbage, Betsy Clark, and Adrian Pitman on December 5, 2019. Held in F-35 interview archive.

12. Interview Murad Bayar, Turkey, with Tom Burbage, Betsy Clark, and Adrian Pitman on April 6, 2019. Held in F-35 interview archive.

13. Joint Strike Fighter: Strong Risk Management Essential as Program Enters Most Challenging Phase, GAO-09-711T, May 20, 2009. Available online https://www.gao.gov/products/gao-09-711t. Accessed January 12, 2023.

14. Joint Strike Fighter: Additional Costs and Delays Risk Not Meeting Warfighter Requirements on Time, GAO-10-282, March 19, 2010. Available online https://www.gao.gov/products/gao-10-382. Accessed January 12, 2023.

15. Jacinto, Leela, "Turkey's Post-Coup Purge and Erdogan's Private Army," *FP News*, July 13, 2017. Accessed January 19, 2022.

Chapter 7

BUILDING THE GLOBAL INDUSTRIAL ECOSYSTEM

The definition of an ecosystem is a system whose members benefit from each other's participation via symbiotic relationships. Ecosystems are complex in nature and are subject to outside environmental factors that can influence their survival in both a positive and a negative way. Strong ecosystems survive, weak ecosystems die. Pestilence comes in many forms to nature's ecosystems. The strength of the F-35 ecosystem is its critical roots in both the military air forces of the United States and our key security allies and the industrial elements that bring together the capabilities of the global industrial base. There may be no better example of the power of the ecosystem than the F-35.

When the US government expanded participation in the JSF Program to include eight partner countries, all those partners agreed on the need to replace their multiple aging fighters. For more than two decades, operating as "the coalition of the willing," the partners had been limited by poor interoperability between air forces and expensive infrastructure. The operational capability that would be leveraged by a common, tri-service, multinational combat force would also allow true burden sharing for allied interests in the future.

In return for that participation, the partners would contribute significant resources to the system development and demonstration (SDD) phase of the JSF program. This brought with it several unprecedented benefits. From a government-to-government perspective, they would participate in defining requirements and providing joint governance over the program. Financially, the international partnership also included substantial financial incentives, including elimination of having to pay traditional research and development recoupment charges which had historically been an additional "tax" on foreign military sales (FMS). In addition, when those charges were applied to future buyers beyond the nine-nation partnership, any revenues generated would be shared with the partners.

Perhaps the most important financial perspective would involve industrial participation, which would be a challenge to the F-35 industry team. Partner countries would be allowed to participate in the JSF project, but only on a "best value" competitive basis. In other words, JSF was committed to providing an affordable weapon system but required a competitive, best-value-based global supply chain. This was a new economic model for nations buying US weapon systems.

Historically, the United States would design and build an aircraft, then sell it to its allies through the FMS process. The secretary of state determined which countries would receive the weapons; the secretary of defense executed the program.[1] Such traditional sales often required industrial offset obligations— contracts from the United States to the country buying the aircraft that would roughly "offset" the cost of the acquisition. Often, offset agreements would require incorporation of the procuring country's systems in the airplane, which tended to reduce interoperability. In addition, the offset projects didn't necessarily need to be related to defense products. An example was the Hilton Hotel in Ankara, Turkey, built as part of the F-16 offset program. The risk of not meeting these offset obligations fully was often included as a financial cost element in the contract price in the event a penalty was levied in the future. This added cost was often a point of contention in the FMS process.

Let's look at exactly how much work would be given to outside companies.

In the past, most prime contractors would usually "make" about 70 percent of the cost of a plane in-house, and "buy" other parts, often including various vehicle and mission system components for installation in the final product. This was referred to as the "Make-Buy" decision process that was used to try to optimize cost and capacity in the industry.

For the F-35, this relationship would be turned on its head.

LM was the F-35 prime integrator and would concentrate on final assembly and checkout. LM would also be the main source to produce the wing and forward fuselage (the cockpit), Northrop Grumman would produce the center fuselage, and BAE Systems would produce the aft fuselage and tails. All three would be tasked to develop a second major subcontractor capable of manufacturing their major assemblies. It was clear that only a very few companies in the world could step up to that challenge.

The second tier of the ecosystem would build the subsystems, subassemblies and components on a competitive, best value basis. That traditional 70/30 split would be reversed for the F-35.

So, why was this strategy required for the F-35?

The first driver was the anticipated need to scale up the global supply chain to meet the very high production rates envisioned for the program . . . annual quantities that had not been seen for decades. If partner industries could step up, it would avoid expensive investments in additional production facilities.

The second factor was a realization that the precision required in the final assembly and checkout process coupled with the integration and test workload for three software intensive variants would require pushing more work down the chain.

Third was the need for multiple sources of supply to reduce the risk of unforeseen global environmental or political events that could disrupt deliveries. A decade later, that risk became very real with the COVID-19 pandemic.

But implementing this new concept was easy to say, hard to do!

★ ★ ★

In the beginning, few realized that the F-35 program wouldn't just recapitalize the fighter inventory, it would transform the West's aerospace and defense industries as well.

Technology advancements in aerospace manufacturing are concentrated in precision metal machining of both soft (aluminum alloys) and hard (titanium) metals and in advanced composite structures. Both were undergoing major technical advancements to meet the precision demands of the F-35.

Composites were especially important. The F-16, by weight, is approximately 2 percent composites. The F-22 is approximately 22 percent composites. The F-35 is approximately 42 percent composites. Composite structure was critical for several reasons, including weight reduction and the ability to introduce new technologies in maintaining low-observability features by including stealth characteristics in the structure instead of applying legacy sophisticated and sensitive treatments to the surfaces of metal skins. This was clearly an area where the F-35 could advance the capability of the global aerospace and defense production industry. World-class advanced composite production facilities would eventually be established in Norway, Turkey, Denmark, and Australia in support of the F-35.

It was clear that successful progress in industrial participation would become the single biggest factor for stabilizing the program within the parliamentary review processes in most of the partner countries. Jobs and their benefits are a universal language around the world. Taking the next big step in this partnership would result in a commitment to procure the airplane and a much larger commitment from everyone's future defense budget. Partner quantities would be additive to the US quantities for production planning purposes. Participating industries that won contracts on the program would reap the benefit of providing their products for a much larger number of airplanes than those just planned for their own country's air force.

Initially, it was difficult to work this awareness down through lower tiers of the F-35 supply chain and their congressional and parliamentary supporters. Additional production commitments would also come from new countries joining the program through traditional FMS.

A new community of stakeholders was now engaged, the partner embassies in Washington. This added a very positive lobbying influence, because their countries were obligating most of their defense budgets to acquire this capability. The US industry understood that this would also stabilize support for the program politically in the U.S. Congress. Annually, LM would gather their supply-chain chief executives in Washington for an update on the program and encourage them to visit their senators and representatives to share the latest program information and to solicit support for funding.

Making the F-35 concept a reality would be challenging and would involve the expenditure of considerable unplanned resources. Like all new concepts, the devil would be in the details, and there were a number of devils out there!

One of the most difficult paradoxes of JSF was the fact that our governing systems for technology transfer control and disclosure management were neither aligned nor motivated to allow the level of international industrial participation offered in the government-to-government agreements underpinning the partnership. US government support would be required at all levels, beginning with the JPO. Strong support from the Department of Defense and the State Department on the disclosure policy requirements was needed to enable any action plan. Strong Congressional support would also be essential. The formation of a "JSF Caucus" under the leadership of Congresswoman Kay Granger, who represents the Fort Worth District of Texas, was formed to bolster support for the program in the budgeting process and involved the members of Congress with F-35 jobs in their districts.

The F-35's new business model also raised concerns for some participants, who were much more comfortable with the more traditional "guaranteed" off-sets. The dilemma was that every partner wanted to work on the program, but no partner (including the United States) wanted to pay a premium for the high-cost producers. There was another benefit that was harder to articulate up front. If the defense industries modernized their capabilities through the F-35 program, it would open new opportunities, not just on F-35, but on many future contracts. To put this in perspective, at the delivery ceremony for the first set of vertical tails delivered by Marand Precision Engineering in Norlane, Australia, CEO Rohan Stoker remarked that before F-35, Marand was a domestic supplier primarily to the Australian automobile industry with no international sales. Today, Marand is a global company competing for opportunities in the global aerospace and defense industry. More on Marand later.

★ ★ ★

A small, nondescript office behind Tom Burbage's executive suite in Fort Worth became the makeshift F-35 strategy center. There, the LM country program managers and the industrial participation supply-chain managers would gather, often after everyone else's work hours had ended, to ponder the puzzles of supply-chain management. One wall had a map of our world that displayed the partner countries and the company locations. The strategists spent many hours discussing the need for a second production facility somewhere in Europe. This might be necessary to go head-to-head with the EU industry giants, especially Eurofighter since work share and labor unions held strong favor.

The requirement to create a "European Appeal" to JSF would be a very complex issue with many minefields. The largest contingent of F-35 partners was European, and most had flown the F-16 (the Netherlands, Denmark, Norway, Turkey, and Italy). The UK and Italy had both flown the venerable Harrier and Eurofighter. But . . . Europe had several different faces.

European industrial dynamics are complex, especially for Americans trying to get concurrence to a new objective. Some of the JSF partners were part of the EU (UK, Netherlands, Italy, Norway, Denmark) but did not adopt the EU's common currency, the euro (UK, Norway, Denmark), one was an EU wannabe (Turkey). Some members of the EU could be obstacles to a coherent EU strategy (France, Germany, maybe even the UK with its Eurofighter ambitions and early rumblings foreshadowing Brexit). Enacting a European JSF solution would be challenging, to say the least. And there were others out there that would later become part of the F-35 family, like Belgium, Poland, Finland, Switzerland, and even Germany. Belgium had been part of the original F-16 European Participating Air Forces (EPAF) group, and Finland and Switzerland had operated the Boeing F-18 Hornet.

If the "European Appeal" really required a production facility on European soil, which country would step up to that opportunity? It was unclear, so initial planning involved a conceptual "floating production facility" somewhere in the Atlantic, not knowing initially where it might land.

But, in the formative years, the key players in Europe would be the Level 2 partners, the Netherlands and Italy. Both had contributed an order of magnitude more money to the F-35 development than the Level 3 partners. In return, not only were they able to compete for industrial participation but they were also given the option of participating in the formal US Operational Test and Evaluation flight test program at Edwards. This would require procuring two test airplanes but would eliminate the need for their national OT&E requirements when they received their own airplanes.

The former chief of the Royal Dutch Air Force, Lt Gen Ben Droste, was a strong advocate for the Netherlands' involvement. One of the original international F-16 pilots, he had flown all the competing aircraft in the Dutch future fighter competition (Eurofighter Typhoon, French Rafale, Boeing F-18, and Saab Gripen). The Dutch Air Force, under his command, always maintained the most current F-16 configuration with the USAF, which allowed them to fly and fight side by side with their US partners. Along with industrial participation, Droste and Burbage roped in academia. In 2007 they created an internship for postgraduate students at Delft Technical University in Rotterdam. Students could come to the factory in Fort Worth to get hands-on experience working on F-35 final assembly and checkout or in the logistics team. The program was a big PR win for the F-35. It wasn't unusual for LM to host visiting Dutch politicians for high-level visits to the factory. The students would be invited to join dinner events, and the interaction between them and the politicians, suitably showcased to the home market by LM public relations, helped solidify the Dutch commitment. All part of the game!

The Netherlands had mature and competitive industries, led by Stork Fokker. The Dutch company had a rich history in both the commercial and military arenas and offered excellent engineering and manufacturing capabilities. Fokker had a very advanced, proprietary electrical wiring capability, and the F-35 was moving toward a "much more electric" airplane to eliminate the legacy hydraulic systems in earlier fighters with its new electro-hydrostatic actuation system. About sixty Fokker engineers relocated to Fort Worth to be part of the design wiring integration process. The Dutch Ministry of Defense also had several world-class laboratories that could be used in the development and test of the F-35. They also had a long-standing interest in the life-cycle support of their fighter fleet and expressed interest in what they referred to as a "Regional Support Center" with the potential to be the European depot facility for the F135 engine.

The other Tier 2 partner, Italy, had a history of manufacturing their own frontline fighters and had invested in production facilities for small aircraft buys in the past. An example is the final assembly and checkout (FACO) line for the Italian Harriers, which was for 18 AV-8B aircraft. As a Level 2 partner and the only one procuring both the F-35A and F-35B, Italy was debating whether to take the option of participating in the formal OT&E program or change their strategy.

Rumors began circulating that the Italians might forgo their opportunity to purchase OT&E jets and opt for development of a European FACO for production of their aircraft in Italy. The facility could be designed as a low-rate production adjunct to the main production facility in Fort Worth with a longer-term objective to be used as a European depot for the F-35. When the pragmatic Dutch got wind of the potential Italian strategy, they were anxious to participate in return for Italian commitment to use the potential Dutch Regional Support Center for their F135 engines. But side deals by partner countries would not be tolerated, and all such decisions would eventually come to rest with the US Joint Program Office.

One thing was clear: the floating European production facility somewhere in the Atlantic was drifting slowly toward the Italian coast.

One of the larger-than-life characters was defense undersecretary Guido Crossetto. A tall, imposing figure who reminded some of Marlon Brando in

The Godfather, he was often heard in shouting matches with Burbage on Italian participation. Crossetto, who represented the region of Piedmont in the Italian parliament, pushed hard for an alternative production facility on the Italian military base in Cameri. Cameri was already established with the Tornado and Eurofighter depot facilities. It was a natural location if the Italian government should decide to change their Level 2 priorities.

Secretary Crossetto and the Italians had two objectives for Cameri. First was to replicate the Fort Worth final assembly and checkout process for the Italian air force and navy. Planes coming off the Italian line would be inspected and accepted by the US government, then transferred to the Italian and Dutch air forces. This ensured quality control across the international fleet. It also sent a strong signal that US leadership supported the facility and might encourage additional commitments to use the Cameri production facility.

Over the longer term, they would hope to conduct depot overhaul and maintenance for all allies operating the F-35 in Europe, including the USAF. In their opinion, this would offer a significant cost advantage for the US forces operating in Europe. In the past, USAF fighters would cycle back to the United States for depot maintenance. If Cameri could become a sanctioned US F-35 depot, allied European F-35 air forces and US F-35s deployed to the European theater could potentially use the Cameri depot facility with significantly reduced costs.

The final decision for Italy was predictable. Industrial participation and jobs won out over the operational test advocates. General Giovanni Fantuzzi said, "We made tough but good decisions. I want all Italians to be proud that our country was able to be a partner of the largest and most complicated program ever. I believe we contributed to make this a reality."

One ominous reminder of the past surfaced during that depot's construction. While Cameri was a military reservation, conducting depot maintenance for Italian air force aircraft on a part of the property, the F-35 facility was planned for acreage that had lain idle for several decades. As the digging began for the foundations, the excavators discovered unexploded World War II ordnance. Cameri had been an Aeronautica base since before World War II and had also hosted a Luftwaffe bomber group late in the war.[2]

But the program had to realize that competing regional interests were also complex. The Nordic partners (Netherlands, Norway, Denmark) have a unique perspective, influenced heavily by their F-16 European Participating Air Forces (EPAF) experience, their Northern Europe NATO responsibilities, and the environmental changes occurring in the Arctic. Norway had a real requirement to accelerate their procurement with the melting of the polar ice cap and the emerging Russian threat and will be discussed in some detail in a future chapter.

The other Mediterranean partner, Turkey, had much different strategic priorities. Turkey was an enigma on the program. Strategically, the country is important to US national interests. Turkey was potentially the largest F-35 partner procurer at 175 F-35s. Their air force had operated about 250 F-16s that they built in their factory in Ankara. While Turkey had been very "offset oriented" in the past, it had become very competitive with the restructuring of the tax laws related to export opportunities. Like all partners, Turkey was very focused on technology transfer and expected to receive an industrial return equivalent to half the eventual procurement dollars for their acquisition. The only realistic way to achieve this was to allocate significant assembly work to major Turkish contractors. Northrop Grumman stepped up, and Turkish Aircraft Industries (TAI) was designated as a second source for production of the center fuselage. TAI was established as an F-16 production facility in partnership with General Dynamics and is the largest aerospace and defense company in Turkey. But Turkey had new political alignments that were problematic for their longer-term relationships with the United States. These would reemerge much later in the program as a major challenge to the partnership.

And then we have Canada and Australia, both covered in detail in other chapters. Canada had enjoyed great trade relations with the United States, and many US Aerospace companies had subsidiaries in Canada. Although Canada enjoys a free trade waiver with the United States, Canada's success on JSF is based on its competitive business practices and not a "favored nation" status. Australia was another interesting story. As a quick overview, its automobile industry was ailing. Saddled with high labor costs and a small domestic market, the major automobile manufacturers pulled out of the country one by one, despite years of heavy subsidies by the Australian government. With expertise in such areas as robotics and specialized machining of parts, several small suppliers were left out in the cold with the departure of the automotive industry and were looking for new opportunities. Creative leaders such as Marand Precision Engineering, Ferra, and several other companies were quick to sign up. Engineering resources, such as GKN Australia, also contributed to the "follow the sun" engineering concept, and to resolving the weight challenges on the F-35B (discussed in later chapters).

Two other countries, Israel and Singapore, were granted participation at a reduced level in a category referred to as security cooperative participants (SCP). Israel was likely to be the country that will in the long run buy the largest quantity of JSFs, outside of the United States. They tend to buy one hundred aircraft per decade. Their industry has some very competitive technology and capability, but industrial participation in the baseline program was limited by their category of participation.

Singapore was an active participant with no real interest in industrial participation. As a customer, they would continue to demand information but were clearly in a different category than other partners in terms of industrial involvement.

As the global partnership matured, it was clear that a new level of governance was needed as the program began to move from design to manufacturing. The JSF executive committee (EC), with senior leadership from all the partners, was formed. The EC was the highest decision-making body within the program at this time, and leadership would be cochaired by the US PEO and a partner lead official on a rotational basis. Each representative was generally the senior acquisition official from their country. Sometimes this was a civilian, sometimes a senior military officer. The EC met twice a year to track progress and look at future development opportunities. Prior to each meeting, subgroups and advisory boards would review progress, prepare updates, and discuss areas where improvement was necessary.

At first, much of the EC's focus was on industrial participation. Its importance in keeping the partners engaged was explained by Dr. Steve Gumley, then CEO of Australia's Defence Materiel Organisation: "Looking back, I found those meetings absolutely vital for the program. . . . There was a lot of administrative effort that went into making them happen. More important than all the formal sessions were all the informal meetings that were going on around the side of it. . . . We spent a lot of time comparing each country's acquisition obligations, strategies—whatever you call it—how you get it through your respective governments, because it was becoming clear—even as early as mid-2004—that it was one of these programs that was at high risk of falling apart if partners started dropping off one by one."[3]

This dynamic drove LM toward a new management structure. Starting in August 2004, it would be led by two LM peer managers. Bob Elrod, formerly the Executive Vice President for the F-16 program and president of the famous

Skunk Works, would be responsible for successful execution of the System Development and Demonstration phase, and the transition to production and operational service. Tom Burbage would be responsible for ensuring that all F-35 customer requirements were defined and fulfilled. He would be the primary point of contact for senior US government leaders, partner countries and worldwide industry as the program moved forward to production. In simpler terms, one would run the day-to-day execution of the contract, and the other would keep the program intact across the tri service, nine-nation partnership.

The EC session in Oslo in May 2006 was one of the most significant because it was the kickoff for the production, sustainment, and follow-on development (PSFD) phase of the program. This phase required a much firmer commitment from each partner to actually buy the plane. The enhanced buy-in was necessary to plan production rates, tooling investments, and capacity expansion.

Of equal importance, U.S. Navy, Marine Corps, and Air Force leadership had to prioritize the program within their respective budget submissions. In the US appropriations process, the development and production budgets are separate budget lines. This allows the "green eyeshade budgeteers" to shift money internally, without disrupting other priorities . . . to a limited extent, anyway.

When the F-35 hit snags—the various development challenges described earlier—the budgeteers had to shift production funding over to offset the additional development costs. As a result, the planned production rates were trimmed back and slowed. As a result, in some years excess funds were returned to the services, which promptly applied the money to other pressing priorities. Though it proved unexpectedly expensive to mature the advanced technologies the new plane would require, no funding was stolen from other programs. The public impression, however, was quite different from the budget realities.

The downside, though, was that the government budgeting process constantly restructured the production profiles to reverse engineer the quantities to meet the residual budgets. This had a domino effect on the partner planners since they tended to follow suit. These changes rippled through the global supply chain, discombobulating everyone, and made some parties skeptical that the program would ever truly meet its obligations.

Despite the turbulence, following Oslo, in the winter of 2006/07, all nine partners signed the PSFD memorandum of understanding. It superseded all previous agreements and codified everyone's intentions for the program. Shortly after, governance was also restructured to meet the new, higher level of partner commitment. A new top-tier management structure called the Joint Executive Steering Board (JESB) was launched, sunsetting the older EC structure. Much like a board of directors, the JESB would provide new governance and oversight for the partnership.

★ ★ ★

For the prime contractor team, the stakes had now increased significantly.

For the first three years, everyone's time and attention had been focused on identifying capable companies within the eight partner countries. They had to possess the skills and technology to build parts and equipment for aircraft of the F-35's complexity. One example: The F-35 required much tighter manufacturing tolerances to meet the new stealth needs. This meant exquisitely accurate dimensional control of metal parts and a whole new technology of advanced curved composite structures. Upgrading to these standards often required significant investment. Some could be provided by the program but some would require investment by the partner country government or the company seeking selection.

The engine contractors had an equally daunting challenge. Ed O'Donnell, Pratt & Whitney's F-35 business development lead, said, "International work share was a major challenge. As an example, GE had long-standing commercial relationships with Phillips in the Netherlands but PW attracted ten much smaller companies in a Dutch consortium to support the F135 engine. There were a lot of different strategies across the international partnership based on the long standing commercial and military engine supply-chain partnerships for each of us."[4]

Every partner country needed a road map with detailed decision points. The individual road maps had to be integrated into a global plan. The plans would be used to increase the level of confidence among partner decision-makers. In addition, industry executives needed a confidence metric that the planning factors for their investment in facilities and personnel would be realized. Corporate executives from LM, BAE, NG, and the engine companies would meet at semi-annual CEO meetings. These meetings included senior US government executives for detailed program reviews and discussions. The program developed a new graphic referred to as "confidence curves" where key decision points could be plotted on a time line and weighted as to the importance of the outcome.

A graph could be plotted and the slope would indicate whether confidence was increasing or eroding in a specific country's progress. The partner "confidence curves" were useful in documenting the international complexity of the program.

Nature is a great teacher. When a complex set of relationships all need to work together, nature forms an ecosystem. Strong ecosystems are resistant to outside destructive influences. Strong ecosystems are able to integrate cultural differences and new technologies and meet the need of its intended beneficiaries. In the long run, they can drive value creation and deliver transformational capabilities.

The F-35 program was about to discover how difficult it is to build a working human ecosystem!

Reference

1.   Defense Security Cooperation Agency, "Foreign Military Sales (FMS)." Accessed February 27, 2022.
2.   deZeng IV, Henry L. "Luftwaffe Airfields 1935–45 Italy, Sicily and Sardinia." Accessed October 6, 2021.
3.   Interview Dr. Steve Gumley, CEO DMO Australia with Tom Burbage, Betsy Clark, and Adrian Pitman on August 19, 2020. Held in F-35 interview archive.
4.   Interview Ed O'Donnell, Pratt & Whitney, with Tom Burbage on April 5, 2019. Held in F-35 interview archive.

Chapter 8

ENGINEERING A NEW GLOBAL CULTURE

As the government international team negotiated the contracts, Burbage tackled the puzzle of the Rubik's Cube. The prickliest difficulty seemed to be the eternal human and corporate tendency to slog ahead with "business as usual." As mentioned in the last chapter, along with building the political and production coalitions, he had to integrate the Lockheed Martin prime industrial team with a long list of foreign and domestic peers (who had often, before, been bitter rivals). If he couldn't do that, enormous friction would result, delaying the schedule and increasing costs. That would most likely doom the program, and maybe Lockheed Martin as well.

All publicly traded companies have a responsibility to their shareholders, as well as to their employees and retirees. As viable business ventures, they must make, or at least anticipate, a reasonable profit. But nowhere is that goal more difficult than in a new major development program with technical and execution risks.

Look a little closer at that question of "risk" (usually meaning, who gets to pay if things go really wrong). Large defense contractors hedge their bets through diversification: a broad portfolio of programs, usually in different stages of development and production. A major effort like the Joint Strike Fighter unfolds in stages, usually beginning with a competitive cost-sharing agreement with the government. It often requires the company to invest enormous sums of its own money. That was how the JSF concept demonstration phase was structured.

The second phase, when the technical promise of the proposal was demonstrated through testing, moved to a cost-plus incentive fee arrangement. The government reimbursed all costs, but paid out any fees according to whether a series of criteria and milestones were met. If the contractor's performance was flawless, the maximum award fee could be earned. (This hardly ever actually happened in real life, though.) During this phase, the government and the contractor shared the risk. But as adjustments occurred, due to technical problems becoming clearer, or other issues, the contractor incentive fee got progressively whittled down.

In the event of a major restructuring, a contract can be renegotiated, but only after extensive review by the Department of Defense and Congress and certification that the system was essential for the future. And almost never without the contractor being made to look bad.

Thus, any real profits were most likely to occur in the production phase. By then the design would be mature and producible; the remaining uncertainties mainly involved managing the domestic and international supply chain. From that point forward, the contracts became more straightforward, generally at a fixed price per delivered unit.

On the downside, though, the government actually owned the final design, since they'd paid for it, and usually reserved the right to bid out increments of production. So, *another* risk was that years later, *some other* company could end up making money building critical parts of the planes LM had designed.

Risk, risk, risk. At every stage of the process.

And performance to contract requirements was going to be tough. Of course! If it wasn't, any idiot could build a world-class fifth-generation fighter in his backyard.

But the most immediate stumbling block was the huge issue of staffing, especially in the specialized engineering disciplines.

The F-35 personnel ramp-up was swift and in some ways brutal. Worse, some of the pain was self-inflicted, at least for LM. In October of 2001, at contract award, the company had about 180 employees charging full- or part-time to the program. One year later, *four thousand* LM employees were working on the F-35, with similar massive hires at partners Northrop Grumman and BAE Systems. But corporate had ordered the engineering team staffed with 50 percent new college hires. This would keep the engineering labor costs within the funding available. In addition, the introduction of new collaborative digital design tools highlighted some generational challenges. The new grads often knew these advanced tools better than their crusty mentors. It got to be common to see "reverse mentoring" going on. Integrating new employees and making them productive was a major human resources headache.

Security was another huge pain, from two perspectives. First was the workload associated with obtaining clearances for all those new recruits. (Remember, hiring started just six weeks after the attacks of September 11, 2001). The government-run security review and approval cycle slowed and complicated LM's need to make the newbies productive as soon as humanly possible. A second security predicament emerged more gradually as the international partners joined up. All were allies, sure, but each country had its unique limited access to the F-35 digital design tools. Several of the partner nations had design responsibility for the part of the airplane they would eventually build. For example, BAE Systems would design the aft fuselage and tails and build them in the UK, Alenia Aeronautica in Italy would participate in the weight-reduction program for the wing, GKN engineers in Australia would be key to efficiently conducting the extensive stress analysis to achieve the extended life projections for the airframes, and Fokker Elmo would embed their Dutch engineers to design the wiring systems in Fort Worth. The responsibility for ensuring that each of these "work packages" was strictly controlled was LM's responsibility, but the daily actions of the engineering team were key to enforcing it.

Along with these daunting requirements came an additional necessity: stay focused on the larger strategic issues that would really determine the program's eventual success. These included forging long-term personal relationships with important (and constantly changing) decision-makers in the United States and all the partner countries.

But looking ahead, Burbage saw clearly that the biggest dangers would probably not lurk in hiring, or security, or even personal relationships. Scaling up and out from "two-dimensional" operation, consisting of the X-35 production and flight testing in the desert and a technology development and proposal effort in Fort Worth—to the full complexity of the Rubik's Cube described in the previous chapter would require a level of integration none of the players had ever confronted.

Some long-standing company norms and traditions would have to be radically altered.

Lockheed Martin Aeronautics boasted a very successful long-term F-16 production program with many international dimensions, but had no recent experience of anything of the scope and scale of the F-35. Engineering a new global culture would not be popular or easy. It would require concentrated and sustained effort from the larger LM enterprise to overcome vested interests, siloed decision chains, and the good old shibboleths of "that wasn't invented here" and "that's how we've always done it."

Dr. Jude Olson, LM's senior organization development analyst and head coach, was a pioneer in advanced organizational development techniques and specialized in the design and development of high-performing teams. Jude's style epitomized the "empathetic coach" whose friendly personality and listening style conveyed a sincere interest in every word, motivated by a deep-seated interest in unleashing the full benefit of human organizations. The F-35 start-up became the research topic for her dissertation—teaching and learning at the same time. In her words, "I was part of a living laboratory on complexity management called the F-35 program, and the program manager was convinced that traditional program management tools and techniques were inadequate to ensure success. . . . He was right!"[1] Jude was a full partner in the start-up of the F-35 industry team and introduced a number of innovative organizational design techniques to enhance collaboration.

Jude described the issues involved in integrating a leadership team from multiple companies:

> You're being managed by people from another company. Who's going to do your performance review and recommend you for a raise? So that became a whole human resources puzzle, how to ensure equity for employees.
>
> There were other barriers. Each of these competitors brought with them their own intellectual property, which they protected fiercely. There was a careful balancing act to work together in designing and building this advanced aircraft but without giving away company secrets.
>
> There were literally hallways in the building that certain employees could not walk down because they might see another company's IP, and so we had to educate employees on how they were able to walk through or exit the building because of the three companies being in one geographic area. And we had to

install separate fax machines because we couldn't send data on the same line. Even in meetings, there were agendas that would say "Everybody can start off from 9:00 to 9:30. At 9:30, BAE people have to leave and then come back in at 10:30 and then Northrop Grumman has to leave." You can imagine the management challenge of trying to do that but still have it be one team.[1]

But "necessity is the mother of invention," as the proverb claims.

The first requirement was to get all stakeholders to fully accept that following a traditional approach would probably wreck the whole effort. All hands would have to sign on. Lip service and a few colorful posters wouldn't be enough. To really make this work, leadership had to identify and iron out the hard points that might slow, frustrate, or even derail creating a new culture across corporate, geographic, national, and language boundaries.

★ ★ ★

In fact, the challenge facing that leadership was one that only a few other leaders of large technology programs had ever faced. Possibly the best historical comparison was the Manhattan Project. Also developed in wartime, and subject to stringent security, the effort to develop the atom bomb presented many of the same issues—though since only one other country (the UK) was involved, the international facets of the cube were much less of an issue.

On the high mesa of Los Alamos and the parched desert of Jornada del Muerto, Dr. Robert Oppenheimer faced the same ordeal as the F-35 leadership: to weld together a team of brilliant peers, from various countries, and to replace academic and military mindsets with something entirely new. How did he do it? By combining openness to new ideas with a fierce focus on solving one of the most difficult problems in physics. As one of his team, Nobel Prize winner Hans Bethe, later wrote:

> To keep the scientific staff current on the project's progress, Oppie established three levels of continuing communication. First was the governing board of about ten people who made the decisions on the scientific program. Second was the coordinating council of about 60 people, including group leaders and other senior scientists, where the participants reported their recent successes and ongoing problems. Often a person from a quite different part of the lab

would make useful suggestions. And third, he established the general colloquium, open to about 300 people, including all the PhDs and a few others who were informed of the progress and prospects of the laboratory.

The result of this openness was that we all felt we were part of the lab and that each of us was personally responsible for its success. The ability to foster this esprit, to get the very best from every member, is what makes a great leader of a large project, not the leader's individual contribution to the solution.[2]

★ ★ ★

Following the comprehensive proposal submittal in June 2001, Burbage and his deputies—Peter Shaw from Northrop Grumman and Martin Taylor from BAE Systems—began preparing everyone for the possibility of contract award later in the year.

Dr. Olson introduced the first of several visioning exercises that Burbage led while awaiting the go-ahead. The magazine *Fast Company* let LM use their format and logo to design a mock cover dated ten years in the future. Two dozen of the early F-35 managers, engineers, and test pilots gathered in a Mexican restaurant in Fort Worth. They propped the oversized cover on a display easel and debated the content of the articles, both positive and negative, that the make-believe issue might contain a decade down the road. This appreciative inquiry exercise started to focus everyone on the process of shaping future outcomes; it would be critical to success.

In a further twist, following contract award, Burbage was doing an interview with a *New York Times* reporter writing about the motivational aspects of management. Her article was read by a senior executive of *Fast Company*, who was so intrigued that the magazine sent a journalist and a photographer to Fort Worth to do a full feature on the F-35 titled "The Risk Issue."[3] (**See Figure 12: Fast Company cover**)

For the first offsite get-together, program managers and chief engineers of every modern tactical development program were invited to the Worthington Hotel in downtown Fort Worth, to discuss the lessons they'd learned in their own programs. Surprisingly, they all RSVP'd, and the F-16, F-18, F-22, B-2, Eurofighter, Harrier, F-117, and Tornado communities showed up. To liven things up, Burbage's British deputy, Martin Taylor, was designated "the High Sheriff of Worthington," charged with keeping the agenda on track. Those who strayed got a dose of "his majesty's" ire. Fines of a dollar were handed out liberally for abusing time limits, using inappropriate words, or abusing the speaker during post-presentation questions. The fines were collected in a bucket to offset the first round of grog at the bar at the end of the day.

Burbage asked each attendee to give a fifteen-minute presentation on the topic: *If you were sitting where we're sitting, knowing you were about to be awarded the most challenging fighter development program in history, what would you take into consideration?*

All the speakers gave compelling talks, but two takeaways in particular would prove prophetic for the F-35 team.

Each presenter recommended scheduling a formal program reset on cost and schedule after about 18 to 24 months, since it would be impossible to predict all the potential problems in the proposal submittal. Unfortunately, since LM's proposal had already gone in, this was a nonstarter. Plus, it probably would have been rejected by government evaluators anyway.

The speakers also all cautioned to be very wary of government demands for changes and improvements after contract award—often referred to as "requirements creep."

Over the next year, lab testing of some of the key technologies needed further work to get up to spec, and, as predicted, the Navy and others demanded so many changes it forced an unprogrammed cost and schedule reset—the exact speed bump predicted by the legacy managers and engineers. But some journalists were quick to leap to the simplistic and misleading characterization of the reset as a "cost overrun." This was the beginning of a hostile media and political attitude that still largely exists as of this writing, at least among the uninformed, or those who resist being informed. Had the inevitable reset been an element of the original proposal, the cost and schedule impact could have been handled in a much less disruptive and unfortunate way.

This first visioning exercise grew into a series of leadership offsites as the pace accelerated and new rocks and shoals loomed ahead. They would continue after contract award as an important strategic communication tool. There was a debate early on whether or not to include the government in the offsites. As Olson recalled, "Several people on Tom's leadership team didn't want the government included because we might have to talk about bad news, but Tom said, 'We're going to be transparent, we're going to have an open atmosphere' and that was a departure from tradition—to not hide things but to include everybody and say, 'Well, we do have bad news, and we've all got to solve it together.' I remember that was a big one and that opened the door."[2]

★ ★ ★

But back to establishing a culture! The first step was to institute a universal language, shared expectations, and eventually common objectives across thousands of workers, engineers, and managers networked literally around the planet. Fortunately, the unprecedented scale and scope of the program gave the management team flexibility in developing this new culture. Sometimes jokingly referred to as a "mix-master that you didn't want to put your hand into" there was a trust factor across the corporate management structure of all three partners that allowed the F-35 management team and Dr. Olson and other key leaders to proceed.

To unify the geographically dispersed team, all of the senior leaders had to buy in and promote the change. Short-term and long-term objectives were mutually constructed, agreed on, and carefully aligned among this multitude of players. Posting them in highly visible areas in every organization created a constant reminder of the need to focus on them. As Jude said, "The idea was that one could walk into any F-35 conference room around the world and confront the same set of objectives. Weekly collaborative meetings, often involving personnel scattered across the globe, started by discussing progress against them to reinforce the common view."

Every culture has its unique norms and expectations. Making sure they're met is crucial in a fast-paced, high-stress environment, where many things can go wrong and the downsides are fearsome. To address this, the team established a set of "F-35 Behavioral Norms and Expectations" or "Guiding Principles." Like the common objectives, these were also displayed in the conference rooms and reviewed as part of the opening remarks in every weekly meeting. And of course, they evolved as various issues took center stage over time. Flare-ups were common, but usually were settled in a positive way, in the spirit of the behavioral norms.

Building trust and involvement across three major aerospace prime contractors without falling into the old prime-sub dichotomy was a daunting test. Everyone involved had to think as if they wore F-35 T-shirts over their old company badges. This analogy underlined the fact that everybody would succeed or fail *as a team*, not as separate companies pursuing individual agendas. The real proof was to place "best athletes" in leadership roles. The LM program director's principal deputies were senior executives from Northrop Grumman and BAE Systems, all colocated at headquarters in Fort Worth. Other pivotal positions were filled by proven leaders from other companies, both American and from the partner countries.

For example: In chapter 4, Simon Hargreaves mentioned how surprised he was to find himself, a BAE Systems chap, the chief test pilot on the X-35. Similarly, Martin McLaughlin, the airframe team leader, said, "I couldn't believe a Northrop Grumman guy would be selected to run the Airframe Design Team for a Lockheed Martin F-35. It was the most challenging and highest accolade I received in my career."[4]

★ ★ ★

Remember all those new hires? Immediately following contract award, the number one risk in the eyes of the customer was the ability to staff up in time to meet early objectives. The other partners had much the same problem in staffing up, since the track record for new-employee effectiveness in aerospace was historically somewhere between disappointing and horrible.

To fix this, the leadership team introduced two innovations. The first was onboarding, taking new employees through a unique three-day introduction and assimilation into the world of the F-35. This included a welcome and overview by the F-35 general manager, Tom Burbage, a lesson on program-specific acronyms, a review of the objectives, behavioral norms and expectations, an introduction to the next-generation digital design tool sets, and immersion in the new F-35 culture. Attendees also participated in specialized training on virtual teamwork. The onboarding ended with the new employee's manager joining the group for a lunch and accepting responsibility for "taking it from there" and making them productive in the workplace.

Dr. Olson recalled, "I remember Martin McLaughlin, F-35 Airframe team leader, insisting on the One Team concept. Martin would tell people 'I don't want anyone to introduce themselves as 'I'm from Northrop Grumman' or 'I'm from British Aerospace' or 'I'm from Lockheed Martin' or wherever. You introduce yourself as 'I'm from JSF.' He just wanted everyone to start getting that we were one team."

The second novelty was to name three experienced developmental engineers (or senior technical fellows) as "coaches (or mentors) without portfolio." These seasoned vets would have no staff but would roam the engineering design teams, encouraging knowledge-sharing and teaching the integrated product teams as the organization scaled up. Nicknamed "the Wizards," their office area was affectionately known as "Hogwarts" after the school of witchcraft and wizardry in the Harry Potter series. They were also responsible for selection of the monthly "Wizards' Award" presented to the individual who best represented the guiding principles of the program.

The initial winner was Andy Boyne, one of the first BAE Systems employees to arrive in Fort Worth—again reinforcing the "One Team, No Company Badge" concept. The award consisted of a small honorarium, recognition at the monthly all-hands meeting and, perhaps most valuable, a parking space at the very front of the employee lot.

Fundamental to making such changes work was ensuring communication channels were open, accessible, and transparent. It was absolutely vital that any serious issues shot up the chain fast and early. Bad news doesn't improve with age! The most critical innovations here were periodic all-hands meetings that connected the principal operating sites. The locally based personnel would gather in a large conference room and the remote personnel would join virtually in similar spaces in their home facilities. All employees could participate.

During this start-up phase, between eighty and a hundred new employees were being onboarded each week, including folks from other companies, both US and international, personnel from the various government teams, and new college graduates. Several of the larger suppliers from the partner countries also sent full-time engineers to onboarding in Fort Worth.

A volunteer, employee-driven workforce vitality team with representatives from all partner companies, calling themselves "the V-Team," promoted cultural awareness and developed various fun activities to blow off steam and help restore balance in this high-pressure environment. These included sports events, international custom appreciation events, and other celebrations. Celebrating differences was one key to gaining a genuine understanding of and appreciation for the plane's global DNA.

Diversity of the workforce was also a corporate and governmental goal in the early 2000s. Remember, it was essentially wartime, or as close as the country could get without a formal declaration by Congress. The program needed all the smart people it could get. HR hired Black engineers, female engineers, Hispanic engineers; in fact, anyone who met the qualifications. The LM VP of engineering was a woman, and the general manager of Marietta (who replaced Burbage) was Black, as was the F-16 program manager. Everyone worked like sled dogs, and no one on the team expected anything less.

Another source of diversity—national identities—was also a wellspring of healthy pride. Sports competitions, in a strange contradiction, became a great method for developing unity. Engineers on-site in Fort Worth from the UK, the Netherlands, Italy, and Denmark embraced the annual F-35 Football World Cup (soccer, to the US team.). The competition was always particularly intense, and even brought national team uniforms on the field, since some of the international employees had been notable players before their current career.

There was humor in those hard-fought matches as well as sweat, screaming, and beer. Dr. Olson remembered one game, in particular. "Soccer became a big bonding experience. because the British were teaching the Americans how to play soccer after work and they would form teams. At the annual JSF family picnic in Fort Worth, there was always a big game between the Brits and the United States. One year, everyone knew that the Brits were likely going to win. At the trophy presentation they brought out the first-place trophy, which was very small. The second-place trophy, which went to the Americans, was huge."

The Netherlands had great pride in their national team. The Dutch chief of the air force, LtGen Jac Jansen, had recently visited Fort Worth and went from there to the finals of the World Cup in South Africa in 2010. The Dutch team were playing the Spanish team for the World Cup championship. General Jansen sent a message to Tom asking for a picture of a Dutch F-35 in national colors (orange) with soccer balls in place of the rondels that normally were on each wing. The Team scrambled to photoshop the picture. Although the Dutch team lost 1-0 in overtime, the picture was a hit.

One of the UK stalwarts from BAE Systems was an engineer, Ian McDonald, who'd earned a reputation as a solid F-35 teammate. Ian's family stayed in the Northern England area near the BAE Salmsbury plant while Ian was on assignment to Fort Worth. Sadly, while there, Ian died of a heart attack. The annual World Cup competition then became the Ian McDonald Tournament. His widow Emma joined the team the following year to celebrate his contributions and to present the winning trophy.

"There was an important purpose behind the teambuilding," Olson added. "Tom Burbage's view of organizations was that they were more like living organisms. His thesis was that real knowledge was largely exchanged through social relationships, so we knew we had to connect people socially and get the trust going, so that technical knowledge would be shared."

The JSF Voice program offered another way for employees to raise issues or concerns, anonymously if necessary. Notes could be deposited in collection boxes set up around the work spaces. Weekly "breakfast with management" events and "managing by walking around" added insight into day-to-day operations. When those managers sensed a problem, they took instant action to keep it from metastasizing.

Strong and responsive leadership was essential in the pressure cooker of the F-35 program. A major challenge was the need to identify and develop the next set of leaders from among the many new hires. Distinguishing leaders from managers and from individual contributors was essential, though all three were important.

Managers make decisions based on data. If a manager can understand trending data, he or she can institute process changes and improve outcomes.

Individual contributors are specialists. They're vital for their depth of knowledge in a specific (though often limited) skill set.

Leadership is different. As Dr. Bethe noted about Robert Oppenheimer, it's a "here and now" requirement to motivate and inspire people under incredible pressure. Peter Drucker, a well-known organizational guru, said "an effective leader is one who can make ordinary people do extraordinary things." Far too often, managers are put in key leadership positions. They can manage, but they often fail as leaders. Burbage was determined this wouldn't happen in the F-35 program. There was far too much at stake.

That early focus on establishing a new culture took time and effort, as did the leadership development and much else—*much* else—that wasn't traditionally understood as aeronautical or production engineering. But was it worth it? Did the effort contribute to the survival and success of the aircraft, or further understanding of how to manage such complex international partnerships?

The jury's still out on some of those questions. But the JSF program was one of the original pillars in establishing an executive master's degree in complex project management at Queensland University of Technology in Brisbane, Australia. Burbage and Olson were both lecturers during the first semesters it was taught. Several F-35 leaders later took yearlong sabbaticals to attend the full immersion course. Burbage was also invited to become a charter member of the International Centre for Complex Program Management, headquartered in the UK. Other major DoD programs have benefitted from the F-35 challenges facing both the industry and government teams..

But the real proof may be in an email Burbage received after he retired. In his words, "It gives me hope that the cultural change has indeed grown roots." It reads:

A woman who sits in the same bay as me has a quote printed and posted on the wall outside of her cube. It reads:

"I go back to—everybody is important and everybody has an important role to play. The more you understand and appreciate that and express that appreciation, the better the performance and the work is. Don't forget the basics of people.—Tom Burbage"

I'm not sure when you said it (as it's not dated), but I love walking this way so I can see it. It is an important reminder of so many things to me—what the basics are, and how much of an impact you make by just doing the basics. It is a reminder of the passion and commitment that you spread when you were here, and that if I make the right choices and the right priorities, I can make a positive impact too long after I'm gone from these walls.

So, for your birthday, I thought I'd share with you the impact you still have on employees here, and how your legacy lives, that you embodied our written values of Respect Others, Do What is Right, Act with Integrity.

The shared culture was gradually starting to roll, with false starts and setbacks, but by 2002 it was gathering momentum. However, welding together disparate international elements, with different national strategies, priorities, and leaders, into a partnership solid as forged titanium would still prove more difficult than anyone had imagined.

And meanwhile, the biggest customer—the US government—still hadn't decided exactly what it was they wanted from this airplane. Should be a pretty straightforward question, right?

Wrong!

Reference

1. Interview with Dr. Jude Olson by Betsy Clark and Adrian Pitman on January 22, 2018. Held in F-35 interview archive.

2. Hans Bethe and Robert Christy, letter to *Physics Today*, June 2000, 15.

3. Bill Breen, "High Stakes, Big Bets." *Fast Company*, March 31, 2002.

4. Interview with Martin Taylor by Tom Burbage on his departure from the F-35 team in May 2004.

Chapter 9

DEFINING A NEW BEAST: CONVERTING GENERAL REQUIREMENTS INTO A COMBAT MACHINE

O ver the years, America's three air combat services had become stovepiped, responding to what they perceived as different missions and thus different operational requirements. As described in the previous chapters, in the early 1990s, all three were on a path to replace their inventory with roughly similar but higher-performance planes. But Secretary of Defense Bob Gates wanted a single family that could meet the economies of commonality, interoperability, and scale that could accompany a creative new strategy. Gates canceled the individual programs and launched the Joint Advanced Strike Technology Program to define the requirements for such an aircraft.

At the beginning, though, such a plane was only a vision, if not a fantasy. The government had to furnish a set of precise specifications, so bidders could determine product design and execution estimates, establish management schedules and time lines, and make some sort of ballpark judgment of the risks, uncertainties, and costs. Once this was done, the bidders would produce the prototypes—the two X planes. And when that was done, and a final winner selected, once again the government had to refine their requirements, and with input from a lot of stakeholders, argue, negotiate, and compromise a way to work with that winner to produce a fighter that could stand in the front lines.

So, this chapter will address how requirements become specifications; then, how specs became the X planes; and finally, how the X-35, in turn, was reimagined and reembodied in metal, plastic, and silicon to produce the F-35 Lightning II.

★ ★ ★

The first task, which the government really had to do, was to specify the high-level requirements for a generic joint strike fighter. What threats would the future hold, and what sort of plane might best meet them?

Paul Wiedenhaefer was an engineer with an ability to convert difficult operational scenarios into critical system level requirements. His friendly and approachable personality, coupled with a slight New York accent and a quick wit, enabled a unique knack for converging different engineering approaches and solutions into a consensus opinion, an unusual skill. Paul had been an integral part of the F-22 program as an employee for Lockheed Martin working for Tom Burbage. Paul worked on the Naval Variant of the F-22, referred to as the Naval Advanced Tactical Fighter and the AF-X, but when those programs were canceled, he found an important role as an operations analyst for a top consulting group supporting the government named Whitney, Bradley & Brown. The company provided tactical analysis to the Pentagon with a specialty in high-performance aircraft requirements development. In short order, Wiede was drafted by BGen Mike Hough to support the Joint Program Office for the F-35. As Paul said,

> Most people go from the government to industry, but the F-35 program was looking for someone to come from industry to the government to provide the critical industry perspective to the unprecedented challenge of the Joint Strike Fighter.[1]
>
> We looked at all the ongoing programs, how the shape of the world was changing . . . The services were all doing their own thing but there's got to be a way we can do some collaboration across the services and do a joint program to make things more affordable . . . otherwise we're just going to be playing with technology and never force it to transition to something usable.

The new defense acquisition strategy required a detailed "strategy to task" evaluation of the services as a single, unified fighting force. The Cold War was over, but what might come next? Wiedenhaefer said "It really forced everyone to take a step back and ask what is our strategy? What was really interesting was going through that process—we were not going to just build another F-16 replacement, not just build another F-18, or AV-8. We were told to go through and really figure out the future. . . . What are the roles and mission that our known forces are going to be good at and where are the gaps that the JSF should be good at and focus on those. The major criteria were to win quickly, to win decisively, and minimize losses. . . . It came down to kills per sortie, how fast can I get to an operational theater, how survivable will I be when I got there, and how lethal will I be in performing my operational mission?"

One of the most interesting tools was the Force Process Teams, where each of the services brought their doctrine and assets to the discussion. Wiedenhaefer:

> They all learned from each other. The Navy guys didn't operate stealth and didn't know much about F-117s and the B-2, and the Air Force guys didn't know much about shipboard operations. The Marines had their own thing with STOVL operations. These process teams forced everyone to understand and ask, "Why did you task those assets to do that and why did you do that?" Everyone started to get real insight into the specialized expertise that the Air Force, the Navy, and the Marines had with their specific assets and then started cross-pollinating that information across the strategic plan. The fundamental question became "What are the roles and missions that the F-35 would have to accomplish to complement the existing force to the maximum extent?"

Unfortunately, this effort would also nurture an entire cottage industry of critics. They judged the new plane based on how things had always been done. They didn't understand the geometric increase in combat power offered by a new combination of technology, electronic warfare, survivability and joint and allied cooperative interoperability. But more on that later!

★ ★ ★

Remember that propulsion system challenge discussed earlier? While more powerful, more efficient engines were the Holy Grail for top-end performance, an even more daunting challenge was the ability to power a viable fighter with vertical or short takeoff and vertical landing capability. There had been forty-five attempts, but only three had gone from R&D into production. Of those, two had very limited production runs and only one became truly operational, the AV-8 Harrier. Many different propulsion schemes have been tried over the years as the physics of balanced, controlled flight in the hover mode competed with the aerodynamics of transitions to and from forward flight. Couple that with supersonic and stealthy and it was darn near an impossible dream.

In 1985 Paul Bevilaqua joined the Skunk Works as the chief engineer of Advanced Development Projects. Paul and his team patented the lift-fan concept in 1993. The concept was innovative but its execution staggeringly difficult. And when Lockheed and Boeing were selected to build the X-32 and X-35, it became quickly apparent that integrating this fan with their engine would be a drastic change from anything Pratt & Whitney had tried before.

As we discussed in chapter 3, the engine for the X planes was the Pratt & Whitney F119. Pratt & Whitney developed a larger and even more powerful engine, the F135 for the F-35.

"I remember the first time the Pratt engineers took me out on the test stand," said Burbage. "It was a huge structure and looking at the STOVL propulsion system without the airplane around it created an image I will never forget. A gigantic test stand, supporting the most powerful conventional military engine in the world, connected to a lift fan which had never been demonstrated before was, in a word, *awesome*. The sheer power of the system defied my imagination to see a pilot climbing up on that structure and sitting there with the engine at full STOVL power." Put an airplane around it, and it is not as impressive as the pure power of the engine on the test stand. (**See Figure 13: F135 Engine on test stand**)

Bob Cea recounted, "When we started running the engine at high power, we realized we needed to reinforce the concrete around the test rig. The vibrations from engine and lift fan combination distorted the data being recorded to verify the engine's performance."

★ ★ ★

Along with power, the engine had to be designed for mass production—unlike earlier high-performance power plants, which had been largely one-off, hand-built "racing engines." From the government perspective, "production strategy" had nothing to do with the actual design or manufacturing processes used to build the engine. It had to do with the best use of the American and allied industrial base to promote competitive pricing and future technology developments. Maj Gen Mike Hough described the government's position as follows:

In 1997, a group was formed to determine the benefits of a second engine for the JSF. Its initial study, and another one conducted in 2002—both validated the benefits. It was not to have a second source for delivery of the same engine, it was to have a competition for new technologies and cost competition over the very long life cycle of the program. Both engines would be part of the program going forward and would provide an insurance policy against a significant issue with one of the engines. The studies paved the way for a plan that would compete the engines in the 2012–2013 time frame. With both DoD's and Congress's support, the JSF engine competition would become a reality and we would see immediate benefits in improvements in engine design, responsiveness of the contractors and reduction in costs. From the war fighter's perspective, the second engine provided not only an interoperable alternative, but a "must have" insurance policy if either engine became grounded due to design, fatigue, or other reasons.[2]

The eventual F-35 specifications took the two-engine requirement a step further. The alternative engine program would require a level of "interchangeability" never attempted before. Both engines would use the same controls, have the same attachment points for installation, and use the same set of hand tools for the maintainer and the same engine trailer to move it, whether on land or on a ship at sea. The controlling software for both would be integrated into the same operational flight program installed in every F-35. The airplane would recognize which engine was installed and only activate the software associated with it. The pilot would not know or care which engine was in the plane. This would significantly reduce the cost of training, sustaining, and future updating of the airplane. But, in General Hough's words, "such interchangability was easy to talk about but very difficult for engine manufacturers to do."

Tom Farmer, Pratt's F135 VP and later president of Pratt Whitney Military Engines, was another Pratt Whitney personality who grew up through the F-22 and was a principal in F-35 development. Farmer agreed, "General Hough's insistence on 'interchangeability' was a very significant challenge. It required sharing proprietary info between the PW and GE/RR teams. As competitors in the commercial and military engine markets, it was very difficult. The drive to have common components was very contentious. The F135 and F136 had different cycles making the reality of common components much more difficult than the concept."[3]

Jean Lydon-Rodgers led the JSF program at General Electric. Jean, who later became president of GE Military Engines, was an exceptionally capable program manager with such a striking resemblance to Princess Diana she'd often garner startled second glances, especially at air shows in the UK.

Lydon-Rodgers:

GE was very much involved in powering many of the military aircraft for Desert Storm. We were very passionate about supporting the warfighter. The downside was that the USAF Industrial base had a concern about GE domination. The selection of the F119 was a major win for Pratt & Whitney, and we knew we had to remain vigilant to stay in the fighter business.

When the F-35 started, the USAF wanted a common engine with the F-22, so in reality there was never an engine competition for JSF. The F119 became the baseline engine for both airframe competitors. In 1995, the USAF was again looking at industrial base challenges, but from a different perspective, with PW powering both the F-22 and the F-35. The USAF provided seed funding to GE and RR to enable a competitor to PW. It was intended to begin to address the need for a backup, but then Congress got more involved. In 1996, the JSF alternate engine program was officially established, and GE, in partnership with RR, started development on the F136.[4]

All of our conversations with the USAF agreed that historically, there were significant benefits to having had two engine manufacturers on the F-16. The US ability to sell F-16 internationally also benefitted from the international commercial engine base. The F-35 propulsion requirements were becoming more defined and demanding which we felt supported our opportunity for the more advanced F-136 engine.

All of these dynamics were in play when the USAF put seed money in their budget for the F136. We went to the JSF PEO, RAdm Steve Enewold, and told him we had an opportunity to make a change in the design of our engine to provide even more thrust. He said he liked what we were doing but he couldn't increase the contract value or time constraints to qualify the engine. We took on the challenge. We made the changes in the engine and we actually got the first engine to test a month ahead of schedule. The Interchangeability requirement was also very difficult for GE but we were committed. Obviously, PW was out in front and we had to live within the PW envelope that had already been defined but it didn't stop us. We recognized and we also owned that challenge.

★ ★ ★

One of the highest risk elements of any new airplane program was weight growth as the design requirements matured. The Marine Corps was in a state of transition to an all-STOVL fleet, and their variant, the F-35B, would be the most sensitive to any weight increase. Wiedenhaefer realized that the strategy of maximizing commonality across the variants could be modified. He recalled, "The Marine Corps does not have the same target set as the Navy or Air Force and did not require an internal weapon bay that could carry 2,000-pound munitions. This allowed us to back off on weapon bay payload requirements for the B Model." Wiedenhaefer's father had been a structural engineer for Grumman "Iron Works" and the weight czar for the lunar module on the Apollo program and often reminded his son that "holes weigh a lot" in airplanes. That was Wiedenhaefer's initial clue to take a hard look at the weapon bay requirements for the STOVL. "We were able the shorten the weapon bay by about fourteen inches, saving several hundred pounds of empty weight without sacrificing the USMC's ability to meet its target requirements."

"Similarly, the Air Force position was they were not as weight sensitive so wanted to be capable of pulling 9Gs, carrying an internal gun and basically have everything they had always had." (Air Force fighter pilots had always prided themselves on the ability to maneuver at the limit of the human pilot in terms of gravity or g-forces). At that point in the maneuver, everything weighs nine times its normal weight. Even the best pilots cannot sustain those forces on the body for long and without physiological efforts to maintain consciousness. The "high-g grunt" accompanied by a tensing of all the muscles in the body along with the inflatable g-suit extended the tolerance in high-g maneuvers.

"For the Navy, 'carrier bring-back weight,' the combination of fuel and weapons that an airplane could 'bring back' to the ship and make a safe arrested landing with, was much more critical. The Navy would trade off a few Gs for higher bring-back capability. So, what you really got was everyone became aware of what the other guy needs, and parameters were negotiated. The result was a very reasonable solution that said let's maximize what's common but what is unique needs to be unique."

Another point of heated disagreement was how to prioritize the key aspects of traditional fighter performance. . . . What should be placed front and center in the new design? Wiedenhaefer said,

I would get them in the room and say "Look, if you don't do this, the engineers are going to make the trades for you." That usually scared them enough that I could get them in a room for three or four days and force them to prioritize these things."

What was very interesting was that the war fighters made their top attributes situational awareness, survivability, range, payload, and interoperability. It wasn't the fighter stuff, what we used to call the white scarf and the knife fight in the phone booth. A key factor was that Lockheed built a series of manned tactical simulators. We learned a very significant lesson. I could stand up there and brief for two days and tell them all this cool stuff, give them all these numbers and plots and charts but if you let them fly the simulator, usually within a day and a half to two days they were like "okay, where do I sign?" Suddenly, the light bulb went on.

The first time we had the Israelis in, we had one colonel—a really gruff guy, just kind of a pain in the ass. And he walks out of the simulator and he looks at me and he goes "Wiedie, if half this shit's true, we've got to buy it." I told him "I can guarantee you half, no problem. Bring that check now." I also had an admiral in the sim once and he said, "Wait a minute. I must be flying the wrong direction. I'm turning away and I maintained all my situational awareness so . . . how's that happening?" I told him he was getting all that information from his EW system and his wingmen's active sensors so when you turn cold, you don't lose situational awareness. You could just see suddenly the light bulb go on.

But . . . where were the warfighters?

The combatant commanders, referred to as the COCOMS, are the most senior operational military commands. They split up the world into eleven geographical areas of responsibility. They also have responsibilities for integrating allied air forces within their regions. In several of the COCOMS, allied nations were also acquiring the F-35. Introduction of the new joint, allied infrastructure made the F-35 a massive new war-fighting capability.

Wiedenhaefer recalled,

Besides OSD, the COCOMs were the biggest supporters of the program. So, when we'd get into certain internal fights, we went out to the COCOMs and explained to them what this aircraft could do. Knowing the interoperability aspects and the war-fighting capabilities of the jet, this is what it would mean to your coalition partners. Historically, our services were always so far superior the COCOM position was "Stay out of the way until we kick the door down, then you can do some things." Well, now, you give them an airplane that lets them be in the front line. That truly leverages the alliance. We can't handle this all by ourselves anymore so the fact that we have effective coalition partners is critical and that's why we must give the best capabilities we can within F-35 to our coalition partners.

★ ★ ★

By the time the final selection of the F-35 had been made, the services were beginning to realize just how radical and effective it could be. While some legacy fighter pilots liked to argue that the dogfight regime was the paramount requirement, that had increasingly little to do with what would be required to fly, figh,t and survive in future combat arenas. This plane would penetrate heavily defended airspace with a full internal payload of air-to-air and/or air-to-ground weapons. It would hold strategic targets at risk and attack and obliterate the most heavily defended targets. Should it encounter an air threat en route, it could choose to avoid or engage. Its sensors and avionics would give it a decisive advantage before getting into close proximity to any enemy air. But should it get into visual range with an enemy fighter, it would still possess the lethality and defensive systems to emerge victorious.

General Gary North was the commander of the Pacific Air Forces from 2009 to 2012. He said,

Most of today's combat experienced veterans grew up in the world of third- and fourth-generation fighters and "know the world through the world that they have known." Very few flew the F-117 Nighthawk and the raw courage of the pilots that flew those aircraft into "Downtown Baghdad" on the first night of Gulf War 1 not knowing whether all the "stealth hype" was reality or not was profound. When they returned unscathed with very accurate delivery of weapons on their high value targets, it became evident that it was a new critical capability. Any other third- or fourth-generation fighter would not have survived that night.

So . . . what does all that mean? Pilots who grew up in third- and fourth-generation fighters had a strict priority in combat—survive the threat environment, then complete the mission. Many pilots did not get the first part right and suffered the consequences. In much the same way that the SR-71 found a sanctuary in the very fast, very high regime, stealth brought that capability back into the main operating environment. The ability to roam in a highly defended enemy environment without detection and share the situational awareness of the F-35 with other aircraft and networked forces, land or sea, in the battlespace has been the Holy Grail which was not achievable from an integrated technology strategy until now. The ability to share that knowledge across US services and allied air forces was the unique challenge of the F-35.[5]

But all that was "PowerPoint promises" until it was proven in the air. And the journey from the X to the F would be long and harrowing.

★ ★ ★

To an outside observer, the most obvious visual changes from the X-35 to the F-35 start with the canopy. The X-35 had a two-piece, side-opening design with a conventional bow frame. Most fast jets have a two-piece canopy, for good reason. The forward thicker piece provides protection from bird strikes. The thinner main canopy allows the ejection seat to safely penetrate the plexiglass. The bow frame separates the two pieces. But those airplanes were not designed with stealth or innovative sustainment in mind. The F-35 incorporated a distinctive forward-opening canopy. The design eliminated the radar reflectivity of the old bow frame, improving stealth qualities and, more importantly, improving reliability and maintainability in several ways.

All ejection-seat-equipped airplanes have had a complex challenge maintaining that system. Historically, the canopy had to be removed to allow the ejection seat to be hoisted out. The new, very precise positioning and forward opening feature allowed the seat to be removed without taking off the canopy. This significantly reduced the time to maintain the seat and reduced the normal wear and tear on the sensitive features of the canopy.

A second visible difference was the nose landing gear door. The X-35A had a large single door like the one on the F-117 Nighthawk. Earlier, this had been essential to reduce the overall radar signature. Advances in low-observability technologies allowed the substitution of two smaller, split doors. increasing control of the airplane when taking off or landing in crosswinds. It had a secondary beneficial effect of downsizing the vertical tails because of the reduced forces imposed by the smaller doors, saving overall weight.

The F-35B would change several more features from its X lineage. It started with the lift-fan upper door. On the X, these were bifold openings that would allow air to be sucked in to provide the forward lift. As the design matured, it became obvious that the X system wasn't appropriate for the higher airflows required for the F version. The bifold doors induced an irregular airflow over the face of the fan, which would significantly reduce the life of the fan. To correct this life-cycle problem, the F-35B design engineers incorporated a rear-opening large single-piece door that would provide increased airflow and eliminate the anomalies experienced in the X-program.

Just behind the lift-fan door is the auxiliary inlet door. When opened, it provides more air for the main engine during STOVL operation, when there's no forward speed. The X-35 had two doors hinged on the centerline of the aircraft. The F-35B has two auxiliary inlet doors hinged on the outboard side of the opening, which greatly improved the inlet performance.

Some significant improvements also took place beneath the fuselage. The airflow from the lift fan was now ejected from a simplified air ejection system through a variable area vane box nozzle. This was like a set of venetian blinds that can precisely direct the thrust. This gave the F-35B pilot much better control in the hovering mode and in maneuvering for precise landings, as well as increasing overall lift.

The Navy or C variant was designed from the beginning to be different from the A and B. The Navy's overarching requirement was suitability for operation off carriers. And the Navy has never supported adopting an airplane designed for another service's needs. There's a direct correlation between lower landing speeds and a reduced accident rate in the unforgiving environment of carrier traps. In addition, the C needed a distinctly beefier structure, for the high stresses of catapult launches and arrested landings. The Navy also demanded high taxiing maneuverability for the tight spaces of the hangar and flight decks. This meant foldable wings and reducing the space required to do major maintenance like changing the engine. For good reason, Lockheed chose to make the carrier version the most unique. (**See Figure 14: JSF Family of Aircraft**)

But engineers are not known for passively accepting others' ideas. Final integration of all these features often led to disagreements across the team.

The senior engineers established the concept of "the woodshed," which would occur weekly. Conflicting ideas that could not reach agreement would go to "the woodshed," where the experienced engineering leaders would review and decide on the path forward. And that was just within the contractor team. There was an additional level of technical alignment that also had to occur with the government program office. This was most critical with the Naval Air System Command, who had the responsibility for accepting any airplane into naval service, especially if it was expected to go to sea.

While the X-planes were the most visible part of the concept development phase, there was much more development work going on. Advanced vehicle systems, integrated mission systems, and low-observability technologies were being developed simultaneously but separately in the various labs. These separate efforts had to be integrated into the air vehicle design.

Sometimes referred to as the "brains" or the "secret sauce" of the F-35, these included fully integrated sensors that would offload the need for the pilot to interpret multiple complex inputs. Instead, the pilot would have a complete picture of the world around the airplane and be able to quickly make decisions and share tactical information with other fighting elements. All the sensors would be carried internally, and the weapon bays would accommodate a wide variety of US and allied munitions, both air-to-ground and air-to-air.

The internal sensors and weapon bays became political pawns in the ever more difficult comparison of cost. Competitors would market their older plane's "fly away costs" without equivalent capabilities, since most of their sensors and weapons had to be carried externally. These systems were needed for combat but were procured as ancillary equipment and not included in their "fly away cost." In the case of the F-35, all sensors and equipment were carried internally and were calculated as part of the F-35 fly away cost. Despite the many uninformed critics, the F-35 has never lost a competition based on the real cost of combat capability.

But hold on. The pilots were also changing! One of the last military communities to recognize that females could compete with their male counterparts was combat aviation. But now women were smashing through this glass ceiling—female pilots in noncombat roles had been very effective, and female test pilots had played a significant though largely unheralded role in aviation development in other nation's air forces. But with the F-35, another issue challenged the designers.

The Martin Baker Company began as a UK aircraft manufacturer, founded by James Martin and Captain Valentine Baker. Captain Baker was killed in a test flight in 1942. This affected Martin so much he decided to focus on pilot safety and rocket-powered ejection seats.[6]

At that time, there was little data on what the body could withstand. Martin designed test rigs to try to understand the limits of explosive trajectory and human limitations. The first live test of an ejection seat was on July 24, 1946. The envelope continued to expand until the development of the "zero-zero" seat, stationary on-the-ground ejection. The road into the Martin-Baker facility today is a journey down a single-lane country road in Higher Denham, Buckinghamshire, England, to a high-technology assembly plant with an electronic counter on display showing the number of lives saved. Martin Baker sponsors an "Ejection Tie Club" for those saved. Today there are over six thousand members of the club. Every ejection within the envelope has been successful.

But Martin Baker and their team would be challenged again with the F-35.

★ ★ ★

Designing the cockpit and the pilot escape system was much more difficult than for any previous combat aircraft. The envelope had to be dramatically expanded to accommodate the new population of female and (small) male pilots. Now the seat had to safely eject personnel from 100 to 230 pounds, from zero speed to very high speeds, without injuring the smallest aircrew from the explosive force of ejection and while ensuring the largest pilots cleared the aircraft. A second issue for the smaller folks involved dangerous neck loads from high-speed wind blast with a heavy helmet.

Especially important was to ensure safe ejection in the hover for the STOVL B variant. If the shaft connecting the main engine and the lift fan should ever fail, the nose-down rotational effect so close to the ground wouldn't allow sufficient human reaction time to initiate an escape. This required an automated ejection sequence for the F-35B when in the STOVL configuration. All these requirements had to be integrated into the system.

As the design iterated to finality, the engine team over at Pratt Whitney wasn't resting on their laurels either. They knew the demands would increase significantly and were busy ensuring that the new engine was evolving to meet not only the new thrust requirements but also the demanding life expectancies.

Especially critical was improvement of the capability and durability for the B model.[7]

From an engineering view, the initial design strategy was to do the simplest version first, the F-35A, then move the design team to the next-closest structural variant, the F-35B, then finally, to the most unique structural variant, the F-35C. This order also paralleled the needs of the services, with the exception that the Marines had the most pressing need for early replacement of their aging Harrier fleet.

The major unknown initially was weight. Minimizing avoirdupois was critical for the STOVL variant, though also important for the F-35A and C.

Engineering evolution moves from conceptual design to detailed design to production released drawings. The design order must be strictly maintained to ensure that the maximum commonality between variants can be achieved. This turned out to be one of the great misperceptions of the program: that complete or nearly complete commonality could be maintained across all variants despite the very different operational environments each had to meet. The structural arrangements required to meet three different and extremely demanding requirements resulted in three airplanes that looked identical from the point of view of the pilot sitting in the cockpit, but which were very different under their skin.

The F-35 design freeze was ten years after the F-22 design freeze. In that decade, rapid advancements in processing power, computer graphics, and computer-aided design had unleashed the potential for global digital design integration. A new concept, which the F-35 engineering team named "Follow the Sun Engineering," allowed teams in distributed time zones to participate as a virtual team. Northrop Grumman engineers in El Segundo, California, and Lockheed Martin engineers in Fort Worth, Texas, could pass design tasks to BAE Systems in the UK and to Alenia Aeronautica in Italy and then on to GKN in Australia that would literally allow design activities to continue on a twenty-four-hour basis. They were connected by integrated computing systems based on advanced three-dimensional design tools referred to as the F-35 Digital Thread.

Lurking in the background was the fact that two of the three variants had to go to sea. They would operate in a harsh saltwater environment without the protection of humidity- and temperature-controlled hangars. The F-35B and C would need to operate on ships ranging from small Marine Corps L-Class amphibs to large Navy nuclear-powered aircraft carriers. Internationally, the UK was designing a new generation STOVL aircraft carrier named after Queen

Elizabeth, and a second ship in that class named after the Prince of Wales. Italy had launched a new STOVL carrier called *Cavour*. Developing a stealth capability robust enough to operate routinely at sea would be one of the most important innovations required.

Maintaining stealth had been a big, expensive headache for earlier stealth planes. Complex materials and coatings, requiring temperature- and humidity-controlled environments for repairs were just not suited to use on ships at sea or makeshift Marine strips in the jungle. Designers and engineers evaluated several alternatives. Large appliques of decal-type finishes went on Navy planes for evaluation. Advances in the manufacturing of complex curved composite structures opened another option. The ability to embed conductive materials in the skins eliminated the need for temperature- and humidity-controlled environments. This was one of the great technical breakthroughs in the F-35 development cycle.

★ ★ ★

And finally, along with all the engineering, the plane had to have a name.

In the United States, naming fighters is the responsibility of the Air Force. In the early days of the F-35 program there was a great deal of speculation about what the jet would eventually be called. For months, potential monikers—like the Black Mamba, Cyclone, Piasa, and Spitfire II—were batted about in the partner community and hotly debated on aviation blogs around the world.

On July 7, 2006, the guesswork came to an end. At a ceremony at Lockheed Martin in Fort Worth, the U.S. Air Force officially announced that the F-35 would be called the Lightning II.

U.S. Air Force Chief of Staff Gen. T. Michael Moseley underscored the historic nature of the name.

This aircraft represents the fruits of lessons learned over a hundred years of flight and aerial combat. We're excited about bringing it into our inventory, and warfighters around the globe are excited about flying it in defense of freedom. Like its predecessors, the Lightning II seeks to provide transformative capabilities. It pushes the edge of the envelope and sets a new standard for modern warfare. With stealth, next-generation avionics, and advanced weaponry, the F-35 Lightning II makes its famed forefathers proud.

The Lockheed P-38 Lightning could reach speeds of four hundred miles per hour in level flight and could approach the sound barrier in a controlled dive. Designed by famed engineer and Skunk Works founder Kelly Johnson, the P-38 revolutionized the aerospace defense industry with smooth metal skin, flush riveting, all-metal control surfaces, and a bubble canopy. Its pilots said it "climbed like a homesick angel" while their German counterparts called it the "fork-tailed devil."[8]

In the Pacific Theater, seven of the top eight aces piloted the P-38. It was ideal as both a gunner and photo reconnaissance aircraft. P-38 pilots shot down more Japanese aircraft than any other fighter and, as a reconnaissance aircraft, obtained 90 percent of the aerial film captured over Europe. More than ten thousand were built during the war, and the fighter would go on to fly more than 130,000 missions in theaters around the world.[9] (**See Figure 15: The Lightnings in formation**)

As the Cold War was heating up, English Electric was quietly developing its own Lightning. This revolutionary aircraft would become the first all-British Mach-2 fighter, and the first aircraft in the world capable of supercruising— meaning it could break the sound barrier without employing its afterburners— thanks to two Rolls-Royce Avon turbojet engines. The Lightning's vertically stacked (under/over) twin-engine configuration, rather than the traditional side-by-side alignment, was a hallmark of its design. Developed to counter increasingly advanced and capable Soviet bombers, the Lightning was built to strike quickly. It boasted renowned climbing acceleration and a top-end speed upward of 1,500 miles per hour.

The Lightning defended the skies over the United Kingdom for nearly thirty years before retiring in the late 1980s. English Electric would eventually become BAE Systems, a principal industrial partner on the F-35 program.[10]

★ ★ ★

Speaking of famed forefathers.

Eric Melrose Brown was born in Scotland in 1919. His father was a balloon observer and a pilot in the Royal Air Force; he took Eric on his first flight at the age of eight, sitting on his father's knee. When World War II broke out, Eric joined the Royal Navy Voluntary Reserve as a pilot serving on the first escort carrier, HMS *Audacity*. On December 21, 1941, *Audacity* was sunk by a German

U-Boat. Eric was the only one of twenty-four to survive. He was awarded the Distinguished Service Cross. Over his flying career, Eric "Winkle" Brown flew 487 different types of airplanes, more than anyone else in history. A significant number were enemy planes he was dispatched to fly following the war based on his qualification of speaking fluent German. Incredibly, he also holds the world record for the most carrier deck takeoffs (2,407) and landings (2,271) performed. One of his most amazing feats was accomplishing more than one hundred arrested landings or "traps" in a single day as the UK was in a rush to deploy her new carriers and each one had ten wires. In today's world, deployed Navy pilots are lucky to achieve one hundred traps (allowing them to carry the proud badge of Centurion) in a full deployment of more than six months.[11] (**See Figure 16: Eric "Winkle" Brown**)

Brown is also the only pilot known to have flown both the Lockheed P-38 Lightning and the English Electric Lightning. In June of 2007, Tom Burbage received a request for Lockheed Martin to sponsor Eric at the Society of Experimental Test Pilots' annual reunion in Los Angeles. As Tom said, "I agreed to the sponsorship but only if Eric would stop in Fort Worth, Texas, and sit in a Lightning II and speak to the test pilots on the F-35. A good negotiator, Eric agreed but only if he could fly first class and bring his fiancée with him. He was eighty-six at the time, and there was no way we would not agree to his terms."

Lockheed Martin was able to bring a P-38 Lightning to Fort Worth for a historic photo op. The highlight of the visit was when Eric joined a roundtable of test pilots and kept an audience captivated with stories. Eric passed on at the ripe old age of ninety-seven, a contradiction of the adage "There are Old Test Pilots and there are Bold Test Pilots, but there are very few Old, Bold Test pilots." Winkle Brown proved that adage wrong.

But the easy part was about done. The Beast had been defined; it had been named, and, in a sense, baptized.

Now it was time to prove it could actually be delivered.

Reference

1.   Interview with Paul Wiedenhaefer by Tom Burbage, Betsy Clark, and Adrian Pitman on April 14, 2020. Held in F-35 interview archive.

2.   Interview with Mike Hough by Tom Burbage and Betsy Clark on January 15, 2018. Held in F-35 interview archive.

3. Interview with PW Executives with Tom Burbage on October 24, 2019: Tom Farmer, President, PW Military Engines. Held in F-35 Interview archive.

4. Interview with Jean Lydon-Rodgers, President, GE Military Engines with Tom Burbage, Betsy Clark, and Adrian Pitman on May 8, 2019. Held in F-35 interview archive.

5. Interview with Gary North by Tom Burbage, Betsy Clark, and Adrian Pitman on May 20, 2020. Held in F-35 interview archive.

6. Wikipedia, Martin Baker Aircraft Co. Ltd.

7. Interview with Pratt & Whitney executives by Tom Burbage, April 5, 2019. Held in F-35 interview archive.

8. Lockheed P-38 Lightning, "The Skunk Works," by Ben Rich and Leo Janis.

9. Lockheed P-38 Lightning, "The Skunk Works," by Ben Rich and Leo Janis.

10. Wikipedia, British English Electric Lightning.

11. "Eric 'Winkle' Brown, Captain R.N.—A Pilot's Story" Isle of Wight College, Main Hall Lecture November 18, 2021.

Chapter 10

THE DEVIL'S IN THE DETAILS

In chapter 5, we introduced Major General Jack Hudson, who became the program executive officer the day after Lockheed was awarded the JSF contract. A former flight instructor and test pilot, Hudson had served as Mike Hough's deputy during the concept demonstration phase. Hudson would remain as PEO until 2004. He recalls, "One of my biggest challenges was integrating the U.S. Air Force, U.S. Navy, U.S. Marine Corps, and members from all the partner countries into a program office that functioned well."[1] He worked with Tom Burbage to identify individuals within the government and contractors who were clear counterparts and could work together on a day-to-day basis.

"My priorities were to spend taxpayer money well, both from the United States and our partner countries, to meet user requirements, to get a good start on system development and demonstration, to cement the relationships among the partner countries, and to keep the services and OSD (Office of the Secretary of Defense) responsible for overseeing defense programs working together." As F-35 development unfolded, OSD was to become an increasingly painful thorn in the side of Lockheed Martin and every government PEO, with pointed and often poorly informed criticism and cost estimates that seemed to most insiders overly pessimistic. Criticism came from various factions within OSD and sometimes became increasingly strident. This was especially true of OSD's operational test and evaluation organization that seemed to report on problems that had long since been resolved.

In addition to staffing the JPO and making sure everyone cooperated, Hudson focused in his first couple of years on spurring the development of the "alternative" General Electric engine. Finally, he had to oversee the setup of the international supply chain. According to Hudson, "Lockheed Martin worked this, but there were sensitivities and expectations on the part of international partners that their industries would be able to do certain work on the program. This led to occasional butting of heads, most notably when expressions of disappointment were made. At times, it seemed like many partners were still stuck in their previous offset experience where work was an obligation and not an earned best value position."

Rear Admiral Steve Enewold, call sign "Smiley," joined the JPO as Jack Hudson's deputy. A former A-6 pilot who'd attended the Air Force test pilot school, Enewold's most recent assignment had been as the program executive officer for fifteen different Navy aircraft, including the V-22 Osprey, the T-45 training jet, and all Marine helicopters.

The sheer size of the F-35 effort flabbergasted Enewold. "I did a people count once of how many people were working on the program, and just on the government side, the Tier One and some of the big Tier Twos, we had 20,000 people, and I'm sure it's two or three times that when you really got down to it."[2] The variety of customers and other stakeholders involved was just as mind-boggling. "I made a customer map of all the different entities that we had to deal with, and it went from the operators to the acquisition side to the Congress to who knows. There were eight major categories, each of which had many people. There ended up being around two hundred and fifty customers that at any one time could ask a question and we had to respond to them."

With Hudson as PEO and Enewold as deputy, the program began to cycle through the standard early milestones demanded of all US defense acquisition programs but with one significant variation from earlier fighter programs. The JSF contract was to be executed in accordance with the well-intentioned defense acquisition reform initiative called Total System Performance Responsibility, or TSPR, that was introduced in the 1990s. The initiative was intended to reduce acquisition cost and schedule by providing greater flexibility for contractors to innovate and develop the technical solutions using their commercial process and standards; the usual detailed contract requirements specifications were replaced with high level performance requirements and government oversight was to be reduced. However, the reality of TSPR was not as intended and the consequences for the JSF are discussed in a later chapter.

But this initial progress hit a big speed bump in 2003.

As the system requirements review came due, Lockheed was hip-deep in the design of the Air Force CTOL variant. The government had agreed that it would be designed first, followed by the Marine Corp F-35B version, then finally, the Navy's F-35C carrier model. The plan was to start with the simplest first, following a "walk, then run" strategy. At that point, everyone recognized that the B was going to be the most complex of the three, with its special lift fan and rotating rear nozzle. The Navy variant would be addressed last, due to the unique structural requirements for carrier operations; specifically, a larger wing surface to permit lower landing speeds, reinforced landing gear, and a stout tailhook.

Several producibility objectives guided the original design. One was to keep costs low by using as many as possible of the same parts across all three variants. A second goal was to make it easy to build the plane rapidly, to quickly generate the thousands of units expected to be ordered by the US services and the international partners. Production would be hastened by building relatively large subsections first. These could then be quickly assembled on a final production line, whether in the United States or overseas.

One of the LM design leads, Art Sheridan, said, "The notion was you'd have large subassemblies coming in that you would bolt and snap together and not require any drilling. We called it 'fully stuffed components' meaning that all the systems would be already installed prior to final assembly . . . you just snap the airplane together very quickly and go into flight operations."[3] Unfortunately, this turned out to entail several serious problems. First, assembling large subsections required large bolts and many added electrical and plumbing connectors. And large bolts and connectors were heavy. While weight's a concern for any aircraft, it becomes a total showstopper for one that must do vertical landings. Simply by the law of physics, the plane can't weigh more than the pounds of vertical thrust generated by the engine.

Beyond the weight conundrum, designing for rapid assembly led to a heavy and inefficient structure for a fighter that had to endure up to nine Gs in combat turns. As the design was fleshed out in more detail, and the weights of the numerous parts were summed, the bottom line revealed a disaster. The B version would turn out to be three thousand pounds (1,360 kilograms) too heavy to perform its key mission objectives.

Forecasting the weight of as-yet-unbuilt aircraft is a demanding occupation. Engineers start with a statistical analysis of past designs with similar requirements and parameters: One engine or two, maximum altitude, G limits, gross weight, and so on. Projections generally fall into three categories: (1) structural, (2) vehicle systems (electrical power, actuators) and mission systems (radar, infrared sensors, etc.), and (3) other (miscellaneous allowances for coatings, sealants, assembly hardware, etc.).

In retrospect, government and contractor estimates for the eventual production weight had consistently tracked with each other plus or minus about 2 percent. With the F-35, stealth brought an additional, nonhistorical element into the "other" category. Because the F-35 involved eight international partner countries, weight databases for stealth development programs were not included in the F-35 official database. In addition, a few new technologies were being introduced, including eliminating main hydraulics in favor of more-electric control systems. These new technologies were hard to capture when estimating weights of the finished aircraft.

Tom Blakely, LM Aeronautics' VP for engineering, rode herd on the work during this period. At first, he felt the "walk-run" CTOL-first strategy made sense. "I think that just about everybody who looked at the program in the late nineties and through the first couple years of the program would have concluded that it's very rational to have the plane order be the A, the B, the C."[4] But toward the end of 2003, Blakely and others would nurse a growing unease as the design grew clearer. The trouble wasn't immediately evident in the A variant, but Blakely could sense several alligators getting ready to bite when the design work would be carried over to the STOVL model.

Weight was the biggest issue, but not the only one. There would be less internal cubic space in the STOVL variant, because of the extra machinery needed to create vertical lift. Blakely: "The other big problem I saw emerging out of our design reviews was that there was no way we were going to get all the parts into the STOVL version unless we optimized the structure around that. The arrangement was challenging in the STOVL because it has the lift fan, driveshaft, and clutch as well as additional actuators and roll posts. We just had to design that STOVL first and get those things installed right. And the weight problem was uncontrollable at that point. Everything we did added weight. With that design, we were never going to get there."

Around this time, Blakely was spending all his Saturdays meeting with Dain Hancock, president of LM Aeronautics. As Blakely's doubts metastasized, he realized he had to surface his conviction the STOVL had to be designed first.

Engineers cherish their reputation for telling the truth, but sometimes those truths aren't welcome. One come-to-Jesus moment in particular is seared in Blakely's memory. "In one of my Saturday meetings, I said, 'Dain, there's one thing we need to talk about. There are many of us in engineering that are of the opinion that the firing order that we've got right now is going to cost a lot more to develop and take a lot more time. We would like to explore the possibility of doing the STOVL airplane first.'"

The news was not well received. "Dain asked me some questions. I could tell he wasn't happy about that at all and I got too esoteric and deep in my answer and he got aggravated with me. He was professional but he said, 'We'll talk about this later.'"

Blakely drove home with worries about his own future now added to concerns about the viability of the design. "I'll never forget that night. I sat by the pool and had a gin and tonic. My wife came out and lit a candle, and I felt the warm Texas wind blowing over me and I thought, *Well, I wonder if I'll have a job on Monday.*"

Monday came and went. Then, "I think it was the next Tuesday evening— I'd just come home from work and my phone rang at home and my wife said, "It's Mr. Hancock on the phone." And he said, 'Tom, do you still have a strong conviction that the firing order must change, that we've got to do the STOVL airplane first?' and I said, 'Yes sir, I absolutely do. It'll take me a little while to generate a more cogent and compelling analysis supporting that recommendation, but I'm absolutely convinced based on the experience and the consensus from the top engineering team that we've got to switch the firing order.' He said, 'Okay, you got it' and he hung up."

The JPO quickly signed off on the change. By this point in time, Enewold had been promoted from deputy to the program executive officer position. In his words, "We decided that if STOVL fell through, then that would drop the Marine Corps out. The Air Force would decide they didn't really need the F-35 either, and then the whole program would collapse. That's how critical we thought the STOVL was to the program." The JPO and LM management worked together to convince the other stakeholders to accept the new direction.

★ ★ ★

The STOVL Weight Attack Team (SWAT) was formed in 2004. To lead it, Lockheed appointed Art Sheridan, who had a wealth of experience in STOVL development over several decades and had been chief engineer for the STOVL variant. Sheridan led a worldwide team of over five hundred engineers. No dietitian or bariatric doctor ever considered more strategies to shave off pounds. The result was some six hundred changes. They reduced the weight of the design by 2,600 pounds. Tom Burbage characterized the effort as a few changes that could reduce the weight by hundreds of pounds and hundreds of changes that could reduce the weight by a few pounds. (**See Figure 17: The Major SWAT Structural Change**)

All the F-35 designers operated from the same digital design tool set and were operating as a single design team. The biggest revision was to the structural modules that originally united the Northrop Grumman built center fuselage and the Lockheed Martin built wing. As Paul Wiedenhaefer, the JPO requirements lead, described it:

> One of the original concepts for the airplane was rapid manufacturing. . . . They had some duplicated structure where the airplane structural break points occurred. Northrop Grumman's original work share included the center fuselage as well as the weapons bays—we didn't want to have a manufacturing break across the weapons bays for stealth reasons, so their piece of the airplane looked kind of funny—it was like the center body and then the full weapons bay and then the wing would sit on top of that. Where those two came together, you had a separate bulkhead on each piece. By changing that design and going to a single bulkhead, we saved about six hundred pounds.[5]

Unfortunately, that not only reduced the STOVL weight, it also reduced the share of the work for Northrop Grumman. Janis Pamiljans was the Northrop Grumman deputy program manager. Janis said, "The work share change was a real issue. I had to go to the president of Northrop Grumman to make the case that we had to give up work share to keep the program viable."[6]

Burbage offered, "Janis was the ultimate teammate. He coined the phrase 'the airplane is the boss,' recognizing the fact we had to optimize the F-35 design to achieve the objectives of the program. Janis put a sign in the Northrop Grumman production facility to remind everyone of this."

★ ★ ★

Another major change was to shorten the internal weapon bays. Santi Bulnes, Lockheed's airframe development lead, explains that effort. "At the beginning of the program, we thought the STOVL would have a thousand-pound bay, and the Air Force and Navy would have a two-thousand-pound bay. The weight reference alludes to the size of the largest air-to-ground weapon to be carried internally in the weapon bay. In our exuberance, we made all the bays common and made them all two-thousand-pound capable. When this weight problem hit, we went back to a configuration that had a thousand-pound bay for the F-35B and that took out roughly three hundred pounds right there."[7] It also allowed some space and weight allowance to meet Tom Blakely's concerns.

Burbage recalled, "Our senior engineers created a special room which we called 'the woodshed.' If you didn't consider all the SWAT requirements, you were invited to 'the woodshed' for a spirited discussion of your engineering skills."

Sheridan described the gradual process of trimming pounds:

We had attack teams addressing weight reduction in every dimension. If you could bring in a hard pound of weight reduction, you could get an award, but the final exam was successful adaptation in the static and fatigue test results. SWAT identified a few large changes that were inherent in the original rapid manufacturing strategy that needed to change to improve load path efficiencies. The rest were many small incremental changes in systems, subsystems, and components that allowed us to remove significant weight from the design.

Santi Bulnes, who led the subsystem weight reduction effort, recalls:

The subsystem weight reduction effort was tough. We had a target to remove two hundred pounds of weight without impacting performance. This did not come easy because there were no singular large weight opportunities in the subsystems. We had to scrub all the components and remove the weight in small increments, with most changes yielding being between 0.5 to 2 pounds. At the end, we successfully optimized all the systems and achieved over four hundred pounds of weight reduction. This took a lot of buy-in and innovative ideas across many teams.

Jon Beesley, Lockheed's chief test pilot, said, "The SWAT changes improved all the F-35 variants. While some may view the SWAT effort as a reduction in capability it was, in fact, the opposite. . . . Every engineering team has always wished they had one more turn on the design, and that was what SWAT enabled."[8]

Tom Blakely added,

If we could just open up the inlet to increase the airflow a little bit, we could accommodate some additional growth in thrust in the future. In 2004, we had that opportunity under the STOVL Weight Attack Team initiative by making some adjustments to the inlet shape to allow some additional air mass flow. That small change could allow additional thrust later in the program and was an enhancing feature for having an alternative engine. I've never met a pilot that didn't want more thrust as his airplane evolved. The GE alternate engine could really be great for the future.[9]

Along with the weight reduction, the PW engine team was able to identify changes to increase installed vertical thrust by seven hundred pounds. Finally, an intense scrubbing and relaxation of some requirements closed the gap by about another 1,200 pounds. An example of "relaxation" was that the fuel reserve requirement for the STOVL airplane was based on a missed landing approach with the jet making another circuit around the pattern with its landing gear down. A missed approach is hard to envision for an aircraft that lands vertically, plus a pilot would normally raise the landing gear to cut drag, reducing the fuel required for the second approach. The government agreed, and the fuel reserve requirement was relaxed.

As noted earlier, in addition to rapid assembly, another major objective was using the same parts across all three variants. This aspiration had to be sacrificed during the SWAT effort. It simply proved impossible to maintain common parts and still meet the unique requirements of each variant. In Art Sheridan's words,

We were trying to reuse as many components as possible. . . . But the requirements had actually diverged, some in subtle but important ways. The Air Force required an airframe capable of pulling 9 Gs. The STOVL requirement was to withstand 7.5 Gs. The initial notion that we were going to reuse some of the parts would add a lot of weight to the STOVL airplane that we just couldn't afford.

And so, we evolved from that to what we called "cousin parts" from one variant to the other that would be lighter weight for the STOVL airplane but still maintain all the same locations for tooling so we could still have a common assembly line and the main tooling fixtures would all still be common among all the variants.

"Cousin parts"? An article in the *Smithsonian Magazine* in 2006 defined them: "A cousin part is manufactured using the same machine, but the computational design information is altered to produce a part unique to a variant. If a part is designed to handle certain stresses arising only during a carrier landing, it can be remade with the same tool for the conventional takeoff-and-landing variant, with only a minor cost increase."[10]

Still, the ideal of commonality persisted in other ways. While the use of shared elements decreased for the airplane structure, the mission systems across the variants—e.g., radar, infrared sensors, the targeting system, communication and navigation systems, etc.—all retained common parts.

The international partnership also contributed to the redesign effort. Italian engineers from Alenia Aeronautica helped redesign the wing structure they would eventually build in Cameri. Stress engineers from GKN in Australia helped in the assessment and analysis of requirements.

The SWAT was largely over by November 2004, and the Five Hundred went back to their day jobs. But the challenge didn't end with their disbandment. Throughout the life of the program, the urge to gain weight would persist, as would the struggle to keep it off. As described by Art Sheridan:

> We stood up a "weight czar," a term we gave to a team of chief engineers who personally reviewed every design drawing before it was released to see if it was at the minimum acceptable weight. That helped to control weight, but the bad news is that if it wasn't at the minimum acceptable weight then it was literally sent back to the drawing board. This was a contributor later in the program to our challenges with meeting the drawing release schedule.

Burbage recalls,

> When we were having our challenges with the F-35B weight issues, General Hough came to Fort Worth and asked for an audience with all the employees working on F-35. We did not have any idea what his message would be but were braced up for a tongue-lashing. I introduced him to the team and he very calmly reviewed the U.S. Marine Corps strategy to develop a new class of carrier based on the capabilities of the F-35B. His appeal to the group was that "We have got to make this work; it's critical to the future of the U.S. Marine

Corps and to our nation and the nations of our key allies, the UK and Italy. Let's make it happen." And he walked off the stage.

The other big change during these first four years was in the top-level leadership structure on Lockheed's side. From the start, Tom Burbage, as executive vice president and general manager, was responsible for interacting with the partner countries and the JPO and for leading the day-to-day execution. This constituted an enormous scope of responsibility, one that had him on the road most of the time. In August 2004, his general manager role was split in two, with Tom serving as the outward face of the program, interacting with the US and international partners, with Bob Elrod assuming the responsibilities for the day-to-day execution. Elrod, a long-term fixture within the former General Dynamics and later Lockheed management structure was revered as a strong program manager but also an exceptional mentor and leader. He was the guy you always wanted to go have a beer with but you better have your act together in the morning. He had served as president of Lockheed's Skunk Works as well as VP of the F-16 program.

Elrod retired in 2005 and was replaced by Dan Crowley, who had helmed LM's Training and Simulation Company in Orlando, Florida. Reflecting on his transition, Crowley remembers, "I got advice from a lot of people. I said, 'I haven't run an aircraft development program before.' and they said, 'Don't worry. No one's ever done a multivariant, tri-service development like this. And you'll get all the help that you can stand,' and that was certainly true."[11]

By the time Crowley took charge, the SWAT team had finished up. The designs for all three variants had been improved. But a lot of the original work had to be redone, setting development back by several years. And money was an issue now as well. When the JPO had agreed to change the "firing order" and do STOVL first, they'd also agreed to delay production, allowing more time to finish the design and develop the hardware and software. Money was diverted from production and redirected to development, but overall, the schedule was now very tight, and so was the budget.

Crowley said, "When I got there, Bob Elrod said 'The teams want an additional eleven billion dollars and the government doesn't have it. All they have is about seven billion. You've got to figure out a way to bring this program in because that's all the funding there is or the program is going to be terminated.'"

In this cost-constrained environment, Art Sheridan got a new title: affordability director. His task, and a loathsome one, was to scrutinize the budget for each team, to identify where Peter could be robbed to pay Paul—that is, where cash could be reallocated to finish the air vehicle design and its production drawings. This latter was no small task, either. The F-35 has about 45,000 drawings for the airframe alone, not counting mission systems. To pay for them, dollars vanished from the mission systems side, particularly software. This was a necessary evil at the time, but it cocked a gun to the head of the mission systems software team. The consequences of this shortfall will be discussed in a later chapter.

Amid these challenges, the original CTOL variant, the A airplane, was well along in its development. Actually flying and testing it in the air could provide the program with a much-needed boost in morale and public relations. More importantly, it would be a significant technical risk-reduction factor. The first production prototype, airframe AA-1, was heavier than the production CTOL would eventually be. It also differed in its internal "bones" structure, but it was very similar in its aerodynamic shape and incorporated several technologies being used for the first time. Probably the most important was the electro-hydrostatic actuation system. EHAS saved weight and space by replacing a traditional main hydraulic system through a combination of electrical power and small, localized hydraulic reservoirs to maneuver individual control surfaces. In Blakely's words, "EHAS was a novel technology that the F-35 is designed around. One time in a design review meeting, a rear admiral asked me, 'What are you going to do if you can't get the EHAS to work?' and I said, 'Admiral, there's no Plan B on this one. This is plan A and that's it. We're going to succeed, sir.'"

"I was a very strong advocate of proceeding with AA-1, because I really wanted to get it up and flying. I wanted to see the EHAS fly supersonically. I wanted to see how the weapons bays design concept was going to work and if the vibration, acoustics and airflow around the airplane would work. I wanted to get data on the diverterless inlet. So, there were a few things like that . . . to significantly reduce technical risk. Whenever I was asked by JPO or anybody else, I advocated for getting the airplane in the air."

Fortunately, the JPO supported the push to get it flying. Enewold remembered, "AA-1 by that time was well along, and we started focusing on first flight. The Congress and the services were using first flight as the milestone for how the program health was. They understood that AA-1 was not a production representative airplane but they also realized it was at least aerodynamically the same and so they wanted to see it fly to prove that the airplane was going to fly. So, there was a lot of pressure on the program office and the companies to get first flight squared away. So, we went ahead and decided to build AA-1 in what I call the heavyweight version. First flight was a key wicket that we had to run through."

But the guy who had most to lose if AA-1 face-planted was Lockheed's Jon Beesley. Crowley said, "It was fantastic to work with Jon Beesley because as chief test pilot, he had this fatherly style that would put everybody at ease and keep everybody from panicking, and yet it was going to be his ass in the seat when it came time to fly, so he more than anybody had a vested interest to make sure it was done right. And we really benefited from his experience and sense of calm and focus."

But would that first flight of AA-1 prove a success? In some ways, it would be another Battle in the Sky.

Reference

1.   Interview with Major General Jack Hudson by Tom Burbage, Betsy Clark, and Adrian Pitman on July 31, 2019. Held in F-35 interview archive.

2.   Interview with Rear Admiral Steve Enewold by Tom Burbage, Betsy Clark, and Adrian Pitman on August 8, 2019. Held in F-35 interview archive.

3.   Interview with Art Sheridan by Tom Burbage, Betsy Clark, and Adrian Pitman on March 23, 2018. Held in F-35 interview archive.

4.   Interview with Tom Blakely by Tom Burbage, Betsy Clark, and Adrian Pitman on July 2, 2018. Held in F-35 interview archive.

5.   Interview with Paul Wiedenhaefer by Tom Burbage, Betsy Clark, and Adrian Pitman on January 26, 2018. Held in F-35 interview archive.

6.   Interview with Jan Pamiljans by Tom Burbage, Betsy Clark, and Adrian Pitman on November 8, 2019. Held in F-35 interview archive.

7.   Interview with Santi Bulnes by Tom Burbage, Betsy Clark, and Adrian Pitman on April 16, 2020. Held in F-35 interview archive.

8.   Interview with Jon Beesley by Tom Burbage, Betsy Clark, and Adrian Pitman on August 28, 2018. Held in F-35 interview archive.

9.   Interview with Tom Blakely, LM VP engineering by Tom Burbage, Adrian Pitman, and Betsy Clark, October 9, 2021.

10. Pappalardo, Joe, "Weight Watchers: How a Team of Engineers and a Crash Diet saved the Joint Strike Fighter." *Smithsonian Magazine*, November 2006.

11. Interview with Dan Crowley by Betsy Clark and Adrian Pitman on January 27, 2018. Held in F-35 interview archive.

Chapter 11

CONTROLLING THE BEAST

Perhaps no other dream has teased the human imagination longer than that of escaping the bounds of earth and perfecting the art of flight. In the myth, Daedalus and Icarus used feathers, thread, and wax to attach wings to their bodies. Most early attempts ended in serious injury or death due to ignorance of the concepts of lift and control.

Sir George Cayley was the first to be called the father of the airplane in 1846. His contributions to aeronautics included clarifying the principles of heavier-than-air flight, understanding the principles of bird flight and the concepts of drag, streamlining, center of pressure, and camber. Cayley defined the modern configuration of fixed wing, fuselage, and horizontal and vertical tail assemblies. He also demonstrated manned gliding and established the principles of power-to-weight ratios for sustaining flight.

Otto Lilienthal, a German pioneer, said, "To invent an airplane is nothing, to build one is something. But to fly is everything." Lilienthal's gliders were controllable by shifting weight, much like modern hang gliders. He would strap himself in by the shoulders and shift his lower body to relocate the glider's center of gravity. During a test flight on August 9, 1896, his glider collapsed, and he fell to his death. The Wright Brothers studied Lilienthal's research early on and credited him as a major inspiration for their pursuit of powered flight.[1]

Many other innovators worked on gliders, wind tunnels, and airfoil shapes, but none could deliver a consistent aerodynamic design until the Wrights' work matured.

The Wrights solved both the control and power problems. They invented wing warping. The pilot could twist the trailing edge of the wing through a mechanical system of cables. They combined this rudimentary roll control with simultaneous yaw control, using a steerable rear rudder. Although wing-warping as a means of control was used only briefly, superseded by Robert Esnault-Pelterie's ailerons, the innovation of combining roll and yaw control was fundamental foe maneuvering. For pitch control, the Wrights used a forward elevator, sometimes called a canard. Although the canard also became outmoded, it's reappeared in some modern fighters like the French Rafale and the Eurofighter.[2]

The Wrights made rigorous wind-tunnel tests of airfoils and flight tests of full-size gliders. In 1902, they came to Kitty Hawk, North Carolina, selected for its constant winds, which helped add lift to their wings, and its hills of sand, more accepting of crashes. They flew over seven hundred successful flights in their unpowered glider.

Having perfected controlled gliding, their next step was to add power. They built their first powered craft, the Wright Flyer, and completed the first manned powered flight on December 17, 1903 at Kill Devil Hills, North Carolina, with Orville at the controls. That first flight lasted twelve seconds and covered 120 feet. (It could be completed today within the interior of the C-5A cargo airplane.) Three more flights were conducted that day, with Wilbur piloting the record flight, fifty-nine seconds for 852 feet. The challenge of flying that early airplane was evident when an exact replica of the original Wright Flyer attempted to reenact that first flight on the 100th anniversary, December 17, 2003, but was unable to accomplish the feat.[3]

These early understandings of the countervailing forces of flight centered on balancing lift versus weight and thrust versus drag. The art and science of aerodynamic engineering introduced two more, elusive critical criteria: *stability* and *maneuverability*.

The tendency of an airplane to maintain steady flight and to return to steady flight if its path is disturbed, is aerodynamic stability. But as maneuverability of high-performance fighters became more and more important, stability became a limiting factor. Very stable planes have limited maneuverability. Less-stable designs allowed the pilot to maneuver more dramatically, but also had a greater tendency to depart controlled flight. This manifested itself in stalls, spins, and crashes.

Analog, mechanical systems of chains, pushrods, and strategically placed weighted ballast limited the stability knowledge base of early designers. Beginning around 1972, computers solved this dilemma by providing automatic and nearly instantaneous recovery from controlled-flight departures. The F-16 was one of the first fighters to employ this "fly-by-wire" technology. As computing power evolved, engineers integrated advanced propulsion systems with the flight control system. These advances dramatically improved airspeed, altitude, and maneuverability envelopes, while limiting unwanted departures.

But an even greater challenge was the F-35 mandate to create a family of next-generation high-performance airplanes. As we discussed in earlier chapters, the CTOL, or Air Force version, would use traditional runways. Where extreme environmental conditions existed, as in Norway, the F-35A would incorporate a drag chute to assist in braking on icy runways. The Marine Corps version, the F-35B, would operate off small carriers or expeditionary short runways. International partners (UK and Italy) would operate the F-35B off their own small carriers. The U.S. Navy carrier variant, the F-35C, would be designed for the hazardous environment of catapult launches and arrested landings.

There were two major issues related to flight controls on the F-35. First, the F-35's engineers had to design a control system that would, in simple terms, make all three variants "fly the same" despite the differences in tail and wing sizes and control surfaces. If this could be done, it would allow pilots to easily transition between variants, significantly reducing life-cycle costs of training across the US services and those of the allies. Making all three variants fly the same wasn't simple. But the F-35 flight control software engineers succeeded by perfecting a strategy they referred to as "dynamic inversion." This concept embedded an optimal response model of "how the airplane should fly" and coupled it to the reality of "how the airplane does fly" through complex software algorithms. The resulting flying qualities of all three variants were thus made very similar. One huge benefit of this was in reducing the cost of ownership for any fixed-wing inventory when the F-35 replaces multiple legacy airplanes. Consider the benefit to the Marine Corps. The F-35 B and C will replace the AV-8B Harrier, the F/A-18 Hornet, and the EA-6B Prowler by 2027.[4] Today, all those aircraft have separate training pipelines and separate, specialized infrastructure and logistic requirements. Such cost efficiencies were fundamental to embracing the concept of the Joint Strike Fighter but are seldom recognized in public discussions.

The second major issue wouldn't be simple either but what made it really hard was that it triggered an emotional and divisive debate among test pilots, pitting those with a Harrier background against those with experience on other airplanes. Any aircraft with vertical landing capabilities must operate in two distinct modes. First, a pure "jet-borne mode" during vertical landings where the thrust of the engine has to lift the weight of the plane. And second, a full "wing-borne mode" where forward speed generates enough lift to sustain flight. But flight dynamics had historically been very unforgiving in the transition between wing-borne flight and jet-borne lift during landing. Approximately a third of the early Harrier fleet had been lost in that fatal gap.[5] An article in the online magazine *Vertical* describes the problem succinctly: "VTOL aircraft face fundamental flight control challenges because they're essentially two vehicles in one—a vehicle that hovers and one that flies forward through the air, with the piloting task changing fundamentally between the two regimes. Conventional VTOL aircraft such as Harriers and helicopters are relatively hard to fly. Even after undergoing extensive training, pilots of these vehicles are subject to high workloads that can, and do, lead to cognitive failures and accidents."[6] A pilot in the Harrier needs to work three controls to fly the airplane—the throttle, the stick, and a nozzle control lever. The X-35B was similar to the Harrier in that respect. Art Tomassetti, who flew Mission X with the X-35B, recalled, "The X-35 was an advanced airframe design but employed a similar propulsion control concept as the Harrier. The pilot had to manage three controls, one to control engine thrust, a second to control pitch, roll, and yaw when the airplane was in conventional flight, and a third to control the movement of louvers under the lift fan to vector the air when transitioning to and maneuvering in the hover."[7] An additional complication in flying the Harrier and the X-35 is that the throttle was used to control speed in wing-borne flight but used to control altitude in the hover (by increasing or decreasing engine thrust). But a new flight control concept for STOVL aircraft had been developed in the UK known as "unified flight controls" that would be at the center of an impassioned debate at LM. The debate boiled down to whether the F-35B should operate the way the Harrier did or was the unified concept a better way to go?

★ ★ ★

During the early days of the DARPA ASTOVL program, a British team was working on the new unified concept to control STOVL flight at the Royal Aircraft Establishment (RAE) Bedford, led by scientist Peter Nicholas and test pilot Peter Bennet. They had conceived the solution that was installed and flown on the UK's vectored-thrust aircraft advanced-flight control (VAAC) Harrier. The VAAC was a test bed flown initially out of RAE Bedford and later the Royal Air Force Test Center at Boscombe Down in Wiltshire, in the UK. The front seat was a legacy Harrier, but a pilot in the rear seat could also fly the air-craft to evaluate new concepts of control, including the unified concept.

Justin Paines was a Royal Air Force test pilot assigned to the X-35 team during the concept demonstration phase and was a project test pilot on the specially configured VAAC Harrier up to that time, and again from 2004 to 2008. An exceptional test pilot and very experienced STOVL pilot, Justin was a very engaging participant in the final design of the F-35B flight control system. Paines defined the unified flight control concept as being "unified" across the flight envelope as the STOVL transitions from wing-borne flight to engine borne in that the throttle always controls speed and the stick always controls altitude. As Paines described it,

> Essentially, the effect of moving either the throttle or stick (we call them inceptors, but I'll just use throttle and stick for simplicity) is the same irre-spective of your speed. So, if you're in the hover or if you're at 50 knots or if you're at 500 knots, you pull back on the stick and you increase your alti-tude—you go upwards. And if you push forward on the stick, you go down-wards. If you push forward on the throttle, you go faster whether you're at 500 knots or at five knots or if you're in the hover. You pull back on the throttle to decelerate or if you're in the hover to go backwards.

While with conventional fighters, engine thrust was controlled by the left hand and altitude was controlled by the right hand, the term "inceptors" was adopted because the left inceptor was no longer dedicated to the engine and the right inceptor was no longer dedicated to the flight control surfaces. With the uni-fied concept, when a pilot transitions from wing-borne flight slowing down to hover, the control of the engine actually changes from the left hand to the right "altitude-controlling" hand, and the left "speed-controlling hand" now manages the venetian blinds under the lift fan that control forward and backward move-ment. What is conceptually simple from a cognitive perspective—the left hand always controls speed while the right hand always controls altitude –is extremely complex from a software perspective. To the layperson, the control of the engine could move from your left inceptor to the right inceptor without you even know-ing it. The magic of software!

★ ★ ★

Buddy Denham was a career Naval Air Systems Command flight control engineer who, like many of the unsung heroes on the F-35 program, was determined to make the F-35B and C the safest STOVL and carrier airplanes ever. The ultimate engineer, Buddy was immersed in his craft . . . to solve, once and for all, the challenge of safe, repeatable shipboard flight operations regardless of the conditions. Buddy's work on flight control theory for advanced short-takeoff and vertical-landing concepts in the mid-1990s would make its way into the JSF Program. When the JSF concept demonstration phase began, the only government technical team that was not divided between the competing contractors was the flight control team, so he was deeply involved with both the Boeing X-32 and the Lockheed X-35.

Toward the end of the decade, Buddy became heavily involved with the UK team. As Buddy recounted "In the US services, we were always battling two things. One was technical, which really wasn't that difficult to implement all these modes in the VAAC. The second and biggest part was cultural and it's how do you change the pilot culture? When you have loads of former and current Harrier pilots, how they have always done it anchors the way it should be in the future. These cultural norms make change very difficult, even if there is evidence that there may be a better way of doing things."[8]

July 6, 2004, was the thirty-fifth birthday of the venerable VAAC Harrier. The airplane had been a tremendous technical asset in the development of future STOVL control concepts and had been reconfigured to support the F-35B STOVL flight control development. A birthday cake awaited the return of the crew. But this birthday flight could be very significant for the F-35B. Now the rear seat replicated the control system of the F-35B. The pilots on this mission would be Royal Navy Cdr Phil Hayde and Tom Burbage. A former Navy test pilot, Burbage had flown the F-35 simulator in Fort Worth but had never flown a live STOVL airplane before. After launch, Hayde told Burbage, "Your airplane, I'm not coming back on unless you're trying to kill me." The two pilots executed several landings and, when the flight was complete, Burbage's comments were "I felt like I had been a STOVL pilot all my life; the airplane was very easy to fly."

Unfortunately, a significant argument about which operational concept would be best for the F-35B was about to erupt.

★ ★ ★

In the summer of 2002, the STOVL pilot communities gathered in Fort Worth for a technical debate on the merits of each concept. It turned out to be a very emotional meeting with very strong positions being taken by "the warriors," who had operational and combat experience in the Harrier, and the "young bucks," who brought deeper understanding of the new technologies and the software advantages of the unified system. The strongest proponent for the Warriors was Simon Hargreaves from BAE. Hargreaves had been the lead X-35B test pilot and was now the contractor team lead STOVL test pilot. Simon was convinced that the older Harrier scheme was the right path for the F-35. Harry Blot, the Lockheed Martin F-35 deputy program manager (and a former Harrier pilot famous for his ability to exploit the unique maneuverability features of the Harrier) agreed with Simon. Blot had perfected the "Blot flop" maneuver and later became the USMC Deputy Commandant for Aviation before retiring and joining the LM team.

Buddy Denham, joined by Justin Paines and the UK team that had developed the unified system, and Joe Krumenacker from NAVAIR were the leading advocates for the unified approach. In their opinion, the mood of the meeting was swinging strongly against the unified proponents due in part to the persuasive personalities of the "warriors" and their colorful language, while the Denham, Paines, and Krumenacker camp attempted a more data-driven argument. The data didn't appear to be landing against a barrage of criticism until, on the last afternoon, Paines gave a technical critique of the warriors' more legacy-oriented proposal—criticism that he and Buddy had held back from meting out until that point.

In the end, the highly energized meeting was a stalemate. The F-35 chief test pilot, Jon Beesley, reported back to Burbage that there was no clear decision. Burbage had complete trust and confidence in Jon and asked him for his unvarnished opinion. In a closed-door meeting in Burbage's office, the two discussed the significance of the decision and the longer-term benefits versus the risk of taking the unified option. Burbage challenged his chief test pilot for his decision. Despite the fact that the unified system might be regarded as higher risk, it offered transformational capabilities that could have profound effects on training and transition costs across the F-35 community. Ultimately, Beesley and Burbage agreed: the advantages outweighed the risk, and the decision was made to implement the unified system. The risk reductions demonstrated in the VAAC Harrier, which both Beesley and Burbage had flown, clearly contributed to their decision.

The Flying Saucer is a well-known watering hole in downtown Fort Worth. It's famous for having more than one hundred brands of beer and tracking customer consumption. Those who taste (or consume) all one hundred brands get a personal medallion on the wall commemorating their induction into the Flying Saucer Ring of Honor. As the favorite gathering place for JSF/F-35 warriors, there are more than a few names on that wall. The warriors and the young bucks were all gathered there following the spirited exchange over the F-35B control strategy.

Buddy Denham recalls, "We were all waiting for the decision to be made at the Flying Saucer Bar in downtown Fort Worth. We were elated, because we had really convinced ourselves with data, not emotions, that unified was the right way to go. And so that decision was made by Tom and others, and key to that was the fact that we flew both of them in the VAAC Harrier. Jon came in as the chief test pilot and he had zero agenda. He came in and said, hey, let's just listen to what both sides of the story are and, Simon, what are you presenting? And okay, NAVAIR, what are you presenting? Jon Beesley's insight as an Air Force guy coming in and decelerating down to a hover and then a vertical landing and Tom's similar experiences showed that the unified concept really was viable. So that I think flying both Tom and Jon Beesley was very beneficial. That decision was monumental, I think, and really changed the course of future naval aviation."

There was a rousing round of applause and a few toasts to the future in the Flying Saucer that night as well as some disappointed warriors, but the decision has proven to be a major factor in the success of the F-35B. Choosing the unified concept was one fundamental change made in the F-35B. Another was to move from the three controls in the X-35 to two. Art Tomassetti described this improvement by saying, "The F-35 is nothing like the X-35. It has two controls, called inceptors, which replace the conventional stick and a throttle. A pilot only has two hands, and two controls are much easier than three. For military pilots in training, it usually takes about three months to learn the basic techniques for safe operation. For the Harrier, that training span is about eight months. Today, in the F-35B, it takes three flights to qualify a new pilot to safely fly the F-35B, a testament to the flight control engineers."

★ ★ ★

Along with the strife over the B version's control system, a parallel but just as intense struggle was taking place over the Navy's carrier variant. Like other pieces of the F-35 puzzle, the F-35C had to combine the design contradictions of developing a maintainable, stealthy, supersonic, internal weapon carriage air vehicle, then empower it with flight control software that would make it the most carrier-suitable airplane ever introduced into the fleet. For the design engineers, the first issue was how to integrate the conflicting objectives of stealth and geometry to routinely launch and recover the airplane on the flight deck of an aircraft carrier. For the software engineers, the second challenge was to make the landing event accurate, repeatable, and as stress-free as possible for the pilot.

But first, a little background.

When the Navy's A-6 replacement, the A-12, was canceled, and the F-14's replacement, the AFX (a variant of the F-22), was also deep-sixed by Secretary of Defense Robert Gates in 1990, the whole future of the big-deck Navy's combat strike capability was suddenly cast into doubt. In terms of national security, this was a huge threat; the carrier fleet was expected to provide a major deterrent capability in the Pacific, and if deterrence failed, it would be the principal source of forward combat power. Carrier suitability was thus the single most important criteria for any new weapon slated for the Navy inventory. With both the U.S. Navy and the Marine Corps planning to operate the C variant, it could determine success or failure of the Joint Strike Fighter concept. But an airplane designed for exceptional carrier suitability was inherently in conflict with the design mandates for stealth. (This was the fearsome contradiction that had sunk the A-12.) This dilemma, coupled with the Navy's apprehension that stealth would be very hard to maintain at sea, made the Naval Air Systems Command a "reluctant bridesmaid" in the F-35 tri-service marriage.

Navy carrier aviators pride themselves on the number of successful landings in their logbooks. The "Top Tailhookers" are regarded as exceptional aviators. One hundred successful landings make you a "Centurion" and allow you to put a patch on your flight jacket. One thousand successful landings puts you in a very rare club of Navy carrier legends. Over time, automation has replaced the raw courage of early aviators who had to lean out of the cockpit to see the flight deck at all, because of the huge radial engines and whirling propellers that obstructed their vision when slowed down for landing.

Every landing is graded by a landing signal officer, a highly trained air wing officer who stands on a platform on the rear of the carrier. He waves the pilot off if there's danger on the flight deck or if the approaching plane is in a dangerous attitude. And the landing interval during normal flight operations is only forty-five seconds. Once on deck, the pilot must follow the directions of the "hook runner," a sailor who dashes out and signals the pilot to raise his tailhook, fold his wings, and taxi rapidly out of the landing area as the next plane approaches. Operations on the flight deck are often referred to as a "ballet," with synchronized movements to prevent horrific accidents. Making this very demanding task simpler was the Holy Grail of engineers designing the C version.

Boarding rate, the percentage of landings completed on the first try, is also an important statistic. Most jets must reduce their landing weight (dumping fuel if necessary) to stay within the ability of the arresting gear machinery to safely "trap" the plane. If they miss the wires and have to go around for another pass, their fuel state may become critical. Normal operations at sea require airborne tankers that can transfer fuel to thirsty jets trying to get aboard. In rough weather or when operating outside of range of shore-based divert fields, more "fuel in the air" is required to ensure safe operations. If the control system on the airplane could increase the accuracy of the landing, ensuring that the tailhook captured the arresting gear with very few exceptions, flight operations could be streamlined, with fewer tanking assets required and faster recovery operations.

The need for the F-35C to integrate internal weapon carriage (for stealth) and concealment of the arresting hook system was a major design challenge for the Lockheed Martin and NAVAIR engineers. In simple terms, the plane had to carry a wide variety of large ordnance in a covert weapon bay. But this intruded on the space normally reserved for the tailhook system.

In legacy, non-stealthy airplanes, it had been easy to just put on a longer hook. The F-18 is a good example of this solution. But the stealth requirement was to cloak the airplane by hiding everything possible inside the fuselage. The requirement for a shortened hook resulted in a technical issue that made early arrested landings very problematic. It took forensic diagnosis of ultra high-speed film taken during the field landing tests to crack this problem. The resulting redesign of the tailhook system would resolve the geometry problem, but advanced flight control software algorithms would be needed for reliable, repeatable landings aboard ship under all conditions.

★   ★   ★

Innovative flight control algorithms and extensive testing to cope with the combination of rapid acceleration on catapult launches and the requirement for safe day and night landings in a wide variety of weather and sea state conditions presented a challenge that Buddy Denham had been working on for years. Successful landings required the already combat-stressed and tired pilot to control airspeed, glide slope, and line up to hit a tightly constrained landing area on a moving ship, with other airplanes and helicopters in close proximity on the same deck.

Buddy had already fought and won the battle on the STOVL flight control laws, making a significant contribution to simplifying the most complicated flight phase for the F-35B. But he wasn't finished. His team had also been participating in the UK's research efforts, again using the VAAC Harrier as well as F-35 simulators, on a STOVL enhancement called Shipboard Rolling Vertical Landing, which could allow for a significant increase in "bring back" payload for the F-35B.

In layperson's terms, that offered the opportunity to land with additional fuel or unused ordnance, not possible with a pure vertical landing. The combination of slow forward flight, contributing some additional lift over the wing, and enhanced by relative wind over the deck, allowed a slow roll-on landing within the confined space available on smaller ships. Buddy was convinced the same theory could also simplify the challenge that high-speed jets landing on carriers experienced.

This work, a UK program that would eventually be successfully tested on the *Queen Elizabeth* British carrier, led to a new concept, in Buddy's mind, that could simplify the CV variant landing phase. He called it the Magic Carpet, an acronym for "Maritime Augmented Guidance with Integrated Controls for Carrier Approach and Recovery Precision Enabling Technologies." In simple terms, it was a complex set of software algorithms that had the potential to make the traditionally hairy carrier landing for the F-35C aboard a nuclear aircraft carrier a repeatable, safe event.

Buddy recalled:

Once again, we were not sure we could overcome the strong cultural issues for the Navy. There is a special badge of courage related to being a Naval aviator. We went to landing signal officer (LSO) school and briefed the LSOs. They became our partners because of the safety implications on shipboard operations. I flew sixteen senior Navy and Marine Corps officers over that period, briefing them and letting them fly it in the simulator. Some were pilots, some were not. The last was the Navy Air Boss, Vice Admiral Dave Buss, who was not a pilot.

He came and flew it and was trapping and three wiring almost immediately and got up and said "OK, we need to get this into the fleet."

In the beginning of 2014, I had been talking to Santi Bulnes at Lockheed and around that time we got to Tom Burbage. After all the admirals, I got Tom to come in and look at this, and that really opened the door. "We need to do this" was Tom's conclusion. The software concept had been started under the F-18 Super Hornet program. It was time to look at migrating the concept to the F-35 as its design was being finalized. I played the fact that we were putting this in the Super Hornet to my advantage because Santi said, "Look, we're not going to field the airplane and turn around and watch the Super Hornet have a better control system than we do." Within two and a half weeks, we had a working prototype that we flew. When the ship operators saw the kind of off-nominal conditions that the pilots were flying and getting right back on, they said, "All right, we want this sooner rather than later."

I think we looked at over 16,000 landings and showed that the boarding rate had dramatically improved. And for the Navy, boarding rate is everything and boarding rate is from approach started to a successful trap and not a "bolter and go around" where you now had to get back in the stack of airplanes waiting to land particularly at night. You had to go back out ten miles and not getting the wire and going back out into the black of night just starts to intensify your heart, and you're running out of gas and you've only got a couple of looks and now you've got to go find the tanker at night. So, you know when you can up the percentage of traps with the boarding rate, it's monumental from the Navy's perspective.

So basically, that's the evolution of how Magic Carpet got into the F-35. They're about to suspend ever having to do manual throttle approaches to the ship beginning later this year, and it really is and has been a remarkable safety improvement. Most of the guys I talked to that are out there now say I will never go flying at night without it. I don't do manual approaches. To quote a fleet aviator, "I'm not afraid of the night anymore."

Buddy Denham and Santi Bulnes, with help from the F-35 test pilots, the Navy LSOs, and the NAVAIR engineering team, redefined shipboard operations, not just from a cost perspective, but in terms of saving lives and making the carrier strike group a more effective weapon system. This is one of the biggest, but most often missed, benefits of the F-35 program.

Reference

1. Royal Aeronautical society Heritage Collection biography Sir George Cayley; Hartzellprop.com/ aviation-pioneers-otto-lilienthal, September 18, 2017.

2. Udris, Alex, "What are canards and why don't more aircraft have them?" Boldmethod.com, August 14, 2014.

3. CBSnews.com. "Wright Reenactment Goes Wrong," August 21, 2003.

4. Burgess, Richard R., "Marine Corps Aviation Plan Reduces Number of F-35s in Some Squadrons, Keeps 420 F-35s Total," *Seapower*, May 3, 2022. Available online https://seapowermagazine.org/ marine-corps-aviation-plan-reduces-number-of-f-35s-in-some-squadrons-keeps-420-f-35s-total/. Accessed January 3, 2023.

5. Valle, Orville; "The Marine Corps' love-hate relationship with the AV-8 Harrier"; Wearethemighty. com; January 29, 2019/

6. Head, Elan, "Q and A with Jacoby Aviation's Justin Paines," *Vertical*, June 6, 2019. Available online https://verticalmag.com/q-and-a/joby-aviation-justin-paines/ accessed January 4, 2023.

7. Interview with Art Tomassetti by Tom Burbage on October 23, 2021. Held in F-35 interview archive.

8. Interview of Buddy Denham by Tom Burbage, Betsy Clark, and Adrian Pitman on March 23, 2020. Held in F-35 interview archive.

Chapter 12

INNOVATION DOESN'T JUST HAPPEN

*F*orbes magazine once described *innovation* as challenging conventional notions of how things have been done before and bringing ideas from one industry to another.[1] It's hard to innovate at any time, but excruciatingly difficult in an ongoing program with critical milestones.

In the case of the Joint Strike Fighter, though, a high degree of original thinking was essential to realize the plane's potential. The F-35 was the biggest design quandary in the history of combat aircraft. Many of the new technologies integrated during the concept demonstration phase had to be refined during the development phase. C. R. Davis, who served as PEO from 2006 to 2009 observed, "Every innovation challenge we had was put in motion the day the contract was signed. Put in place a program with three new variants, three new engines when you think about the Pratt & Whitney F135, the GE/RR F136 plus the Rolls-Royce lift fan, three US services, eight partner countries, and many new technologies less than TRL 6."[2]

Davis's remarks may take some unpacking. In the engineering world, technology "maturity"—that is, how ready a given innovation is for prime time—is defined in TRLs, technology readiness levels. TRL 6 means that specific technology has been demonstrated in a laboratory or simulated environment. TRL 8 means it's fully ready for production and combat use, and TRL 9, the highest level, means that the technology has been proven in the operational environment. The need to parallel F-35 design development with corresponding releases of software forced everyone to accept yet another level of risk.

Further complicating everything was that the original proposal, done decades before the plane could be fielded, inevitably lagged behind rising expectations (and requirements) over time. Which meant *more* innovation (and thus, additional jeopardy) was continually called for to meet the new, even tougher expectations.

Three areas most urgently demanded innovation: packaging everything, uniting human and machine, and ensuring suitability for service at sea.

★ ★ ★

Paul Park, the lead design integrator, was faced with the need to incorporate everything required into a relatively small, single-engine airplane that had to meet incredible performance specifications. Park was a tall, soft-spoken until challenged, highly respected design engineer. He could be fiery in meetings when defending his decisions, but very accommodating to young engineers needing mentoring. LM and PEO peers used to tease Park about the U-Haul the new fighter would need to rent and tow behind it for all the "parts that wouldn't fit in the plane." It was a joke, but it reflected a real problem and an increasing source of anxiety as the design matured.

Begin with the fact that, due to the life-cycle cost limitations, the JSF absolutely had to be a single-engine fighter. But twin-engine planes offer a natural channel or void between the turbines where wiring and piping can be routed. The single-engine design meant everything had to be snaked around that single huge power plant somehow. A two-engine design also results in a more or less natural cavity where the weapons bay can go. Yet another problem child was the cockpit air-conditioning system. For weight and balance reasons, it had to be located aft, but the cool air it generated had to go to the pilot, who was of course sitting up front.

And making everything twice as hard was the necessity for stealth. For the plane to remain unseen, everything had to fit within its skin: bombs, missiles, fuel . . . since any and all external stores immediately compromised the Lightning's biggest advantage: its near invisibility to radar. Changing the outer mold line or compromising the weapon bays was not an option.

★ ★ ★

One of the elusive technology goals that had always bedeviled designers of high-performance fighters was the inability to integrate the separate, often heavy and large, onboard vehicle management systems. The F-35 Integrated Vehicle

Systems laboratories had been working hard on this objective throughout the JAST phase, targeting three major systems. First was the auxiliary power system needed to operate the aircraft without the engine running on the ground and to provide starting power for the main engine. Second was the emergency power system to keep critical systems running if the main engine quits in the air. Third was the environmental control system that provided air-conditioning and pressurization life support to the cockpit. Separately, each required precious volume and weight margin and, remembering the single-engine challenge highlighted in the above paragraph, each could compromise needed internal space or force a stealth tradeoff. If successful, the integrated power pack (IPP) would also have the potential to increase reliability and provide much needed packaging efficiency to help unload Park's U-Haul.

On April 29, 2005, the F-35 IPP successfully started the F135 STOVL engine in the Pratt Whitney test facility in West Palm Beach, Florida. The Lockheed Martin and Pratt & Whitney teams involved personnel from Hamilton Sundstrand, providing engine external accessories and the engine start system, Rolls-Royce, supplying the shaft-driven lift fan and Honeywell International, provider of the integrated power package. Bob Elrod, then the LM F-35 Joint Strike Fighter program general manager, commented, "Combining such diverse functions into a single system like this is a lofty technical challenge, but this engine start shows that cooperation among industry leaders can bring great success."[3]

But there was another innovation that might circumvent the physical challenges to the stealth mandate. Just *get rid of* a lot of the traditional hydraulic piping. The electro-hydrostatic actuation system (EHAS), sometimes called "power by wire," had the potential to do away with a traditional hydraulic control system's tanks, accumulators, and piping, as well as the maintenance issues related to leaks.

Consisting of a cylinder, feedback unit, variable speed pump, servo motor, electric drive, and control components,[4] EHAS offered significant space and weight savings along with lower life-cycle costs, sustainment advantages, and increased survivability. Hydraulic systems on combat aircraft have always been an Achilles' heel, since the fluid is flammable, and complete loss of it renders the aircraft uncontrollable.

How does it work? Manipulation of the flight control inceptors (formerly known as "the stick and throttle") by the pilot sent an electrical signal to a small hydraulic actuator, no bigger than a boxer's fist, located right at the control surface. Moog-Parker designed and developed these actuators. While other aircraft today have moved to similar systems, the EHAS development on F-35 was a first. EHAS replaced hydraulic tubing and fluids with electrical cables. They weighed less than pipes with fluid in them and were much less susceptible to fragment or bullet damage or other leakage.

However, such cables presented a different complication. Traditional piping could be bent at right angles to go over and around obstacles, while the thick cables driven by the 270-volt system demanded by the "more electric" architecture can't make 90-degree turns. Suddenly there was a need for wider turning radii for routing in constrained spaces. This was yet another challenge for Park and his designers, but EHAS was an absolute requirement to meet the weight and dimension constraints. To quote Tom Blakely, "There was no Plan B."[5]

As the designs matured, EHAS was further complicated by the unpleasant realization that all three variants had to have different flight control surfaces. This meant the actuators had to deliver custom-tailored amounts of force and stroke distance. The USAF variant required a 9G capability, the ability of the flight control surfaces to generate nine times the force of gravity. The B-model only had to sustain 7 Gs. The carrier variant or C-model was the most challenging. It required much larger control surfaces for slow-speed- flying qualities for safe shipboard landings, but also needed to sustain 7½ Gs.

So, what is all this G-stuff about? In short, one of the keys to maneuverability and agility of a fighter is its ability to accelerate in the turning environment of air-to-air combat. If I can outmaneuver you, I can defeat you. To do that my airplane must be able to outperform yours. The differences in G-design criteria for the three variants involved a tradeoff with other key design requirements of the control surfaces. The F-35B had to have smaller control surfaces for weight constraints on a STOVL design. The F-35C control surfaces had to deal with a larger, heavier airplane optimized for carrier operations.

LM engineers then discovered they couldn't just scale up the actuators for the larger and heavier variant. That became evident in the flight simulators and in the integrated vehicle system laboratories. The result: they had to redesign the C-variant actuators, something else to go into Park's fictional U-Haul.

The next big problem was the weapons bays. They were the plane's reason for being, so they had to be right, and their space had to be protected from the many demands that would press to intrude on them. The inventories of the three

US services and eight other partner nations contained dozens of different bombs and missiles, and more were being developed.

Every weapon also required an internal clearance margin to prevent its slamming into the plane when it was ejected. Ejection speed and other dynamics were different depending on the bomb or missile being employed, complicating the challenge even more.

The new three-dimensional design tools really paid off now. Ben Rich, the former patriarch of the Skunk Works, often said "holes are the most difficult part of designing a combat airplane." To cope, the weapon engineering team developed what they called the 'blob of bombs,' a 'keep out' volume that accommodated all the weapons envisioned. The rest of the airplane would be 'shrink wrapped' around the blob.

★　★　★

Before the F-35, the streams of data entering a cockpit were monitored and evaluated by an onboard organic supercomputer: a highly trained human brain with many hundreds of flight hours. But when that three pounds of fat and neurons became overloaded, fatigued, stressed, wounded, or otherwise impaired, it had been known to neglect some inputs, based on the overriding priority of pilot survival.

Very-low-altitude combat maneuvering was a good example. There, avoiding a catastrophic impact with the ground took precedence over everything else. The pilot would look past momentarily less-essential sensor and threat data to make certain he or she did not die in the next half second. If this tunnel vision effect could be removed, it would revolutionize aerial combat.

Thus, the most elusive dimension of fifth-generation technology was to define and develop the interface between the fighter and its pilot. Integrating all the components of a combat machine—propulsion, flight controls, vehicle systems, and mission systems—was a monumental task. Many believed it would be too much for a single-seat plane.

Over the years, there had been plenty of examples of both single-seat and two-seat fighter and attack aircraft. In some cases, versions of both were ultimately fielded. One reason was that for high-performance airplanes, a second experienced aviator was often judged to be a necessary safety factor, especially for young pilots entering the community. Once trained, that newbie could transition into the single-seat variant for some missions.

Early fighter and attack aircraft dropped "dumb bombs" on a visual target, which a single pilot could do. As sensors and weapons became more sophisticated and "smarter" and raw airspeeds increased, a second systems expert was often needed for navigation, sensor management, and targeting, when pilot skills were saturated in high-threat scenarios. Some even required up to three additional systems experts, as in the EA-6B, a twin-engine four-seater, to monitor a wide portfolio of sensors.

Thus, fighters increasingly tended to need a second organic supercomputer (human brain) in the cockpit, as "surviving the ride" and "completing the mission" both required full attention. Over time, engineers worked hard to automate various pieces of this puzzle, with varying degrees of success.

The Holy Grail of truly making human and machine one turned out to be directly connected to the steady growth of sheer computing power.

★   ★   ★

Moore's law was formulated by Intel cofounder Gordon Moore. He observed that the number of transistors on a microchip was doubling every eighteen to twenty-four months.[6] That dramatic increase in processing power was accompanied by a reduction of about 50 percent in cost. Steadily increasing power at a steadily dropping cost is an unexpected concept, but recall that anyone who bought a smart TV ten years ago for about $9,000 can buy one today, with much more capability, for about $1500.00.

Unfortunately, the Defense Department acquisition process means one may see four or even five cycles of Moore's law before a new weapon system can be fielded. This dynamic had bedeviled the F-22 Raptor program. The revolutionary computing architecture of the Raptor was based on the Intel i960 Chip. The Raptor Common Integrated Processor was the equivalent of two Cray supercomputers. It was truly the state of the art at the design freeze of the F-22 mission system, but it was obsolete by the time the airplane finally went into production.

Extending production of "yesterday's chips" for the small military market made no business sense for large manufacturers. Eventually, it drove new supply-chain terms such as diminishing manufacturing sources (DMS) and lifetime buys of baseline chips.

Both of these phenomena, progress and obsolescence, would have a marked influence on the development of the F-35.

The Lightning's human/digital interface started with the individual pilot. His or her helmet-mounted display would receive inputs from a night-vision camera, multispectral sensors and infrared cameras mounted at various locations on the airplane, providing the pilot with a globe of situational awareness around the airplane. The distributed aperture system, or DAS, consisted of a series of infrared cameras positioned around the fuselage, looking out. Predigested and interpreted information was projected on the visor, so the pilot didn't have to focus on the cockpit displays. Now, they had an unobstructed view of the surrounding environment, as if the airplane itself wasn't there. When they looked back, the wing and tail were invisible. When they looked down, they saw the ground or the sea. No longer did the pilot have to roll the airplane to assess the impact of his bombs, a maneuver that might compromise the plane's position. No longer was the flight deck hidden from the F-35B aviator conducting a landing. And the view was the same day or night. Just as importantly, the DAS was a fantastic sensor for target detection. When fused with the electro optical targeting system, radar, and the electronic warfare sensors, this created a God's-eye view of the world around the plane.

But innovation sometimes proceeds by fits and starts. The Helmet Mounted Display System encountered a number of technical setbacks, even enduring the threat of cancellation or replacement with a lesser-capability helmet. So, why the disconnect? It came down to understanding human physiology in the new world of technology. Think about the evolution of pilot-vehicle sciences. Early fighters had an array of dials and instruments in the cockpit, demanding that the pilot scan integrate visual cues searching the environment and heads-down interpretation of a variety of instruments. Enter the head-up display (HUD) technology that placed a display of critical information in the outside field of view, relieving the human brain of the sometimes disorienting effects of being the resident integrator. Now move the HUD to your head. Suddenly there is a jitter problem affecting pilot interpretation of the displayed information. Larry Lawson's experience in complex integration systems introduced a potential cause. Larry recalls, "Turns out the human body and brain played a direct role in the legacy HUD effectiveness. The human body absorbed any vibrations imputed by the airplane ride and the brain compensated. Take that vibration damping chain out of the equation and jitter results."[7] Once again, software algorithms had to be developed to replace what the human body did naturally. The technology matured, and it became the glue that finally bonded human and machine. (**See Figure 18: The F-35 Helmet-Mounted Display System**)

★ ★ ★

All this integrated information could also be shared, transforming the F-35 into an information node on the combat web. This enabled the second level of combat capability . . . connecting the Wolfpack. F-35s flying as a multi-ship force of four to eight, often in a widely dispersed formation, were connected through a sophisticated, covert data link.

At yet a third level, they could also share information with the rest of the force. That sharing came in two flavors. Lesser-capable third or fourth generation planes, which still constituted a large portion of allied air forces, could leverage that information flow to become much more effective. They could "see" far more of the battlespace than was visible out of their cockpits. Finally, the F-35's ability to roam at will throughout high-threat environments let it hand off reconnaissance information and targets to distant seaborne and ground-based assets. Such precise intelligence greatly expanded the lethal range of their weapons.

But making these concepts operational was tough. Software integration is a complex science. Before everything else, it required stability in the basic architecture. A system that crashed was useless. That stability was disrupted every time an anomaly popped up or a new requirement was defined. Every change had to be fully evaluated through regression analysis to make sure it hadn't compromised another capability. As the volume of code increased, the more difficult this became.

In the future, the most elusive dimension of technology may no longer be in developing sensors that can see farther, although that will always be a driver. The newest frontier will be to continue to simplify the interface between the capabilities of a machine and the skills of the pilot, while preserving the advantages of both . . . and sharing more information faster, to permit fully coordinated air, sea, land, and space operations.

But first the best software engineering minds in the industry had to tame the onward march of Moore's Law and attack the cost of obsolescence that had accompanied that unforgiving dynamic. It was probably the most complex challenge the program would face. The mission systems software was designed from the beginning to enable efficient replacement of older computer processors with newer, more powerful ones. This replacement was done twice during the development phase, thus providing more processing power to support the continually more sophisticated and growing amount of software.

★ ★ ★

Finally, there was the issue of taking the plane to sea. As noted in a previous chapter, the last US military service to accept the benefits of stealth was the U.S. Navy. Low-observable Air Force platforms like the F-117 Nighthawk and the B-2 Spirit were celebrated for their combat effectiveness but dreaded for their nightmarish maintenance demands. The F-22 Raptor was better, but still required specialized facilities to maintain full stealth.

Yet two of the three F-35 variants would have to go to sea, and cramped space and open-air, salt-water environments were anathemas to specialized care and materials. To be successful, any solution would not just have to *work* at sea. It became apparent that there would also have to be a fundamental technical and a cultural education process if the F-35B and C were going to succeed in the carrier environment. The Navy technical and engineering communities would have to embrace any solution . . . always a tall order.

The first technical concepts were structured around "appliques," essentially large decals that could be glued to critical areas. The materials went to sea on A-6 Intruders for evaluation. The results were not good.

By 2004 stealth technology simply had to move on from external coatings applied to traditional metal skins. Considering the proliferation of advanced composite structures, the engineers opened a dialogue with the 'super yacht' community. The light, strong hulls of those boats were largely composite, and, moreover, showed few of the tiny layer-on-layer fabric defects that would compromise stealth.

To build a modern boat, the composite fabric structure is placed in a mold. Through an engineered process of applying alternate layers, high strength and durability can be "baked into" the eventual part. This meant a major change from traditional manufacturing, but it was critical. If LM could bake into the skin of the F-35 what in the past had required an extensive process of sophisticated coatings, stealth could be maintained in a shipboard environment. In retrospect, this was one of the program's most important breakthroughs.

Recognizing this challenge, Dr. Bill Grant set up a supportable low observability team. Grant was a Lockheed Martin tech fellow (the highest accolade an engineer can receive) in advanced materials. Tech fellows are recognized experts throughout the aerospace fraternity. He summarized his team's focus this way:

"In 'legacy' stealth, the stealth in effect was a parasitic application of a multiple stack-up of material systems done in the final finishes stage after the actual airframe is built and completed. In the case of the F-35, we've been able to incorporate much of the LO system directly into the air frame itself. The materials have been manufactured right into the structure, so they have the durability and lifetime qualities of the airplane itself. It makes them much more impervious to damage. It is a much simpler system with fewer materials to contend with."

Under Dr Grant's leadership, the program implemented the most extensive and aggressive material qualification program in history. Dr. Grant continued, "the testing process has led to changes in the repair approach as well as the manufacturing approach for the program. When we found deficiencies, we suggested changes to the manufacturing processes.

Getting to the point where historically conservative senior admirals with thousands of flight hours would trust the new technology was a whole 'nother ball game'. To prove it would work, LM built a test operation in Daytona Beach in northern Florida. Three hundred sample panels of F-35 skins were propped in the surf line. A number of them were intentionally damaged, to simulate wear and tear that would likely be sustained during a typical carrier cruise. After several years of testing there was very little degradation. This began to convince the skeptics that the Navy's ability to project power from the sea could be preserved.

But proving stealth was durable was only the first step. It also had to be maintainable within the constrained cubic of the hangar deck.

Again, virtual modeling helped enormously. The basing and ship suitability team built a digital replica of the hangar decks for both the small L-Class carriers as well as the larger nuclear fleet. They used "avatars," simulated human maintainers of various sizes, to evaluate all the maintenance activities envisioned. One of the most demanding was the "engine change box." This modeled the removal and replacement of the large F-135 engine. These simulations, based on exact dimensions of hangar bays and the human maintainers, allowed the F-35 to be integrated into shipboard operations without the normal extensive learning curve.

★   ★   ★

NAVAIR was very protective of their responsibility. Their insight into the unique requirements of the flight and hangar decks made them skeptical of the JPO/LM development of the next-generation carrier fighter. It was very clear they would make the final decision about accepting the F-35B and C into the Fleet . . . or not.

Based on Northrop Grumman's reputation as the principal subcontractor on the Navy's F-18, Lockheed Martin tasked them (partnered with Stork Fokker in the Netherlands) with developing the new plane's arresting gear. While both the F-35A and the F-35C have tailhooks, the F-35A uses long, land-based runways, and will only deploy its hook in rare emergencies, such as a brake failure. The C, on the other hand, would have to use its hook system multiple times in a single day. This required a different approach. The solution would require a combination of detailed engineering of the tailhook and development of software to ensure repeatable, safe landings in all weathers.

The engineering was complicated by the need to hide the hook for stealth. But real estate inside the airplane was already at a premium. The retracted landing gear, the weapon bay, and the tailhook competed for cubic. The result was a stubbier hook than built into previous Navy fighters. But then the engineers discovered a new problem.

The initial "roll-in testing" was done at the Carrier Suitability Test Facility in Lakehurst, New Jersey. The new, shorter hook didn't catch a single wire in eight attempts. Uh oh . . . NAVAIR, despite having approved the design, had its antibody rejection triggered. To quote a senior NAVAIR engineer, "F-35C will never be a carrier-suitable airplane." Clearly, the contractor needed to bring in reinforcements.

Tom Blakely, the chief engineer at Lockheed Martin Aero, was drafted. He had a long history with NAVAIR and was respected there. Blakely pulled the system back from Northrop Grumman to Lockheed Martin. His program review concluded that a satisfactory solution required a detailed engineering model combining many technical issues including flight deck response, arresting cable response, hook "hold down" dynamics, and more.

He recalled, "After we redesigned the tailhook system, the F-35C conducted sea trials aboard USS *Nimitz* in November 2014 off San Diego. After ten days of sea trials, the F-35C test pilots made approximately a hundred traps with no 'bolters' or missed arrestments. To my knowledge, this was a first in Navy carrier aviation." In addition, the flight deck crew were impressed by the differences between the F-35C Lightning II and its predecessors. Maneuverability on the flight deck, ease of parking, quick and safe catapult hookup and arresting gear exit all left the "green shirts" smiling.

Going from zero arrestments to the most successful sea trials in the history of naval aviation was a testimony to the Lockheed Martin and NAVAIR engineers. As Blakely said, "Forming a partnership with NAVAIR is not easy and neither is developing an innovative solution to enable a stealthy, supersonic capability to the Big Deck fleet that meets their rigorous standards for shipboard operations. I really think this may be the most rewarding career accomplishment to me personally."

Innovation doesn't just happen, no less in aviation than in any other field of engineering. Yet those who build defenses for the West can never rest on their laurels. They have to challenge conventional notions of how things have been done before. They have to look at bringing in ideas from other industries. They must not just respond to, but *anticipate* how technology, threats, and budget priorities are going to change. Their solutions will define the next steps in a never-ending journey.

But the F-35 challenges were far from over.

Reference

1. Greenwald, Michelle, "What Exactly Is Innovation?" *Forbes*, March 12, 2014.
2. Interview of CR Davis by Tom Burbage, Betsy Clark, and Adrian Pitman on July 29, 2020. Held in F-35 interview archive.
3. News.lockheedmartin.com, PRNewswire First Call, Unique Integrated System Starts F-35 Engine in Joint Test by Lockheed Martin, Pratt & Whitney, April 29, 2005.
4. Helbig, Achim, "Electro-Hydrostatic Actuation," Moog White Paper, 2014, accessed June 5, 2022.
5. Interview with Tom Blakely by Tom Burbage, Betsy Clark, and Adrian Pitman on February 12, 2018. Held in F-35 interview archive.
6. Gianfagna, Mike, "What Is Moore's Law?" *Synopsi*, published June 30, 2021.
7. Interview of Larry Lawson by Tom Burbage on December 26, 2022. Held in F-35 interview archive.

Chapter 13

TESTING THE BEAST

Operational Test and Evaluation (OT&E) is conducted by independent agencies within each military service using realistic combat scenarios. Their objective is to determine if a system is effective and suitable for its intended missions. In layperson's terms, ready for combat. It is the ultimate "seal of approval" for a new system.

To help insulate the process from service politics, Congress directed that the Director OT&E also separately report to them. This added another step to the approval process, often an extensive one, to carry out a thorough evaluation, write a report, and review it before release to the public. At the same time, it provided an opening for congressional politics, both pro and con.

For the F-35, the most complex weapon system ever attempted, issues that surfaced during testing would often be resolved long before the report was published. The so-called "deficiency" would then pinball through the press, Congress, and the multinational partnership, jangling nerves and generating more heat than light. Hostile commentators would seize on it to malign the program, long after the initial shortfall or glitch had been remedied.

A second organizational dynamic presented a stumbling block for introduction into naval service. Because of the unique nature of aircraft carrier operations, certifying naval planes was the responsibility of the Naval Air Test Center at Patuxent River, Maryland, not the F-35 Joint Program Office (JPO). This, despite the fact the JPO was staffed to the most senior level with personnel from both Naval Air Systems Command and the Air Force Systems Command.

As a result, the Lightning II faced the most extensive and demanding test program in history. Long before the first F-35 went wheels-up, engineers were doing exhaustive simulations at the component and subsystem level. They ran wind tunnel tests with small-scale models across a variety of low speed and supersonic regimes. Some of these facilities were government-owned and others contractor-owned. A few were provided by international partners. The

Figure 1: Lockheed P-38 Lightning

Figure 2: F-117 Nighthawk

Figure 3: B-2 Spirit

Figure 4: F-22 Raptor

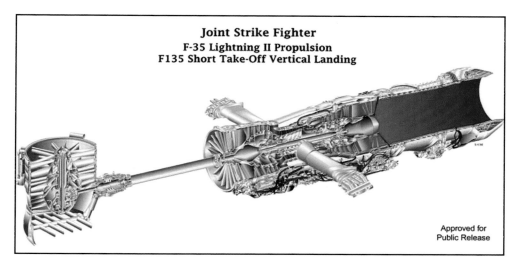

Figure 5: The Lift–Fan Concept for the X–35B STOVL Variant

Figure 6: X-32 and X-35 side by side

Figure 7: Simon Hargreaves performs first hover in X–35B. Note Hat Trick logo on tail.

Figure 8: "The Winner is . . . Lockheed Martin" at the Pentagon

Figure 9: "The Winner is . . . Lockheed Martin" in the Fort Worth Conference Center

Figure 10: Danish F-16 Chase Plane with JSF Program Tail Flash

Figure 11: Dutch piano burning celebration

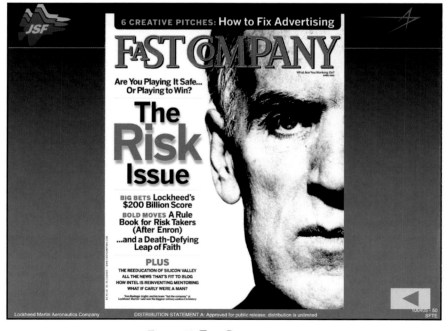

Figure 12: Fast Company *cover*

Figure 13: F135 engine on test stand

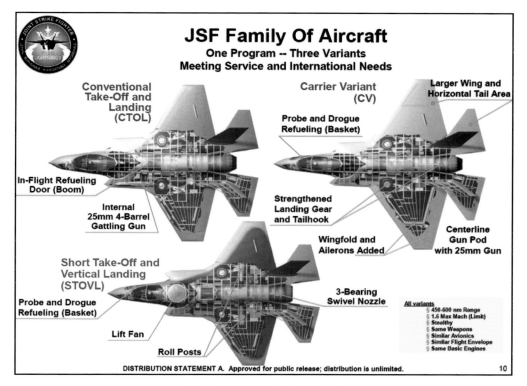

Figure 14: JSF Family of Aircraft

Figure 15: The Lightnings in formation

Figure 16: Eric "Winkle" Brown

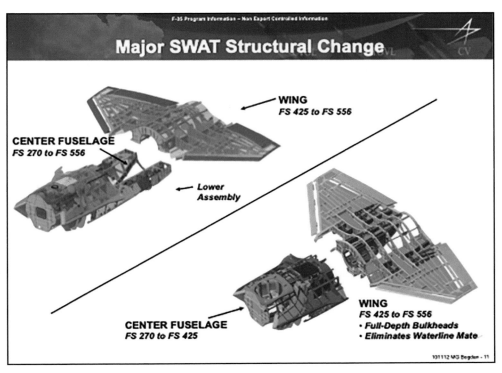

Figure 17: The Major SWAT Structural Change

Figure 18: The F-35 Helmet-Mounted Display System

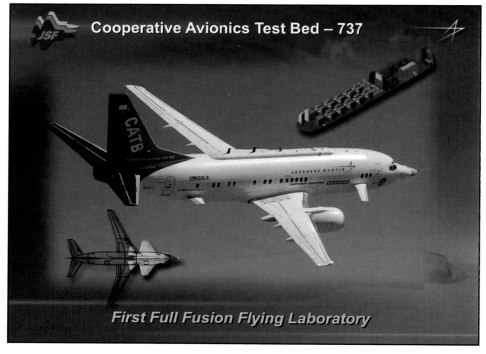

Figure 19: Cooperative Avionics Test Bed or Cat Bird

Figure 20: The challenge of going to sea with stealth

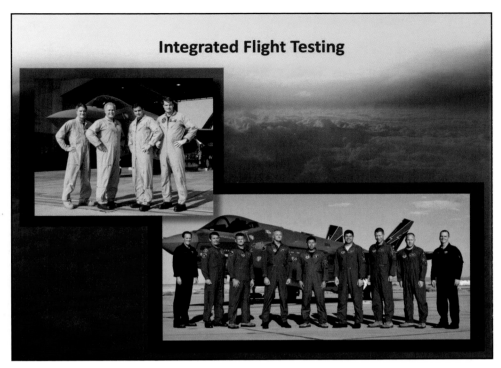

Figure 21: F-35 test pilots

Figure 22: Bill Gigliotti in cockpit with UK flag following first flight of UK F-35B

Figure 23: F–35C aboard U.S. Navy supercarrier

Figure 24: USMC L–Class carrier USS America

Figure 25: HMS Queen Elizabeth *underway*

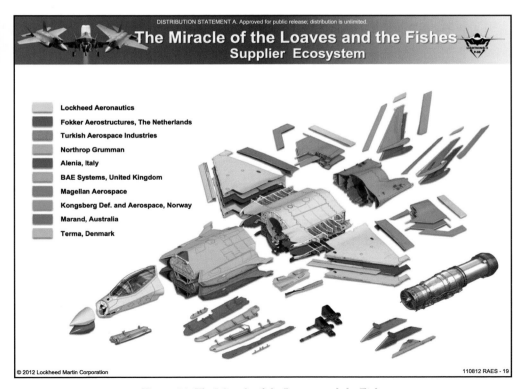

Figure 26: The Miracle of the Loaves and the Fishes

Figure 27: Lockheed Martin Final Assembly and Checkout Operation

Figure 28: Factory Move of AA-1 . . . First Flight?

Figure 29: Marand Precision Engineering engine trailer

Figure 30: F-35 weapon loadout

Figure 31: Bucket List Item 1

Figure 32: My Dutch rowing partner

Netherlands Research test facility, for example, provided key aerodynamic, aeroacoustic and aeroelastic data as a full test partner.

Subsystem suppliers had to prove their equipment could meet the extraordinary demands for reliability, maintainability, and connectivity to the software-intensive control systems being developed in Fort Worth.

The initial cadre of test pilots worked as engineers in the development labs years before actually getting to fly the plane. At the Integrated Vehicle Systems Lab, with a human pilot in the loop, engineers could evaluate how the systems would react in actual flight. Mission systems integration and development stressed individual systems as well as the integrated cockpit. This lab's high-fidelity simulators let the engineer/pilots prove out the transformational abilities of the integrated systems. A secondary benefit was that non-test pilots, often from partner countries, could fly simulated missions in high-threat scenarios long before their air forces would take delivery.

Along with these integration labs, other assets contributed to developing individual sensors and flight dynamics. For instance, advanced flight control and inlet development work was carried out on a specially configured F-16, radar development was done on the BAC-111 at Northrop Grumman, and electro optical targeting systems testing on their Gulfstream II.

★ ★ ★

As the hardware and software matured, it became obvious a full flying test bed would be essential to test the complete integrated capability of the new design.

Lockheed tasked Paul Metz to find a commercial platform for the flying test bed. In a former life, Metz had been the Northrop Grumman YF-23 chief test pilot during the Advanced Tactical Fighter competition. When Lockheed won that competition, he joined the team and became the F-22 Raptor chief test pilot, piloting its maiden flight in 1997. When the F-35 program approached flight test, he hopped cockpits again, becoming the first VP for flight test in Fort Worth. After some research, Metz identified a Boeing 737-300 formerly operated by Indonesian Airlines as an airframe which could become an "F-35 in a 737." Its official name was the Cooperative Avionics Test Bed (CATB), but everyone called it "the Cat Bird."

This entailed one of the most extensive modifications ever attempted. The interior was rebuilt with racks to house the avionics and a full F-35 cockpit where a test pilot or engineer could operate the systems as they would look in the new fighter. Farther aft, twenty individual engineering stations were installed. Along with the 737 pilot, a co-pilot, and those twenty engineers, the crew included a test director and a test conductor. In addition, racks containing extensive electrical components and wiring were installed in the 737 cargo bays to provide power to the F-35 mission systems, laboratory equipment and engineering workstations.

The weirdest-looking feature was the forebody of an F-35 grafted to the 737 front end. Strange as this appeared, it reproduced the geometry between the radar and electronic warfare sensors and helped work out their fusion from a software perspective. The Cat Bird also got a distributed aperture system (for 360-degree situational awareness, day or night) and the electro optical targeting system. Additional sensors, data links, and comm systems went in a "spine" on top of the airplane, in a "canoe" added to the belly, and in a pair of strakes aft of the wing.

Wayne Elbers managed the plane from 2006 until 2009. "Our CATB team always thought it was interesting that everybody looks at the Cat Bird and sees the outside stuff—the forward wings, a little stub back wing and the nose extension—and very few realize that the inside modifications are probably more complicated than the outside. The inside is not sexy and it's a lot of wires, equipment racks and workstations but we've got a real F-35 cockpit in the middle of the airplane. The pilot or engineer sitting there sees the real displays from all the F-35 sensors while the pilots up front are flying the 737."[1]

All these mods coupled with the additional weight changed the flying qualities of the 737. So, the Cat Bird had its own test requirements. First, it had to pass baseline flight tests to determine its normal flight dynamics. Then, following the modifications, the flight tests were repeated with some added test requirements to pinpoint changes and ensure safety precautions were understood before certification as a test asset.

BAE Systems, at the Mojave, California Air and Space Port, got the job of doing the modifications. The director was Paul Nafziger, a retired Air Force test pilot. Paul had been an exchange officer and instructor pilot to the Navy Test Pilot School in the mid-1970s. One of the students he worked with was then-Lt. Tom Burbage. Thirty years after flying together as young test pilots, Paul and Tom flew together once more in the baseline trials at Mojave. (**See Figure 19: Cooperative Avionics Test Bed or Cat Bird**)

★ ★ ★

Previous fighter aircraft had been designed to a six-thousand-hour structural life before an upgrade was needed. The F-35 team's goal was a structural design that could endure for eight thousand flight hours. The difference between these life expectancies could be a major weight driver but also a very significant life-cycle cost reduction.

Testing this stouter, hopefully longer-lasting structure required complex rigs to reproduce forces and moments anticipated over the jet's lifetime. Each of the three variants underwent static testing. This applied extreme loadings, past the point of failure. Each step of the static tests expanded the envelope for the flight test airplanes, so it was essential to finish them on time. The static testing would also ensure that structural weight was optimized for the required strength.

Evaluation of the three variants was distributed across six airplanes and three test facilities. The F-35A static and durability testing would occur at BAE Systems' excellent facility in Brough, England, which had tested the Eurofighter Typhoon. In early 2009, a barge made its way up the South Channel of the River Humber to deliver the next-generation stealth fighter. The journey to Brough was an interesting one with curious onlookers wondering why a fighter airplane was barge bound and the challenge of timing tidal flows for unloading the precious cargo. The 350-ton airframe structural test rig was built to "fly" the F-35 through a series of scenarios, over and over, to replicate its future life. Over twenty miles of wiring, 2,500 strain gauges, and 160 actuators subjected the aircraft to the stresses it would experience in actual flight. The F-35B and C static and durability testing would be done in similar test rigs at Lockheed's Fort Worth facility and the unique F-35 C landing gear structural tests would be done at the Vought Aircraft Industries facility in Grand Prairie, Texas. In what is referred to as "drop tests," the airplane is literally dropped from various heights to simulate the hard landings experienced on carriers at sea.

The three durability test vehicles would provide assurance that the F-35 could achieve their predicted life projections of eight thousand flight hours. In their test rigs, they would tolerate thousands of routine operations: raising and lowering the landing gear, flaps, tailhook, and other moveable parts, as well the dynamic loads of pulling Gs in combat. Failures were expected. (As Elon Musk says, "If things are not failing, you're not innovating enough.")[2] When an element broke or showed fatigue, either the structure had to be "beefed up" or a stronger material had to be substituted. Repeated many times, this process ensured the design was optimized for weight versus strength. Connected electronically, the testers would share information across the globe.

In a world where failures were misrepresented by hostile interests, a simple explanation often trumped trying to explain why a crack or deformation occurred. Bob Burt, chief structural engineer, used the analogy of a metal coat hanger. "While it's a solid structure in normal use, you can cause failure by repeatedly bending and unbending it. The same physics apply to a comprehensive air vehicle structure when it simulates three lifetimes of use."

So . . . why "three lifetimes"? Past combat aircraft had suffered from premature stress cracking and other failures. This had driven up the sustainment costs over decades of demanding use. By testing to three lifetimes, the *probability* of achieving the required eight thousand hours was significantly improved.

By November 2017, the F-35A had completed three lifetimes of durability testing, the equivalent of flying 24,000 hours. The airframes should last well beyond 2050.

★ ★ ★

Pilot safety is a special challenge in high-performance aircraft. That challenge was squared when the population expanded to include female (and smaller male) aviators. Previous ejection seats accommodated pilot weights from 150 to 250 pounds. The new minimum was a hundred pounds. The system had to eject the small pilot without injury but still be able to safely handle a much larger pilot.

It also had to extract the aviator throughout a flight envelope that extended from zero knots to supersonic speeds, with the plane damaged, upside down, sideways, or in a spin. It had to save him or her from the STOVL F-35B if the lift fan failed in a hover. While the chance of that happening was small, the dynamic loss of control coupled with proximity to the ground meant no human could react in time. As mentioned in a previous chapter, LM called on the Martin-Baker Company to develop an auto-eject capability.

Developing a new seat progresses from a static (nonmoving) test rig to high-speed testing on a rocket sled. Lore had it that in the old days, a muzzled black bear was the perfect "test pilot" as it had about the same dimensions as a slightly overweight human. The first ursine was bundled into the cockpit without much objection. It rocketed down the rail, ejected, and the parachute floated it back to earth. But the attempt to get it back in the sled for a second run was met with bared teeth, claws, and a fight that resulted in the test being canceled.

★ ★ ★

Meanwhile, another issue had surfaced. As noted previously, the P&W F135, the most powerful jet engine in the world, was derived from the F-22's F119. It came in two versions. The F135-PW-100 powered the F-35 A and C variants. It generated 28,000 pounds of thrust in military (non-afterburning) mode and 43,000 pounds with afterburner. This output matched the combined thrust of the two engines in a F-18. Its sister, the F135-PW-600, which powered the F-35B, also had to drive the lift fan in the STOVL mode. It generated 27,000 pounds of thrust in military power and 41,000 pounds in afterburner. In the hover, the engine/lift fan combination can generate a total of 40,650 pounds of lift.

Unfortunately, noise is a major by-product of that power, as the engine accelerates all that air over a distance of nineteen feet. The associated physics generates such a din it can be viewed by some as a threat to sanity. Some feared it would prove unacceptable to communities that had developed near military airfields, despite the strips having been there first.

This concern, amplified by press misrepresentations, was shared by a number of the partner countries. Happily, testing proved it shouldn't be a significant factor. Although the shaping of the airplane, driven by the need to survive in high threat environments, did provide increased noise on specific angles from the airplane, the way it flew in takeoffs and landings would make sound less objectionable than that of previous aircraft. The F135's single-engine thrust equals the combined thrust of most twin-engine fighters. This let the new jet take off with military power as opposed to the afterburning requirement for most fighters, including its European competitors.

This was shown dramatically when senior politicians from the Netherlands visited Fort Worth. They were at the flight line to observe an F-35 test being chased by a Lockheed Martin test F-16. The F-35 made a short takeoff run and vanished over the employee parking lot. Nothing untoward happened. A few minutes later, the F-16 departed on the same flight path in afterburner. As it streaked over, hundreds of car alarms began to bleep and blare in the lot. Since F-16s had long been operated without major objections, this made a case that for the new plane, noise wouldn't be an overwhelming issue either.

One of the most vocal US critics on this fear was the Panhandle community of Niceville, Florida (yes, its actual name), home of Eglin Air Force Base. When Eglin Air Force Test Center was named as the first F-35 training facility, the mayor and city council demanded a town hall meeting with its commander to discuss noise pollution. To prepare, LtGen C. R. Davis, the Eglin Test Center commander and former F-35 program executive officer, asked for a prototype to come down and fly over the town all afternoon, including multiple takeoffs and landings. At the meeting he asked innocently, "You have a community concern about F-35 noise. Did the noise today really bother you?" The response was "What noise?"

Case closed!

★ ★ ★

Carey Lohrenz, the first female F-14 pilot, said, "A carrier landing is similar to a controlled crash. The touchdown is enough to destroy most other airplanes. As the arresting hook snags a wire, your body is slammed forward with such force at times it feels as though your legs and arms are going to separate from your body."[3]

The flight deck of an aircraft carrier is one of the most dangerous places anywhere. Launching high-performance fighter and attack planes from a small platform, in a variety of weather and sea states, is never easy. Early catapults employed pneumatic, hydraulic, and flywheel-powered systems. As carriers grew larger, the real estate available also increased, allowing a longer and smoother stroke. Steam catapults were an improvement, but complicated construction with boiler fittings and piping. The newest designs use a linear induction motor rather than steam. Catapult launching requires precision maneuvering to align the airplane with the launch system. The launch imposes severe stresses on the undercarriage with each stroke.

Meanwhile, at the carrier's stern, an equally complex and dangerous operation is going on as planes are recovered. Four thick steel cables cross deck pendants and attach to longer purchase cables that run to the arresting gear engine rooms. The arresting gear engine is made up of a fixed crosshead and a moveable crosshead that the purchase cable connects to through a series of sixteen cable windings. As a plane lands, its hook grabs a pendant on the flight deck. As the pendant is pulled out by the airplane, that energy is transferred to the arresting gear engine, where the moveable cross head is pulled toward the fixed cross-head. The airplane's rollout on the flight deck is then regulated by a mechanical valve that slows the movement of the moveable crosshead. A young sailor, connected by a set of sound-powered phones, manages each of the four arresting gear engines and resets the mechanical valve for each landing airplane since all are landing at different weights and speeds.

It sounds complicated but here's the way it works (much simplified). An observer in the tower identifies the next plane to land. The pilot acknowledges, and gives his fuel state. A quick calculation confirms the setting required for the arresting gear engines for that aircraft and its specific speed and weight. That information's passed to the arresting gear operators (the young sailors mentioned above), to set the braking valve. A too-light setting would result in the system not stopping the airplane in time and dumping it over the angled deck. Alternatively, if it's set too heavy, it can snap either the pendant or the plane's tailhook, also with major damage and possibly a dead or injured pilot.

Landing also requires very precise flight path control. The tailhook has to engage the arresting wires just so. This also stresses the tailhook and landing gear. Then, the pilot must quickly raise his hook and clear the landing area, as the next plane is already on final approach. And remember, this is all happening every forty-five seconds!

One of the most incredible aspects is that the majority of the flight deck crew are in their teens and early twenties. Observers often refer to it as a "ballet," with all personnel wearing color coded jerseys to identify their roles. They're connected by a radio system that allows anyone, no matter what rank or position, to suspend operations if they anticipate danger.

Following recovery, respotting operations rapidly reposition aircraft around the deck, so they can be refueled, checked, and rearmed for the next launch. Navy planes, including the F-35C, are designed with folding wings to hoard the limited space in both the flight deck and the hangar deck below it. (**See Figure 20: The challenge of going to sea with stealth**)

Watch all this for hour after hour, at night, in stormy weather, with the ship itself a moving target, and you begin to grasp the challenge of designing a Navy airplane and get an idea of how hard it is to earn the naval aviator's Wings of Gold.

Planes grew steadily heavier as they progressed from propeller to jet propulsion and added fuel and weapons. Making them both stealthy and supersonic added even more complexity. Evaluating a new design's ability to operate efficiently and safely from carriers is a demanding specialty, one that for good reason is jealously protected by the experts of the Naval Air Systems Command.

Testing a next-generation high-performance aircraft for carrier suitability consists of both shore-based and shipboard events. The center of excellence for carrier-based engineering and testing is the Naval Air Test Center at Patuxent River, Maryland. The major testing site for the interface between the plane and carrier is the Naval Air Warfare Center Aircraft Division at Lakehurst, New Jersey. Both were extensively involved in testing the F-35C.

All the facilities provided the confidence that would allow the early production planes to enter the most critical test phase: flight testing. At that point, the spotlight would shift to an elite breed: the test pilots.

When the concept demonstration phase ended with the submission of the Joint Strike Fighter proposal, it would be six years before the next group would fly the production F-35 Lightning II. As mentioned earlier, they spent those years designing the cockpits and man-machine interfaces and developing the flight control laws.

Finally, in 2006, flight tests began in earnest, and the contributions of these men and women called "testers"—engineers, test directors, data analysts, maintainers and pilots—took the helm. To quote Doc Nelson, the first F-35 pilot to reach a thousand hours, it was time to populate "the best seat in the house."[4]

Reference

1. Interview with Wayne Elbers by Betsy Clark and Adrian Pitman on June 17, 2017. Held in F-35 interview archive.

2. *The Economist*, "Ad Astra, on the Cheap," February 19–25, 2022, 64.

3. https://careylohrenz.com/be-fearless-what-night-carrier-landings-can-teach-us-about-high-performance/.

4. https://www.lockheedmartin.com/en-us/news/features/2017/nelson-100-hours.html.

Chapter 14

THE BEST SEAT IN THE HOUSE

Test pilots' devil-may-care, white-scarved image endures from movies like *Test Pilot* with Clark Gable, *The Right Stuff*, and even *Top Gun*. The reality's different. Today they're highly educated engineers who can both help design superb flying qualities into aircraft and push those planes to the edges of their envelopes.

Consider the process of becoming a military test pilot. After completing a squadron tour, gaining flight experience, they go through a rigorous application and acceptance process to attend one of the formal test pilot schools. They will attend either the Air Force Test Pilot School at Edwards Air Force Base in California, the Naval Test Pilot School at Patuxent River, Maryland, or the British Test Pilot School at Boscombe Down in the UK where they face a year of intense academic and flight training in the techniques of testing high-performance military airplanes. Most contractor test pilots come from this fraternity of military-trained pilots.

Often, test pilots get the opportunity to fly multiple aircraft, and most will recount experiences that are often dangerous and unpredictable. Their Test Pilot School experience was critical to learning and often surviving in developing these powerful machines.

To be chosen to participate in developing and testing a next-generation fighter is the plum job in a test pilot's career. A select few pilots had test flown the X-35. Tom "Squid" Morgenfeld took the X-35A plane aloft for the first time in 2000. The second, and first government, pilot to go wheels up, was USAF Lt Col Paul "TP" Smith. The first Marine was Major Art "Turbo" Tomassetti. Fourth was LM pilot Joe "Irish" Sweeney. Simon Hargreaves, BAE pilot and decorated RN Harrier veteran, took the X-35B STOVL up for the first time. Sixth was RAF squadron leader Justin Paines; he flew all three of the variants. Seventh was Navy LCDR Brian Goszkowicz, and eighth was LCDR Greg Fenton. Sweeney, Goszkowicz, and Fenton did most of the carrier suitability testing at Pax River. Only two of the eight were Lockheed Martin employees, and, as mentioned in chapter 4, this fact was not lost on the other pilots.

This early band of brothers completed the most aggressive X-Plane flight test program in history, setting a number of records and setting up the program for the 2001 Collier award for the performance of Mission X. Then there was a pause while the program waited for a decision and then completed the design and development phase that would determine the real family of F-35 variants. This would introduce the next set of engineering test pilots.

Jon Beesley was the best and most experienced test pilot Lockheed Martin had, and possibly the most experienced in the industry. He'd put the F-117 through its paces in the "black program" days, and had been one of the original test pilots on the YF-22. As chief F-35 test pilot from 2002 to 2011, Beesley burned up many hours helping design the Lightning's flight control systems and said,

> Early in a program, it's very critical to get it right because quite honestly, you can't afford to go back and fix very many things after the fact or you'll kill the program.
>
> I always used to tell the young test pilots, first thing you do . . . you invite yourself to meetings, you go find the meetings, you go to them, and after a while they'll actually tell you when the meeting is and then they'll get to the point where they won't hold the meeting unless you can be there. I was the guy who spent many hours every week working with the engineers and refining how we wanted the airplane to fly. Making airplanes very easy to fly is very, very hard.[1]
> (See Figure 21: F-35 test pilots)

The scale of the F-35's flight test program was unprecedented. Previous designs had been evaluated at a single site. The Lightning would operate from three primary sites and ten secondary sites designed to test very specific aspects of the airplanes. Where older planes had dealt with a single test organization, the new plane had to coordinate with several, including those from the partner countries. While historical programs had to certify one platform, the F-35 had three airframe variants and "two and a half" engine variants: the CTOL/CV engine, the STOVL engine, the lift fan, and the integration of the fan and the basic engine. While traditional programs had typically scheduled 2,000–3,000 flights and

3,000–4,000 flight hours, the F-35 had 7,000 flights and 12,500 flight hours. The biggest previous programs had flown seven to nine instrumented test airplanes. The F-35 would fly fifteen. Most unusual of all, the tests would be managed by LM, the prime contractor, not by the government.[2]

Data collection was also extraordinary. Onboard instrumentation was capable of recording nine terabytes of data on each flight. To put that in perspective, all the books in the Library of Congress together contain twenty terabytes. Shuffling that many bits between Pratt & Whiney in Connecticut, the JPO in Washington, Lockheed Martin in Fort Worth, the Navy at Pax River, the Air Force at Wright-Patterson and Edwards Air Force Bases, and others was a huge task. The task of archiving it in case of a later issue was monumental, made even more complex considering the security required for much of the data. But it was essential to keeping the test program within a reasonable time line.

All three airframes basically performed similarly across the middle of the flight envelope. But significant differences lurked at the edges of the variant regimes. High angle of attack and departure from controlled flight characteristics had to be deeply explored. Also, the STOVL environment for the B model and the "Big Navy" carrier environment for the C model needed special attention.

Of course, that all worked against the original acquisition reform objectives of reducing testing costs with flight dynamics modeling and high-fidelity multi-axis simulators.

But back to the test pilots. Everyone who's ever had the chance to test a next-generation aircraft considers it the ultimate opportunity to ply their craft. In this case, the pilot group had the unique opportunity to fly *all* the variants. (In the past, the services had jealously guarded the operational demands of their specific environments). Since all three were designed to "feel" the same, aviators could hopscotch from the A to the B to the C model. This came from the hard work on the flight control integration and was a significant piece of the aircraft's promise.

But now someone had to prove those promises were valid.

★ ★ ★

On December 15, 2006, without a white scarf but in his blue LM flight suit, Beesley caught the bus out to the Fort Worth flight line, along with Tom Burbage and Dan Crowley, the F-35 program general managers. The F-35A was ready for its long-anticipated maiden outing. The first flight test "article" (airplane) was designated AA-1. Several thousand people lined the fence, mainly LM employees, a few dignitaries and journalists and a number of "bird-watchers," aviation enthusiasts who trotted the globe anxious to watch and record significant events. The weather was clear, the airplane was ready, and there was a palpable excitement in the air.

First flights always feel dramatic. A lot is at stake. The media's there, either to record a success or cover a historic disaster. Dan Crowley remembers that day well: "I said a prayer for the whole team. We all knew that there was so much fly-by-wire, electronic technology and so many things could go wrong. We'd done all the ground taxi tests, we'd done all the simulations but until you fly it, you really don't know. And it was a huge leap forward from F-22 so you just didn't know."[3]

Beesley finished his walk-around, climbed up into the cockpit, and was strapped in. The canopy closed around him, the engine whined upward at the direction of the plane captain, and the pre-taxi checklist was completed. As AA-1 slowly taxied out and turned to head for the hold short line on the runway, he was only a few feet from the onlookers along the fence. A chorus of applause and cheers erupted from the men and women who'd toiled for so many years for this day. Photographers jockeyed for position, aiming huge zoom lenses where they expected the plane would lift off.

The program managers, Burbage and Crowley, ran up the stairs to the observation tower. They'd be on the radio to Jon during the flight.

"That day was very special, particularly seeing all of the employee turnout," recalls Beesley. But . . . "On rotation for takeoff, I got an alert in the cockpit at about 150 mph. The alert was an Air Data Degrade message. At that point, I said 'We're going, and we'll sort it out in the air.' As luck would have it, the first flight team had briefed that very failure in the preflight briefing. On first flight, everything is new. Especially on F-35, since there are so many new systems."

In the tower, Burbage heard the pilot say, "I have an Air Data Degrade light, but I'm going." "Very cool voice, completely in control, pure test pilot talk. I was much more concerned than Jon but I knew we were in great hands." The flight continued for the half hour that that had been planned, reaching 15,000 feet and conducting a series of flight maneuvers. In engineer talk, the flight was judged "nominal," which means it "went according to plan and thank God, nothing bad happened."

The reason for the degrade on rotation? Lockheed had employed lessons from the F-117. That and other early stealth designs had required a large, one-piece nose wheel door to reduce the front sector stealth signature. The Fort Worth runway on that day was experiencing a crosswind, which resulted in the one-piece door on the F-35 temporarily blocking the airflow to the pitot static sensors that feed airspeed data into the flight control computers. Once the landing gear was raised and the door closed, the fault was cleared. Jon's subdued reaction to what could have been a major malfunction was typical of the expertise and sangfroid of the test pilot community.

AA-1 was being built when LM convened the STOVL weight attack team. The SWAT effort would significantly improve the structural arrangement of all three variants, including a change in the nose wheel door configuration. The remaining test planes would incorporate those changes, but AA-1 would continue to be valuable in maturing the flying qualities and internal vehicle management systems.

★ ★ ★

Jeff "Slim" Knowles, whose physical stature reflected his call sign, was one of the original engineering pilots. He was in the cockpit for the first developmental test that experienced a major malfunction in the air. On the rare occasions when things go south, a pilot must call on all their years of training while coping with the adrenaline rush of a life-or-death situation. One such event was flight 19, conducted at the test range near the Fort Worth production facility on May 3, 2007. Knowles says, "Jon Beesley, our chief test pilot, built our team early on. Five of us were the mainstays. Jon, Graham Tomlinson from BAE Systems, a very experienced STOVL test pilot, Doc Nelson (former USAF test pilot), Bill Gigliotti, (former Navy Test pilot), and me."[4]

A sidenote: When Tom Burbage entered Navy test pilot school in 1974, a real estate agent named Pat Gigliotti sold him his first house. A year later, after completing the Test Pilot School, Tom joined the test center, and his chief engineer was the same Pat Gigliotti. Some twenty-five years later, when the F-35C program relocated to Pax River to conduct carrier suitability testing, Tom and

Pat were reunited. The connection was made even stronger when three of Pat's sons joined Lockheed Martin and were members of the F-35 test team. Bill was one of the key test pilots mentioned above. Ken was a test engineer. Jim would eventually lead the test force at Pax River. (**See Figure 22: Bill Gigliotti in cockpit with UK flag following first flight of UK F-35B**)

Knowles goes on, "Jon launched a concerted effort early on to get the test pilots involved as engineers. We were very involved, and our focus was that once the jet rolled out, that it would be fantastic to fly. We all had different assignments under Jon. We all flew all the variants. . . . The cockpits are all the same. If you blindfold a pilot and put them in the cockpit, they wouldn't know which variant they were in. . . . I spent the most time on developing the USN F-35C variant, but we all spent a lot of time on the first production prototype AA-1.

"Jon flew AA-1 for the first ten flights. I was programmed to fly as a backup to Jon and was the second pilot to fly AA-1. Flight nineteen was my sixth flight on AA-1. I was very comfortable with the airplane in general, but still a little new."

Eventually he comes to the hairy part. "Our test objective on flight 19 was to go to 38,000 feet, .78 Mach as part of the flight envelope expansion testing. Everything started normal, and I was being chased with an F-16 and photographer. I climbed to 38,000 feet and started maneuvers, cross checking air data with my chase. I did 60 to 60-degree rolls, followed by a maximum-rate 360-degree roll, and about halfway through the roll I started getting alarms. I continued to roll until I was level and then settled out—I had eleven caution and warning lights. The flight controls page on my screen showed four red (failed) surfaces and three yellow (degraded) surfaces. Horizontal tails, Flaps, rudders, leading- edge flaps were all affected."

He was still flying, but so the fact that so many lights were red wasn't good news. "I still had communications with the control room, declared an emergency and headed for home base. I was most concerned about the right-hand horizontal tail, which was inoperative and at an angle that could make control for landing very difficult."

His wingman in the F-16 was "Doc" Nelson, one of the other test pilots. "Doc could see the horizontal tails were asymmetric, he could physically see the tail issues. . . . The flight control surfaces that were indicating red were frozen in place (four of them). The ones indicating yellow could move but were limited. One of the nice things about the F-35 flight control system was its design to allow for adapting to combat damage. As long as its surfaces can move, it will find a solution to keep flying, using any available surface. The airplane was now flying with one horizontal tail, one rudder and the wing trailing edge flaperons."

Knowles knew from simulator runs that he was operating in an emergency mode now. But to make matters worse, the control room informed him that he was now on a ten-minute timer.

> When flight controls are degraded, and the "brains" were not getting the signals it needed, it switched to a backup solution. The flight controls were going to degrade in ten minutes to a place we did not want to be. Forty-five miles from home at 35,000 feet, I had to land in less than ten minutes.
>
> My technical problem had now become a real operational problem. . . . There was an adrenaline constant, but I was thinking strictly about execution, which was complicated by the limited maneuverability. My speed brakes didn't work, and the electrical failures caused the engine to have excessive thrust at idle. We were operating under a speed restriction of 350 knots. It would be hard to descend as fast I needed to. I tried to reset the generator, and that didn't work.
>
> I was at ten thousand feet and knew I would not make it. I leveled out and slowed to landing angle of attack, but the airplane was acting peculiarly and wanted to roll off. I wanted to reset the flight controls but had been waiting for concurrence from the control room. The leading-edge flaps were stuck. I was finally able to reset the flight controls and got everything back except the right tail. At ten thousand feet I set it for the runway and dove, trying to make the ten-minute window. I touched down at 190 knots, well over normal landing speed.

It was a good test of the brakes. He thought of trying to use the tail hook as well but decided not to press his luck by using another untested system.

> I was finally able to stop at the last brick of the runway. The fuse plugs on the tires blew because they were so hot. In final analysis I had thirteen seconds left to spare. I did not know that at the time, I just knew it was close. I did what I had to do to get it on the ground. That was not the worst part. There was a momentary dual generator failure—with a gap of fifty milliseconds

to switch to backup power, but the battery had shorted out, so that backup failed. If the second generator had been offline another seventeen milliseconds, that would have been the end of it.

Jon Beesley underscored the potential gravity of this failure.

> This incident was related to our electric actuators, which had the unfortunate characteristic that the tail will continue to drift to the stop due to aerodynamic forces on it. This meant that the flight control system would position the other tail to counter it and it would hit the stop in the other direction. At this point, which would happen quickly, the aircraft would go out of control. Even though failure was considered virtually impossible, I was adamant that we needed to install the horizontal tail lock to catch a failed tail before this could happen, especially in the A models. I got agreement for at least the flight test aircraft. The airplane Slim was flying had the lock installed. If we had not had this feature installed, Flight 19 would have been the first loss of an F-35. Slim would have never gotten close to the runway.

During flight 19, Dan Crowley was returning from a meeting in Dallas along with a few other Lockheed executives, one of whom was Frank Cappuccio, the head of the famed Skunk Works. Dan Crowley recalls,

> We were looking out, and Frank turned to me and said, "Is that your airplane on the ground over there surrounded by fire trucks?" And I said "No, that can't be ours," and sure enough it was. The "fence sitters" were there taking photos. Before we could even park the van, there were photos all on the internet. Had we lost that aircraft, I don't think the program would have been canceled, but it would have been completely restructured. It was an incredible day for the team. The airplane saved itself, and the pilot lived, and the program lived. Afterward, I talked to Slim and his wife. We had a laugh about it, but it was almost tragic.

Seven months went by before the plane flew again. The ten-minute timer was eliminated, and certain electronics were redesigned. A stripe was also painted on the tail, so the chase pilot could quickly assess whether the configuration was kosher.

As painful as it was, the incident brought out shortcomings that, had they emerged later, could have derailed the program. It proved the importance of keeping AA-1 funded and flying. It's why the test program is so important.

Knowles concludes,

> Flight 19 was on my mind for quite a while. You're always more critical of yourself after an event like that. I sat with the control room folks, kicked everyone else out and reviewed how to make our emergency response better. . . . At the time I was going on what I had to work with. The control room folks were very focused on trying to understand what was happening with the aircraft, and the group learned that the priority was to land the airplane safely and figuring out the "what and why" could come later. Working together is key, especially when it does not go smoothly."

When Beesley retired in 2011, Al Norman replaced him. After a career with the U.S. Air Force flying F-16s, Norman joined Lockheed Martin and was a test pilot on the F-22 for twenty-two years. He had short white hair, a strong, almost stocky build, and an infectious smile. His enthusiasm for flying permeated every sentence.

Norman described his objectives in testing a new aircraft.

> The one thing you never want is a street named after you at Edwards, because that usually means you aren't around anymore.
>
> Tests start by systematically opening the "envelope" to verify the airplane's performance parameters, including maximum altitude, speed, gravitational (or G) forces, and angle of attack. In a very measured way, we move out by increasing altitude and speed while testing for something we never want, which is the unbounded oscillation of a surface known as "flutter."[5]
>
> We have systems on the jet that we can use to excite a flutter condition by making surfaces move independently so they act in a certain frequency and amplitude. . . . And there is an army of engineers on the ground who are looking at real-time data from the aircraft for any indication that uncontrolled oscillations could occur.

Actually, flutter would probably happen so fast no pilot could do anything about it. So, you're looking for those telltale signs before you get it. Those engineers are all there talking to you.

"Once we're satisfied that at a condition [specific combination of speed and altitude] everything is going to be okay, we go back to that condition and we move the flight control surfaces ourselves to make sure they respond correctly. Then we increase the G loads in the aircraft, both symmetric and asymmetric. Once we do all that, then we've opened up that piece of the sky. and we'll move to the next piece of the sky. That's the basic way we do envelope expansion.

Beesley had once experienced the frightening results of flutter as a test pilot for the F-117 when a vertical tail broke off in flight. "If you imagine one of the tails made out of glass, it was like it was being hit with a hammer and it shattered. . . . That was a very unpleasant ride." That he managed to land safely was a testament to his superb flying skills.

The next piece of testing involves decreasing the air speed and increasing the angle of attack (or "alpha" in pilot speak). As the nose goes up, the airplane slows until, at some point, the flow of air over the wings is disrupted and the plane stalls.

Norman once more:

What I found unusual in how we tested this jet for our high alpha program is, because of the nature of the combined program, we took everybody's needs, wants, and the way they do things into account. The U.S. Air Force does high alpha testing one way and the Navy does it a different way. There is no right or wrong way, there's just two different ways to do it, so we ended up doing both. The Air Force employs a departure-resistance program to determine how hard it is to make an airplane stall. You march your way up in angle of attack trying to make the airplane depart [stall]. And then we label the airplane as "departure resistant," "extremely departure resistant," or "there's no way you can get the thing to depart."

The Navy approach is quite different. The basic question is "What if you do end up in a spin? Can you get out of it?" So, we test that by turning all the features off on the F-35 that prevent you from going into a stall, we get the airplane to spin, and then we turn on all the protective features, and the airplane pops right out of it.

From a pilot's perspective, one of the great things about this airplane is it's really easy to fly. All our white scarf bravado. . . . You can toss that out the window. To teach somebody to fly this airplane and fly it well, doesn't take long. That translates into training savings and, above all, safety.

The F-35 even has its own form of cruise control for flight and for landing. "What makes a fifth-gen airplane so great is I can fly it if I want or I push some buttons and not worry about flying the airplane which frees me to concentrate on managing the battle space."

Reflecting his age, Al describes the F-35's sensor fusion capabilities with a *Star Wars* analogy. "I'm Luke Skywalker sitting there with help from R2D2. And in this case, R2D2 is the sensor manager." In previous fighters, the pilot had to integrate real-time data from different sensors in his head in order to identify an object. "In a fourth-generation airplane, if there's nothing else out there and I'm very, very experienced, maybe I've seen this object before and know what's going on. But if I get too many objects, I get bogged down and slowed down. And I'm trying to paint pictures in my head based on what my wingmen are telling me as well."

Beesley described the F-35's advantage this way.

You don't want to make the pilot the data analyst. He's not the guy to debug the system. He's the guy to make the decision on whether or not to deploy a weapon system that is going to destroy targets, and that's a big decision. . . . I always used to tell people that when you fly an airplane, the things you have to do you ought to be able to do going down a flight of stairs in a rolling desk chair. . . . And the software makes that possible.

Jeff Knowles agrees.

I've flown many planes, Tornados, Jaguars, most of the U.S. Air Force and Navy fighters, and the F-35 is by far the best airplane to fly. It doesn't do too much, or too little. Pilots say it is responsive, it does what I want it to do. It has a lot of power, it snaps more G's really quick. . . . When I was in a USN squadron, we would spend 25 percent of our annual budget practicing shipboard launch and recovery operations. We would rather have spent that money in air-to-air combat or weapons deployment tactics. The F-35 is turning all those legacy rules on their ear. You just don't need all that practice in the F-35 and you can concentrate your training resources on the mission.

Beesley thought it important to comment on the stress pilots face.

> One of the challenges you learn early on when you fly single seat airplanes is when things go wrong, does it rattle you? The answer is yes. And you want to turn to the other person in the airplane and say "Why don't you take over while I compose myself?" Well, unfortunately, there's nobody there. So, you're left to yourself, and your first thought is "I wish I wasn't here right now." But you are. So, you spend a tremendous amount of time working through all the possibilities of what can go wrong and then practice those scenarios in the flight simulator."

Remember the fin that broke off in the F-117? Jon had spent hours in the simulator preparing for exactly that scenario.

★ ★ ★

Flight testing is the crucible. Most Americans live expecting everything to go as planned, but in the sky there's always risk. Test pilots like Beesley, Knowles, Norman, Nelson, Gigliotti, and the others, accept the challenge. That, in the end, makes the airplane better for future pilots, who'll take it into combat.

Once, Norman was addressing an audience of pilots from all three US services and the eight other international partners. He began with a question: "How many of you have flown a fifth-generation fighter?" Only a few raised their hands. "How many have flown *against* a fifth-generation fighter?" Most raised their hands. "How did you like the experience?" The response was unanimous: it wasn't a fair fight.

Achieving that overwhelming advantage was due, in large part, to the engineering expertise and raw personal courage of the test pilots.

Reference

1. Interview with Jon Beesley, F-35 chief test pilot by Betsy Clark and Adrian Pitman on August 15, 2018. Held in F-35 interview archive

2. www.F35.com, F-35 Flight Test Program Specifics, accessed November 10, 2020.

3. Interview with Dan Crowley by Tom Burbage, Betsy Clark, and Adrian Pitman on January 27, 2018, held in F-35 interview archive.

4. Interview with F-35 test pilot Jeff Knowles with Tom Burbage, Betsy Clark, and Adrian Pitman on September 17, 2018. Held in F-35 interview archive.

5. Interview with Al Norman, F-35 chief test pilot, by Tom Burbage, Betsy Clark, and Adrian Pitman on November 17, 2017. Held in F-35 interview archive.

Chapter 15

ROLES AND MISSIONS MATTER

T o every branch of the US military—and no doubt of the militaries of
other nations as well—very little is more sacrosanct, to be cherished and
defended, than its role and its missions. Their *roles* are the broad and enduring purposes of that service, as defined by the 1948 Key West Agreement and
the 1986 Goldwater-Nichols Department of Defense Reorganization Act. Their
missions are the unique functions each service must accomplish to carry out its
role.

Speaking very generally, roles and missions were initially defined by
where operations took place. "The Army handles ground combat, the Air
Force and Space Force manage air and space operations, and the Navy and
Marine Corps run sea and amphibious missions."[1] But the lines between
them are blurred. Each service flies aircraft, runs cyber activities, and owns
or at least uses boats, space, and other intel assets . . . and logistics is a whole
different animal. There's a lot of overlap and many gray areas, which can lead
to either wasteful duplication or necessary redundancy, depending on one's
point of view.

Still, the bottom line is that its role and its missions are each service's justification for existing. The reason Congress funds it decade after decade. Weapons,
recruitment, personnel management, logistics—basically everything—are built
on this bedrock foundation. Yet, since "Wants are infinite and resources scarce,"
as the Iron Law of Scarcity has it, from time to time one service has been known
to slowly move in on the roles and missions of another, especially if technology
makes it feasible.

In which case, it triggers an existential crisis for the threatened service.

The F-35 turned out to be just such an existential threat.

★ ★ ★

November 16, 2012, dawned hot in the Arizona desert. To most of the nearby residents of the military base in Yuma it would be just another day, but to the Green Knights of Marine All Weather Fighter Attack Squadron 121, it was anything but. The first two operational F-35B aircraft were inbound to their new base. The VIPs gathering on the flight line included Senator John McCain, a frequent critic of the airplane's cost and performance, calling it both "a scandal and a tragedy" in political circles.[2] Also in attendance were General Jim Amos, Commandant of the Marine Corps, Arizona Governor Jan Brewer, and Under Secretary of the Navy Robert Work.

As the first aircraft taxied in, Amos set the stage.

"For the first time in aviation history, the most lethal fighter characteristics, supersonic speed, radar evading stealth, extreme agility, short takeoff capability and vertical landing, and an impressive array of twenty-first-century weapons have been combined in a single platform."[3]

Secretary Work added that with the addition of the F-35B to the Marine inventory, the United States would now have additional carriers capable of launching first-day, supersonic, stealthy power projection, essentially doubling US striking capability from the sea.

Even McCain seemed to have changed his tune. "Today marks the beginning of Joint Strike Fighters flying over the skies of Arizona for perhaps the next fifty years. That's another fifty years for the city of Yuma, and the state of Arizona, to do their part to help ensure this great nation remains strong and secure."[4]

But the celebration would ring the bell for a knock-down-and-drag-out fight over the respective roles and missions of the U.S Navy and the Marines.

★ ★ ★

After World War II, the centerpiece of the Navy was its large attack carrier fleet. And since then, Marine fighter and attack squadrons had been integrated into their air wings. The sister services combined their efforts to accomplish a shared mission. (**See Figure 23: F-35C aboard U.S. Navy supercarrier**)

But progress tends to call received wisdom and long-settled issues into question. The smaller L-Class carriers operated by the Marines had originally been built as helicopter carriers, to hasten transfer of troops ashore during amphibious operations, or to act as platforms for relatively short-ranged and short-duration raids, strikes, evacuations, or humanitarian missions. That capability was expanded in the 1970s with the addition of the Harrier VSTOL fighter. It increased again with the introduction of the V-22 Osprey, a hybrid platform that was larger and much faster than a helicopter with the qualities of both an airplane, in terms of speed, and a helicopter, in its ability to take off and land vertically.

But the F-35B threatened to endow the Corps' L-Class carriers with a far heavier punch. "Blue Suit" Navy leadership viewed this as a threat to the unique and very expensive nuclear carrier fleet. (They had been down this road before with the submarine- and destroyer-launched Tomahawk missile). (**See Figure 24: USMC L-Class Carrier USS** *America*)

This quickly led to battle lines being drawn as the Department of the Navy's tranche of the defense budget had to fund both the USN and the USMC. Competition for precious funds was an annual fraternal wrestling match. The internal contradiction grew even sharper with a similar controversy within the United Kingdom. The launch of the UK's very capable Queen Elizabeth class carriers, while smaller than the US supercarriers in terms of displacement, carried a flight deck landing area that was significantly larger than the ships the Marines deployed on. This would have implications for the USN/USMC internal squabbles, a story played out in a later chapter.

Thus, what once had been a specialized and limited air element now threatened to become a major force on the allied stage. The Italian *Cavour*, designed a few years earlier, also hosted an F-35B striking force. And more to the point for Big Navy, it threatened the existence of the crown jewels.

Some would call the Navy a reluctant, even recalcitrant partner throughout the development of the JSF. In the early 1980s, the sea service pushed its own favored supersonic attack design. The McDonnell Douglas/General Dynamics A-12 Avenger II was a flying wing designed for deep attack, intended to replace the A-6 Intruder at a time when the fighter and attack missions were done by different and specialized airplanes. But the Avenger had ignominiously cratered during development and was canceled by then Secretary of Defense Dick Cheney in 1991.

Likewise, the Navy's experience with trying to adapt an Air Force–designed airplane into a carrier-suitable sibling was littered with failure and compromised performance.

The Advanced Tactical Fighter (ATF) effort was launched in the mid-1980s to develop an air superiority fighter for the Air Force. As with most new programs, larger buy numbers and thus multiservice involvement are often critical to obtaining broad DoD and Congressional support. The ATF was no different. It included a variant referred to as the Naval Advanced Tactical Fighter (NATF).

Although NATF was included in the ATF selection process, it never really had a fighting chance. In the end, adapting the jet to shipboard life would have required a completely different design. The ATF program eventually produced 187 USAF F-22 air superiority fighters, but for the Navy, zilch.

As tactics and technology advanced, it became apparent that the traditionally separated attack (also known as air-to-ground) and fighter (air-to-air) missions (and their pilot tribes) could be combined. A slow transformation of carrier-based aviation was emerging. The Navy's F planes (fighters) such as the F-4 Phantom and F-14 Tomcat, and A planes (attack aircraft) such as the A-6 Intruder and A-10 Thunderbolt II from the 1960s and 1970s gave way to the dual-role F/A-18 Hornet in the 1980s (usually referred to simply as F-18). Meanwhile, the ballistic and cruise missile systems of near-peer adversaries were pushing the carrier battle group farther and farther back from their strategic targets. The need for more "fuel in the air" to extend the range of the striking force and the duty to protect "home base" were driving a reduction in the different types of aircraft constituting the air wing.

Defense Secretary Gates decided to face up to the reality of the post–Cold War reductions in the defense budget. He canceled the separate service development programs and put all his chips on the Joint Strike Fighter program. This made the only remaining option for modernizing the Navy air wing the Super Hornet upgrade to the F-18.

But still, the Navy was the last service to embrace the F-35, or, indeed, stealth aircraft entirely. Some solid rationales existed for this hesitation. As mentioned in previous chapters, the at-sea environment was harsh, and the original stealth coatings were fragile and tough to maintain. Carrier suitability was the domain of the Naval Air System Command and would not be delegated to some Johnny-come-lately called the JPO, at least not without a fight. And in terms of accomplishing the Navy's mission, sortie generation rate (the ability to launch and recover many aircraft quickly) was traditionally a much more important criterion for aircraft carriers than an individual plane's effectiveness in executing the end mission.

Not only that, the cost of modifying legacy ships to accommodate both the B and the C variants was initially projected to be horrendous. Media-fed rumors of the F-35B burning holes in the flight deck and blowing sailors off the deck in the hover were rampant. For the C, ship alterations would also be costly. For example, the jet blast deflectors, large water-cooled panels that are raised behind a launching aircraft to protect the aircraft and sailors behind it, would have to be redesigned and rebuilt. Why? The F-14, A-6, and F-18, all twin-engine aircraft, had a much different heat dissipation profile than the F-35. Their two engines distributed the heat in two spots compared to the F-35C, which concentrated the heat, equivalent to both engines on the earlier aircraft, in a single blazing spot.

Another issue was the protective coatings of the flight deck itself. Carrier decks are paved with a thick, rather flexible nonskid coating, primarily to prevent sliding of the aircraft when taxiing once oil and grease build up. When landing vertically, the B variant's very hot exhaust would impinge directly on this carefully maintained surface. Any tendency to break up or degrade these various special coatings creates the potential for foreign objects to be ingested and damage the engines of other aircraft operating off the deck.

Since the early days, the STOVL variant had been the F-35 program's problem child. Its future was still far from certain. Not only had there been the bulkhead cracks, but airflow problems had been caused by the auxiliary inlet doors that sat on top of the center fuselage. They allowed additional air into the engine during hovering and short takeoffs. These doors had required a redesign. While flight test was proceeding as planned for the other two variants, testing was lagging behind schedule for STOVL.

In January 2011, Gates announced that he was putting the STOVL "on probation" for a two-year period. If the problems, including the cracks in the bulkhead, weren't fixed by then, "I believe it should be canceled."[5]

It was paradoxical that the variant that had contributed most to Lockheed winning the JSF contract was the one that was now on death row waiting for a reprieve.

★ ★ ★

In July of 2011, Gates retired and was replaced by Leon Panetta. Probably the most unsung and critical inflection point on the program came later that year.

With the STOVL variant under probation and seemingly destined for cancellation, something had to go right for the jet. A much-needed success emerged from three weeks of sea trials on the amphibious assault ship USS *Wasp* in October. The *Wasp* was outfitted with instrumentation to measure various aspects of the jet's performance at sea, including noise levels and deck temperature during vertical landings. Two STOVL test jets performed flawlessly, completing seventy-two short takeoffs and vertical landings during this period.[6] No sailors were blown off the ship, and its deck was undamaged. The following January, Panetta lifted the STOVL's probation, citing sufficient progress in flight testing and in maturing the aircraft design.[7] Finally the Marines' much-wanted jet and the program's most complex variant appeared to be off the chopping block.

As the strongest advocates for the F-35, nothing would deter the Marine Corps' fight to introduce the new B-variant into their inventory. In retrospect, the dark days of "probation" for the F-35B, the exceptional *Wasp* demonstration and its subsequent effect on removal of the probation tag and the stand-up of the first Marine Corps F-35B wing in Yuma may be recorded in history as the pivotal point in the F-35 journey.

★ ★ ★

Not surprisingly, there began a slow awakening in the larger Navy that the big-deck nuclear carriers had better also show some benefit from the transformational capability of the F-35C, or they could be left behind in the eternal competition for budget dollars. The alternative was stark: The carrier fleet could be threatened both operationally and politically. Standing off the enemy coast at a comfortable distance with their fourth-generation air wing while the Marine Corps led the close-in knife fight with F-35s was unacceptable.

USS *Carl Vinson* and the "Argonauts" of Strike Fighter Squadron 147 were first to deploy with the Navy's maiden F-35Cs. At the same time, the Black Knights of Marine Fighter Attack Squadron 314, the Corps' first F-35C squadron, were going through refresher training prior to deploying aboard USS *Abraham Lincoln*.

This continuation of the integrated Navy-Marines air wing concept significantly increased the carrier's lethality. Additionally, interoperability problems due to different configurations of the USN and USMC aircraft would no longer be an issue. Not only could the merged air wing fight as a single unit, but other

F-35As or Bs from the other US services or allied air forces could also join seamlessly. This was fundamental to the F-35 concept, but a new trick to the old dogs of the carrier community.

USMC Major Mark Dion, a Marine F/A-18 Super Hornet pilot, was one of the first to transition to the F-35. Dion had the unique perspective of being one of the only operational pilots to fly both the F-35B and the F-35C. In a former assignment, he was part of the first US F-35B combat deployment, which saw Marine pilots flying F-35Bs off USS *Essex* to conduct strikes in Afghanistan.

Of all the jets he's flown, Dion has a favorite. "The F-35C brings more capability than the B. It has more fuel, allowing for more time on station and the ability to carry different weapons. To have an F-35 squadron on a carrier integrated with F/A-18s tactically makes the carrier much more lethal."[8]

The world-famous U.S. Navy Fighter Weapons School, better known as TOPGUN, is the ultimate training experience. TOPGUN trainees study fighter tactics in the classroom. They then fly their aircraft to put into practice the skills they've just learned. But they also have another mission: to take what they've learned back to their squadron mates.[9]

The Lightning II represented a major step-change for the Navy as it blended a low-observable plane into TOPGUN and the fleet for the first time. Gone were the traditional scenarios of detecting an opponent via radar, then playing cat-and-mouse with AIM-120 AMRAAMS versus Russian Vympels and Chinese PL-15s. The F-35 could operate practically with impunity in full low-observable configuration, picking off its foes without ever being "seen." The F-35C also added the capability for deep strikes into highly contested environments to the carrier air wing.

As NATO air forces move from the F-16/F-18 to the F-35, their roles and missions are also evolving. While differing older allied configurations and tactics limited their participation, all are now able to participate on day one with the F-35. Allied forces have historically been led by US military commanders, but now there was a real opportunity to share the burdens of combat on a more equitable basis. The roles and the missions of the alliance itself remain under continuous revision. As new nations such as Belgium, Finland, and Sweden join NATO, they're also joining the common F-35 user family.

Alliances evolve with changing threats. Old threats evolve as new geographical and strategic challenges reshape the security picture. The melting of the Arctic mentioned earlier, the resurgence of a paranoid and revanchist Russia, the emergence of China as a world power and their expansion into the South China Sea—these will also reshape alliances.

In the Indo-Pacific region, there is no NATO-like formal alliance system. There are security partners. Australia has been a principal partner since the start. Japan is now building F-35s in their own final assembly and checkout (FACO) facility in Nagoya. The Republic of Korea is now building major assemblies as they prepare to take delivery of their F-35s. Singapore, one of the original security cooperative participants, has begun the process to become the fourth F-35B operator.

Singapore also has the unique operational environment of being a territorially minuscule state with essentially no large airports. Their interest in the F-35B model offered the potential to use highways for takeoff and landing in the event the airports were unusable in a conflict. Interestingly, the Marine Corps has been rumored to be getting out of its comfort zone recently. Leaders are looking to short stretches of road and improvised landing spots to prove the aircraft's ability to fight from austere and hastily established locales. In early December 2022, two USMC F-35Bs conducted a series of test events under the nickname "Obsidian Iceberg" at the Helicopter Outlying Field at Camp Pendleton, California. The tests were designed to further the tactical understanding of operating F-35Bs from remote locations with little logistical support. Being able to operate the aircraft from these sorts of locations could prove essential in a high-end conflict in the Indo-Pacific, and certainly would support Singapore's operational employment.

With a common capability now resident with the F-35, these global realignments will drive updates in their roles and missions.[10]

As the first few planes for each partner were delivered to Luke Air Force base in Arizona, they were swiftly integrated into a composite squadron to train that country's pilots as an integrated force. Newly qualified, they then returned home to stand up squadron operations.

★ ★ ★

Still, no new capability becomes a reality until it's in the hands of the operators.

The morning of December 12, 2016, dawned crisp and clear as four pilots walked to the briefing room at Fort Worth. They were about to deliver the first operational craft to two key overseas partners, Italy and Israel.

Uniquely, the pair of Italian aircraft had been assembled in Cameri, at that time the only production facility outside the United States. They'd been flown back to Fort Worth for additional testing before delivery.

Ferry flights often travel in groups to efficiently take advantage of inflight refueling assets. While ferrying airplanes produced in the United States to allies overseas is pretty much routine, this one in 2016 was different. It was traveling as a flight of four: two F-35As for the Italian Air Force, flown by Italian pilots, and two for the Israeli Air Force, flown by Lockheed pilots. A USAF tanker, referred to as the Pathfinder, would provide several in-flight refuelings en route to Italy. Their first actual stop would be Amendola Air Base on the Adriatic coast, marking the first operational delivery to an international partner. The milestone would not be announced for several days to avoid public attention focused on the first delivery to Israel.

All four landed in Italy on schedule in the early afternoon of December 12. The Israeli jets refueled there and the pilots enjoyed a welcome stretch after a very long flight sitting on a hard ejection seat. They would continue on to meet a crowd eagerly waiting at Nevatin Air Base in the Negev desert. That was the second delivery to an ally.

General Amir Eshel, commander of the Israeli Air Force, had pushed for his country to acquire a fifth-generation fighter. Eshel hosted a gathering of senior dignitaries at Nevatin. U.S. Secretary of Defense Ash Carter, Israeli Prime Minister Benjamin Netanyahu, Lockheed Martin CEO Marilynn Hewson, and F-35 Executive Vice President Jeff Babione were all present. Unfortunately, the weather at Amendola turned bad. The official party waited patiently for hours. Finally, the F-35s arrived.

"It was a very eerie and amazing sight," Eshel said. "It was a cool, clear night in the moonlit desert, and the F-35s almost appeared to be spaceships with their lights as they approached the runway"[11]

As the airplanes taxied in and shut their engines down, it was time for the speeches. Eshel went first. "The 'Adir,' or Mighty One, (the Israeli name for the F-35) is about to become a powerful accelerator for the entire IAF. We plan on leveraging our systemic abilities to new heights in attack and defense. Our aerial force will be much deadlier, combined, and more relevant than ever."

Prime Minister Netanyahu added, "The Adir F-35 stealth fighters will be able to operate in every arena, near and far. Our goal is to obtain supremacy in every theatre: in the air, in the sea, on the ground, and in the cyber arena. We build our force and sharpen our abilities in defense, attack, deterrence, and decision."[12]

After dinner with the US delegation, Eshel headed to Ben Gurion airport for a midnight flight to Arizona. He spent two days getting outfitted, flew a series of high-fidelity simulator flights with Lockheed's Chief Test Pilot, Al Norman, and went home anxious to get his first flight in the Adir.

Meanwhile, back in Israel, the Lockheed ferry pilots had turned the jets over to the IAF.

Sixteen hours later, on December 13, 2016, the first two F-35 qualified IAF pilots, the squadron commander and operations officer, flew the first operational mission. This sixteen-hour turnaround after taking delivery was an amazing accomplishment, never before equaled. As Eshel told the world, "Airplanes have to go to work."

Eshel became the first and likely the only Chief of Air Force of any of the allied nations to fly the Lightning II.

In May of 2017, Eshel made his last visit to the United States as chief of the IAF. The USAF chief of staff, David Goldfein, hosted a dinner with Secretary of the Air Force Heather Wilson. There was a lot of discussion about the F-35. As the only one who'd actually flown the airplane, Eshel dominated the conversation. After returning home, he received a video in the mail of the chief and secretary testifying in front of the Senate Armed Services Committee. One comment was "Two weeks ago we had dinner with the chief of the IAF who, unlike USAF generals, gets to keep flying." They then shared Amir's experience with F-35.

In Eshel's words, "On August 4, 2020 we received four more F-35s including a test airplane which will be stationed at our domestic Flight Test Center at Tel Nof Air Base. This makes us the first non-US air force in the world to have an operational test airplane. Our initial F-35 pilots were experienced F-16 and F-15 pilots, but in quite a short time new pilots will be able to move to F-35 without a lot of experience. . . . Young pilots will have fun really learning how to employ this weapon system; they are much better than us old guys."

The F-35 program has had many similar rollout and first-delivery ceremonies, each tailored to meet the unique traditions, cultural norms, and specific needs of the acquiring nation. They mark the beginning of a new era in global security and a revolutionary and ongoing redefinition of roles and missions for all the principal players.

As to how these new planes will force our peer competitors to redefine *their* own roles and missions . . . well, *that's up to them.*

Reference

1. Cohen, Rachel, "Time to Rethink Roles and Missions?" *Air Force Magazine*, September. 1, 2020. Accessed April 28, 2022.

2. https://www.cnn.com/2016/04/26/politics/f-35-delay-air-force/index.html.

3. DVIDS News, "First operational F-35 Squadron honored in historic ceremony," November 21, 2012.

4. DVIDS News, "First operational F-35 Squadron honored in historic ceremony," November 21, 2012.

5. McLaughlin, Andrew, "F-35B STOVL JSF 'on probation,'" News Update, Australian Aviation, available online http://www.pilotaptitude.com/files/F-35B%20STOVL%20JSF%20on%20probation.pdf, accessed August 11, 2022.

6. "F-35 completes first sea trials on USS Wasp," PEO(JSF) Integrated Test Facility Public Affairs, NAVAIR, October 24, 2011. Available online https://www.navair.navy.mil/node/18041. Accessed January 20, 2023.

7. Australian Aviation, "F-35B off probation," January 24, 2012, available online https://australianaviation.com.au/2012/01/f-35b-off-probation, accessed August 11, 2022.

8. Ibid.

9. Hunter, Jamie, The Warzone, "How the F-35 triggered Topgun's biggest syllabus revamp in nearly four decades," July 9, 2020.

10. Parken, Oliver, The War Zone, "Inside how the Marine's island hopping F-35B playbook is being written," January 19, 2023.

11. Interview with Gen Amir Eshel by Tom Burbage on October 15, 2020. Held in F-35 interview archive.

12. Interview with Gen Ido Nehustan by Tom Burbage, Betsy Clark, and Adrian Pitman on June 21, 2019. Held in F-35 interview archive.

Chapter 16

REMAKING HER MAJESTY'S ARMED FORCES

The British Empire built its global reach as a seafaring nation with a strong navy. On July 4, 2014, at the naming ceremony for the new HMS *Queen Elizabeth* aircraft carrier, Admiral George Zambellas, the 100th First Sea Lord, said, "Prime Minister David Cameron has described us as a small island with a big footprint in the world. We want to be a nation that is influential in the world, that can compete strongly in the global race, helping to deliver national security and prosperity objectives. We live in a world that is increasingly globalized and inter-connected and where almost all UK trade, by volume, is still carried by the sea."[1]

Years later Zambellas explained,

> But the UK ambition to build a future carrier battle group striking force with jets in some form is a messy tale. Our transatlantic relationship with the U.S. Navy goes back to the early 1950s with the signing of the UK-US Defence and Security Agreement, which got us into our nuclear partnership. After that, the next most important element was intelligence sharing, which has served both of our nations very, very well. The U.S. Navy didn't have to help the UK with carriers, but in my humble view, they did so out of respect for our long partnership.
>
> Our relationship with the U.S. Marine Corps is much more subtle. The USMC looks for strategic partners that can help further their ambitions.[2]

How the UK went about building its future carrier-based strike force is a complex and tumultuous journey. The relationships between the UK and the U.S. Navy and Marine Corps and how they interacted provide a look into how the two close allies represented, negotiated, and at times fought for their slightly different interests.

★ ★ ★

The Marine Corps and the Royal Air Force had been allied operators of the AV-8 Harrier for decades. The Royal Navy's aviation division, the Fleet Air Arm, had flown the Sea Harrier since it was introduced into service in 1980. By 1983 the UK's Harriers were growing weary from the high flight hours pulled during the Falklands conflict the year before. The British decided to join up with the United States to develop a supersonic replacement. This would become a formal collaboration, the Advanced Short Takeoff and Landing (ASTOVL) program. Both the Marine Corps and the Royal Air Force/Royal Navy Fleet Air Arm needed STOVL capability to operate from their small-deck carriers. (This class of ship had neither the power nor space for catapults and arresting gear.) The first phase of this work, done under contract with the Defense Advanced Research Projects Agency (DARPA) evaluated different powered lift concepts and concluded that none were satisfactory. They then approached Lockheed's Skunk Works in an initiative to develop a powered lift concept to meet the requirements as a covert part of a Phase II study of the ASTOVL program.[3]

In 1993, the Joint Advanced Strike Technology (JAST) program was launched, and the US and UK's STOVL requirements were incorporated into the JAST development plan.

★ ★ ★

Simon Henley was a career Royal Navy officer, a friendly, engaging personality who made friends quickly. Over his twenty-five years in the Royal Navy as an engineer, he'd introduced innovative maintenance concepts into the Fleet Air Arm and was a participant in the ASTOVL program. He was pulled into the new JSF JPO in Washington in January 1999 as the first UK national deputy. Since the UK was the only top-tier partner, Henley and his team helped define the operational requirements. He said, "There were four participants, each with a 25 percent vote, the USAF, USN, USMC and UK."[4] The fact that both the USMC and UK needed the STOVL version gave the USMC added leverage in the formative years.

Henley served with the JPO team for three years, pushing innovative logistics and support concepts, until the F-35 contract was awarded to Lockheed Martin in 2001.

Air Commodore Mark Green from the Royal Air Force (RAF) joined Henley in the JPO in 1999 and replaced him as the UK National Deputy immediately after the contract was awarded to Lockheed Martin in 2001. Tall, good-looking, and sporting an alluring Oxbridge accent, Green could make an instant connection with anyone willing to listen to his point of view. He was also a very experienced Harrier pilot. Although he was with the Royal Air Force, he had extensive involvement in the Royal Navy's Sea Harrier replacement effort. Prior to joining the JPO, Green had been in the UK working with the Royal Navy to jointly define the requirements for the Sea Harrier replacement. "They had a Navy operational requirements guy and they decided that the best way to take the program forward would be in conjunction with the Royal Air Force and that we would drive the requirement together jointly." At that time, in addition to the JSF, alternatives being considered for the replacement were the F-18 Super Hornet, a marinized version of the Eurofighter Typhoon, the French Rafale, and a "super Harrier," which involved adding a more powerful engine to the existing airframe and other enhancements.

When Green was posted to the JPO, the Concept Demonstration Phase was in full swing. With his previous experience in writing operational requirements for the Sea Harrier replacement in the UK, Green was appointed to the team writing the operational requirements for JSF. "I was wearing a joint hat— RN and RAF. My job was to influence the Joint Operational Requirements Document [JORD] with the UK requirements while at the same time in the UK, run the analysis of alternatives and get the funding for whatever program we were going to do. While a team in the UK was working out whether the Joint Strike Fighter was the best aircraft for the UK, my role was to influence the JORD so that if we decided to go with the Joint Strike Fighter, it would meet our needs. That culminated in me being invited to be on the source selection as one of the operational requirements folks to oversee the Boeing design and the Lockheed design. I was very privileged in that role."

One of the UK's early requirements for the JSF created a near-impossible constraint on both Lockheed and Boeing. The JSF was to operate from the RN's light carrier class, Invincible, which required that it fit in the lift (elevator) on the carrier. Green described the problem by saying, "They were originally helicopter carriers for amphibious landings and were no longer fit for purpose. Both contractors were having a real difficulty meeting that design requirement. That was constraining size which meant that range and everything else had been

compromised by the UK telling everyone that it needed to go down in the lift."
But the Royal Navy was initially hesitant to waive that requirement because that
would necessitate a new, larger carrier class and, in Green's words, "They could
be accused of requirements growth . . . and the real cost of the program would
be tens of billions as opposed to just buying a new aircraft."

Eventually, the requirement to operate from the Invincible class was
removed as work began in the UK on a new, much larger Queen Elizabeth class
carrier comprising two ships, the *Queen Elizabeth* and the *Prince of Wales*. The
three Invincible class ships were decommissioned between 2005 and 2011. At
the same time, the Royal Air Force was fighting the Treasury for more funding
for the Eurofighter Typhoon. Green added, "The Ministry of Defence was keen
not to allow JSF to disrupt the Typhoon procurement. If people were allowed to
question Typhoon, and JSF did not work out, it would likely compromise both
programs. We needed to keep our JSF commitment to the STOVL variant to
keep all these political options clean."

Green concluded, "Within the program, we felt pretty good. The Royal Air
Force got the Typhoon, the Royal Navy got their carrier replacement program,
and we were able to relax the design constraints on the F-35 STOVL."

★ ★ ★

When the contract for the F-35 was awarded to Lockheed Martin in 2001, the
UK made the decision to go with the F-35, and the B appeared to be the obvious
choice. Green said,

> Our involvement was not a significant investment from the US perspective,
> but it was very significant from a UK perspective. Our new strategic reshap-
> ing was based on retaining our status as a global power and a staunch ally of
> the United States with a primary requirement to maintain a strategic mari-
> time force. Our involvement with the USMC in developing a replacement for
> our STOVL fleet was central to that theme.[5]

But as Green recalled, "The choice of aircraft was a political and interservice
minefield with hidden agendas." The Brits have an expression, "going around
the buoy," which means that a lot of activity occurs without making a decision.
That's exactly what happened when it came to settling on the UK's choice of

F-35 variant. Henley recalled, "Between my three years at the JPO and four years back in the UK, we went around the B versus C decision buoy. I took it to the ultimate committee that decides these things at least three times." A primary point of contention focused on the range of the STOVL compared to the CV variant. Henley continued, "The evidence was always there that in order to meet the requirement we had, the range of the B aircraft was more than adequate."

The C had a longer range than the B but that came at a steep price. Henley: "The range of the C, which a number of people touted as being a significant advantage, was a luxury that was questionable whether we wanted to pay for it. The C aircraft came with a very significant cost of ownership in terms of building the carriers with catapults and arresting gear and then maintaining that capability because there's a great deal more exercising of landing and taking off required to keep a CV capability than there is for a STOVL deck." And a few of these CV devotees were very vocal and had the ear of politicians in the Conservative party.

In 2006, the Sea Harriers were taken out of service, and, as Green noted, "We ended up with RAF squadrons with RN individuals embedded in them."

★ ★ ★

The UK is famous for its rowdy and argumentative political process, with opposition politicians anxious to prove any previous decisions were unfounded, if not actually criminally negligent. The F-35 program was not immune to this dynamic.

The impending government change in 2010 from the Labour to the Conservative party in charge brought to the forefront the debate on whether the Royal Navy's future carrier class should be equipped with catapults and arresting gear for the C variant. The Royal Navy had once operated *HMS Ark Royal*, an Audacious class capital ship equipped with conventional catapult and arresting gear. *Ark Royal* was substantially smaller than US carriers, but had introduced several novel features, including the angled flight deck, steam catapults, and the hurricane bow (a completely sealed hangar deck). These became integral to the designs of the first US supercarrier, USS *Forrestal*. *Ark Royal* had been decommissioned in 1978, but would still influence F-35 decisions years later.[6]

But that debate and decision was fair game for political challenge. One of the questions now being asked was, "Should we change our shipbuilding decision and go for the C-model or stay with the B?" The drama of this sudden change in UK military strategy would play out in a high-stakes poker game involving both the United States and the UK and their military services.

★ ★ ★

Green recalled, "Among the great world-class navies, there's an ongoing dispute between those who advocate smaller STOVL platforms and the larger catapult and arresting gear equipped supercarriers. To some, it was a measure of manhood to be one of the few navies that could afford to operate the more capable capital ships. At one point, some in the Royal Navy were even considering forgoing the F-35 completely in order to save money which could be used in equipping the new carrier class with catapults and arresting gear. After all, Boeing had loads of F-18s, and the UK could probably lease them for about ten years and then move to unmanned systems. And, after all, the show of force of a major aircraft carrier had a certain status in the new world order. It was even said that some felt that supporting the smaller STOVL carrier was a commitment to the nonsense of taking our launch and recovery energy with us to visit the Queen's enemies when we should instead be leaving that energy with the catapults and arresting gear back on the ship and taking more fuel and weapons!"[7]

★ ★ ★

One strong advocate for the flexibility provided by the F-35B and its role in truly joint Allied forces was the Marine Corps' then BGen Jon Davis. From 2008 to 2010, Davis was the Marine Assistant Deputy Commandant for Aviation. A former Harrier aviator, Davis had been squadron mates with Green when Davis served as an exchange pilot with the RAF. He recalled,

> As the one-star deputy, I felt strongly that the ability of the F-35B to operate off any deck offered unprecedented strategic advantage, especially considering fifth- generation capabilities and Allied cooperation. I also felt that the Queen Elizabeth class ship design was truly a snapshot to the future for an affordable and highly capable carrier force. With 34 F-35Bs, additional tiltrotors, helicopters, and potentially UAVs, it was a formidable power projection capability at one-fourth the cost of a CVN and manned by one-fifth the personnel.[8]

Davis went on to explain,

> Our initial thinking began in 2009 when we started looking at the opera-
> tional benefits of employing a coalition fifth-generation force. Our planning
> coalesced around an integrated air wing of RAF and USMC F-35B aircraft
> for deployment aboard HMS *Queen Elizabeth* on her maiden deployment.
> This would be a huge commitment by the USMC but the payoff would be a
> demonstration of true integrated fifth-gen operations from a single deck.

And the Marines were ready and willing to invest in this vision. Davis continued, "To build the partnership with the UK and to ensure that the UK
had enough STOVL pilots to man their new F-35B fleet when it arrived,
the USMC would provide nine to ten pilot slots for RAF/RN pilots in active
Marine Harrier squadrons to help them maintain their STOVL skills when
they shut down their early model Harriers. This came at the expense of precious flight time limitations on the Marine units. This became even more
critical when the UK government shut down their entire Harrier force in
December of 2010."

★ ★ ★

But the hard work to solidify the USMC-UK partnership was about to receive
a severe setback with a sudden change in direction by the new Cameron
government.

The 2010 general election ushered in a Conservative government, with
the party leader, David Cameron, becoming prime minister. That October,
he signed a comprehensive study, *Securing Britain in an Age of Uncertainty: The
Strategic Defence and Security Review*.[9] The study outlined three key new aspects
of Britain's defense strategy going forward: (1) construction of two new Queen
Elizabeth class aircraft carriers would be completed (HMS *Queen Elizabeth* and
HMS *Prince of Wales*), (2) the remaining (RAF) Harriers would be retired, and
(3) the new aircraft carriers would be fitted with a catapult and arresting gear
for the F-35C variant. Suddenly, the F-35Bs were out, and the Cs were to be the
future of the Royal Navy's sea-based strike force. However, this sudden change
in direction would be difficult to implement, particularly with its budgetary
implications.

Green recalled, "It did get very tense around 2010—the beginning of our austerity period to balance the budget—and they made some really radical changes to the RAF's order of battle. They disbanded the RAF Harrier force. The RN was extremely concerned because the RAF could redistribute their Harrier guys and girls around the Typhoon force but the RN had nowhere to go. They didn't have any other fast jet."

Zambellas recalled, "It was a miserable time . . . I recall vividly the Commander of the Royal Navy Fleet Air Arm, standing on a table at the Yeovilton Officers' Club, speaking to all the aviators he could muster. His emotional message was, 'If you fixed-wing aviators have decided there is no future, let me tell you, there is a future, but if all of you go, there will be no future.' At that point, he was literally down to counting on one hand the level of expertise that eventually stayed and allowed us to rebuild a maritime capability instead of starting from scratch." In addition, there was still an undercurrent within the civil service community that fielding a strategic carrier force was unaffordable, and the funding to procure and support such a major capability could better be diverted to decrease the ongoing defense budget deficits.

Green notes, "It was apparent that this decision was not well thought out. Suddenly, the RAF thought such a switch from the STOVL to the CV variant really did threaten the very existence of the RAF. It would build up the RN carrier task force with power projection and let the Royal Navy take the lead as the combat force in Her Majesty's military striking capability. There was also a lingering concern that the U.S. Navy might not be fully committed to the F-35C program."

But some in the RAF understood the importance of maintaining a maritime strike force. Green recalled,

I think it was Air Chief Marshal Glenn Torpy who went up to Cottesmore to talk to the joint Harrier force and told them, "Unfortunately, the decision is that the Harrier force is going to be disbanded literally in months, but don't worry, Royal Navy, we will do our best to look after you and ensure that there is a Royal Navy fast jet force of the future to move into JSF." I think they were fully expecting him to say "Royal Air Force, move over to this side. You've all got a job. Royal Navy, you're on your own. Go and be helicopter pilots." But he didn't. The RAF, although it had its problems with money going to aircraft carriers, it understands power projection from the sea. We'll always keep that capability. It was just in the early days a concern about how it might impact other procurement programs.

While the RN pilots still had jets to fly, there were major repercussions from the decision to go with the F-35 CV variant both at home and in the US.

★ ★ ★

Interestingly, a parallel and simultaneous disagreement was percolating within the American services, with the big-deck U.S. Navy concerned that an F-35B operating off a small-deck USMC amphibious carrier could compromise the justification for the much more expensive nuclear supercarriers. Also, if the Brits moved to the C-model, reducing their buy of the STOVL variant, the F-35B would become vulnerable to a non-affordability argument, raising the tempta-tion to cancel it. So, the U.S. Navy welcomed the UK shift to the F-35Cs with open arms and created billets aboard US carriers as well as in the catapult and arresting gear technical schools for enlisted UK maintainers to gain experience.

The Marine leadership felt personally affronted after going to great lengths to support the F-35B partnership during very difficult times. The immediate reaction of the Deputy Commandant for Aviation, LtGen "Trouser" Trautman, was dramatic. He terminated UK staff assignments within the Headquarters Marine Corps Department of aviation, as well as those of the UK pilot billets in Marine Harrier squadrons.

Green described the Marines' reaction by saying,

> The UK has fantastic relationships with the Commandant of the Marine Corps downwards. They had been massive supporters of us and the STOVL program. . . . They'd given us real access and influence. The fact that I was in the JPO defining requirements for STOVL with the Marine Corps—all of that was an indication of just how much they valued the UK being on board. And then, of course, when this decision was made, they felt like they'd been really kicked in the teeth, big-time.

Admiral Zambellas said, "Marine Corps leadership felt personally affronted after going to great lengths to support the UK STOVL partnership. The dressing-down of the Brits resident in the Marine Corps operational and administrative billets working the F-35B program was a singular event in Air Arm history and was viewed as a rejection of the US-UK partnership. We went back with our tail between our legs."

But there was soon to be a major problem with the plan to add "cats and traps" to the two Queen Elizabeth class carriers. The major critical unknown was the cost of modifying the two new carriers already under construction. To incorporate the new electromagnetic launch system being developed for the much larger US carrier platform, install its separate gas-generating engine system to power the catapults, and install the arresting gear engines and cable systems was probably not feasible without a complete redesign of the ship. The carrier office that had originally estimated 400 million pounds sterling for ship alterations had grossly underestimated the cost, and the estimate became 2.5 billion pounds sterling. Even that estimate was challenged by some decision-makers as being too optimistic. Adding even more risk was the immature technical status of the new catapult system.

And while the U.S. Marines were irate about the UK's switch from the B to the C, they weren't about to give up but rather, continued fighting hard on the opposite front.

★ ★ ★

LtGen George "Trouser" Trautman USMC was the epitome of a focused, aggressive, "take no prisoners" leader, and Gen Jim "Tamer" Amos was the highly respected Commandant of the Corps. Amos said, "We were taught by an old war horse four-star warrior that, while command relationships are an important annex in an operations plan, as we become more senior, the most important is not command relationships, it is the relationships between commanders."[10]

"There were several points of tension in the F-35 saga at this time," Trautman recollected.

In October 2010, sensing blood in the water, the 'big deck' carrier Navy was mounting opposition to the F-35B. In the midst of that tension, on October 19 I received a call from a two-star Royal Navy admiral saying they were going to go with the C. The UK embassy knew it was going to happen and was feeding false narratives into London papers. Stories like the UK defence attaché being escorted out of the Pentagon by armed guards and removing the desks and personal effects of the UK liaison staff from their office and depositing them in the hallway of the headquarters appealed to the tabloids but were completely untrue.[11]

This new assault on the F-35B led to extraordinary Corps efforts to keep the program viable even with the potential loss of the UK. Trouser and Tamer led the fight.

The B's sea trials on the USS *Wasp* would prove to be pivotal. Amos recounted,

> The F-35B was back on track. Sea trials were starting, and I flew out to the USS *Wasp*, which was positioned in the Atlantic off the Naval Air Test Center. We were up on "Vulture's Row" observing flight operations and saw a lot of perfect landings and takeoffs, all executed flawlessly When I returned, I told my staff to get all the photo and movie clips and put it to the movie *Top Gun* music. Unfortunately, my legal watchdogs reminded me there were copyright restrictions to using that music, so we found some good music and made a highlight film.
>
> Fast-forward and I have a trip to Afghanistan about a month after the sea trials aboard *Wasp*. I received a call from UK General Sir David Richards, the Chief of the Defense Staff and advisor to the Prime Minister, David Cameron.

General Amos landed late at night at the British airfield in Helmand Province called Bastion. Sir David was just finishing visiting his troops and was heading back to the UK as General Amos was arriving to visit his Marines. The Marines based their aircraft on the British base. The two of them went into an austere adjacent room just off the runway to discuss the F-35 program status.

"Sir David, you have to see this," said Amos. He pulled out his CD with the music video of the sea trials on *Wasp*.

Richards watched intently. Finally, he said, "I need a copy of that. If I am successful, would you support Her Majesty's carrier battle group striking force coming back to the B program?"

Amos nodded eagerly. "We absolutely will! We'll put your pilots in our training squadrons, using our airplanes, and we'll allow you to get head-of-the-line privileges on the production line so you don't have to go to the back of the line. . . . We can make this happen, and we'll put USMC airplanes on your *Queen Elizabeth* flight deck."

The deal was sealed. Amos reported the exchange back to Trautman, and several months later it became public in the UK. British pilots showed up immediately and joined the Marines for training.

Getting agreement on the air assets was a huge redirection. But there were still some big decisions yet to come on the actual ship construction. The first decision was that the Queen Elizabeth class carriers would not incorporate catapults and arresting gear but would be optimized for STOVL operations. Their systems and power projection capabilities would be designed to fully exploit the F-35B. The second decision involved a major change in British strategic policy.

The original plan was that the new class would consist of two carriers, one operational and the second in a "mothballed" state of readiness that would require extensive time to become fully operational. To the Royal Navy, that significantly limited the strategic value of the centerpiece of their fleet. The ultimate objective would be to have the second carrier online and ready to deploy in the event UK commitments to both the transatlantic and NATO relationships demanded it.

Tamer and Trouser and their "old war horse four-star warrior" mentor had done what many considered impossible: bringing the critical allied STOVL program back from the brink.

But manning the new force would need some help.

★ ★ ★

In 2014, LtGen Davis received his third star and returned as the USMC Deputy Commandant for Aviation. He described the reversal this way:

> Once the UK returned to the F-35B as their variant of choice, the vision for an integrated operation with the Marines was reenergized. It still took lots of convincing, coordination and detailed work to make a maiden deployment like this a reality, but that hard work paid off. We now know exactly what it will take to employ and generate combat power from a coalition fifth-generation sea base. The importance of resolving this chapter in the STOVL journey

for the USMC and the UK and eventually the Italian Navy was one of the real keys for keeping the F-35 program viable for both allies.

While the generals' relationships broke the ice, these five—Henley, Green, Davis, Trautman, and Amos—shaped the partnership for both allies at critical points in the program.

★ ★ ★

As noted in the opening to this chapter, at the naming ceremony for HMS *Queen Elizabeth,* the Queen herself was the guest of honor with the First Sea Lord as her escort. Admiral Zambellas's keynote speech was unforgettable.

> Across the channel, our people are already serving within the French Carrier Strike Group. And, across the Atlantic, our nation's pilots, engineers and deck crews are being trained in the art of jets from sea. And for that we are deeply indebted to the United States Navy and the United States Marine Corps. Their generosity is astonishing. It is the generosity of strategic partnership and common strategic responsibility. . . . She may be commanded by the Royal Navy but she is a Defence ship. The Royal Navy *and* the Royal Air Force will both operate the Lightning II jets from her deck. And, when she gets operational, she will be the beating heart of our nation's strategic armada—the Joint Expeditionary Force. So, today, she waits impatiently for the beginning of an extraordinary maritime journey. A journey that is global. And a journey that is completely tied to the United Kingdom's strategic ambition. That means HMS *Queen Elizabeth* will be a national instrument of power. That means she will be a national symbol of authority. And that means she will be a national icon too . . . helping to keep the "Great" in Great Britain, and the "Royal" in the Royal Navy.[12]

Zambellas grinned as he said,

> When Prime Minister Cameron and his Chancellor heard that speech, nobody was going to cancel the carrier program. They suddenly saw and smelt their strategic responsibility to have a carrier ready at all times. After Her Majesty had had a cup of tea and broken the bottle of fine single-malt Scotch on her

namesake, I knew there was no way the carrier program wouldn't go through. The oppositionists were screwed.

For the Prime Minister, I believe this "wake-up" occurred at the naming ceremony, and he was a great supporter subsequently. Indeed, without reference to any policy plan, Prime Minister Cameron committed to a very significant change for the second carrier at the NATO Ministerial Summit at Cardiff, Wales in October 2015 when he stated, "And today I can announce that the second carrier—HMS *Prince of Wales*—will also be brought into service. This will ensure that we will always have one carrier available, 100 percent of the time."

In the end, it really boiled down to national ambition. The carrier program was an outrageously ambitious act. Interestingly, I was regularly asked, as were the other former Sea Lords, why not get rid of the carriers and spend it on frigates? The nature of our ambition for the carriers had to be continuous and strong. My first day on the job, senior civil servants tried to leverage my language to be less interested in carriers. The question is why. I think it was a combination of diverting funding to pay down liabilities and that those guys simply did not want to see the Royal Navy taking on a strategic role again.

But ultimately, the liability isn't with admirals or civil servants, it's with the government at the strategic level. It's with the Prime Minister and the Chancellor. Do you or do you not want a Navy that works?

In 2018, the first four F-35Bs arrived at RAF Marham, in East Anglia. Later that same year, the UK declared land-based initial operational capability. The Harrier force could now operate off land bases while it was awaiting sea trials for the *Queen Elizabeth* to complete its full operational capability certification. In April 2019, the RAF deployed six of its seventeen F-35Bs to Akrotiri, Cyprus, for exercises and combat missions over Iraq and Syria. The stealth fighters flew thirteen combat missions that June. Each involved a pair of F-35s and, presumably, a pair of Typhoons. "The F-35s are the most advanced jets our country has ever possessed and will form the backbone of British air defense for decades to come," Defence Secretary Penny Mordaunt said in her public statement. "They have passed every test their training has thrown at them with flying colors, and their first real operational mission is a significant step into the future for the UK."

At the same time, the *Queen Elizabeth* deployed to the U.S. Naval Air Test Center in Maryland, to conduct F-35B flight trials aboard ship. In 2020, the Royal Navy declared maritime IOC for the F-35B, a precursor for the full carrier strike group IOC declaration a few months later.

In the end, the *Queen Elizabeth* was built to fully exploit the capabilities of the F-35B. Although considered a small carrier from a displacement perspective, her flight deck acreage was only slightly less capacious than the US supercarriers. She was designed for normal operations of about forty aircraft but could carry up to seventy-two. The deployed air wing would consist of 24 F-35Bs and fourteen helicopters of various types, depending on whether the specific mission was anti-submarine warfare, power projection, or humanitarian relief. (**See Figure 25: HMS** *Queen Elizabeth* **underway**)

The new battle group first deployed in October 2020 on Exercise Joint Warrior, with nine UK ships in company and a flight deck that included fifteen F-35Bs. Five were UK and ten were USMC. Additionally, it had eleven helicopters. This was the largest number of aircraft embarked on a British carrier since 1983, and the largest number of F-35Bs ever at sea across the globe. In January 2021, The UK Carrier Strike Group declared IOC.[13] Later that year, the *Queen Elizabeth* deployed on her maiden combat cruise, with ten USMC and seven UK F-35Bs, bringing the vision of Allied integrated combat operations created some ten years earlier to life.

On 22 November, on *Queen Elizabeth*'s return trip through the Mediterranean, two Italian Navy F-35Bs joined the embarked air wing for a day of operations. The flights by the Italians meant the new carrier had hosted jets from three different countries since leaving home in May, with the Italians the first European partner to land on the UK flight deck.

Everything considered, the success of the UK's strategic transition to the new carrier with the fifth-generation F-35 was due to exceptional leadership and the iron strength of the partnership between the USMC and the RAF/ RN. Navigating the ever-fluid technical and political landscape required careful attention from all the players, but most importantly, the only Tier 1 partner, the United Kingdom. Making a long-term commitment while the technical challenges were still unresolved took courage, but the triumph of HMS *Queen Elizabeth*'s maiden deployment meant the risk had paid off.

Reference

1. *QE2* Naming ceremony speech on July 4, 2014, at Rosyth, Scotland by Admiral Sir George Zambellas, First Sea Lord and Chief of the Naval Staff.

2. Interview with First Sea Lord Admiral George Zambellas (ret) by Tom Burbage on January 18, 2022. Held in F-35 interview archive.

3. Advanced Short Take-Off/Vertical Landing (ASTOVL) 1983–1994, GlobalSecurity.org. Available online https://www.globalsecurity.org/military/systems/aircraft/astovl.htm. Accessed January 13, 2023.

4. Interview with RAdm Simon Henley by Tom Burbage, Betsy Clark, and Adrian Pitman on June 21, 2019. Held in F-35 interview archive.

5. Interview with Air Vice Marshal Mark Green by Tom Burbage, Betsy Clark, and Adrian Pitman on July 20, 2019. Held in F-35 interview archive.

6. Military-historyfandom.com/HMS Ark Royal. Accessed 28 December 2021

7. From interview with Admiral George Zambellas.

8. Interview with LtGen Jon Davis, USMC (ret) by Tom Burbage on December 20, 2021. Held in F-35 Interview archive.

9. UK Ministry of Defence. *Strategic Defence Security Review–GOV.UK: Securing Britain in an Age of Uncertainty: The Strategic Defence and Security Review*; Foreword, dated October 2010.

10. Interview with Gen Jim Amos by Tom Burbage on January 10, 2022. Held in F-35 Interview Archive

11. Interview with LtGen George Trautman by Tom Burbage on December 28, 2021. Held in F-35 interview archive.

12. *Queen Elizabeth* naming ceremony speech July 4, 2014, at Rosyth, Scotland by Admiral Sir George Zambellas, First Sea Lord and Chief of the Naval Staff.

13. www.Royalnavy.mod.uk/HMS *Queen Elizabeth*, November 22, 2021.

Chapter 17

THE PERFECT STORM

The elation after AA-1's maiden flight was short-lived. Certainly, the SWAT redesign had reduced all three variants' weight and improved the fighter. Yet it consumed enormous amounts of cash and time, while the delivery dates remained the same.

To meet those milestones, the remaining work had to be done very quickly, and with less money than anticipated.

With the first prototype, AA-1, now flying, three additional aircraft designs were nearing completion—the redesigned CTOL, the STOVL and the CV (the A, B, and C variants). Lockheed had to stand up the supply chain and production line, and the Air Force, Navy and Marine Corps had to prepare maintenance and support facilities at multiple bases. Lockheed Martin and the government had to supply training simulators and training facilities. Also of vital importance, someone had to write a huge amount of software, both to fly on the jet and to run on ground-based computers, to support mission planning and debriefing, maintenance instruction, and parts supply.

No one, either at DoD or Lockheed, wanted to put his head on the block and say more time and cash were needed. The fate of the A-12 and other suddenly guillotined defense programs (Safeguard, Sergeant York, Crusader, Comanche, etc.) was in everyone's mind.

A time-tested strategy to speed up development was to schedule some activities to occur in parallel—what's called increasing concurrency. The downside was added risk. Concurrency had been part of the F-35 development strategy from the beginning. Management had assumed that problems could be avoided through advanced modeling and simulation. But the degree of concurrency was especially high in software development, with overlapping releases, each providing more advanced war-fighting power and lethality.

Brig Gen C. R. Davis consulted with LM to brainstorm other ways to save time and money. He recalled, "Maybe we can cut out six months of the test schedule here, maybe we don't need these extra two flight test jets because the technology can be mature enough. . . . The flight test schedule was compressed with the hope that we would actually have more maturity than we thought. . . . Everybody got put under some pressure to work within the confines of the budget and schedule we had."[1]

But all the positive thinking in the world wasn't a match for reality. There were fierce battles on the political front as well. The sheer number of dollar bills being burned attracted criticism and second-guessing both inside and outside DoD. Most annoying, Davis had to keep rebutting the canard that the Lightning II was no better than the venerable F-16. Even expert critics, experienced aviators and engineers, had a fourth-generation mindset. Foremost among them were Pierre Sprey in the Pentagon and Carlo Kopp and Peter Goon in Australia. They were hyper-focused on dogfighting ability, which they knew and understood, to the exclusion of other capabilities more relevant to modern air combat.

Davis recalled,

> We had to spend so much time comparing an F-35 to an F-16, and I got so exasperated every time we had to do that, having flown a lot of hours in the F-16 as a test pilot. The critics would point to the F-16 and say, "It's got nine Gs, it can turn a lot better." But this wasn't an apples-to-apples comparison, because they were comparing a bare, unloaded F-16 (what is referred to as "the air show configuration") with the F-35, which carries its weapons internally and contains a full suite of sensors within the aircraft.
>
> I would point out that you have to put the same load on an F-16 as what the F-35 carries internally including a targeting pod, four external missiles plus an electronic countermeasures pod. Then, when you did that, you had an F-16 that on a good day could maybe get 350 knots with a G limit of about four or five just to get to the same configuration as an F-35 with full internal fuel and full weapons . . . to try to compare the two just did not make any sense.

Meanwhile, the picture within Lockheed wasn't rosy either. And the most pressure was falling on the software teams.

The F-35 has been described as an "interactive information node on the battlefield" and as a "flying supercomputer." The amount of software on the aircraft is five times more than that aboard any previous fighter. Just to control the systems and surfaces needed to fly totaled close to two and a half million lines of code. The engine required nearly a million lines. An additional six and a half million controlled the sensors and integrated their data into a coherent picture of the battlespace. Overall, this added up to nearly ten million lines of code. And it had to be flawless, to react instantly and correctly in life-and-death situations.

The software was delivered in three "blocks" of capability. Each block consisted of a number of releases, sent first to the integration and test labs, and then to flight test.

The first block controlled the flying systems. As Dan Crowley explained, "Block 1 required over a thousand software releases to the laboratory and to the aircraft. A lot of people don't realize how much work went into just the basic flying qualities software. And because the initial focus on the program was so heavy toward the first flight of all three variants, just getting Block 1 released was a monumental effort."[2]

As the design came together, the next key piece was mission systems. These turned the plane from "just" a high-performance flying machine into a combat-ready weapon. There were five mission systems that together provided the pilot with unprecedented awareness of the battlespace and the ability to identify and immobilize threats. These mission systems include:

- An active electronically scanned array (AESA) radar
- A set of six infrared cameras mounted around the aircraft, with real-time imagery projected onto the pilot's helmet visor (the display aperture system (DAS)
- An advanced electro-optical tracking system (EOTS) for tracking and targeting threats
- An electronic warfare (EW) / countermeasures (CM) system, and
- A communications, navigation, and identification (CNI) avionics suite.

These sensors covered both the radio frequency and infrared spectrums. Fusing their outputs presented the pilot with a coherent, real-time depiction of the combat environment, which could also be shared with other platforms through the multifunction advanced data link (MADL) and the older Link 16 tactical data link.

The objective was to help the pilot focus on executing the very complex mission of destroying heavily defended strategic targets. A book on the F-35 published by the American Institute of Aeronautics and Astronautics described it like this:

> The concept for the F-35 developed by Lockheed Martin centered on returning the pilot to the role of tactician. . . . One of the F-35 Mission Systems team's design goals was to develop a set of sensors that could collect information across multiple spectrums. Another goal was to develop a sensor control scheme of autonomous sensor management. This, along with a next-generation cockpit, would provide the pilot with an unprecedented amount of information distilled to an easily consumable format. Prior to this, the pilot spent precious minutes setting up radar scans and adjusting tilt, gain, and refresh rates, while also monitoring multiple displays to run an intercept. With this new suite, the pilot is able to view a picture of the multispectral battlespace in a consolidated format.[3]

But writing the software to control the sensors and fuse the information as well as manage the communication links proved to be a massive job. Hundreds of software engineers and programmers from LM and Northrop Grumman worked endless hours to develop the algorithms and then the code written primarily in the programming language C++.

The engineers delivered the mission systems software as new pieces of the second and third blocks released to the airplane. But they got hit with a double whammy. The SWAT redesign ate up a full eighteen months of schedule, and, as noted in the chapter on the SWAT redesign, funding had been taken away from the mission system software to fund the design activities. But both Lockheed Martin and the JPO realized there was no choice but to short-sheet the software, if the program as a whole was to stay alive.

Crowley recalled,

> The software team was short on manpower. [Lockheed Martin] Aero didn't have a lot of software depth and the team was probably staffed at 80 percent of what they needed and had 120 percent of the workload. . . . The concurrency hit the Mission Systems team really hard because of Block 1 sliding and then Block 2 and 3 getting right on top of it and that became the critical path on the program. So, I would just say the Mission Systems team, in particular, was really overstressed by the concurrency, the number of releases, and the complexity of the effort.

Bob Hanson's first exposure to the F-35 was as a member of a corporate review team in early 2010. He was asked to stay on and help with the mission systems software. Bob embodied the intensity and competence of the engineer that he was. He started as director for Mission Systems software and then lead engineer in 2010. He was shocked at the low morale.

> Dan Crowley and his management were put in a very difficult situation. They had to get weight under control, or there wouldn't have been an F-35. That affected production, it affected everything at the expense of software development. They had to make some tough decisions, and it really did cause a tremendously bad environment. I'd never seen a bunch of engineers that were so low. They didn't have the staff and they weren't meeting their schedules.[4]

The JPO stood by as the software team was starved of money and time and let them sink or swim. In Hanson's words, "They saw our budgets being cut. It was 'deal with it. We've got to get the aircraft redesigned.'"

And so, the software team struggled on. But then several setbacks arrived together, to create a perfect storm of bad news.

In 2009, Davis's term ended, and his deputy, Marine MajGen David (Duncan) Heinz, became PEO. He faced pushback from both the Air Force and the Navy.

> The budget was in crisis from the sheer number of procurement programs. You had the Air Force trying to buy F-22's; you still had the Navy trying to buy more Super Hornets, and those were playing against the JSF program. And a lot of what you saw in the press were stories about the other airplanes being better and predominantly efforts to try to buy more of the alternatives. I think some of that was the contractors. You had Boeing and other folks in their pitching their aircraft over the others.[5]

But the major battle for Heinz centered around the F-35's engine, whether P&W should be a sole supplier or whether GE, with their less mature but more technologically advanced power plant, should also be funded. Heinz felt strongly that acquiring engines from two sources was the preferred path. This was based on his experience with the Harrier when an engine problem had grounded nearly every AV-8 in the fleet.

That belief would cost him his job.

Heinz recalled, "When the Obama administration came in, the alternate engine was on the chopping block. The first words out of my mouth were always 'I support the President's budget,' but if asked for my personal opinion, I said that this is not a good bet."

Let's look at the alternate engine story in a little more detail.

Jean Lydon-Rodgers, GE's F136 Program Director, recalled,

We were awarded a contract for the alternate engine in the summer of 2005. In 2006, it was evident that the DoD had serious budget challenges. The DoD budget submittal to Congress did not include funding for F136. Congress, however, felt strongly about the need to strengthen the industrial base and understood the advantages experienced in the F-16 engine competition. Congress overturned the DoD position.

This was called the "Gold Watch game," where DoD recognized the powerful lobbying capability of both Pratt & Whitney and GE and counted on them to provide funding for the alternate engine program. This allowed DoD to show a reduced budget request with a high probability the extra funding would be provided by Congress. The same scenario played out in 2007 and 2008 (and in other major defense programs). The unfortunate fact is that defense appropriations are sought-for prizes in the brutal game of federal-level politics.

Bennet Croswell, the F135 program manager said, "In Pratt's opinion, GE had a very strong congressional lobby and was able to get Congress to add funding to the annual DoD budget for the alternate engine development after the DoD had suspended their funding."[6]

Jean Lydon-Rodgers didn't disagree:

We spent a lot of time in discussion with members of Congress, and we had tremendous support from key players. In 2008 we completed a major milestone in our Preliminary Design Review and had actually done some STOVL engine testing. We kept our F136 team focused on demonstrating the key capabilities of the engine. We also had a technical breakthrough when we demonstrated a new material called ceramic matrix composites (CMC). It was the first time we had ever introduced a new material into high-pressure turbine manufacturing that was not metal.

It had two very real benefits. It enabled significant weight savings as well as the opportunity to not have to cool this material so we could redirect cooling air into additional thrust for the engine. It really redefined the engine world, and we started the use of CMC in all of our engines. When we were designing our strategy to increase thrust without increasing weight, this CMC material became the essential technology. We did major battle internally to provide this revolutionary technology for this very important military program.[7]

2010 was our most difficult year from a funding standpoint but Congress again provided funding. In 2011, there was a tough vote in Congress, and Secretary of Defense Robert Gates felt JSF just could not afford a second engine.

The shifting winds of politics also played a role. A new Republican conservative movement was voted into power. The "Tea Party," as it was referred to, was bent on lowering taxes and eliminating Congressional "earmarks." Earmarks is the colloquial term for funding add-ons above the administration's budget request, often considered "gifts" to supporters.

With Congress considering cancellation of the second engine, LtGen Hough urged legislators to reconsider, saying,

> I have watched with disappointment over the last few months as those advocates of sole-sourcing the F-35 with only the Pratt & Whitney engine have attempted to spin a tale of myth and innuendo to deliberately muddy the waters around the issue. Let me set the record straight. First, there was no JSF engine competition as part of the overall air frame competition. . . . it never happened! Second, I have never been an advocate of a single-engine solution for the JSF. It simply is not good business and I believe it would fail to drive behavioral changes with the contractors and render potential decreased "aircraft availability" down the road. As we have seen during the last few years, the positive aspects of competition have improved engine reliability, cost, and maintainability, and our entire JSF program will be better for it.

But LtGen Hough and GE lost this battle. Lydon-Rodgers remembered it vividly.

> One late afternoon in April 2011, I received notification that the F136 had been terminated. It was a very tough day. The hardest part was going into my office the next day to inform the team.

In retrospect, we learned a lot and benefitted greatly from our experience with the F136 alternate engine program. I couldn't be prouder of our team and the innovative ideas they have brought forward. That team is thriving today because of the opportunities F136 provided for us.

★ ★ ★

MajGen Heinz said,

As a Marine Corps and as a nation, we didn't have a significant problem with a single engine supporting the Harrier because it only represents 15 percent of the tactical aviation fleet. But, when you take 80 percent of that fleet and 100 percent of the fleet for some of the eight partner nations and you tie that to one motor, do you want to take the risk of grounding that entire fleet? So, my view was, let's keep an alternate design in the program. In the F-16 case, we increased the competition between the two motors. The price went down 20 percent in the first year. It creates an environment of competition where the cost of technology upgrades are not passed on to the government, the government doesn't have to subsidize every improvement because each manufacturer is trying to figure out a way to distinguish their motor. My entire point was that an alternate engine is an insurance policy. It will promote competition, it will keep the price down, but most importantly, do you want to bet 80 percent of the US and allied partner nations on one engine? If asked for my personal opinion, I am going to give my personal opinion. And my perspective is, this is not a good bet.

But the last word on a second engine may not have been spoken yet. One of the questions that continues to be asked is, "Is there any chance the F136 will come back in the program?" The opinion among all stakeholders is almost always "yes."

Tom Burbage believes, "The F-35B STOVL model is the most challenging to upgrade, because it requires a balance between the engine and the lift-fan system, which is complex. But technology has a way of solving those problems. The Air Force and Navy will always strive for additional thrust. There will always be a demand for a second engine."

There have not been any major engine problems yet, but most of the operational experience is still ahead of the program, and latent defects could still become a future issue. In addition, there is always a need to be able to increase thrust over time to meet the installation of new sensors and weapons. The PW engine is limited in its growth potential, and any decision to grow the engine would likely require an open competition. This will be discussed in a later chapter about the future.

★ ★ ★

During this turbulent period, USAF Maj Gen C. D. Moore came in as Heinz's deputy and was taken aback at the interservice strife.

> I had run the F-16 program, I had run the F-22 program, so I understood big programs. . . . So, I came into it, probably a bit naïve, thinking "I'm an Air Force guy but I'm going to put my joint loyalty up there on top to really focus on the interests of all the parties to include the allied partners and all three of the Services," and I really didn't appreciate the tension between the Marine Corps and the Navy. I wasn't getting calls from the Navy, who own the budget process for both the Navy and the Marine Corps. I was getting calls from LtGen George Trautman and the Marines. He was the Deputy Commandant for Aviation, and they were driving hard. They were a demanding customer, and you knew that they wanted this platform and they wanted it bad and they wanted it soon. So that was the dynamic.[8]

Adding to those tensions, the program was under attack from a number of other quarters. As Crowley said,

> There were a lot of people trying to gain control of the program. The OT&E crowd were uncomfortable with the amount of concurrency and the dependence on simulation for retiring a number of the test points. The old guard test community wanted to do exhaustive testing and have a very expensive test program that flew every point in the sky and the program was never premised on doing that, both schedule and cost. The Navy was trying to gain control of the JPO at that time because they were never comfortable with the Joint Program Office construct and made that very clear.

As different camps within Defense tried to wrest control from the JPO and Lockheed Martin, Crowley remembered one time in particular as the darkest on his watch.

There was a milestone event in the Pentagon during an all-day review on a Sunday. It was with Ash Carter and OSD. I would say that's the day when they basically changed the trajectory of the program. They decided to slow down the program, reduce the planned production ramp and procure fewer airplanes in the near term. We knew those actions would trigger a Nunn-McCurdy breach. It's just math.

"Nunn-McCurdy" may not be a topic of discussion in living rooms across America. But it's a huge deal in the Pentagon. Introduced as an amendment to Title 10 by Senator Sam Nunn and Congressman Dave McCurdy in the FY 1982 National Defense Authorization Act, its purpose is to draw Congressional attention to large defense programs that significantly overrun their budgets. A "breach" would require the Pentagon to provide assurances that the programs were essential and that costs would be brought under control. A breach occurs when the development and unit costs for a program go over the originally planned amount by a certain percentage. An overrun of 25 percent triggers a "serious" breach, and an overrun of 50 percent triggers a "critical breach."[9]

At the rate the F-35 budget was being spent, and with the slowdown in the production ramp, the unit costs had increased to the "critical" threshold. (Unit costs are highly sensitive to the rate of production cost such that slowing down the rate of production increases the cost per plane.)

When a critical breach is triggered, the Hill requires DoD to take significant steps to report and address the overrun. In order for that program to continue, the Secretary of Defense must declare it essential, identify the root causes of the overruns, and take steps to address them.

Meanwhile the administration was facing heavy expenditures for current military operations, mainly the war in Afghanistan. Secretary Gates took this as an opportunity to restructure the F-35 program, only eight months after Heinz had started as PEO.

★   ★   ★

The *New York Times*, February 1, 2010:

Defense Secretary Robert M. Gates said Monday that he was replacing the general in charge of the Pentagon's largest weapons program—the F-35 Joint

Strike Fighter—and withholding $614 million in award fees from the contractor, Lockheed Martin.

The surprise announcement came from a Pentagon chief who has sought to impose accountability across the department's senior leadership and who himself had promoted plans for the new plane last year in persuading Congress to kill the more expensive F-22 fighter jet. But a special Pentagon review team has since warned of possibly billions of dollars in cost overruns on the plane, and Mr. Gates announced that he was restructuring the program and requiring the company to cover some of the extra costs.[10]

In Heinz's words, "I was advised by several senior officers to stop talking about the need for a second engine, and I said, 'Look, I am not trying to make a big deal of this.' I expressed my opinion, it was in the press, I was definitely not on Gates's good side as a result of that. And I think when the first opportunity came when he could let me go, he did." Heinz became the sacrificial lamb to give the appearance that the Pentagon was taking action to put the program back on track. Heinz stood by a sincere conviction of the need for a second engine at great personal cost. Reflecting back, he said, "I really, truly hope that I am wrong in this, but we are now with one engine and I fear for that day when we discover the unknown."

The day of Heinz's firing, C. D. Moore was visiting Lockheed Martin. As he recalled, "I was just starting to learn about this very complex program. I was at Fort Worth, walking the production line with Dan Crowley, and I got a phone call. It was my wife, and she rarely calls me in the middle of the day because she knows that I'm typically pretty busy, and her question to me was, 'Do you have a job?' And I said, 'Why are you asking?' and she said, "Well, I'm online right now and the Marine general just got fired." And I said, "I don't know." I flew back to DC not knowing what was going to transpire. I got back there and I got a call from Dr. Carter [then Undersecretary for Defense] that night saying, 'OK, you're in charge now. Fix it!'" But the program couldn't be "fixed" without more time and more money. There was nothing Moore or anyone could magically make happen without either of these resources.

Moore served as interim PEO until the Navy appointed a new one, a period he described as "the longest four and a half months of my life. . . . The dynamic between the Navy and Marine Corps became very crystal clear to me when I ran into a retired Navy four-star at the airport about a week afterward. I'm in the driver's seat trying to get us through this period and he cornered me and said, 'We will never let this happen again—the Marine Corps running one of our programs.'"

Along with the turmoil on the government side and the financial penalty, other hard times loomed. Crowley described a sea change in how the government managed the program. "The players changed out across the board—the Secretary of the Navy, the Secretary of the Air Force, the Secretary of Acquisition, and the leaders that came in at that point really listened more closely to OT&E and OSD than they did to the people running the program—the PEO, the JPO—and our inputs became less important in the decisions that they were making."

The new guard in charge had much less tolerance for the risk and would revisit the whole acquisition strategy. The concurrency overlap of development and testing with early production had been fundamental to the acquisition reform initiatives that were baselined in the program. They felt that production needed to slow to allow any latent problems to be discovered in flight test. The Undersecretary of Defense in charge of all military acquisitions, Frank Kendall, was famously quoted as referring to the high concurrency of the F-35 as "acquisition malpractice."[11] Lockheed Martin and the JPO braced for a change in philosophy and a slowing down of the program. The program was soundly criticized from numerous quarters as negative reports appeared one after the other in the press like sharks circling a wounded animal. But the most damaging criticism came from within the US government with a string of disparaging reports from the GAO that served to erode confidence within the international partners and even resulted in an immediate about-face by the Canadian government after Ottawa had just announced plans to buy the F-35.[12, 13]

Dan Crowley reflected on this period by saying, "For those of us that had really labored through a very difficult phase and then to be criticized as roundly as we all were was disappointing. There were a lot of divorces that came out of JSF; people spent so much time away from their families. That core team kept it powering through. Duncan's treatment was exceptionally poor."

While Heinz was indeed treated poorly, he held no grudges against the program and offered a personal story:

My son is a Marine aviator. He has been flying F-18s for a very long time. I said from the beginning that the F-35 is about the warrior and that the greatest thing that can happen for me would be to have my son fly that airplane. He was at the cake-cutting ceremony when I took over as the F-35 PEO. Second Lieutenant Heinz cutting the cake with me was a very special moment from that standpoint. He got into the F-18 and has done extremely well with the F-18, and at one point he came to me and said, "Dad, I don't think I am going to sign up for the F-35: I said, "This is your life, I'm not going to push you either direction on it."

And a few months later he got to fight against one. Within a few weeks after that he got to have one join him in a division fight against a dissimilar group. After that he called me back up and said, "I get it. It was amazing. It was truly amazing. I'm in." Today, my son is at Lemoore California; he recently finished the F-35C training at Eglin AFB and is one of the first instructors with the Navy group out at Lemoore teaching the next cadre of people to fly F-35C.

With Heinz out and with C. D. Moore temporarily at the helm, the JPO waited for a new PEO to be selected. Who would step up to the challenge during this tumultuous period? Would they be able to restore the tattered reputation of the program and regain the confidence of the services and the international partners? Given the tensions of that period, the person who became the next PEO and the one to restore trust in the program came from the most unlikely of places.

Reference

1. Interview with LtGen CR Davis by Tom Burbage, Betsy Clark and Adrian Pitman on August 11, 2019. Held in F-35 interview archive.

2. Interview with Dan Crowley with Tom Burbage, Betsy Clark, and Adrian Pitman on January 27, 2018. Held in F-35 interview archive.

3. Lemons, Greg, Karen Carrington, Thomas Frey, and John Ledyard, "F-35 Mission Systems Design, Development, and Verification." Chapter in book edited by Jeffrey W. Hamstra, *The F-35 Lightning II: From Concept to Cockpit.* American Institute of Aeronautics and Astronautics, Inc., Reston, VA, 2019.

4. Interview with Bob Hanson with Betsy Clark and Adrian Pitman on February 27, 2015. Held in F-35 interview archive.

5. Interview with MajGen David (Duncan) Heinz with Betsy Clark and Adrian Pitman on November 29, 2017. Held in F-35 interview archive.

6. Tom Burbage Interview with PW Executives on October 24 2019: Bennett Croswell, President PW Military Engines.

7. Interview with Jean Lydon-Rodgers, president, GE Military Engines by Tom Burbage, Betsy Clark, and Adrian Pitman on May 8, 2019. Held in F-35 interview archive.

8. Interview with Lt Gen CD Moore by Betsy Clark and Adrian Pitman on February 25, 2017. Held in F-35 interview archive.

9. Schwartz, Moshe, and Charles V. O'Conner, "The Nunn-McCurdy Act: Background, Analysis, and Issues for Congress." Congressional Research Service Report 7-7500, dated May 12, 2016.

10. Drew, Christopher and Shanker, Thom, "Gates Shakes Up Leadership for F-35," *New York Times*, February 1, 2010.

11. Butler, Amy, "Kendall: Premature F-35 Production was 'Acquisition Malpractice.'" *Aviation Week*, February 7, 2012.

12. US Government Accountability Office Report to Congressional Committees, GAO-11-325, Joint Strike Fighter: Restructuring Places Program on Firmer Footing, but Progress Still Lags, April 2011.

13. US Government Accountability Office, GAO-10-382, Joint Strike Fighter: Additional Costs and Delays Risk Not Meeting Warfighter Requirements on Time, March 19, 2010.

Chapter 18

TRANSPARENCY, TRUST, AND REALISM

In June 2010, Vice Admiral Dave Venlet, USN, became the new F-35 program executive officer. Tall, with an understated, approachable demeanor, Venlet was the program's first three-star leader. In the rank-obsessed environment of the military, this translated into increased respect and clout. (Actually, it was ironic that the step up in leadership came from the Navy, then a strident critic.)

Venlet was a respected leader whose most recent posting had been commanding NAVAIR. Both he and Tom Burbage were fellow Annapolis grads, and both had been test pilots at the Naval Air Test Center in Pax River. That shared history made the PEO and LM mesh more smoothly than might otherwise have been the case. The move to F-35 PEO was in some respects a demotion for Venlet. He had been looking forward to retirement and, as he said, "pulling on my waders and doing some fly fishing." But the largest defense program in the world badly needed strong leadership. He accepted the challenge and moved up the road from Patuxent River to Arlington, Virginia.

It was clear by now that someone would have to take firm corrective action. The program had been declared in a Nunn-McCurdy breach. It was more obvious by the day that it needed more money and more time if it was to continue. Powerful voices in Congress were calling for its cancellation. And in that post–Cold War era, no program was safe from abrupt termination. Secretary Gates had deep-sixed two ambitious initiatives in 2009, the Missile Defense Agency's Kinetic Energy Interceptor and the Army's Future Combat System. (The FCS had already been in the System Development and Demonstration phase; its cancellation zeroed out almost $19 billion in sunk costs.) In 2010, the Navy's ambitious Next Generation Cruiser had also been led to the chopping block.

Clearly, the JSF program was operating within a kill zone.[1]

One of Venlet's initial meetings was in the Pentagon, with Defense Secretary Gates. Gates told him,

> "Dave, we've made adjustments to this program over the years—small ones—and we keep being disappointed. If I need to make a big adjustment, just tell me. All I want to know is how long it's going to take and how much it's going to cost. That's your test."
>
> I left that conversation realizing that I had his support to really get to the ground truth. How hard can a test be with only two questions on it? But it was a very complex question. Get it wrong and it's over, for me and likely, for the program.[2]

Venlet had only a few months to find the answers. The next fiscal year's budget was due to Congress that December. Would the additional appropriation needed be so large that the plane would be nixed entirely? He couldn't worry about that. His only concern was to come up with the most accurate estimate possible and let the chips fall where they might.

He turned to his just-appointed chief engineer.

★ ★ ★

Doug Ebersole was career civil service. He'd been the lead flight tech engineer for the F-117A and F-15E. His most recent job had been as director of engineering for the F-22 at Wright-Patt.[3]

Ebersole hasn't forgotten their first meeting.

> He (Venlet) didn't have a whole lot of time or patience for shenanigans. He's a very straightforward guy. . . . He talked about how we were going to run this program going forward with three foundations. The first was sound, disciplined systems engineering. When you're the director of engineering, that's like music to your ears. The second foundation was to treat planning with realism. And third, we're going to be transparent with everything we do. And he stopped and said, "Those are the three things. For any decision, if you follow those three things, you're in."
>
> That was the best first meeting I've ever had with a boss because not only did he communicate what he was about and how he was going to run this

program but then he immediately communicated to the workforce, "It's easy. This isn't complicated."[4]

Venlet tasked Ebersole to find out "how long" and "how much" to complete SDD. The first priority was building the team to answer those two questions. Ebersole had extensive knowledge of experienced acquisition engineers and professionals at Wright-Patterson who could contribute. However, he did not have knowledge of comparable people at NAVAIR who could do the same. He turned to his deputy, Jim Ruocco, a seasoned NAVAIR technical leader, to help identify candidates to join the team. In short order, Ebersole and Ruocco pulled together over a hundred experts and called the team's activities the technical baseline review, or TBR. "We brought in folks who were outside the JPO from Wright-Patterson and from NAVAIR. These were very senior folks who had done complex development all their careers, people who had worked on the F-22, the F-18, the E-2, and various weapons programs. They had seen messes and been through them. We had systems engineers, software engineers, and flight test folks. We also included Lockheed, BAE Systems, and Northrop. . . . It wasn't just a government thing. We had to do it together and, to their credit, industry contributed immensely." Ruocco continued to play a key role in the TBR actively managing task lists, risks, and action closures.

The contractor team was also undergoing a leadership change. Larry Lawson replaced Dan Crowley as the Lockheed Martin F-35 general manager. Lawson was a smart and forceful leader who had faced similar recovery challenges on the F-22 Program. His reputation as a hard-driving, technically astute program manager facilitated attacking the aftereffects of concurrency that were bedeviling progress. While the program re-baselining team was replanning the future, Lawson attacked the major developmental challenges of the helmet, arresting hook and, most importantly, the STOVL variant.

Venlet's re-baselining team microscoped every major cost component. Ebersole recalled, "They were living in Fort Worth for four months basically inquiring, challenging, understanding, going back looking at different models, really trying to assess the eight hundred-some cost accounts that we chose to do a deep dive in . . . based on their risk and their dollar value."

The team immediately zeroed in on two areas for special attention: software and flight test. With nearly ten million lines of complex code on the plane, and close to five hundred engineers designing algorithms and writing that code, software was high-risk and high-cost, and the diversion of resources from it to reduce the plane's weight hadn't helped. Flight test was a second obvious target because of its sheer expense. As Ebersole described it, "The issue with flight test is the burn rate of that infrastructure is extremely expensive. You miss that by six months, that's a big bill." A complicating factor for flight test is that each service wanted a larger slice of the new testing program. A new revision of the testing assumptions had been proposed to each service but had not been agreed to. The USAF test community was the most difficult to reconcile. Lawson recalled, "On F-22 we had an accident trying to demonstrate a nearly impossible test point conceived by the Operational Testers. It involved a nine-G rolling missile launch. Very unfortunately, the LM pilot lost consciousness in the maneuver and awoke too close to the ground and was killed trying to eject."[5] That accident may have influenced the fact that negotiating a new test program with the services would prove to be a major obstacle.

After the team had analyzed and estimated each of the cost components, Ebersole briefed his boss. But Venlet told him to go back and do it again, looking for anywhere they might have counted something twice.

Ebersole: "That was on a Friday. I was going to fly home to see my wife. I canceled the flight, and we spent the entire weekend recovering. But it was that kind of commitment . . . a 24/7 thing. It was like what they say about the greenskeeper at the Masters Tournament—you work from when you can until when you can't."

TBRers went through the cost accounts a second time and, again, Ebersole brought the results to Venlet.

And got put down once more. This time, the vice admiral told him to do one more scrub, this time focusing on areas where the team had low confidence in their estimates and places where Lockheed Martin disagreed with their conclusions. Venlet described his rationale for the second scrub as providing him with a "spine stiffener" for when he had to deliver the results to Gates and DoD. He told Ebersole, "I need to stand firm and look them in the eye with courage and confidence. If that's the number, then that's the number, but I want to say we've scrubbed it twice and the best possible people on planet Earth have done this."

★　★　★

With the results of the second scrub in hand, Venlet and his deputy, C. D. Moore, went to the Pentagon to brief the higher-ups, including the service chiefs, the service secretaries, the undersecretary of defense, Ashton Carter, and his deputy, Frank Kendall. It was a make-or-break moment for the program. Venlet:

> We gave the presentation, and I ended it with my rehearsed pitch that "I know this is a lot of money, and I know you may not have that much, but please don't ask us to do it for less, because that's what's going to drive the program in the ditch again." . . . And then I just waited and held my breath, and the room got real silent, and then the only person who made a comment was the Marine Corps Commandant, Jim Amos. I think the world of him and he said "Wow. Dave, that's a lot of money. Are you sure?" . . . I said, "We've scrubbed it twice, and the best possible people on planet Earth have done this. If not these people, where else would you go? You're not going to go to Krypton, to extraterrestrials." And that was it. Everybody said OK.

With the OK of the higher-ups, OSD added an additional $4.8 billion to the F-35 line. President Barack Obama sent the budget to the Hill. Just to add more last-minute angst, House Majority Leader John Boehner threatened a government shutdown, wanting more cuts in abortion programs and environmental protection.[6] But after more compromises and cuts, the Defense budget finally passed both houses, and was signed into law in April 2011,[7] including the new money for the F-35. Looking back at the TBR, Venlet underscored Ebersole's immense contribution: "I told Doug we could not have walked that road without him. I am forever in his debt."

For really the first time, the industry partners now had a realistic budget and schedule going forward. No more need for Peter (hardware and SWAT redesign) to rob Paul (software). JD McFarlan, LM's VP of Flight Test, said, "If Lockheed had come forward and said we need this, they probably wouldn't have gotten it, but it was outside experts saying the program needs this. . . . That was the brilliance of the TBR."[8]

The budget now reflected that change, but opposition would continue to demand a strong lobbying campaign to keep the appropriation intact. The contractor team, led by Burbage, and the Lockheed Martin Washington operations team, and the government team, led by Dave Venlet, all began working their contact base to ensure a positive outcome.

Venlet credits his predecessor, VADM Joe Dyer, with teaching him the value of transparency. "I had seen people run programs with data close to their chest. Then I saw people like Joe who operated very transparently, and I saw the difference in the result. There are risks to operating with transparency. People can take your money if they know your failures, but I see the risk of that versus the value of establishing trust and trust as worth taking that risk."

More bad news quickly put Venlet's promise of transparency to the test. In November 2010, cracks were discovered in a rear bulkhead during ground-based fatigue testing. Venlet recalled,

> When the bulkhead broke on the STOVL fatigue test, after I first told the Defense Department, I went right over to Congress and said, "Listen, guys, we just had a big crack. It's a big deal. Let me tell you what I know and what I don't know." I needed to gain their trust that it was under control because if the media finds out, stories get written, everybody will start making assumptions until they know the ground truth, so I worked hard to push information to them and I did the same thing for each of the eight international partners.

In reality, static and dynamic structural testing was critical to ensuring that the weight issue on the STOVL variant had been safely resolved. Finding a weak point before the plane was in the air was actually a good thing. But such details would have been overlooked or glossed over by those focused on finding failures.

Venlet visited each of the international partners, briefing government officials and members of various parliaments. His most memorable visit took place in Italy. Venlet:

> The meeting that stands out most was with the head of the Italian Navy, Admiral Giampaolo Di Paola. We went into his office, which was massive and ornate, as you can imagine given the history of the Italian Navy. It was a large room with a conference table full of people. . . . It didn't take me more than a minute to realize that we weren't going to be flipping any charts. His

eyes just bored right into mine, and it was very uncomfortable. I'd break eye lock just for relief and it was like he had the powers of some science fiction movie to grab my eyes and bring them back. And I think he was trying to plumb the depths of my soul wondering, *can I trust this man*? And I said to myself, "I've got to be able to tell this without even looking at the charts."

Another of Venlet's transparency initiatives was setting up what he called the "command information center" in the JPO. This "war room" contained multiple charts and data sets showing the status of every part of the program from software development, flight test, production, and sustainment. Any international partner or service was welcome to assess the current status for themselves. "It made folks nervous, because I said this room's got to be available to the government oversight agencies, the inspectors general, the Brits, the Australians, and everybody else who wants to do a review, because they've got to trust us. That made a lot of folks real nervous but I said 'If we can't stand that scrutiny, we won't be trusted.'"

Little by little, Venlet regained that trust.

★ ★ ★

But the program still had its share of challenges. Since the early days, the STOVL variant had been the problem child. Its future was still far from certain. Not only had there been the bulkhead cracks, but airflow problems had been caused by the auxiliary inlet doors that sat on top of the center fuselage. They allowed additional air into the engine during hovering and short takeoffs. These doors had required a redesign. While flight test was proceeding as planned for the other two variants, testing was lagging behind schedule for STOVL.

In January 2011, Gates announced that he was putting the STOVL "on probation" for a two-year period. If the problems, including the cracks in the bulkhead, weren't fixed by then, "I believe it should be canceled."[9]

It was paradoxical that the variant that had contributed most to Lockheed winning the JSF contract was the one that was now on death row waiting for a reprieve.

One other important change occurred in day-to-day management at about that time. Venlet had brought with him Matt Mulhern, whom he knew and trusted from NAVAIR. Although a Colorado Springs Air Force Academy graduate, Mulhern had decided against the Air Force. "When I walked into the Marine Corps, I fit in right away. I don't know what it's like now, but in those days, it was like a football team. It was a rough bunch, no doubt, which always added color. But I just fit in better there."[10] He flew F-4s and F-18s, then left the cockpit to join the Navy's F-18 program in Pax River, where he worked with Venlet. Then he became the program manager for the V-22 Osprey.

Mulhern had hit thirty years and was about to retire when he sat down with Venlet, then ending his term at NAVAIR, for his retirement interview. The vice admiral said, "Matt, I've got a question for you. I just got asked to do something pretty hard and I'm going to need some good folks. I can't promise you a promotion. You can probably make a lot more on the outside."

Venlet asked him to be his program manager. While the senior was the outward-facing PEO, Mulhern ran the program from day to day. He immediately got to work to restore the confidence of the people working within the JPO.

At that point, the staff were demoralized. Mulhern described them as consisting of three "flavors."

> There were the ones that had lost any authority to influence anything and they were curled up in the fetal position and somewhat useless. There was another body of people who were still trying to exercise what I considered typical government authority in a program. And they weren't allowed to for whatever reason before Admiral Venlet came in, and they were just getting progressively more frustrated. And then there were people at NAVAIR and Wright Pat who had been that second kind of person who got more and more frustrated to the point where they had gone back to their home systems command. And they were holding a grudge and fighting against the program.

To build confidence, Matt clarified for his staff what their authority was to make Lockheed do what was needed . . . the government oversight role. He emphasized that it was better to act and screw up than be paralyzed by overanalysis. "If someone made a mistake, the wheels turn so slow, we could unwind it. I would tell folks, 'In the worst case, if you don't know anything, you've got a 50/50 shot.' I was a pretty strong believer that they had more information than that so the odds were good that they were going to make a good decision." As a result, the JPO became more assertive with the contractor.

In Mulhern's view, one of his greatest challenges was the sheer complexity of the partnership. "I used to say we have three services and eight allies, and they each think they get 51 percent of the vote. The Marine Corps was under constant stress with the F-35B as they really wanted the airplane. . . . The Air Force was tied to the F-22, the Navy was tied to the F-18 E/F. They all saw their airplane budgets atrophying, and there were tensions both between and within the services."

Looking back on his time as PEO, Venlet offered the following advice.

> How many management books have been written about the importance of knowing where your time is going and not wasting where you invest your time? I think that's off the mark. I think someone in a stressful job needs to manage their personal energy more than their time. Take care of yourself. Eat right, sleep right, exercise because then you won't lose your temper, your judgment won't get skewed. Silly things like revenge and all that stuff creep into your life when you don't take care of yourself. . . . It's important to be calm, because if you're not approachable, you're not going to get that bad news when you need to hear it.

Venlet was a key figure in the journey of the F-35. In the words of his mentor Joe Dyer, "Dave Venlet has never gotten quite the credit I think he should because he was the bearer of much bad news."[11] On the contractor side, Lawson provided similar stability to the contractor team. The newest challenge, mission system software, was still heading down the road to disaster. It needed new resources, new ideas, and new leadership. But Burbage wasn't sure it could arrive in time.

Reference

1. Stephen Rodriguez, Stephen, "Top 10 Failed Defense Programs of the RMA Era," *War on the Rocks*, December 2, 2014. Accessed August 4, 2022.

2. Interview with VADM David Venlet by Betsy Clark and Adrian Pitman, on September 19, 2017. Held in F-35 interview archive.

3. AF.mil, Biographies, "C. Douglas Ebersole," accessed August 3, 2022.

4. Interview with Doug Ebersole by Betsy Clark and Adrian Pitman on May 10, 2017. Held in F-35 interview archive.

5. Interview with Larry Lawson by Tom Burbage on December 2, 2022. Held in F-35 interview archive.

6. Adams, Richard, "Government Shutdown 2011," *The Guardian*, April 8, 2011. Accessed August 11, 2022.

7. Silverleib, Alan, "Obama Signs 2011 Budget Deal into Law," CNN, April 15, 2011. Accessed August 11, 2022.

8. Interview with J. D. McFarlan by Tom Burbage, Betsy Clark, and Adrian Pitman on January 11, 2022. Held in F-35 interview archive.

9. McLaughlin, Andrew, "F-35B STOVL JSF 'on probation,'" News Update, Australian Aviation, available online http://www.pilotaptitude.com/files/F-35B%20STOVL%20JSF%20on%20probation.pdf, accessed August 11, 2022.

10. Interview with Matt Mulhern by Tom Burbage, Betsy Clark, and Jeff Morris on February 18, 2018. Held in F-35 interview archive.

11. Interview with VADM Joe Dyer USN (Ret.) by Betsy Clark and Adrian Pitman on February 18, 2017. Held in F-35 interview archive.

Chapter 19

IT'S ONLY SOFTWARE

The Lightning II's software had to accommodate a next-generation level of integration across nearly every dimension of the aircraft and its supporting systems—for operation, training, and sustainment. At the same time, developers would face an uphill battle, thanks to rapidly advancing computer design and manufacture.

As mentioned earlier in this book, in 1965 Gordon Moore, the cofounder of Intel, recognized that the growth of microprocessors was exponential. The number of microprocessors that could be etched on a chip was doubling every two years, while the cost per transistor was being halved. The availability of faster and more powerful chips incentivized manufacturers to move to the newer models as soon as possible, or find their products obsolete. The upside, of course, was that computers, and machines that depended on computing power, would become smaller, faster, and cheaper over time.

Unfortunately, this "law" would operate to the detriment of military systems, whose development and production spanned many years.

The decades it took to develop, test, and field the F-35 meant multiple cycles of Moore's law would occur before the plane became operational. Computers specified for the aircraft, or for supporting systems on the ground, would quickly become difficult or even impossible to purchase. It also meant F-35 software would need to be independent of the underlying processor improvements.[1] Designing the software to be independent of the underlying processors would be a major discriminator for the emerging "fifth-generation" moniker that critics seldom understood and which allowed for the continued evolution of a fighter with increasing computer power.

The various pieces of equipment, including the computers and software onboard the plane, are organized into two major categories: *vehicle systems* and *mission systems*. Because their functions are so different, let's look at them as two separate but connected design challenges.

F-35 engineers understood that systems critical to managing combat air-craft, referred to as vehicle systems, had traditionally been "federated," mean-ing they were operated separately. Merging them offered the potential to reduce equipment and weight, dramatically improve performance, and reduce cost. Three areas offered the greatest potential. Flight controls and the systems that ran them; electrical systems; and environmental control systems, which regulated such aspects as cockpit temperature. But integrating and simpli-fying these systems would introduce a new level of complexity in software development.

Let's get a bit more specific here. The Lightning's vehicle systems are con-trolled by three independent and redundant vehicle management computers. The trio are physically separated in the aircraft for redundancy in the event of damage. Supplied by BAE Systems, they were designed from the start to be expandable by adding core processors. The early jets had two core processors, while the VMC can be expanded to six over the life of the jet.

In 2011, Dan Crowley left the program to take over as chief operat-ing officer of Lockheed Martin Aeronautics. Orlando Carvalho was brought in as his replacement. With intense dark brown eyes and a genial expression, Carvalho had spent his career to date managing the development of naval-based air defense and ballistic-missile defense combat systems including the Aegis Combat System installed on the Ticonderoga Class Cruisers and Arleigh Burke Class Destroyers. He was immediately struck by one piece of good news. Despite delays in getting the vehicle systems software written, tested in the lab, then loaded onto the flight test aircraft, it was in pretty good shape.

Carvalho recalled,

One of the things that struck me was that the software for the vehicle systems was very stable. And having been around a lot of weapons systems devel-opments over the years, your productivity is directly proportional to stabil-ity. If the system you are building is stable, you can get a lot of work done. Conversely, if the system you are building has a lot of stability issues, then every time you turn around the software is going down, or it is reloading, or it is restarting and it just kills your productivity. I remember thinking that this is a good sign.[2]

But a combat airplane that could fly well was only the beginning.

Integration was also key to improved performance for mission systems, but this would be a much different and even more complex issue. Mission systems software turns the F-35 from being "just" a superb airplane into a true war-fighting machine.

The sensors would have to be integrated and networked to provide the situational awareness the pilot needed to meet exacting future mission scenarios. The underlying software would need complex algorithms in four critical dimensions. *Data fusion* would unite the inputs from multiple sensors to provide improved information about specific targets of concern. *Sensor fusion* would create a blended solution, simplifying tactical decision-making for the pilot. *Information fusion* would create an integrated view of the environment.

The final test would involve converting all of this information to meaningful graphic displays on the panoramic screen in the cockpit and on the aviator's helmet-mounted display. While all of these would dramatically improve mission execution for an individual jet, the fourth dimension would involve information sharing among other members of the flight and other sensors and shooters in the battlespace.

While (as Carvalho noted) the air vehicle software was already stable, which was definitely good, the bulk of the remaining software fell into the area of mission systems. And *that* team was in a world of hurt. The weight reduction redesign had diverted resources, and without enough people or time, they were burning out.

★ ★ ★

While Vice Admiral Venlet was instilling his three principles—transparency, realism in planning, and engineering discipline—into the culture of the JPO, a similar transformation was underway in the mission systems software development team in Fort Worth. There, hundreds of engineers were developing millions of lines of code to be tested first in test laboratories on the ground and then on the plane. The software would be delivered in four blocks called 2A, 2B, 3i and 3F, with each delivering more capability.

Programming like this was extremely hard to write and test. It had to process data and respond instantaneously, without delay. Software engineers routinely discuss carrying out tasks in thousandths or millionths of a second. Yet everything still has to be processed *without error.* Pilots' lives and mission accomplishment depend on it.

Most large military projects follow a succession of activities known as the "systems engineering V." The algorithm begins with an operational concept document (OCD) that describes what the system does in the context of specific war-fighting scenarios, along with a high-level set of requirements—statements declaring specific things the system will and *must* accomplish. Written by the government, the OCD and the high-level requirements are handed over to the contractor during the original proposal stage. Once a contract's awarded, engineers analyze the core requirements into progressively more detailed tasks. They then map those tasks into a hardware and software system design. That design is then further split into even smaller subtasks.

For software, the steps to accomplish each of these smaller tasks are precisely described in a programming language, using English-like words trained humans can understand. A compiler translates these words into the ones and zeros that tell the computer what to do. The mission systems software, working with the sensors on the aircraft, forms a closed-loop system. It can automatically detect various objects of interest in the air or on the ground, then focus and tune the sensors on each to gather as much data as possible for identifying, tracking their movement. . . and targeting them.

As the technical baseline review was underway, there was a shake-up in leadership at LM. A search began for a new head for the mission systems software development. Jeff Morris, at the time a Lockheed VP based outside Philadelphia, was asked to move to Fort Worth to take on this challenge. Morris had moved his family ten times over his career already, and had promised them there would be no more relocating. He recommended one of his directors, Mark Dotterweich, based in Denver, for the position instead. Dotterweich moved to Fort Worth at the end of 2010. Just two months into the job, though, he suffered a fatal heart attack on Superbowl Sunday of 2011. Jeff felt he had to complete what Dotterweich had started, so once again, it was moving day.

Morris arrived in April 2011. His instructions from Lockheed's chief technical officer were "fix the software problem in Fort Worth." Morris had a Maine accent that reflected his farm-boy roots, and a calm, friendly demeanor. Probably no one else in the industry was better suited to the task. Morris's nearly forty-year career had been spent working to get various troubled software programs back on track. He'd earned his reputation for turning around problem programs as a young programmer for General Electric in the 1980s. When the Air Force's Over the Horizon early warning radar system languished, Morris was given a squad of programmers and told to get it working. Within a few months, they were able to demonstrate a correctly functioning system. A decade late, Morris was sent to Melbourne to turn around the Jindalee Operational Radar Network, to help the Australian Air Force and Navy protect their northern border.

By the time Morris arrived, the crisis in mission systems had come to a head. As soon as he reached Fort Worth, he asked his administrative assistant to randomly select forty engineers and schedule each for a one-on-one interview lasting an hour. Jeff held these over the next three weeks, asking each engineer three questions: What's slowing you down? What upsets you in your daily routines? What do you think my priorities should be?

After the sit-downs were over, he convened the entire LM mission-systems software team of several hundred in one room. He listed the inefficiencies and problems he'd been told about. Had he gotten it right? After a resounding "Aye," he laid out a set of initiatives to help them work more efficiently and effectively.

One of the biggest bottlenecks for the software engineers who designed the algorithms (the set of steps the software would execute) and for the programmers who wrote the actual code had been fixing errors discovered in the integration laboratories and during flight test. These were hard bugs both to diagnose and correct. Also, when individual programmers had tweaked the software in one place, unintended errors surfaced elsewhere, a phenomenon known as the "ripple effect." Unfortunately, the engineers and programmers had stopped doing peer reviews of each other's design and code, as earlier management had pushed them to just get the damn code written.

As Morris recalled, "The design problems dated back to 2007 to 2010, during a period of intense schedule and cost pressures. There were lots of discussions about the program being terminated. These were big decisions that were made to just keep cutting code and throw it on the jet."[3]

Morris set about providing better coding and test tools, and put in place a set of rigorous quality checks. He also ordered his entire team to stop what they were doing and review every bit of code to run on the airplane. For three months, that's all they did. The result? They discovered over two hundred errors, bugs that had been lurking in the software for years.

Another of Morris's initiatives was the way he tracked progress. With hundreds of programmers writing code, evaluating progress was far harder than, say, measuring the progress of novelists writing books or artists painting masterpieces. Morris introduced an objective method for measuring precisely what percentage of the software was complete.

When he got the result, it was a shocker. Progress was significantly behind where the engineers had been reporting to Lockheed and the government. They'd estimated they were 56 percent of the way through, when in fact they were only 45 percent done. This translated into $84 million dollars more to complete the development of the mission systems software than everyone had previously believed.

Morris went to his boss, closed the door and said, "I have to de-book eleven percent of my $780M budget." ("De-book" is corporate-finance-speak meaning the money's been spent but the work hasn't been done, so additional funds must be taken from a special pot labeled "management reserve.") "My boss went through the roof and called me every name in the book. After he finished his little speech—there were just the two of us—I said, 'As the software manager, I'm telling you, this is what we need to go do to fix it. You can shout, you can scream, you can call me anything you want but I'm not backing down because this is the right thing to do.'"

And that's exactly what was done.

Bob Hansen, Morris's deputy director, said Morris was one of the best VPs he'd ever worked for. "He was so fair and so calm. He wasn't mean but he was going to make it happen. And I can't emphasize enough how much morale improved. Jeff would do walkarounds. He'd make anyone feel like a million bucks in three minutes. It's his leadership style. If you could bottle that and give it to all the VPs and directors, the corporation would zoom."[4]

As a result of the technical baseline review and the additional $4.8 billion Congress added to F-35 development, mission systems was finally able to hire more personnel. Hansen recalled, "We staffed up over a hundred people. We were hiring like crazy, because we didn't have enough people to do the job."

One of the new heads brought in was Sam Russo, who'd worked for Morris before. Morris put Russo in charge of the most complex part of the software, the fusion piece that integrates or fuses the terabytes of data from the plane's sensor systems to present the pilot with a coherent and comprehensible picture of the battlespace.

Russo recalled a story to explain what he first observed on the fusion team. "When I was in high school, we played games on Friday nights and then on Monday, the coach would show us films of the game. I remember one time, he stopped the play when we were at the line of scrimmage, and he asked us, 'What play are we going to run here?' And we all told him."

Russo was an offensive end, and the tackle and guard were friends.

The coach said to the tackle, "So, Donald, who are you supposed to block on this play?" Donald tells him. The coach says, "Okay, roll the tape." Donald was supposed to block this guy but he didn't. Instead, he blocked another guy. And the person Donald was supposed to block came through the line of scrimmage and sacked the quarterback, wholly untouched. The coach said to Donald "So tell me what happened. You clearly knew who you were supposed to block; why didn't you?" Donald was this big mountain of a guy, and he said, "Because the guard, Gene, kept telling me in the huddle how much trouble he was having with his guy, so I tried to help Gene out." And when he helped Gene out it created a wide opening for the defense to just walk through and ruin our play. And the coach said, "I understand why you did that, but that is not your job. Your job was to block this guy, right? All those guys up in the booth with the headsets that are watching the game, that's their job to identify and spot problems, and who's having trouble with who. Then we can make game adjustments from the booth. But when you choose to compensate for that on your own without our involvement, then we don't see what the real problem is."

Russo said the same thing was going on with the software engineers. "People were working on all sorts of stuff that was important but not in our plan. They were getting so distracted by all the other shiny problems that float around. I just put an end to that and held them accountable for the tasks that were assigned to them. And if they had problems executing them, they needed to come to me to get help."[5]

Morris and his staff, folks like Hansen and Russo, solved the software puzzle, resulting in impressive gains in productivity and fewer errors. For the first time, mission systems was meeting their schedules.

★ ★ ★

Another jigsaw piece also proved surprisingly difficult. The F-35 embodies a complex set of capabilities developed over time. Part of the journey involved how to plan and describe the sequence, timing, and maturity of these capabilities, and, especially, how to communicate expectations among Lockheed, the JPO, and the test pilot community.

When defense executives talk about the "capabilities" of a system, they mean what outcomes it can achieve given a specific set of conditions. The Lightning's capabilities are so complex it took hundreds of software engineers and system engineers to develop them over more than a decade.

While Lockheed was making improvements in software development, the JPO and Lockheed weren't on the same page regarding the maturity of the result. Aside from that, the test pilots needed to know exactly what capabilities were being delivered and how mature those capabilities would be in order to plan their test flights.

In 2012, Will Urschel joined the JPO as the software director after serving as a technical director at Wright-Patterson. With a wide grin and glasses, he strikes one as boyish in spite of a three-decade career spent designing systems for the F-16, B-2 bomber, and even a stint with the JSF in the late 1990's. Urschel recalled, "The JPO was starting to have three-star forums on a monthly basis between the Air Force, Navy, the Marine Corps and Lockheed because they could not come to an agreement as to the status of the software or even where we were heading to.

"I went to one of those sessions. We spent the first half of the day with Lockheed explaining what they had going on in terms of the blocks and the increments and why they felt like they were in good shape. The second half of the day was the Program Office and NAVAIR explaining why they weren't . . . By the end of the day, there was no meeting of the minds as to where we were even though we'd spent the whole day and a lot of people's time . . . I met with Doug Ebersole and he said, 'I desperately need you to help sort this out because it's a "he said, she said" sort of thing and I don't know where the truth necessarily lies in this but we can't move forward because we have no agreement on how to move forward at this point.'"[6]

Urchel faced several gnarly obstacles in trying to discern and communicate the software's actual status. First was the sheer number of people involved. "This was the largest program we'd ever done. We had a program office [the JPO] that was 2,500 people, distributed across the United States in multiple sites, and a distributed test force in multiple sites, and we had no means of communicating fundamentally how we were planning on doing development and how we were going to execute that development."

The test community, which included pilots from the JPO and LM, were based at Edwards and Pax River, with some testing at the weapons range at Eglin AFB. They were used to evaluating fully mature capabilities. They would then score them using basically a yea or nay, pass-fail score on specific discrete indicators.

It was the ultimate complexity concurrency challenge- software releases needing real world testing for maturity development but not ready for ultimate pass/fail tests handed over to a test community chartered to evaluate it as a final exam.

Each capability needed to be flown and data gathered in real-world circumstances to take back to development. This was especially true of the mission systems fusion area. The laboratory just couldn't provide as much information as taking the still-immature capability onto the aircraft and flying it against realistic threats and with additional nodes in the sky to share data with.

A second group that needed a precise understanding of what capabilities were being delivered and when was the production team. They were churning out airframes as part of the low-rate initial production (LRIP) phase. Over time, those LRIP aircraft should become increasingly more capable as the major blocks completed flight test and were ready to be loaded onto the jets coming off the production line.

Urchel wanted to achieve a meeting of the minds.

For four years, I did a hundred trips a year. Every Monday I went to the program office from my home in Dayton, Ohio, and met with all the teams, and then I went from there to Lockheed every Wednesday. I said, "This is what we're talking about at the Program Office now. Let's talk about what's happening here" in order to get some feedback from the Lockheed team. Every fifth week I went to Edwards to sit down with them and say to the test community, "This is what's coming. Do you understand that? Give me some feedback in terms of what you're seeing."

Before Urchel came on board, Lockheed had been driving the ship on what capabilities would be delivered and when. At times, they would delay a capability because it wasn't ready. This frustrated folks in the JPO and the test community.

"For whatever reason, after the Nunn-McCurdy there was a decision made that we had laboratories at such a high fidelity that they would be putting fully mature capabilities out for flight test and all we would be doing then is testing for score in the flight-test program." But this was not the case. "The capabilities coming out of the lab were not ready for that."

Lockheed and the flight test community quickly came on board to put together a plan for precisely what capabilities would be delivered to flight test, when they would be delivered, and how mature they would be. The JPO and LM defined five levels of maturity, the lowest of which was "early engineering." The highest one, ready for pass-fail testing, was termed "verifiable." The "build plan" showed the number of incremental releases to flight test and the planned maturity of each of those releases.

This became the communication vehicle between the development team at Lockheed, the JPO, the flight test community, and production. Eventually, the build plan concept was expanded to include not just the onboard software but all the parts that made up the entire F-35 air system. That included pilot training, the autonomic logistics information system, and ground support equipment for maintenance. A formal block review board, chaired by the PEO, met monthly to review status. This gathering gave the government and Lockheed a common, transparent means of tracking progress and was attended by members of the test community as well.

★ ★ ★

Advanced software turned the F-35 into a war-fighting platform able to penetrate dangerous airspace undetected, accomplish its mission, and get out. It also resulted in a safer flying machine than older fighters.

Jack Hudson was introduced earlier as the first PEO for the program following contract award in 2001. Later, as the director of the Air Force Museum at Wright-Patterson, he said,

I did lots of museum tours for senior people and not-so-senior people. Sometimes, people would say, "Hey, you know, back in the fifties, we could build and fly experimental airplanes and prototypes in a matter of months or maybe a year. We could do things really quickly. What is our problem now?" So, I would tell people, back in the forties, fifties, and sixties, those were all analog airplanes. They were just mechanical airplanes without all the software that modern airplanes have. And we killed a lot of people in test programs.

It's all different today. We do not kill people in development programs and do not crash airplanes. Our modern safety record in development programs is outstanding; it is rare to crash an airplane and even rarer to have a fatality. If you look at the F-35 program, we went all the way through development without killing anybody and without crashing an airplane. That's pretty amazing with the complexity of this system.[7]

It's sobering to realize that the first F-35 (the AA-1 CTOL) was flying in 2006. It took another decade to write and mature the millions of lines of software that make the F-35 unmatched as a combat aircraft, sharing information to make fourth-generation jets more effective.

Orlando Carvalho recounted a lesson learned in Syria and Iraq:

The F-22s went into a combat area first, because they were the one airplane that could go in and not be seen by the radars. The F-22 can determine if there are any air defense radars that are up and operating, and if there are, the airplane has the ability to attack those air defense sites, but if not, that allows the fourth-generation airplanes like the F-16s, F18s, and Eurofighters to come in . . . that is the value of stealth, in that it allows you to operate in these environments that have air defense radars and to use the fifth-generation aircraft to engage it and destroy it.

The F-35 goes beyond even those impressive capabilities. From the beginning, it was designed to fuse and share information, leveraging its abilities in acquiring and communicating situational awareness across a much broader force in the air, on land, and at sea, to forge all the disparate elements of allied power into one great mailed fist.

After all, it's only software!

Reference

1.   Hamstra, Jeffrey W. *The F-35 Lightning II: From Concept to Cockpit*; Lockheed Martin Corporation; chapter 12: *F-35 Information Fusion*. American Institute of Aeronautics and Astronautics, Inc., Reston Virginia. Volume 257, Progress in Astronautics and Aeronautics, 2019.

2. Interview with Orlando Carvalho on February 26, 2015 by Betsy Clark and Adrian Pitman. Held in F-35 interview archive.

3. Interview with Jeff Morris on February 26, 2015 by Betsy Clark and Adrian Pitman. Held in F-35 interview archive.

4. Interview with Bob Hansen on 26 February 2015 by Betsy Clark and Adrian Pitman. Held in F-35 interview archive.

5. Interview with Sam Russo on 28 February 2015 by Betsy Clark and Adrian Pitman. Held in F-35 interview archive.

6. Interview with Will Urchel on 29 March 2017 by Betsy Clark and Adrian Pitman. Held in F-35 interview archive.

7. Interview with Jack Hudson on 1 August 2019 by Tom Burbage, Betsy Clark, and Adrian Pitman. Held in F-35 interview archive.

Chapter 20

EXECUTING TO THE NEW PLAN

Though the program overcame multiple challenges in development, by 2012 it hit an inflection point. It had to move from technology maturation and risk reduction to a clear focus on execution.

Unfortunately, history's littered with programs that got bloody noses while trying to vault this barrier. "What went wrong" postmortems usually attributed such failures to an inability to refocus an ingrained organizational culture on a new task. Excellence in execution is not the same as excellence in innovation! Without insightful leadership and a coherent vision for the future, the transition can fail.

From the government perspective, as discussed in the previous two chapters, VADM David Venlet was faced with navigating the shoals of the Nunn-McCurdy breach amid a tsunami of horrible publicity. He needed to re-baseline the program, while keeping the "long knives"—the Pentagon budgeteers—at bay. In project management speak, a baseline refers to the planned scope (or work to be done) within a certain cost and schedule. A baseline is an immovable standard—a line in the sand—against which a program's performance is measured. In cases such as the F-35, in which it became clear that the original baselined schedule and cost estimates were insufficient, a new baseline must be formally established against which future program performance is measured. Last, but certainly not least, Venlet had to rebuild *trust* in the program, not just for the United States, but in eight other partner countries.

Orlando Carvalho took over the reins of the Lockheed Martin prime contractor team shortly after the restructuring plan was being implemented. Carvalho recalled,

> The program needed someone who was going to come in and bring everybody together. Dave Venlet was what the program needed at the time. But below his level, there was a tremendous amount of antagonism that was going on

267

between the government and ourselves as the prime contractor . . . there were many people in the government who felt that we had been dishonest in characterizing the status of the program. . . . The truth of it is that there wasn't anyone on the company side that was trying to be dishonest, but there was a tremendous amount of optimism that in fairness was overstated.[1]

Carvalho believed what was construed as dishonesty by some stakeholders was due to the fact the program had constantly been in recovery mode ever since the STOVL weight crisis. Despite everyone's best efforts, they'd been unable to catch up, and continually chasing their tails made it difficult to understand exactly where the program was.

★   ★   ★

In July 2012, Maj Gen Chris Bogdan became the deputy to VADM David Venlet. Bogdan was an imposing, no-nonsense Air Force test pilot and acquisition executive with a notably abrasive, even adversarial demeanor. Bogdan took the program on a different path, one focused on delivering on the new commitments. But his "take no prisoners" style created tension across the government-industry-international partnership. He quickly gained a reputation for publicly presenting often-harsh assessments of issues he felt were hindering progress.

As one example, shortly after arrival, he made headlines by characterizing what he called a "dysfunctional relationship" between Lockheed Martin and the other stakeholders as "the worst I have ever seen."[2] This comment came as a surprise to many, including the contractor team, and created considerable outrage when it was publicly reported. But the blunt comments, it seems, were part of Bogdan's game plan to regain control of the program (for which he was being held accountable) from the contractor.

He went on to explain. "When I first got here, I saw things that I really did not like. The biggest concern for me was culture, culture across the whole enterprise." He felt that the culture and the behavior he observed were very dysfunctional. "The stakeholders and Lockheed were pointing fingers at each other. And sitting right in the middle was this JPO. When Admiral Venlet came along, he recognized that problem, but he needed planners who could put realism into the new baseline in terms of cost, schedule and performance. They were good, but they were planners; they were not [program] executers."

In Bogdan's view, there were two reasons for the dysfunction. "The first reason was, from about 2003 to 2010 this program was based on the concept that the contractor would run the program."

The second was what he considered a lack of accountability by both Lockheed and JPO team members. He, and other program executives, believed that the root cause of the relationship and accountability issues was the Total System Performance Responsibility (TSPR) reform, introduced in the late 1990s. As mentioned in an earlier chapter, the JSF contract was aligned with TSPR acquisition reform principles that intentionally provided the contractor greater flexibility and scope to make design decisions, so long as key performance parameters were met.

The mantra of "acquisition reform" seems to cycle in and out of vogue as budget pressures increase or wane. Often, it's advertised as a cost-reduction initiative to deal with the political headwinds of a postwar "peace dividend." As part of this iteration of "reform," TSPR promised to cut costs and shorten schedules by reducing bureaucracy and commercializing the acquisition process. This allowed contractors to use more streamlined industry standards and practices, and to adopt a more flexible, less government-regulated management approach. While increasing the role of the contractor, though, TSPR reduced the degree of government oversight in the systems engineering development process.

Trade space decisions are meant to ensure that a capability solution is cost-effective, viable, feasible, and within program constraints. Reducing oversight and reporting and allowing contractors to leverage industry best practices to enable trade space decisions were central to the JSF program from the beginning. Bogdan described the impact:

> It was written into the contract. Give the contractor the money and let them go. And this JPO, despite its best efforts, was caught in that paradigm shift, and Lockheed and Pratt—much more Lockheed than Pratt—operated the program and ran the program from the early years to 2010 like they were in charge. Like it was their money, it was their requirements, it was their program to manage. So, the JPO needed to learn how to behave like that. They were simply overseeing with no input, with no direction, just watching.[3]

This problem had also been recognized earlier by the JPO PM, Matt Mulhern, who was encouraging JPO staff to become more engaged with the contractor in making decisions.

The JPO attitude Bogdan and Mulhern observed had been reported by other unsuccessful TSPR-based programs. TSPR was predicated on greater government *insight*, rather than *oversight*. However, the "insight" concept, which needed skilled and knowledgeable government staff working with the contractor, was seldom realized. This often resulted in further cost blowouts and schedule slippage.[4]

To the contractor team, Bogdan's criticism seemed overstated. They'd solicited full participation from their JPO counterparts, NAVAIR technical experts, and other stakeholders, with endless reviews by groups that weren't part of the original budgeted events. Bogdan's attacks also surprised some senior managers in the JPO who'd been working with their counterparts at LM to improve the relationship and share responsibility. Was it *really* the worst situation Bogdan had ever seen in his acquisition career? Maybe, but in the opinion of many participants, the situation was a hell of a lot better than what was being broadcast.

Venlet, Bogdan, and Mulhern had identified the unintended impacts TSPR was having on the program and staff. They then focused on implementing changes to address them. Over a three-month period, responsibilities and accountability were clearly identified, responsibility matrix diagrams were drawn up, and individuals assigned to their counterparts in the opposite team. Staff exchanged email addresses and phone numbers with their counterparts. System engineering fundamentals were reinstated, and external experts were appointed to chair technical reviews, while responsibility for outcomes was shared between contractor and government team leads.

While TSPR originated as a well-intentioned reform, it remains moot whether a more traditional government-led approach could have avoided the downsides that nearly derailed the program. However, the initiatives by Venlet and particularly Bogdan—making JPO staff more responsible and accountable, establishing a Block Review Board process to manage capability development and improving flight test program management did improve overall execution.

Bogdan believed another constraint to getting things back on track was a government edict capping the tenure of the PEO appointment to two years. He felt that was too brief a time to make the cultural changes needed to achieve greater government control. After he got permission from Under Secretary of

Defense Kendall, he amended the program charter, leaving the period of future appointments to the respective service chiefs. As he recalled, "That gave me the ability to turn to Lockheed Martin and Pratt & Whitney and say 'I'm going to be here ten years, so don't try to wait me out. You better get on board with what we're doing and where we're going. That was a big deal for me."[5]

While Bogdan didn't stay for ten years, the change to the charter resulted in extending his tenure as PEO until May 2017.

★ ★ ★

In February 2013, after two months in the PEO seat, Bogdan again made headlines when he flamed LM and P&W during a briefing at the Avalon Air Show in Melbourne, Australia. He told the audience he wasn't there as a salesman for the F-35. Instead, he'd report "the good, the bad and the ugly" and let them decide. He allowed that technical issues were being solved, and milestones were being met. While software remained a concern, it was improving, and the time taken to remediate concurrency issues—i.e., retrofit airplanes from earlier production with the latest developments—was better too. He went on to identify the unit cost of an airplane coming off the production line as his main concern. It wasn't dropping as much as he'd expected, and production lot negotiations were too drawn out.

Reflecting on that briefing, Bogdan expressed frustration. "We were in the middle of Lot 5 negotiations and it was going on for like, seventeen months. I came in the middle of it and the behavior I saw from Lockheed Martin was just amazing to me. I made a comment there where I said, 'I am just tired of Lockheed Martin trying to squeeze every nickel out of the US government as if it was the last F-35 they were ever going to sell us and not realizing they're going to sell three thousand more airplanes to us.'"

Again, the contractor community had a different view. They'd been taught a hard lesson on earlier programs, such as the F-22, which required significant private investment. Lockheed had pushed its chips into the pot, with the expectation to turn a profit over a run of some 750 airplanes. But Congress had blocked any possible future sales of that fighter to other countries following revelations Israel might have shared technology with China (the 1998 Obey Amendment). This, along with the fading of the USSR as a competitor and the demands of counterinsurgency operations after 9/11, had decreased buys and thus increased unit costs to the point the F-22 had been terminated after only 187 were produced.[6] Northrop's B-2 had suffered similar reductions, with Secretary Dick Cheney canceling production at only twenty-one planes.[7]

Both experiences had reduced the business cases for the massive investments demanded of contractors, especially in buying and setting up the new infrastructure required for mass production.

Most acquisition program managers understand that development phases will require significant investment, yet provide puny, if any, returns. But mass production should allow the recovery of those inputs, while beginning to provide yield to stockholders. For the industry teams, negotiations that required such heavy investments placed them in a dangerous position . . . much like the failed gambles that had wrecked other aerospace companies, such as Northrop.

Regardless, Bogdan's "squeeze every nickel" dis sparked a worldwide press and social media response. Some responses were critical, concerned that his statement might harm the defense industry relationship with the Pentagon. Other stakeholders expressed appreciation at his openness, while still others speculated that he might have overstepped his authority in expressing those views.

While the first two years of Bogdan's appointment as PEO were directed at reestablishing government control, other issues had to be dealt with too. Along with transitioning the culture from planning to execution, technical problems remained, affordability in terms of the cost per plane (unit cost) still needed addressing, and the Marine Corps was hot to achieve initial operating capability.

Within two months of his appointment, Bogdan started his campaign to reestablish trust, based on the foundations established by Venlet.

Bogdan recalled, "I told my JPO and the contractor that this program runs on only two things—money and trust. If you don't have money, you don't have a program, and if you don't have trust, you also don't have a program." He applied this principle as he visited every international partner twice in his first two years. "I took very few people with me, and I just stood up in front of their Defense Ministries and their Air Chiefs and, if they let me, their parliamentarians."

The same open and transparent approach was being practiced by Lockheed Martin. Adrian Pitman, Director of Acquisition Engineering Improvement in the Australian Department of Defence, and his colleague, Dr. Betsy Clark, a principal consultant to the department and expert on development of software-intensive systems, visited Lockheed Martin's F-35 sites on multiple occasions after the Nunn-McCurdy breach to conduct status reviews. Pitman recounted,

Each time we visited we were briefed on new issues that had arisen and the "get well" status of the problems discussed on previous visits. We were impressed with Lockheed's honesty and willingness to openly discuss new problems they had identified, solutions planned, and the "fixes" they had successfully implemented. This gave us the confidence to report back to the Australian DoD that, based on Lockheed's willingness to identify the problems and their success in resolving them, we strongly believed the program would be successful and was unlikely to delay the Australian IOC target of 2020.[8]

The reports generated blowback from the strong Boeing influence in Australia but the finding was realized in December 2020 when the Royal Australian Air Force announced that their F-35A IOC had been achieved.

LM's transparency also allowed the JPO to anticipate many of the issues and concerns raised by the US director of operational test and evaluation (DOT&E) in his annual report to Congress and the secretary of defense. As noted in an earlier chapter, DOT&E conducts independent assessments of major defense acquisition programs. The reports, on occasion, can create a dispute with a program office or service OT&E agencies regarding the effectiveness of their OT&E program. Furthermore, the F-35 report often included problems that had since been resolved. Consequently, when the reports were released publicly, they created the impression the program was in a worse position than was really the case.

When asked if DOT&E was helpful, Bogdan said, "There was nothing ever in the DOT&E report that we didn't know about and there was nothing in the reports that we weren't already working on." If the reports had exposed issues held close by Lockheed Martin but unknown to the JPO, the effort and time needed to immediately investigate and respond to them would have been much greater.

As Bogdan completed his term in 2017, the program was well on the road to recovery. He'd led the F-35 enterprise to achieve both U.S. Marine and Air Force IOC, production rates were increased, and unit cost had been reduced . . . albeit perhaps insufficiently for his liking. While his sometimes-controversial public statements weren't appreciated by his targets, the program did, at last, achieve consistency in adhering to schedule and budget that had been sadly lacking in its early years.

While DoD was responsible for determining and planning the response to the Nunn–McCurdy breach, it would be wrong to think recovery could be achieved solely by government action. Buy-in, support, and strong leadership from LM and its subcontractors were essential. Although the government provided additional funding and schedule relief, recovery would largely depend on the industry partners' ability to execute the re-baselined plan. This responsibility fell to Lorraine Martin and Jeff Babione, who were appointed to lead industry's effort during the four and a half years of Lt Gen Bogdan's tenure.

Lorraine Martin, a straightforward, articulate, unflappable, talented leader and skilled program manager, joined the program to lead the contractor team in February 2012. As a USAF officer and twenty-five-year veteran of LM, she brought experience and credibility. Martin had successfully run other large LM efforts, including the C-130 Hercules and C-5 Galaxy modernization and production programs. "I was brought on in part because of my ability to successfully partner with customers. I was perceived as someone who was able to build effective partnerships and work through very difficult challenges, arriving at gain for both parties. No one had to lose for others to come out ahead."[9]

She knew she had her work cut out for her after Bogdan's "the worst I've ever seen" statement. "I was sitting in the audience in the front row when he said it. He was referring to our inability to close contracts and work problems together." She set about to address the issues with Bogdan to make sure both the Lockheed and JPO teams were in sync to solve problems and execute to the plan. She and Bogdan cochaired a twice-weekly meeting via teleconference, each with their leadership team. "I was so proud of our team and their efforts to establish confidence and rebuild trust through every commitment, on every day."

The re-baseline out of Nunn-McCurdy required Martin and Bogdan to simultaneously execute on three main program tasks: completing development and test, ramping up production, and standing up supply and infrastructure around the world to support delivered aircraft and Initial Operational Capability (IOC) for each of the US services and international partners. These efforts included complex and interdependent activities that had to be managed within cost and schedule.

One aspect Martin viewed as essential was a common set of metrics and plans so that both the JPO and Lockheed were singing from the same sheet of music, so to speak. "We have joint metrics and status to plans, we don't have two different ways of saying where we are anymore. There is one set of data. And that is hugely important so that we can accurately represent to our stakeholders where the program is against the re-baselined plan and it's the same story. We are dedicated to getting things resolved and not letting them fester."

Lorraine considered Bogdan a "hands-on leader" who had to get into the details—what she referred to as "full-contact program management." However, she believed his in-your-face management style required her and her team to lean into the relationship, not away from it. Over four years, she and Bogdan weathered some of the most critical aspects of program recovery as they partnered to execute to plan. Some have reflected that she was exactly the right contractor counterpart at the right time. When later asked for his opinion on their working relationship, Bogdan reflected,

> Lorraine Martin was indeed an excellent partner as the LM F-35 PM during my very tumultuous first few years as the PEO. She knew how to handle my aggressive leadership style and spent many hours building a trusted partnership with me and the JPO. I knew at times she was taking big risks by giving me insights into Lockheed Martin's thinking and actions. It helped me understand their motivations so I could devise strategies where the government and LM could both succeed even though success looked somewhat different for each of us. I am proud of what we accomplished together during those first few years, and Lorraine should get a lot of the credit for that.[10]

In January 2016, Jeff Babione succeeded Lorraine as program manager after serving as F-35 deputy program manager. His commanding physical stature, technical acumen, and focus on motivation made him an excellent leader during a difficult period. When asked to comment on his relationship with Bogdan, Jeff said:

> General Bogdan is a very hard driver, and his leadership on the JPO side has added accountability that wasn't there before. I don't really like it when he gets into the details, because it can be painful—but the guy really understands it, he's incredibly smart and detail-oriented. So, I think he took it back, in his mind, from just watching it happen to having an influence over the outcome, and given the two types of customers, I'd much rather have the customer who's engaged and who feels like they have a role in the destiny versus just constantly blaming us for what we haven't done.[11]

In discussing the technical challenges, Babione described the F-35 as a "once-in-a-generation program." Its three different customers (Air Force, Navy, and Marines) with three different operating domains (conventional, vertical, and carrier landings) requiring three aircraft variants. There were also different certification requirements for Air Force and Navy.

"New technologies had to be developed. The electrohydraulic actuators, the integrated power pack, the helmet mounted display, and the distribute aperture system added complexity. These systems, plus the mission system fusion capability, multi-role weapons integration and the autonomic logistics information system, necessitated an extraordinary level of software development."

Babione's grasp of the F-35's technical complexity and his engineering acumen built on twenty-five years of experience with the F-22 program prepared him for his leadership role in executing the program. His value as a senior leader was reflected in his subsequent appointment as vice president and general manager of the Skunk Works in 2018.

★   ★   ★

In December 2016, RADM Mat Winter became the new deputy PEO under Bogdan. Earlier in his naval career, Winter had served operational tours as an A-6E Intruder bombardier/navigator and later as a technical lead in the JPO as chief engineer for the Joint Strike Fighter Integrated Flight and Propulsion Control. He also had extensive acquisition experience on several other defense programs and as Chief of Naval Research. This all paid off when he relieved Bogdan as PEO in May 2017.

In planning his approach, Winter emphasized that the F-35 program is a global enterprise with a global customer base and a global supply chain. The jet was faced with a growing international demand coupled with the need for capability growth to maintain air superiority in a rapidly evolving threat environment. The program had to continue parallel lines of effort for production, new development, and sustainment, for many decades to come . . . not the typically sequential phases of "design it, produce it, sustain it" for the typical single-service customer program. The Lightning II would call for a far more rigorous resourcing strategy in terms of funding and availability of skills, manpower, facilities, and material, and it would extend over many decades.

One of Winter's first tasks was defining and funding the follow-on modernization. Block 4 would be the first upgrade following initial development. It would require integrating a complex set of new requirements, many originating from the diverse F-35 customer base.

Digging into the requirements, he soon saw that the cost estimate and implementation schedule for the Block-4 upgrade had been underestimated. As they updated the onboard mission systems with new capabilities, designers also needed to modernize the ground-based support systems including ALIS (now called ODIN).

Winter's analysis showed that the cost to fully incorporate the Block 4 capability was far greater than it would have been to simply upgrade the plane. When the associated off-board systems were included, the price tag more than doubled.

Another concern he had about Block 4, as well as future upgrades, was the relationship between an upgrade's scope and the time it took to develop, test, and certify it. Larger scale upgrades took longer, a major factor to consider when trying to field new capability.

So, Winter introduced a more agile approach. He proposed frequent, incremental delivery of new capabilities, versus the original plan of a major software upgrade at the completion of Block 4 development. He explained, "Done well, this will allow the war fighter to prioritise capability delivery to match [and keep pace with] the changing threat environment."[12]

In April 2018 the JPO and Lockheed Martin announced the completion of development flight test. In a public statement, Winter recognized how extraordinary this was. "Since the first flight of AA-1 in 2006, the developmental flight test program has operated for more than eleven years mishap-free, conducting more than 9,200 sorties, accumulating over 17,000 flight hours, and executing more than 65,000 test points to verify the design of all three F-35 variants. Congratulations to our F-35 Test Team and the broader F-35 Enterprise for delivering this new powerful and decisive capability to the war fighter."[13]

The achievement was also recognised by Greg Ulmer, LM's vice president and general manager of the program. "The F-35 flight test program represents the most comprehensive, rigorous and the safest developmental flight test program in aviation history. The joint government and industry team demonstrated exceptional collaboration and expertise, and the results have given the men and women who fly the F-35 great confidence in its transformational capability."[14]

During Winter's three-year leadership, the enterprise passed a significant number of major milestones. They included completing the mission system software, expanding sustainment and establishing international repair depots around the world, continuing the ramp-up in production, finishing the development flight test program, and achieving initial operating capability for the U.S. Navy and several partner countries.

★　★　★

Since the Nunn-McCurdy breach recovery began, the cost per airplane has decreased significantly. At the time of writing, the unit cost of a multi-role F-35A is *below* that of an equivalently configured and less-capable fourth-generation jet.

The bottom line may be that this program had the good fortune of having the right people at the right time to navigate stormy waters. The change agents Venlet-Lawson and the JPO recovery team of Bogdan-Winter, in partnership with Orlando Carvalho, Lorraine Martin, and Jeff Babione, and their Pratt & Whitney counterparts, were essential to the Lightning II's survival of the rockiest and longest acquisition process in history.

Reference

1. Interview with Orlando Carvalho on February 26, 2015 by Betsy Clark and Adrian Pitman. Held in F-35 interview archive.

2. Clark, Colin, "F-35 Program's Relationship with Lockheed 'Worst I've Ever Seen', says Gen. Bogdan," Breaking Defense, September 17, 2012. Available online https://breakingdefense.com/2012/09/f-35-programs-relationship-with-lockheed-worst-ive-ever-seen/, accessed November 30, 2022.

3. Interview with Lt Gen Chris Bogdan on March 25, 2017 by Betsy Clark and Adrian Pitman. Held in the F-35 interview archive.

4. Johnson, Ashley, "The Implementation of Total System Performance Responsibility to Avoid a Weakened Systems Engineering Department," (2010). LMU/LLS Theses and Dissertations. 403. https://digitalcommons.lmu.edu/etd/403, accessed December 20, 2022.

5. Interview with Lt Gen Chris Bogdan on March 25, 2017 by Betsy Clark and Adrian Pitman. Held in the F-35 interview archive.

6. Wikipedia. "Lockheed Martin F-22 Raptor," accessed April 6, 2023.

7. Wikipedia. "Northrop Grumman B-2 Spirit," accessed April 6, 2023.

8. Statement included by F-35 book contributing co-author. Entered on December 12, 2022.

9. Interview with Lorraine Martin on February 25, 2015, by Betsy Clark and Adrian Pitman. Held in the F-35 interview archive.

10. Statement by Chris Bogdan December 28, 2022, in email correspondence with Adrian Pitman. Held in the F-35 interview archive.

11. Interview with Jeff Babione on February 27, 2015, by Betsy Clark and Adrian Pitman. Held in the F-35 interview archive.

12. Interview with VADM Mat Winter on November 15, 2017, by Betsy Clark and Adrian Pitman and interview on December 5, 2018, by Betsy Clark and Jeff Morris. Held in the F-35 interview archive.

13. VADM Mat Winter and Greg Ulmer quoted in United States Air Force website article "F-35 program completes most comprehensive flight test program in aviation history," published April 13, 2018, by Joint Program Office Public Affairs. Accessed December 20, 2022.

14. Ibid.

Chapter 21

BUILDING THE BEAST

A mericans may have our shortcomings, but over the last two centuries the world's agreed on one thing: We're geniuses at mass production. Eli Whitney pioneered it. Henry Ford developed it into an art. We win wars and defend democracy with it.

The building of the F-35 was another illustration of that national talent.

Lockheed Martin's plant in Fort Worth can stand as an example of many other manufacturing enterprises in the Lightning's ecosystem. In June 1941 a railroad spur was laid from the main track five miles north to a new airstrip and industrial plant to support the war effort. The spur would deliver construction materials for the plant, then parts to build bombers, then fuel to fly them out. Originally named Fort Worth Army Air Field, it later became Carswell Air Force Base.[1] The factory, first called United States Air Force Plant 4, was later occupied by Convair, then General Dynamics, and finally Lockheed Martin.[2] It produced over three thousand B-24 Liberators, the B-32 Dominator, the B-35 Peacemaker, the B-58 Hustler, and the F-111 before entering the modern age with the F-16.[3]

Scenes from the James Stewart movie *Strategic Air Command* were filmed on the flight line. In 2008, the Texas Historical Commission designated Plant 4 an historical landmark limiting how much Lockheed Martin could modify the plant's structure. This would be a challenge as the new need to mass-produce F-35s would drive innovative production strategies and global facility lash-ups.

By the early 2000s, it was the only place on earth an observer could watch three successive generations of fighters rolling off assembly lines at the same time. The three planes were the F-16, the F-22, and the F-35.

The YF-16 had won the lightweight fighter competition in the early 1970s. Later named the F-16 Fighting Falcon, it has been in production for the USAF and allied nations since 1976.

The Falcon introduced several innovations, including fly-by-wire flight controls that increased maneuverability in a dogfight. It also debuted the bubble canopy. (The old multipiece design protected the pilot from bird strikes but limited his visibility—not a great feature in a visual dogfight.) Technology and materials had evolved to the point where thickness could be varied without hurting optical quality. Designed as an air superiority day fighter, it evolved through many upgrades to be a superbly effective all-weather, multi-role aircraft, and the workhorse for more than thirty air forces. Its manufacturing involved vertical integration, traditional metal machining, assembly in a single position on the assembly line without moving from station to station, and incorporation of proven systems from previous planes. Parts would arrive at one end of the mile-long factory, and a Fighting Falcon would be assembled in pace and then roll out the other end about two years later.

The loser of the lightweight fighter competition had been the Northrop YF-17. Northrop later teamed with McDonnell Douglas to compete for the Navy Air Combat Fighter. That entry became the very successful F-18 Hornet. With the downselect of the F-35, McDonnell Douglas was acquired by Boeing, and Northrop Grumman became a principal partner of Lockheed Martin on the F-35. Boeing and Lockheed Martin would now find themselves, as the two remaining prime contractors, competing over the next four decades for the global fighter market.

Further complicating the "friend vs. foe" business dealings was the F-22 Raptor program. The Raptor was the first fifth-generation fighter, incorporating low-observability technology evolved from the F-117 Nighthawk and the B-2 Spirit. Lockheed, General Dynamics, and Boeing had agreed to team up to win and then execute the contract. The F-22 was a much larger, two-engine aircraft compared to the F-16. Its construction required the fabrication of advanced hard metal structures, and it began the expansion of the use of modern composite materials.

While the new requirements for stealth dramatically expanded operational capability, it imposed tough manufacturing demands. Producibility engineers had to make sure the design could actually be built at a reasonable rate and cost. Scalability, the ability of the supply chain and production processes to move to high rates of production, has been the demise of many production promises and remains a unique capability of the US prime manufacturers.

The F-22 was crafted from three major subassemblies. The General Dynamics Fort Worth piece was the center fuselage. This structure incorporated internal weapon bays and main landing gear. A set of "hard toolings," large and heavy structural jigs, had to be designed and built to maintain tight alignment when the "big pieces" came together.

Thus, a stroll down that mile-long factory floor was already a lesson in the steady advance of aerospace manufacturing.

But the biggest jump forward was yet to come.

★ ★ ★

In the Fort Worth facility, the F-35 shared the same factory with the F-16 and F-22 in the early days of building the test planes and developing the technologies needed for eventual mass production.

In 2004, Don Kinard got the job of revolutionizing traditional production concepts as the F-35 production engineering director. Kinard eventually became a production senior fellow, which is a rare honor for Lockheed Martin employees. Kinard's sense of humor and genuine concern for mentoring the younger manufacturing engineers coupled with his depth of technical knowledge made him a perfect fit for this assignment. Don had worked in production for twenty years on the F-16 and F-22. He understood how new materials and manufacturing techniques could speed production. And one of the greatest challenges facing the JSF team was the government's expectation of higher production rates and quantities than any previous program, at least in peacetime.

But as Kinard came aboard, the program was confronting the stark realities of the weight issue, and the truly frightening fact that it might wreck the original concept of a common production line assembling all three variants.

The F-35 had been sold as an affordable fifth-generation fighter largely based on the use of common parts across the three variants. With the redesign during the SWAT activity, the designs diverged and relied on what were called "cousin" parts, meaning they were no longer identical but they could be produced with the same manufacturing tooling. The cost savings were real, but critics of the F-35 focused on the disappearance of identical parts.

★ ★ ★

Kinard remembers,

> While operational and weight reduction requirements were driving significant
> changes in the underlying structural differences, there was a belief that those
> challenges could be offset by the new digital process enhancements. This was
> a change and generated political challenges and social media trumpeting of
> the move away from piece part commonality that were difficult to counter.
> Advanced manufacturing and machining technologies could soften the impact
> of these changes and could accommodate production of different part specifica-
> tions and assemblies on the same machines. Additionally, digital integration of
> common structure and major subassemblies offset any differences at the part
> level. These revolutionary changes to traditional manufacturing lore were dif-
> ficult to explain to the critics but withstood the test of time. The development
> of 3D digital models for all parts significantly reduced form, fit, and function
> changes common to new programs and dramatically improved fabrication and
> assembly processes.
>
> Today, all three F-35 variants are produced on a common production line.
> Digital virtual assembly of the major structural elements is conducted while
> they are still in their individual production factories before they are ever deliv-
> ered to the final assembly operation in Fort Worth. The assembly facility in
> Fort Worth employs automation, robotics, and other advanced manufacturing
> technologies to a level not seen in other defense programs, dramatically reduc-
> ing assembly time and cost while improving quality.[4]

One of the most significant reasons all of this became possible was the F-35
"Digital Thread."

For previous designs, up to and including the F-22, computer technology
couldn't support three-dimensional modeling. While engineering specifications
were very precise, the two-dimensional drawings had to go through a translation process to design the tooling that would fabricate the parts, hold the subassemblies in place, and complete the final assembly. In essence, the airplane was
built to the tooling tolerances, not to the engineering drawings. As the tooling
aged, mismatches and gaps between various parts grew and had to be patched
over. The smallest imperfections had to be dealt with.

For a stealth design, this was a major issue. It contributed to the early reputation of stealth aircraft as difficult to build and maintain.

But, as luck would have it, the convergence of these new complexities would align with the rapidly evolving computer-aided design technologies.

In the early days, there were several different 3D design tools. They weren't compatible and were fiercely protected as intellectual property. All three of the F-35 industry partners used different tools. For the designers, the rub was that the tools didn't work together well. Complex details could be lost at the interfaces. To make the digital thread really powerful, designers would have to use identical, or at least compatible, 3D computer programs throughout the engineering, manufacturing, assembly, testing and sustainment phases. But to convert all the industrial partners would require heavy investments, which few had anticipated.

At the time, Tom Blakely was VP for engineering for Lockheed Martin Aeronautics. Blakely recalls,

> I was worried about the core architecture of the digital thread called the product design data system, or PDDS, which is wrapped around all of the Joint Strike Fighter for development and production. I had been responsible for investing company money to get the PDDS system up and operating. The PDDS tool had been under development for five or six years at that point and I just didn't feel like we had the requirements right but I could see how critical it was for the success of the program. I just had a very uneasy feeling about whether we in engineering were doing all the right things.
>
> The way PDDS works is that we would release the engineering models that were mathematical digital images and in very complicated graphics format. Then when we were confident that the design of the part was right, that it was going to fit in all dimensions, we vaulted it in PDDS, and our subcontractors were given a password and they would come in and pull that model out and then they would fabricate the part and ship it to us. No paper at all was transferred to the subcontractors. And these companies might be in Turkey or Australia, or all over the world. And I just wanted to see, is this going to work? Is this tool that is so complicated going to work or have we just created a monster that we're going to fight forever?
>
> Our first assembly was a starboard forward fuselage, a part of the integrated forward body around the cockpit area. It had some metal substructure and then

composite skin panels. And the thing went together like a Lego. I mean zero shimming, no cutting, no line drilling. You just can't imagine my relief, because I worried that maybe we had missed something because none of us had ever done it before.[5]

★ ★ ★

The second big producibility breakthrough was outer mold line control.

What's the "outer mold line"? When you look at your profile in the mirror, your outer mold line is on display. (We all wish we could control that!)

The F-35 used composites (sophisticated plastics) for all its skin surfaces. As outer mold line control matured, it became clear that the skins could be manufactured with sacrificial plys, or excess material, that could then be "shaved" from the inside to present an outer mold line with no variances (they cause radar reflections).

Thus, this plane could be repeatably built to the engineering specifications, instead of to the limitations of the tooling. The composites could also incorporate classified characteristics impossible to achieve with the old-style metal claddings. All this resulted in a dramatic reduction in expensive coatings and the maintenance thereof . . . and made it possible for the fighter to operate from U.S. Navy, Marine Corps, Royal Navy, and Italian Navy ships.

Kinard recalled, "There were a lot of other complications. US government International Trafficking in Arms Controls laws required different levels of access to the design database for every partner country. This meant that, although engineers across the world were operating as a team, each country could only access certain sections of the overall design database."

Complicating things even more, the temperature at every major assembly factory had to be compatible. This was to prevent thermal mismatches when major assemblies built in geographically distant facilities came together for final assembly in Fort Worth. (**See Figure 26: The Miracle of the Loaves and the Fishes**)

Kinard added,

The digital thread was also an enabler of several key advantages once higher production rates were achieved. It had a great advantage in employment of digital systems like auto drilling, robotic systems and automated application of final finishes.

Our first objective was to try to automate the "3D" processes: dull, dirty, and dangerous. These were tasks that people were not suited for or did not want to do. For example, there are some seventy thousand holes that need to be drilled and countersunk on the F-35 in the final assembly process. Automating that eliminates the human factors of fatigue and boring, repetitive tasks as well as the complicated human factors limitations of trying to manually control drills in very constrained spaces.

Historically, the aerospace worker referred to a large paper book to guide him- or herself through detailed assembly tasks. Now the digital thread plus an optical system projected assembly sequence information directly on the part being worked. Thus, no continual back-and-forth to the book, reducing the chance of human error.

One major adjustment that had to be made was modifying the original strategy of designing for rapid assembly, needed to accommodate the anticipated high production rates. Some of those rapid-assembly features had to be changed to fix the weight issues as they surfaced.

"The bottom line of those changes was that F-35 was a lighter, more efficient fighter . . . The SWAT redesign also helped to allow more time to complete the complex software requirements for the airplane," Kinard said.

★ ★ ★

Midstream changes became the bane of the production people. At some point, management had to "break the pencils" of the engineers—who focused on the (unattainable) perfect solution—to get a decent product out the door on time and within budget.

To stay abreast of the changes, the three primary partners, Lockheed Martin, Northrop Grumman, and BAE Systems, had to set up common digital tools with every supplier of the parts for their subassemblies. That included international second sources. These second sources were required for two critical reasons. First was to meet the potential future high production rates which would stress the global aerospace manufacturing supply chain and, secondly, to meet industrial participation expectations which were politically important for keeping program sold in the partner countries. Northrop Grumman's center fuselage partner was Turkish Aerospace. Lockheed Martin's alternative wing producers were the LM Marietta facility in Georgia and the Cameri production facility in Italy. BAE vertical tails were supported by Marand in Australia. The second source for the outer wings on the C variant (the part that folds up for parking on the flight deck) was Magellan Aerospace in Canada. The second sources all required support and training to meet the same quality standards as the primes.

★ ★ ★

The F-35 PEO, BGen CR Davis, was in the hot seat during the introduction of the program's novel manufacturing practices. In his words,

> The design of the airplane and the integration of complex systems may have been the easy part. Putting together this brand-new state-of-the-art manu-facturing line that incorporated all the new technologies of the past twenty years was monumental. When we started building the F-35, everything was new. . . . The design tools were new, the machinery like the five-axis milling machines, the use of advanced composites was new. It started revealing a lot of the challenge that we had with maintaining commonality of parts across the airplane. I remember very well a lot of the parts that the engineers could design with the Digital Thread had very complex intricate design shapes and radiuses. Historically these parts would have been very difficult to produce. But now you could take it to a five-axis milling machine company, and they could figure out a way to program their machines and go mill the thing.
>
> I still marvel at the challenge of creating the manufacturing line on top of a very new, very complex design. It really took up a lot of the time getting ready to build the very first variant.[6]

★ ★ ★

Capacity management also reared its ugly head as the volume of production fluctuated. All the international partners had signed the memorandum of understanding indicating their intention to buy a specific number of airplanes in specific years. But design challenges, politics, changing threat perceptions, and budgeting priorities meant the final order numbers were always in flux.

The key to stabilizing production was to have an efficient growth plan for the main factory, while managing the parallel European production facility in

Cameri, Italy. As other strategically important allies beyond the initial partnership signed on, additional assembly facilities had to be planned for, built, and started up.

Initially, management planned for Fort Worth to make the wing and forward fuselage, receive the other two main subassemblies from Northrop Grumman and BAE Systems, and conduct the final assembly and checkout. The forward fuselage was where everything came together for the pilot. It incorporated most of the classified interfaces, and building it "at home" made sense. The wing was a major subassembly too, but it could be second-sourced as production rates increased and factory acreage for final assembly and checkout grew scarce.

With the end of F-22 Raptor production in 2011, two opportunities emerged. The F-22 center fuselage production space became available at the main factory in Fort Worth. This would allow the needed space for the extensive checkout processes once the airplane was assembled. The Raptor final assembly area at LM Marietta, Georgia was freed up as well, along with a skilled workforce, making it the ideal place to move the F-35 wing assembly. The Cameri facility could also produce the wings for planes that would be built on that line.

The factory that had once produced the F-16, F-22, and F-35 at the same time was slowly becoming home for just one.

The last legacy design to sunset in Fort Worth, after over forty-five years in production, was the F-16 line. The USAF had long since stopped procuring the lightweight plane. The international market was still active, but at a much lower level of demand. As Lightning II manufacture ramped up, Falcon production moved to another building, then eventually to another site entirely, completing Fort Worth's transition to the F-35 exclusively. In the past few years, the F-16 line has been restarted in Greenville, South Carolina, and is due to deliver their first aircraft in 2023 with more than a hundred more in the queue.

But building such a complex, densely packed, tight-tolerance plane in volumes not seen since World War II required lean manufacturing and a thorough and ruthless rethinking of process flow. LM hired Toyota production system engineers to take a critical look. Soon phrases like "Kaizan events," "green belts," and "black belts" peppered conversations in the factory. Management also invited Formula One race experts to describe their rapid turnaround techniques. When a Formula One race car showed up on the factory floor and the mechanics showed how rapidly things had to be done to be a winner, it was a very visual lesson on the value of concentrating on process improvement.

Most important, the precision of the digital thread allowed a virtual assembly process before the major subassemblies ever left their home factories. As a result, potential mismatches were corrected before they arrived in Texas. Precision leveling devices, required only to align the components for final mating, replaced the massive, complex hard tooling previously necessary to fix mismatches on the shop floor.

But true success depended on rethinking the entire supply-chair "ecosystem." Alternative sources had to be in place. Uncertainties had to be guarded against. It was clear to everyone that there would be "unknown unknowns," to borrow former secretary of defense Donald Rumsfeld's quirky phrase. Enough resilience had to be built in to accept and overcome unanticipated shocks.

Here's one example. Turkey was slated as the biggest buyer of the international allies, with plans to buy 175 F-35s. But in 2019, that longtime ally and critical NATO partner decided to procure the Russian S-400 "Triumph" surface-to-air missile system.

Granted, Türkiye—the country's preferred spelling these days—had an urgent need for air defense, considering the American invasion of Iraq, the civil war raging in neighboring Syria, and other unrest in the area. (Oddly, President Recep Erdoğan didn't seem to consider Moscow a threat, despite Russian air incursions.)[7] They were frustrated by the unwillingness of the United States to provide the latest technology. Finally, the mercurial Erdoğan signed on the dotted line for the S-400.

But . . . Turkey was a NATO member! The S-400 would compromise NATO's integrated air defense. Even worse, it might allow critical F-35 technical data to be fed back to Russian intelligence.

In response, the United States terminated Turkey's industrial involvement in the F-35 in 2020. And that involvement had been substantial. Turkish Aircraft Industries was a second source for the center fuselage. Several other Turkish companies also had key roles. Fokker Elmo, a Dutch company, made complex wiring systems. To reduce costs, they'd built a factory in Izmir, Turkey, to produce the harnesses. Pratt & Whitney had formed a joint venture with Kale Aerospace to produce parts for the F135 engine, also in Izmir. Actually, Kale Aero, an offspring of the industrial concern Kale Kalip, was one of the strongest partners worldwide. They had parts on every F-35, including the first production prototype, and were the most cost-competitive source in the global supply chain.

Congress's decision to drop-kick Turkey was understandable from a national security perspective, but it was a loss to all concerned. With the decision to terminate, all Turkish work had to be recontracted—a sudden and violent migraine headache. Even worse, this upset occurred just as production was scheduled to ramp up.

The program had to steer around other icebergs as well. Who could have predicted the COVID-19 pandemic, and the monkey wrenches that virus threw into the global supply chain? The impact of port dynamics on unloading seaborne shipping? Worldwide chip shortages? Not to mention the diversion of resources to war in Eastern Europe, global inflation, and shortages of rare earths, industrial metals, and other commodities?

One thing was for certain: Every bit of the robustness and flexibility that had been built into the supply chain turned out to be badly needed.

★ ★ ★

We've talked about engineers and digital threads and even robots. But what remains to be discussed is what MBAs call the human capital—the men and women who comprise the F-35 workforce. They're the ones who manufactured the parts, built the subsystems, created the major assemblies, and brought it all together.

So, who are these people?

At Fort Worth, the spirit of building quality airplanes to protect the nation has been handed down from generation to generation. It creates a mindset that's different from that of any other workforce. It's not out of the ordinary to see a grandparent, a parent, and a daughter or son all busy at Lockheed Martin. The roots run deep and the commitment deeper still.

The program did encounter one brief work interruption. The skilled manufacturing and production workers are a represented (unionized) workforce. A bargaining process occurs every four years when contracts come up for renegotiation. Workers seek better pay and benefits, while management tries to control the costs of delivering the airplanes within government budget constraints. In April 2012, members of the International Association of Machinists and

Aerospace Workers District Lodge 776, which represents most of the manufacturing and final assembly technicians, voted to walk out.

In May, not knowing how long the strike might last, LM began hiring temporary workers. Employees from other positions on the program were also pressed into temporary service to maintain progress. All would stop working whenever the union members returned.

The time-out also had a bright side. Larry Lawson, the F-35 general manager at the time, was able to reconfigure the factory and renovate both the production line and the flight line.

On June 28, the union voted overwhelmingly to support a new contract. Joe Stout, the spokesman, said, "We're pleased that our union members will be back on the job, doing work in support of US and other military forces with what we believe are the world's best fighter planes."[8]

Aside from that single brief disagreement, something not out of the ordinary in any labor/management relationship, our Fort Worth folks have been steadfast. Building the world's best combat aircraft is in their DNA. Without them, the most precise engineering, the most advanced robotics, and the guts of the test pilots would be in vain. Their ability to produce these incredible machines in large quantities is one of the most significant differentiators between the United States and other nations, though over time, that level of commitment has been shared across a global manufacturing and production base, something never before achieved.

★ ★ ★

That same Fort Worth factory floor looks different today. The most modern production line in the world is in full swing. Three separate variants are being built for three US services and eighteen different countries, all in "random flow," meaning any variant can be assembled in any position in the flow. After assembly, each jet is delivered to the final finishes facility (another state-of-the-art manufacturing process where coatings are applied with robotic precision), then to the radar cross section (RCS) building for low observable acceptance testing, then to the fuel facility, and finally to the flight line for ground and flight testing by company and government acceptance pilots prior to delivery. **(See Figure 27: Lockheed Martin Final Assembly and Checkout Operation and See Figure 28: Factory Move of AA-1 . . . First Flight?)**

The process seems to go so smoothly now. But few outsiders understand the bureaucratic and technical efforts that ultimately made this possible. These were the inputs that finally brought this remarkable plane into full production.

But they were about to be challenged like no program before them. When the COVID-19 pandemic hit in early 2020, once again, innovation was required. Focus was on the dual challenge of strengthening the global supply chain and dealing with the new and sometimes unprecedented labor challenges of a contagious and uncertain disease and government-mandated policy impacts. Originally planning to deliver 141 fighters in 2020, it quickly became clear that that wasn't going to be possible. That year, 120 were produced, a shortfall that appeared minimal and would largely avoid the worst of the supply-chain disruption linked to bottlenecks at backed up ports. Perhaps the biggest challenge involved principal partner BAE Systems building the F-35's aft fuselage in Lancashire, England. The UK imposed even stricter lockdowns than the United States, affecting both their labor force and their ability to produce. For many suppliers in both the United States and the UK, people just weren't allowed to go to work.

So how does a major program manage a slowdown on the global magnitude of COVID-19? Slowdowns don't last forever, and laying off skilled, experienced employees is sure to affect the ability to start again. The challenge would traditionally strain the partnership between company management and the unionized workforce. They developed a new work schedule that would allow production to continue but stretch out the labor routine. F-35 work shifts were divided into three groups. Each group would work two weeks on, one week off and employ social distancing parameters. By the end of the summer of 2020, normal work could resume without incurring layoffs or loss of pay and benefits. Management and union leadership viewed the alternate schedule as a success.

Suppliers, especially small ones, were experiencing the same difficult impacts. To keep them operating, the F-35 implemented a forward-funding strategy to pay them a few months early. Otherwise, many of the "mom and pop" suppliers would have gone out of business. In March 2020, government progress payments were increased from 80 percent to 90 percent. In 2021, the contractor averaged about $400 million in accelerated payments each week to it suppliers, particularly the small and vulnerable ones.[9]

American resourcefulness is embodied in a deeply talented global workforce willing to embrace new processes and technologies, applied over endless years of work and personal sacrifices. Rising to new challenges and driven by a gritty dedication to the needs of the future warfighter and the workforce that must deliver it, F-35 production made it through the pandemic.

But the long-term impact would reappear not long after as the F-35 partnership demand exploded with the potential of war on the European front.

Reference

1. https://www.airplanes-online.com/b36-at-carswell-afb.htm.

2. Wikipedia, "Carswell Air Force Base." Accessed April 12, 2022.

3. https://www.lockheedmartin.com/en-us/news/features/2017/celebrating-75-years-of-innovation-in-fort-worth.html.

4. Interview with Don Kinard by Tom Burbage, Betsy Clark and Adrian Pitman, April 26, 2021. Held in F-35 interview archive.

5. Interview with Tom Blakely by Tom Burbage, Betsy Clark, and Adrian Pitman, July 2, 2018. Held in F-35 interview archive.

6. Interview with CR Davis by Tom Burbage, Betsy Clark, and Adrian Pitman, August 11, 2019. Held in F-35 interview archive.

7. BBC News, "Turkey's downing of Russian warplane—what we know," December 2015. Accessed April 7, 2022.

8. https://www.cleveland.com/business/2012/06/lockheed_machinists_ok_new_lab.html.

9. Defense News, F-35 Costs have been declining. That's about to change, by Stephen Losey, November 18, 2022.

Chapter 22

SUSTAINING THE BEAST

In 1995, following the decision to select Boeing and Lockheed Martin to move from the JAST phase to the JSF Concept Demonstration phase, the JSF Program Office minted a challenge coin. Following a military tradition dating back to the Roman Empire, these heavy, ornate medallions were typically passed from one member to another in a handshake, exchanged in the palms. The ritual was a morale booster, a conversation starter, and linked friends, shipmates, and squadron mates across the years. Most importantly to drinkers, if a stakeholder called "challenge!" in a bar, any member who couldn't produce their coin had to buy the next round.

The JSF coin was inscribed *Lethal, Survivable, Supportable and Affordable*. *Lethal* and *Survivable* referred to the focus on new technologies to evade an evolving threat. *Supportable and Affordable* referred to new ways of reducing the lifetime cost of ownership.

This chapter will focus on the latter part of the challenge. The motto on the coin recognized the historic fact that two thirds of the price tag for any new weapon system typically resided in its life-cycle sustainment costs. The images of both the X-32 and X-35 were on the coin. Over the course of the program, many more versions would be issued.

From the beginning, the F-35 government and contractor team resolved that their program would drive down this steep cost of ownership. They would research the legacy cost drivers for fighter aircraft sustainment, challenge the inefficiencies and redundancies, and do their very best to minimize each in turn.

The main tool was to be the autonomic logistics global sustainment (ALGS) concept. The word *autonomic* was important to explain the concept. Much like the human body, which does not have to consciously think about blinking or breathing, the ALGS system, in theory, would function in a similar fashion, continually monitoring the software on the plane and sounding an alert when something had to be done.

The brain of the ALGS would be the autonomic logistics information system, affectionately known as ALIS. ALIS was a breathtakingly ambitious undertaking, since it would have to amalgamate what had historically been totally separate fiefdoms. The most demanding issue, from a technical, cultural, and even political perspective, would be fusing operational data across the global F-35 fleet.

It was an attractive and even a radical idea. But the effort to bring it to fruition would become one of the most exasperating dimensions of the entire JSF program.

★ ★ ★

Sustainment meant keeping airplanes ready to fly. One might see an aircraft sitting on a ramp, ready to go, but the supporting infrastructure and systems behind its presence there were largely invisible. (Though not inexpensive.)

Traditionally, every squadron had its own life-cycle ecosystem. It began at the operational level, referred to as "O-level" maintenance—meaning, any task that could be performed by the operating squadron's own mechanics and maintainers.

Consider the ritual of preparation for flight. The status of each plane needed to be recorded, reviewed, and either released for flight or assigned to scheduled maintenance. Once it was released, prior to starting the engine, the maintainers refueled the airplane, responded to any "gripes" identified by the previous pilot, and repositioned the jet for launch. On the flight deck of a carrier, these actions had to be tightly orchestrated to meet demanding time factors for launches and recoveries. Massive elevators lifted planes coming out of maintenance to the flight deck and shuttled those needing work down to the hangar deck, all without disrupting the ballet of tightly timed launches and recoveries during a typical day at sea. But having a fully capable, mission-ready fighter without a qualified pilot ready to hop in was a hollow statistic. Matching pilot qualifications to mission requirements had always been a challenge for all three services that operated advanced fighters. Traditionally, it had been done by a laborious process of human research and a series of reasoned judgment calls, carried out by the squadron operations officer. But if a computer could integrate qualifications (recorded in individual training records) with the maintenance and flight scheduling, pilots could be matched with planes just like engines, or tires, and be mated to mission requirements rapidly and efficiently. Risk could be minimized and readiness maximized at the same time, lofty goals for the autonomic system. It would also provide a weighty incentive for aviators to maximize their personal qualifications and readiness.

The next "step" began when the pilot stepped to his or her plane. After a visual walk-around or preflight inspection, they climbed into the cockpit and initiated the start-up sequence. At that point, onboard diagnostic systems ran self-test software to ensure all systems were in the green. If something failed at this late point, the ability of the squadron mechanics to do rapid corrective maintenance was essential to making the mission.

But what if such failures, once the pilot was onboard, could be eliminated, or at least substantially reduced? A subset of ALGS called prognostic health management (PHM) promised to *predict* which parts or systems were about to fail. This could replace ad hoc, hurried repairs on the flight line with scheduled maintenance in the hangar, eliminating last minute aborts. Such a capability would fulfill the dreams of flight line managers.

But effective PHM wouldn't be easy. The Lightning's highly integrated system software would make it difficult to predict failure of an individual component. What was initially viewed as an advantage could become a nightmare if false alarms resulted in parts being replaced while they were still serviceable.

In the long run, depending on internally generated data only was just not able to prevent false alarms, and was deemed not good enough by the ALGS team. As the sustainment system matured over time, new technology algorithms exploiting "big data" increasingly looked better than the original PHM concept. In other words, massive computing power changed the approach to understanding and exploiting the data. Similarly, internet browsers began with a basic word search capability, but now they could predict what individual users might want to see next. Perhaps the PHM vision could be achieved through a different approach.

So much for O-level maintenance. At the next level up, for repairs that exceeded in-house capabilities, was an infrastructure consisting of both government and contractor facilities, referred to as intermediate level (I-level). The government-run operations were conducted in a network of aircraft intermediate maintenance departments (AIMDs). AIMDs were located at air bases, but serviced both local and regional operational units. In some cases, as components and equipment grew more complex, the original manufacturer was a more capable and economical place to do these repairs. At the I level, complex repairs could be performed, and parts could be reissued. In addition, and importantly, it could also splice in any upgrades at the same time.

But I-level maintenance was historically governed by very restrictive management rules. They mandated meticulous tracking and return of controlled inventory parts, which had been issued to specific operating units and had to go back to them and only them.

Again, ALGS set out to work smarter. If those bean-counting rules could be relaxed, and components and systems freely moved between operating units, and better integrated with the production line supply-chain inventories, I-level processes could be streamlined, maybe even eliminated. This promised quicker turnaround and higher readiness. At the operational level, the squadron technician could diagnose the impending failure, remove the faulty component, and hand it to a sustainment representative to be logged into ALGS. If the part was in the local base inventory, it would be delivered and installed at the squadron level. If it wasn't, a replacement would be automatically identified within the consolidated production and sustainment inventory and overnighted to the squadron. Meanwhile, the faulty component would be on its way back to the manufacturer to be repaired and subsequently reentered into the global inventory. But this innovative solution would require relaxation of the old "I want my part back" mentality that required *that very same part* to be tracked and returned to the unit.

The third level of sustainability was depot level (D level). Depots were chartered to perform major repair and overhaul of the entire airplane. These would normally be driven by accumulated flight hours or major structural damage repair.

One of the biggest changes in the F-35 structural design criteria, mentioned in an earlier chapter, was an eight thousand flight hour structural life. This was significantly longer than that of legacy fighters, designed for six thousand hours. Making the basic airframe last longer would reduce the need for depot level overhaul, again minimizing life-cycle costs.

Optimizing the depot infrastructure of the three US services and the nine-nation partnership would save on repair and overhaul. But major investments would be required in the depots designated for the F-35. These depots would be refitted with the overhaul and testing equipment needed to refurbish the airframe and the sophisticated low-observability features, capabilities legacy depots lacked.

Three US depots were chosen, one for each service, which also meant one for each variant. In addition, the Italian final assembly and checkout facility would be the principal airframe depot for F-35s operated by the European allies. The Dutch were awarded the European F135 engine depot. If the two European facilities could also process US F-35s and the F135 engines, it could be both faster and cheaper to return planes to operational status. USAF, USN, and USMC F-35s operating in the European theater could also be repaired there instead of sending them all the way back to the United States. Spreading depot investment across the international community would also build partner country political support. Australia was chosen as the airframe, engine, and parts repair depot for the Pacific region.

The remaining depots in the United States would continue to support the inventory of other military aircraft. But hard lessons had been learned over the years about the downside risk of paring away critical military infrastructure. Accelerated op tempo associated with a surge or wartime flight ops could quickly outstrip repair capacity. But the F-35 wasn't just adding another platform to the current inventory, it was replacing most of the current fighter fleet. Thus, as Lightning numbers grew over time and the older jets were retired, their depot capacity could be modified to accommodate the new fighter.

But pushback on this idea was immediate. The individual services and the legislators who represented districts where existing depots resided, jealously protected their local supply chains and repair facilities. Ditto for the international operators, since depots quickly grew political roots based on jobs. Consolidation of infrastructure was viewed as a threat with dangerous repercussions.

As Elon Musk often says, "A high production rate cures many ills." The very high and very long-lasting production rates projected for the new fighter opened up another prospect for innovation: coupling the production and sustainment supply chains.

These had long been managed as separate entities, forgoing economies of scale. As legacy planes aged and their production lines closed, bureaucratic organizations with expensive infrastructure had evolved to make and manage the inventory of parts required to "keep 'em flying," often for many decades past their originally intended life span.

The global footprint of the F-35 program was to be different. If a Lightning II was grounded for want of a critical part, instead of sourcing it from the manufacturer, perhaps that part could come more quickly from the shelves of a sister squadron, from one of the partner production facilities, or from a regional warehouse, dramatically reducing the time to get the jet back in the air. But this vision ran head-on into the barriers of export licensing, trade compliance, and many years of regulations controlling the exchange of data and parts between the Unitd States and foreign nations.

The new plane's global operating model, with full partnership for participating allies, was a foreign concept to the traditional process architecture. It opened up the possibility of a new function for the depots, but someone would have to break a lot of rice bowls to make it a reality.

★ ★ ★

All these sustainment innovations had great promise. And ALGS was well funded from the very beginning. But over time, two major problems emerged.

The first was the difficulty of convincing partner countries and historically independent operational communities to share failure rates and other trends in maintenance data. Countries didn't like divulging what they considered sovereign information. Nor were warfighters fond of spilling the beans on their readiness for battle. And finally, multilevel security had to be borne in mind, with cyber penetrations a continual worry.

The second issue was a more insidious cultural challenge called the "sleeping stakeholder" phenomenon. New and often politically driven decision-makers would suddenly enter the program, demanding changes and special accommodations long after the basics seemed to have been decided.

It has been said that a program moves from a complicated challenge to a complex undertaking when politics enters the daily domain of the program manager.[1] A new area of technical study was founded in 2007 by the Australian Department of Defence, establishing an academic focus on managing large and complex government programs. It was supported by the UK MoD, the U.S. DoD, the Canadian National Defence, and supporting global defense industries. The F-35 became the initial case study for the first cohort of students. The curricula included guest lectures in Canberra and cohort visits to Fort Worth.

But education is a slow process, and few in leadership positions recognized this new politically driven challenge.

★ ★ ★

One of the biggest shillelaghs the program's political opponents found to belabor it with was its projected life-cycle cost.

One of the major unknowns for any revolutionary new system is how to predict the life-cycle costs of the total fleet over its operational lifetime. This had never really been attempted in a rigorous way before, even with single-service platforms. It was a monumental challenge with the F-35 and subject to significant variables entirely outside the control of anyone at LM, or even at DoD, for that matter. For example, the cost of fuel to operate the fleet depended on assumptions (frankly, guesses) extending fifty years into the future. But part of trying to minimize overall cost had to be coming out with a final figure, fuzzy (for the reasons above) though it might be.

The initial calculation was that the cost of producing, sustaining, upgrading and operating the global fleet over its projected lifetime of half a century would be about a trillion US dollars. (A trillion, in US parlance, is a thousand billion.) This massive number hit the public consciousness like a clout on the head. Seizing on it, the media was Lightning-quick to label the F-35 the "Trillion Dollar Jet." In reality, the life-cycle cost estimate for the multiple planes it was replacing, using the same guidelines, was three to four trillion. In addition, consolidation of the unique training infrastructure for the many different airplanes the F-35 was replacing, and the reduction in the operational cost for both war-fighting and peacekeeping operations with a single class of highly interoperable F-35s, never entered the public cost debate. There was no apples-to-apples comparison that would have shown the benefit of the F-35 concept.

On April 2, 2010, USMC Maj Gen James Flock, 2nd Marine Aircraft Wing commander, addressed military, civilians, and community leaders at Eglin Air Force Base at the stand-up ceremony for the first Marine F-35B training squadron. He pointed to one side of the bleachers, where an F-18, an EA6B, and an AV-8B, the current USMC tactical inventory, were on display. On the other side was a F-35. He underlined the fact that the single F-35B and its global sustainment concept would replace the three separate training and support elements then required to support USMC tactical aviation.[2]

But those comparisons were lost on the public, and the moniker became a significant sound bite to overcome.

★ ★ ★

The first step on the journey to field the new sustainment concept took place in 2006, following the plane's maiden flight. Two major milestones had been reached earlier that year. Both the overall ALGS support system concept and the autonomic logistics information system completed their critical design reviews. F-35 ALGS would officially begin by supporting the aircraft at the multiple test sites across the United States. These included the Lockheed Martin facility in Fort Worth, Edwards Air Force Base, and Patuxent River Naval Air Test Center. In addition, a number of secondary, specialized test facilities would be included, such as the Navy's Carrier Suitability test site in Lakehurst, New Jersey.

Several other firsts also occurred that same year, including the ribbon-cutting for the Sustainment Operations Center at Fort Worth, establishment of the first spares warehouse, inauguration of pilot and maintainer training, and delivery of tools, support equipment, and technical data to support production and flight operations.

Initially, ALGS was led by an aeronautics program vice president as a key element of the Fort Worth structure. A sister company, Lockheed Martin Mission Systems and Training (MST) based in Orlando, Florida, was the corporate center of excellence for training systems and simulation and was supporting the design and development teams in Fort Worth.

Dan Crowley, who'd later move to LM Aero and run the whole F-35 program, recalled,

> In 2003, I was selected to be the president of MST. The F-35 ALGS program had been under development for three years in Fort Worth by then, and I had a large engineering team there. They had a comprehensive concept, a preliminary design and had developed some of the key modules when I took over. At MST, our main responsibility was to develop the Autonomic Logistics Information System, a subset of the overall ALGS program. I remember traveling to Fort

Worth to meet with the F-35 program executive, Bob Elrod. He told us that, under the budget pressures, there was only so much more money to finish ALIS.

Two years later, in 2005, I became the F-35 program manager and relocated to Fort Worth. By then the core engineering team was growing rapidly to deal with the SWAT redesign. We had 8,500 engineers working on the program and there wasn't space in the main building at Fort Worth for everyone. The decision was made to move the ALIS team to a satellite facility on the other side of the Fort Worth campus. I don't think it was a great move. They became somewhat isolated from the integrated product teams that had been the hallmark of the development program.

They were led by a guy who I think struggled a little bit in that role and because it was all new, their software releases were always lagging the aircraft releases. And the requirements were also evolving, creating the need to develop new functionality that didn't exist before. They were good people but this program demands exceptional folks and so I think ALIS . . . I won't say it was a stepchild, but it didn't get the level of attention it really needed until later . . . until actual operational squadrons would begin to really use the airplane. Once that happened, the program started to put more energy into it and to see where the gaps were in development.[3]

As initial operational capabilities milestones approached, there were several shifts in requirements as well.

Marines deploy to remote, expeditionary sites. They wanted transportable servers to manage their data. Oops . . . ALIS's servers were designed to manage the global fleet, not to be humped through the boonies in a backpack. Then the Air Force piled on. They wanted a wireless flight line system for communication with maintenance control. This would be a lean process improvement initiative that would preclude walking flight line changes back into maintenance control for adjudication and would speed up launches.

The stress continued to build. ALGS and ALIS were essential to fielding a transformational system of the envisioned scale. But the fact was, a lot of the criticism wasn't actually the system's fault. Its outputs were dependent on the accuracy of input. Yet operational units had widely varying quality standards for recording and forwarding maintenance data. The old computer saw applied: "Garbage in, garbage out."

Maj Gen Heinz recalled,

If you take a look at the time frame from essentially 2007 to 2010, it was really a significant period of transition. There were a number of key building blocks. One of the key ones was to take a look at how we were really going to do the supply system for sustaining the global fleet. We started doing some simulations to try to understand what's the right combination of contractor support, contractor supply as well as using our own depots, using the capabilities within the ICPs—inventory control points—that are provided through the different services."[4]

Simplifying this bureaucratic infrastructure that had been built up over decades was a real struggle.

★ ★ ★

At the time of publication, over a thousand F-35s have been delivered to all three US services and allied nations. Production facilities in three countries—the United States (Fort Worth), Italy (Cameri), and Japan (Nagoya) are assembling the planes. By 2030 more than four hundred will be operational within NATO alone, and many more with the services of other allies. The two-level maintenance structure, based on elimination of the I-level intermediate-stage depots, has been implemented. The global depot infrastructure for both the airframe and the engine is running smoothly, with European airframe depot capability in Italy, an engine overhaul depot in the Netherlands, and an airframe and engine depot in Australia. But the process hasn't been easy.

Perhaps the most frustrating aspect was the impact of Moore's law, described in chapter 11. The ALGS architecture began as a separate, ground-based, stand-alone system using the best technology then available, tightly coupled to the airplane's own software. Nearly two decades later, IT system technology had dramatically evolved, leading to changes in programming languages, processing speed, storage capacity, and miniaturization. Who could have envisioned cloud computing back then? As the global fleet continued to expand, the data management requirements ballooned as well. Eventually, the original design architecture had to be upgraded.

In January 2020, DoD tried to replace ALIS with a new architecture called the F-35 operational data integrated network (ODIN). However, due to budget cuts, lack of access to proprietary code, and ongoing improvement to ALIS, the Joint Program Office decided to incrementally modernize ALIS instead of replacing it. DoD officials stated that when key elements of the ALIS system are significantly improved, they intend to rename the system ODIN.[5]

These days, that original, revolutionary vision—changing the paradigm for supporting a complex weapon system worldwide for over a half-century life cycle—faces additional challenges. These include determining the government's and the contractor's optimal roles in sustainment, assessing the construct of future contracts, deciding on the approach to modernizing the F-35 engine, and transitioning oversight responsibility from the JPO to the individual services.[6]

★ ★ ★

So, let's talk to a modern maintainer. The real task was how to introduce the next generation of maintenance procedures for this new asset. Historically, maintainers had specific specialties they were trained on, such as avionics, hydraulics or engines. But those trades were stovepiped, and their maintainers were also. This next-generation jet was highly integrated. After all, fuel was used as a hydraulic fluid to reduce weight, electric energy replaced traditional hydraulic fluid, and, like modern day cars, software had replaced mechanical systems. Today's maintainer became a general practitioner, not a specialist. Much like the pilot no longer needed to integrate separate systems to figure out the tactical situation, the maintainer had the same new challenge. Lt Gen Michael Loh, director of the Air National Guard, spoke to reporters at the Air and Space Forces Association's Air, Space, and Cyber Conference at National Harbor, Maryland. He highlighted the fact that the new maintenance requirement was very different from the legacy aircraft. It was a new kind of maintenance that could support any fight in a possible war against China or other distant foes. Single domain specialists, proud to have graduated from specific skill training, would now need to learn integrated avionic specialties. One of the differences between the F-35 and legacy jets is that maintainers can hook up a laptop and run diagnostics and internal checks. One of the benefits of a self-diagnosing jet is the elimination of the exploratory problem process of elimination, which significantly reduced maintenance time and the human issue of misdiagnosis.

The software elegance blurs the line between maintenance specialties, resulting in a new generation of maintainers learning a novel concept called "the F-35 nose to tail" program where maintainers adapt skills outside of their normal specialty.

Figuring out how to get the maintainer job done with fewer people is one of the major challenges for the services as their recruiting challenges mount.

Nobody ever said sustainment would be a walk in the park!

Reference

1. ICCPM.com

2. King, Samuel, "First JSF Marine squadron stands up at Eglin," afmc.af.mil, published April 2, 2010.

3. Interview with Dan Crowley on January 27, 2018, by Betsy Clark and Adrian Pitman. Held in F-35 interview archive.

4. Interview with MajGen Duncan Heinz on 1 January 2020 by Betsy Clark and Adrian Pitman. Held in F-35 interview archive.

5. GAO-22-105128 Published: April 25, 2022. Publicly Released: April 25, 2022.

6. GAO-22-105128 Published: April 25, 2022. Publicly Released: April 25, 2022.

Chapter 23

THE MEDIA WAR AND THE SLEEPING STAKEHOLDERS

W ithin the glass house of government programs, communication generally aims at two goals: influencing political decisions and steering public
opinion (usually in that order). The two are related, but require different strategies.

When there's too little government money to satisfy everyone, the "have-
nots" or "outs," those not funded to their needs, naturally try to get some money
back from the "ins," those that are carrying the lion's share of the budget. They
may create imaginary problems to swing opinion to favor their own interests.
Correspondingly, the "ins" should expect endless attacks on their agenda and
their fitness to administer it.

When the program in question is the largest in the Department of Defense
portfolio, these dynamics are magnified tenfold.

One tactic used by the "outs" was to smear their opponents with an unflattering
but catchy label. Since reporters often quote one another (a dynamic sometimes
referred to as "shared talking points") that label is quickly repeated ad nau-
seam. Derogatory adjectives such as "troubled," "inferior," and "unproven" are
hammered into the public consciousness. With globalization, such memes can
quickly propagate around the world and stick for years. Hence, the "ins" must
respond instantly and convincingly to unfair characterizations—or live with the
negative portrayal.

This dynamic is common in military acquisition. The opponents' goal, of
course, no matter how loudly they push "savings," is to justify diverting resources
to their own favored programs. Sometimes the rationale's based on cost growth,

at other times, on maintaining an industrial base. Often, it's based on supporting a legacy constituency.

The F-35's gauntlet began with the "Swiss Army Knife" moniker, first applied by stakeholders in the last-generation fighter who were now threatened with obsolescence. (Much the same dynamic happened with the introduction of every new weapons system.) This phrase acknowledged that the Lightning was a multiservice design, intended to replace several types of tactical aircraft. But it also implied that anything able to do many things would do none well. It hadn't been possible before (e.g., with the TFX) and wasn't now. It was a "jack of all trades, master of none" argument.

When it began to look like the plane *really might succeed* at its various missions, the naysayers abandoned that point for a while and shifted to cost. The "trillion-dollar jet" took flight. The accusation was unjustified, but the slur stuck.

The F-35 would make a great case study on the effects of competing strategies between the "ins" and the "outs," and how that was influenced by the globalization of social media that occurred during the program's formative years. This book doesn't have room to recount the whole war, but let's briefly sketch out a few of the salient campaigns.

★ ★ ★

The first formal Lightning II training squadron was set up at Eglin in 2010. A highly decorated squadron, VMFA 451, "The Warlords," was reactivated to form Marine Fighter Attack Training Squadron 501. This marked the launch of the operational phase of the program.

The operational commanding officer of 501 was LtCol David "Chip" Berke. Berke started his career flying F-18s from the USS *John Stennis*. He deployed to Iraq and then Afghanistan after 9/11, then spent three years as a TOPGUN instructor. After serving as a forward air controller in Ramadi, then as an operations and executive officer in another F-18 squadron, he was selected as an F-22 exchange pilot, becoming the first and only jarhead to fly the Raptor.

As the CO of the lead F-35 training squadron, Berke also became the first operational pilot to fly the new jet, earning him a unique ability to discuss its transformational capabilities. Three years later, he declined the opportunity to return to command the same F-35 squadron as a colonel, retired, and started his own company, working fifth-generation fighter issues. By any measure, he was an informed source.[1]

But the opponents were forming ranks and interlocking shields. A group in the Pentagon called the "Fighter Mafia" had developed the concept of the lightweight fighter back in the 1970s. They were influential in developing such legendary planes as the A-10, F-16, and F-18. Their de facto leaders were John Boyd and Pierre Sprey.

Colonel John Boyd was a Korean War USAF fighter pilot, instructor, and military theoretician known for developing the energy-maneuverability theory of dogfighting and the rapid-decision cycle known as the OODA loop (for observe-orient-decide-act). Sprey was an influential Pentagon civilian analyst and military reformer. Both men, along with others, were steadfastly committed to the post-Vietnam lesson that agility (maneuverability, speed, and power) should be the dominant criteria for a fighter. Boyd died in 1997, but Sprey continued to carry his banner as the requirements for fifth-generation aircraft were firmed up and persisted until his death in 2021.[2]

★ ★ ★

The birth of the JSF in the late 1990s and early 2000s also coincided with the explosive expansion of the internet and the rise of a new form of online communication called social media. Like printing or the telephone, it brought significant changes to the way society communicated and accessed information. While many of these changes had a positive effect, some didn't.

The conflict of opinion that erupted between Berke and Sprey—and between the Fighter Mafia and the F-35 team—exemplified the new reality that in the unmoderated space of the internet, any source, informed or not, could pontificate to millions, whether their opinions were based on objective reality, self-interest, hearsay, or the simple desire to harass and destroy. (These latter, Loki-like creatures of narcissistic malevolence became known as "trolls.")

Berke said,

Something I've just come to accept is that the people who are the most critical of the airplane are the people who are farthest from it. . . . It clearly doesn't help us to have a bunch of advocates for the program who have never flown a fifth-generation fighter say things that don't express directly why the program is unique. We caught ourselves in a position where we were constantly comparing us to our predecessors.

The reason people make that comparison is because (the F-35) looks like an airplane. Thirty feet wide and fifty feet long and ten feet tall and it uses JP-8 fuel, so it's just an airplane, just the next one in line. The worst thing you can do to the F-35 is to compare it to a predecessor because it marginalizes the capability of the F-35.

The lightweight fighter mafia's position was that the best plane was the one that could outturn, outclimb, and out-dive everyone else in a dogfight. Countering that superficially appealing yet simplistic argument with the F-35's more operationally relevant advantages was a Sisyphean task.

One example. In January 2015, an early F-35A was conducting initial basic flight maneuvering against an F-16 in a controlled test. The F-35 was in its flight expansion phase, evaluating high angle of attack maneuvering, and did not have its final flight control software installed. *War is Boring* journalist David Axe got hold of the test report and wrote that the F-35 was outclassed by the F-16. The story went viral and created a lot of blowback.[3]

The USAF response was given by Lieutenant Colonel Christine Mau. Mau had led the first combat mission planned, briefed, and flown entirely by women in the F-15, and was the first woman to pilot the F-35.[4] Her take went like this. "That was a single test point. It was not supposed to be 'Let's see who wins.' It was designed to test the control laws on our airplane. How often do we draw conclusions from single data points? It's not exactly statistically significant and that wasn't the purpose of the test. Give it some time and you'll be impressed."[5]

Not surprisingly, Sprey piled on, immediately denouncing the new program as a failure. "It's one of the worst airplanes we've ever designed for a lot of reasons. But the most important reason is because it was compromised by having to do three different jobs. You can never make a good airplane if you don't focus on a single job, single mission."[6] The Swiss Army Knife argument was alive and well.

The secretary of defense countered that argument. Secretary Gates had decided much earlier that single-mission or single-service fighter programs were no longer affordable.[7] Berke also rejected the assertion.

It's a laughable concept that the F-16 can outperform the F-35 in the visual arena. Talk to some who have flown F-16s for their entire career and are now flying F-35. They're going to tell you that the F-35 is superior to the F-16 in every way, shape, and form. It's just as powerful. It's got much better weapons system integration. But, when our response to a public statement to the contrary is "well, it'll never get into a dogfight," that's really a weak argument.

So, the program's supporters had to learn to argue smarter, not harder.

Early on, then, the PR problem was multifaceted. Those familiar with the new fighter knew it was transformational. They expected the world to understand and accept that. Unfortunately, the new plane *looked like* its predecessors. Self-proclaimed experts weren't shy about voicing uninformed opinions, and the new level of connectivity through the internet provided them a free global audience.

No one has ever argued that qualified experts shouldn't be free to comment on a new program. We live in a democracy, after all. The operative word, though, should be "qualified."

In point of fact, F-35 capabilities were highly classified in a number of areas and not available to public scrutiny. In a perverse way, criticism is sometimes helpful in diverting close scrutiny from adversaries. Obfuscation of real US game-changing capabilities, particularly if they seemed to be having significant challenges, might divert or at least provide a short gap in the close scrutiny of our adversaries.

While other aspects of the public criticism focused on the design's weight growth—a problem with every new fighter, submarine, tank, or ship—as requirements grew, development risk was retired, and especially as new manufacturing technologies and processes were introduced, the F-35B's STOVL requirement super-sharpened that focus on weight, but redesign was taking care of that.

The critiques of the plane on the grounds of its so-called lack of maneuverability and agility, highlighted in the F-16 vignette above, showed either ignorance of or willful blindness to the hard facts. Earlier fighters had to carry critical sensors and weapons externally if they were headed for combat rather than an air show. The additional drag substantially reduced their maneuverability and agility. But the internal carriage of weapons and sensors on the F-35 meant an improvement, not a reduction, when it was in a combat configuration. This reality many critics either ignored, or, when informed of their error, refused to cite.

In Australia, as discussed in a later chapter, the Air Power Australia group was headed by Carlo Kopp and Peter Goon, experienced engineers and pilots. They made a more closely reasoned (if ultimately flawed) argument for "evolving" the Australian F-111 instead of buying the F-35.

Paul Wiedenhafer, introduced in an earlier chapter, was the JPO requirements czar. He commented,

> Air Power Australia was incentivized to be F-35 critics for some alternatives they proposed related to the F-111. They were historically one of the real negative factors we had to fight in Australia, and I had a number of personal debates with each of them. They were connected through the internet to a guy in the Netherlands through the website F-16.net. There was a growing community of conspiracy theorists who were convinced that this whole thing was Lockheed trying to jam an airplane down everybody's throat that no one wanted. It was tough to deal with and I used to say, "Hey, you're wrestling with a pig. You're going to get dirty and the pig's going to enjoy it."[8]

★ ★ ★

The internet thus offered a free forum to a newly empowered fraternity of loud-mouthed but basically ignorant quasi-experts. This phenomenon wasn't limited to the F-35, or even to aviation in general, but a plane like the Lightning II was particularly vulnerable to their attacks. Each nation in the global partnership suddenly had its own domestic resistance group, and in a very short time those groups began to work hand in hand. Someone in the Netherlands or Japan could quote seemingly authoritative foreign sources in their efforts to derail their own country's purchase. While most mainstream journalists treated the program critically but fairly, a few of them also fanned the flames of discontent. Their networking amplified any negative criticism.

No previous weapons program, except possibly the late-1980s basing of the Tomahawk land attack missile (TLAM) and Pershing II ballistic missile in Europe, had caused such a furor. Someone had to counter this negative messaging with the facts.[9] But mounting a successful response involved a delicate balance. Set the record straight . . . sure. But "protest too much," and the critics were quick to complain that the prime contractor was "overselling," ignoring the shortcomings of both the plane and the program in order to defraud the public and line its executives' pockets.

★ ★ ★

So . . . who were the major contributors to communicating the facts across this broad community of both involved stakeholders and critics? Both groups had to be addressed. The naysayers had to be rebutted. The stakeholders had to have their confidence bolstered. Neither task was to prove simple or easy.

In the early days of the program, three major channels of communication existed: government agencies, Congress, and the domestic and international trade press.

Two agencies were particularly influential, the Government Accountability Office (GAO) and the director of operational test and evaluation (DOT&E). GAO was established by Congress in 1921 to provide independent evaluations and audits of government expenditures. Numerous GAO reports are available to the public.[10] DOT&E was set up by Congress in 1983 to oversee operational test and evaluation of weapons systems and to report the results to the Secretary of Defense and Congress. DOT&E reports are also available to the public.

While these offices weren't part of the general media, their reports were widely distributed and their critiques often taken out of context by the critics. Since they often implied a lack of confidence in the program, these reports were a major concern for the partner nations.

The U.S. Congress, especially its defense critics, also carried a big hammer. Perhaps the most vocal detractor was Senator John McCain, who served on the Senate Armed Services Committee. Widely respected and viewed as a defense hawk, he was nevertheless critical of many DoD programs when it came time to set budget priorities. He was quick to quote excerpts from the GAO and DOT&E reports, and when he took a dislike to what he considered a boondoggle, his attacks were relentless.

On May 19, 2011, in the Armed Services Committee hearing on the Defense Authorization Request for Fiscal 2012, he commented that "Even after these production problems are solved, we still have to contend with potentially huge costs to maintain all three versions of the JSF. As the chairman mentioned, right now it's estimated to be about $1 trillion, adjusted for inflation. This jaw-dropping amount may be about twice as much as the cost to maintain other roughly comparable aircraft."[11] His comment was picked up by the trade presses with no mention that the $1 trillion calculation was for the replacement of fourteen different aircraft for a fifty-year operational life. The "trillion-dollar jet" slur was back.

The domestic and international aerospace and defense press was widely read and influential in the partner nations and often quoted in political debates. Personal relationships with key journalists became necessary to counter the criticism. Program leaders made sure that their every visit to an international partner included sit-downs with prominent journalists. For example, on every visit to Turkey, Tom Burbage made sure to meet up with Hakki Aris, general manager and publisher at Monch Media, to make sure he was updated on the program's progress.

So far, so good; setting the professional press straight was possible. But dealing with the daily cascade of websites, Facebook posts, online news aggregators, podcasts, apps, YouTube videos, and so on was a monumental challenge for the program office and the contractor teams. Constantly forced on the defensive, they would have to adapt or die.

The JPO and LM communication team realized this had to be a combined effort. After a "put a toe in the water to see how hot it is" phase, they developed a comprehensive communication strategy focused on both supporting the stakeholders and countering the critics.

★ ★ ★

Why was criticism such a thorn thicket for this particular airplane?

Dan Crowley, the former LM program manager, explained:

> Because these programs are so long cycle, there are very few people that were around to live the development challenges of the predecessors, the F-16 and F/A-18 and F-22. The F/A-18 had an abrupt wing stall problem and center fuselage cracking problems that almost tanked the program. F-22, when it did its first flight at Edwards, it had to be disassembled and flown across the country in the back of a C5A. The first two F-35s flew to Edwards Air Force base and landed Code 1, ready to fly again the next day.
>
> The F-16 at one point was over a hundred aircraft behind schedule, and it was developed with essentially no avionics or weapons capabilities. It took years

through block upgrades for them to get basic capabilities. One of the causes for this dynamic is if you don't do any new development for two decades, you get this pent-up demand of new requirements that you want to put into the next fighter. And this follows the procurement holiday where defense budgets paid the "peace dividend" to social programs. All the aircraft that were aging now drive the importance of fielding the F-35 quickly.

But when you haven't done a new aircraft in a long time, you put into the aircraft every improvement that you'd ever possibly wanted because you believe this may be the only new start you'll get for another twenty or thirty years.

Lt Gen Dave Deptula (USAF, Ret.), dean of the Mitchell Institute for Aerospace Studies, was the principal planner for the Desert Storm air campaign. A 2020 congressional report titled *F-35 Joint Strike Fighter: Ensuring Safety and Accountability in the Government's Trillion Dollar Investment* drew this comment from him.

The portentous title implies the question, what is going on with this program? Given the money, time, and effort invested in this aircraft and its associated systems, expectations should be for real results, not negative headlines and flight line setbacks. The reality is that the Air Force, Navy, Marine Corps, allies and partners all need this fifth-generation fighter to work as advertised. . . . Given those stakes, the reality—according to those actually flying and employing it—is that the F-35 is tracking far better than the hearing title might suggest.[12]

Complex programs, like human children, take time to fully develop. And again, like children, they can suffer existential trauma if their "parents" argue, fight, separate, divorce, or die. Their expectations are suddenly shattered.

Similarly, the F-35 was born into a somewhat dysfunctional "family" of three US services and eight allied partners. It had to mature though dramas of industrial participation, upgrade commitments, and through-life sustainment. Each crisis would reverberate with long-term, ingrained political constituencies. It also had to live with a series of "foster parents"—downstream decision-makers who had little or no regard for earlier commitments, possibly made by their political opponents. Within the program, these new players were referred to as the "sleeping" stakeholders, essentially, folks who inherited key roles in the innovative program's later stages, but who often tended to revert to their more traditional or parochial positions. The passage of time, budget realities, and clashing personalities all meant such changes of heart threatened the healthy growth of the program.

One of the early recidivists, as mentioned previously, was the U.S. Navy. Crowley recalled,

> The Navy believed that the STOVL would damage the decks of the landing ships and blow sailors off the ship when it came in to land. And they would put out that disinformation, as did their test community. We had to go refute it. We had test data—something called the frying pan—it was a skillet with temperature sensors all over it—we put it underneath the nozzle in the back and we'd show that the temperatures would not burn the deck or affect the nonskid coating. We also showed that the outwash when the aircraft was at hover coming in would not blow over people.

Why was the Navy so negative? Crowley:

> The perception was that the Navy wanted control of the program and were going to prove that the platform couldn't meet its mission objectives because they had other agendas—either keeping the Hornet flying or wanting to run their own test programs. It was a real paradox since the Naval Air Systems Command had sent their best people to be part of the F-35 JPO. We just had to prove them wrong.

Another area of controversy was through-life sustainment. Often referred to as the "cost of ownership," minimizing it was a major objective of the JSF program from the beginning. This was treated in detail in an earlier chapter, but efforts to this end included optimizing the footprint of the plane's support depots, justifying production and sustainment inventories, and leveraging "virtual repair," with small technical teams that could evaluate repair damage through remote visual systems and deploy the right technical team to perform field repairs. But to do that effectively, a number of sacred cows would have to be sacrificed.

While these concepts had once enjoyed at least lip-service buy-in from everyone, as fleet introduction neared, the sleeping stakeholders suddenly jerked awake. Their traditions—"The way we've always done it"—were being challenged! They began to doubt, then question, and finally resist the novel structures and routines coming down the pike at them.

One example: Depot bases are huge employment centers. They garner massive, largely bipartisan political support, with backing from local unions, cities, suppliers, and other special-interest groups. The F-35 offered DoD an opportunity to downsize some of that expensive infrastructure. But delegating that responsibility to a third party, specifically to Lockheed Martin, was, to some, unacceptable.

As the plane neared delivery, this friction got hotter.

To quote Lt Gen Tome Walters, Director of the Defense Security Cooperation Agency, overseeing all international foreign military sales,

> So far, this program survived because it is too important to fail. We need to get to this optimized way of operating together as a joint, coalition force. We have a huge number of challenges to deal with. It took a lot of work to bring everyone together but it will take a lot more work keep everyone together. If we can't do that, we will not achieve the full potential of the program.[13]

Unfortunately, keeping the Lightning's dysfunctional family together until the plane reached adulthood was anything but a foregone conclusion.

Reference

1. Interview with David Berke by Tom Burbage, Betsy Clark, and Adrian Pitman on July 10, 2015. Held in F-35 interview file.
2. Mulloch, Eran, "The Fighter Mafia," *Famous People*, October 6, 2019, accessed on www.fightson.net on July 16, 2022.
3. Axe, David "Test Pilot Admits the F-35 Can't Dogfight," www.warisboring.com, accessed on July 13, 2022.
4. National Air and Space Museum, "Lt. Col. Christine Mau." https://airandspace.si.edu/multimedia-gallery/hero1jpg. Accessed July 19, 2022.
5. https://Worldwarwings.com/f-16-vs-f-35-dogfight, accessed on July 13, 2022.
6. https://Worldwarwings.com/f-16-vs-f-35-dogfight, accessed on July 13, 2022.

7. Clark, Colin, Editor AOL Defense, "Robert Gates Completes Cancellation of Targeted Weapons Programs", April 25, 2011, in Huffington Post, accessed July 19, 2022.

8. Interview with Paul Wiedenhafer by Tom Burbage, Betsy Clark, and Adrian Pitman, July 11, 2018. Held in F-35 interview archive.

9. https://www.realcleardefense.com/articles/2017/06/12/ "The TLAM: a counterproductive anachronism for Europe."

10. https://www.gao.gov/reports-testimonies. Accessed January 17, 2023.

11. May 19, 2011—Senate Armed Services Committee Hearing on the Proposed Defense Authorization Request for Fiscal 2012 and Future Years for the F-35 Joint Strike Fighter Program, Accessed on July 16, 2022.

12. https://www.forbes.com/sites/davedeptula/2020/07/20/f-35-problem-child-or-on-track-for-success/ accessed on July 5, 2022.

13. Interview with LtGen Tome Walters by Tom Burbage. Held in F-35 interview archive.

Chapter 24

SPY VS. SPY

A ntonio Prohías, Cuba's leading political cartoonist, fled his country for New York three days before the free press was nationalized by the Castro regime. He ended up employed by *Mad*, a satirical magazine that became part of the cultural landscape of the twentieth-century. Prohías's *Spy vs. Spy* cartoons featured a duo of secret agents constantly one-upping each other. Reflecting the Manichaean ideologies of the Cold War, it parodied the never-ending battle of international espionage.[1]

Spying is often viewed as the most reliable source of information about what enemies actually intend to do, since that often contradicts their public pronouncements. Common tools of the trade used to include binoculars or telescopes surreptitiously poked from a nondescript apartment window overlooking a sensitive site. Sometimes it involved seduction by gorgeous members of the opposite (or same) sex. Slowly, over time, technology played a greater role, from Thomas Jefferson's disk cipher mechanism to the first telephone tap in 1895, to the tiny Minox camera beloved of 1940s spies and the famous "bombes" that broke Nazi ciphers during World War II.

A more recent example involved the titanium required to build the SR-71 triple-sonic Blackbird. At the time, the only place to source that metal in bulk was the USSR, which obviously would have been unwilling to provide it for that purpose, if asked overtly. The CIA arranged a series of shell games and shell corporations, clandestinely purchasing titanium via various intermediaries. The Skunk Works used the metal to build thirty-two planes whose primary mission was to spy on the Soviets.[2] The family of mysterious black spy planes were known for their high-tech camera systems. Ben Rich, former Lockheed head of the Skunk Works, often said that the U-2 *Dragon Lady* could fly over the Rose Bowl and take a picture from eighty thousand feet, and you could read the word "Spalding" on the football.

But in the tradition of Antonio Prohías's cartoons, the next frame showed the other side winning. A few years later, Navy carriers operating in the Mediterranean experienced meaconing, a form of spoofing navigation signals in the cockpits of airplanes trying to find home base in a vast ocean. Small Russian fishing trawlers, operating close to the carrier, were the source of that electronic interference.

During the gestation of the F-35, the ancient profession evolved once more. This time, into the newest realm of technology, cyberspace . . . the hypothetical environment in which computer communications take place.

Cyberwarfare is generally defined as the use of cyberattacks against a nation-state, causing significant harm up to and including disruption of vital computer systems, financial loss, strategic misdirection, tactical confusion, and potentially even loss of life. While cyberwarfare proper generally refers to attacks by one nation-state upon another, it can also describe intrusions or damage by terrorist groups, hacker groups aimed at furthering ideological goals, or individual criminals in search of loot from ransom or blackmail. Cyberattacks usually come in different flavors. An intrusion can take a system down completely, leave it operating but subject to covert eavesdropping for intelligence purposes, corrupt it, insert false and misleading data to subtly curb its effectiveness and erode confidence, or flood it with traffic that makes it inaccessible to legitimate users.

While HUMINT—human intelligence, or actual inside information from within the enemy camp—remains the most basic and reliable source, the dramatic expansion of computer technology has opened a whole new arena of combat. Jamming that once threatened the operation of a single ship or airplane can now disrupt space-based satellite systems and cripple global communication and navigation networks. And military systems are not the sole possible targets. Cyberattacks can also wreck or disrupt critical infrastructure—electrical energy sources or grids, telecommunication networks, banking systems, water supplies, hospital records and services, nuclear plant operations . . . any and every software-controlled environment. Denying essential public services may replace the high cost in lives and dollars of traditional air campaigns or ground invasions or may accompany them to soften the adversary's will and capacity to resist, as Russia did during its 2022 invasion of Ukraine.

This novel realm of warfare has spawned a whole new vocabulary with terms like viruses, malware, phishing, spearphishing, honeypots, computer worms, catfishing, troll farms, and bots.

Obviously, programs that promise significant military-technical advantage are high-value targets for such attacks.

The F-35 Lightning II became such a target when it introduced fifth-generation airpower, promising an asymmetric, game-changing new capability that made it a significant new threat to anyone who might be on the receiving end.

But the F-35's promise went beyond raw airpower. Much, if not most, of the jet's advanced performance is founded in the advanced computing technologies resident in the fighter. That programming offered the ability to gather data from the electromagnetic spectrum, evaluate it in real time, and deliver the results to the pilot in a helmet-mounted display. It could also relay that information to other nodes on the battlefield. The transformation also included high-fidelity simulators that reduced training hours and the ability to exploit maintainer information to predict repairs and manage the availability of spare parts.[3] All this constituted a quantum-leap advantage over peer competitors.

Cyber warfare against the F-35 had two overarching objectives for a putative enemy. First, if the plane's capabilities could be understood and essentially copied, the large investments required to develop them from a blank drawing board to finished plane could be saved. Secondly, spying could elucidate whether the plane had vulnerabilities that could be exploited. Experience taught that every computer-based system has weaknesses. Clearly, potential foes would be heavily incentivized to try to find them.

The F-35's airborne systems run approximately nine million lines of code. That software's made up of two categories. The vehicle systems software controls the flight characteristics: flight controls, the engine, fuel management, and all electrical and mechanical subsystems. Put simply, it manages all aspects of flight once the pilot decides which way to aim the pointy end. It's aggressively tested and uses triple-redundant fault-tolerant software.

The mission systems software controls the navigation, communication, identification, and war-fighting payload. This includes the radar, weapons, electronic warfare, distributed aperture system, defensive systems, and the sensor manager, which processes all the information and displays an integrated view of the environment.

In the cockpit, both vehicle and mission systems are orders of magnitude more complex but more intuitive to the pilot than those of any previous fighter. The need to protect them as the ultimate crown jewels was built into every aspect of the program. The layers of protection began with the limited set of participants and government overseers engaged in the integration phase, the top secret facilities they inhabited, and strict, rigidly enforced need-to-know rules.

Another barrier to hacking is password protection and user authentication checks. When it's time to go, the F-35 pilot feeds unique mission authentication and personal codes into the airplane when he or she climbs into a cockpit.

A third barrier was the imposition of multilevel security (MLS). Software had to be written by the subcontractor responsible for that subsystem well prior to its delivery to the F-35 system integration laboratories. While most of the major systems were produced by US contractors, some elements came from foreign partners. An MLS capability allows information at different classifications to be stored and accessed within a single system with the assurance that the separation is effective.[5]

Managing the multilevel security across the global supply chain was critical to hardening the JSF enterprise. MLS enabled "joint" development and access to operational capability at the level commensurate with an individuals approved national and personal security clearance levels and permissions.

And finally, if an intruder somehow made his way past these safeguards, critical adaptive hardware was in place that would keep working even if there was a successful hack. A 2017 article in the *Jerusalem Post* describes this safeguard as follows: "The solution for both aircraft and other systems . . . is to design the hardware to function even in the event of a successful hack. . . . For aircraft this means installing an engine that the software in the jet cannot turn off."[4]

But there was much more to the story than just the onboard systems.

To take full advantage of the new paradigm of a tri-service, multinational force, F-35s needed to be "connected" even when they weren't flying. A second set of off-board software-based systems were essential to capturing and sharing knowledge across operators and maintainers. It would also provide periodic software updates, essential for fine tuning the plane's sensors to keep up with evolving threats, and to allow new sensors and weapons to be carried and employed. It would also be critical to controlling the fleet's life-cycle costs.

The F-35's original sustainment concept was the autonomic logistics information system, discussed in detail elsewhere. To review briefly, this software included approximately twenty million source lines of code, providing the information backbone to operate, support, train, and sustain the fleet. Connecting all operational units to the IT backbone and keeping the ecosystem functioning smoothly would fall, in large measure, on the prime contractor team, supported by the global supply chain. Both production parts and subsystems and spare parts had to flow unimpeded. But those benefits didn't come without risk. Like any device that connected to the internet, but on a much grander scale, the off-board systems presented a critical vulnerability to hackers . . . and the possibility of disruption.

Cybercriminals' success can be measured by their ability to take down (or hold hostage, for ransom) critical infrastructures. When those infrastructures connect to confidential military or business information, the payoff can be strategic at a national level. Disrupting normal logistics, the industry supply chain, or spare part management could wreck mission readiness. The flow could also be corrupted by entering false data. For example, a bogus update on demand for more engines could create substantial confusion and inefficiency in the global supply chain.

★ ★ ★

So, it's not surprising that literally thousands of cyberattacks were carried out against the F-35 program. Most have been stopped at the front door. But there are several examples of incursions that did succeed. Perhaps the best-known example was that of Su Bin.

A Chinese entrepreneur based in Canada who ran a business called Beijing Lode Technology Company, Su Bin conspired with Beijing to penetrate corporate systems and steal sensitive data. His operation was both advanced and broad-based, covering not only US defense[5] companies but also those in Taiwan and Europe. "According to one of Su's emails, they had control of an unidentified defense company's file transfer protocol server. Jump servers, also known as 'hop points,' were set up in France, Japan, Hong Kong, Singapore, South Korea and the United States. According to emails, these were set up to avoid 'diplomatic and legal' difficulties for China."[6] Specifics of what Su managed to access are classified, but he was alleged to have obtained F-35 test plans and "blueprints" that would "allow us [China] to catch up rapidly with US levels . . . [and] stand easily on the giant's shoulders."[7]

More specifically, his operation may have been part of a much larger cyber campaign later dubbed by US intelligence officials "Operation Byzantine Hades." This campaign, which may have begun as early as 2006, has been attributed to technical reconnaissance bureaus operating as part of the People's Liberation Army's Third Department. Many terabytes of data related to the F-35 program are believed to have been stolen by Chinese hackers, including information on the F-35's radar design—such as the number and types of modules used by the system—and its engine, including the method used for cooling gases, leading and trailing edge treatments, and aft deck heating contour maps.[8]

★ ★ ★

As mentioned, a second "soft underbelly" was the supply chain. The requirement to generate industrial participation across the original nine-nation partnership opened potential sneak circuits for incursion through channels that weren't as well protected as the major US primes.

In late 2017, Australian and US officials confirmed that an Australian company had been hacked by suspected Chinese intruders trying to retrieve F-35 and other data. While the breach didn't compromise any classified data, it was believed to include commercially sensitive information as well as some detailed schematics. Although the press highlighted this as a vulnerability, detecting the intrusion was a testimony to the multilevel security protocols, in that no supplier had access to top-level program data.[9]

The challenge also expanded to include insider threats. Feeding on the most basic human weaknesses, greed and lust, stealing sensitive information was much easier if an insider was part of your team . . . and money whispers sweetly to the weak.

In 2017, Mozaffar Khazaee was sentenced to ninety-seven months of imprisonment for trying to send secret US defense technology to Iran. A dual citizen, Khazaee was employed by three different defense contractors between 2001 and 2013. One was Pratt & Whitney, who manufactured the engines for both the F-22 and the F-35. US authorities became suspicious when he tried to ship a large container to Iran. Inspecting it, they found thousands of pages of documents, including diagrams, test results, and jet engine blueprints. When the suspect attempted to board a flight to Iran, agents found additional information, as well as $60,000 in undeclared cash, in his checked and carry-on luggage. Spy vs. spy was taking on a new dimension.[10]

Recognizing this new danger, the Department of Defense and major contractors instituted new training and employment protocols. It was clear the F-35 would not be immune to this threat either.

Today the program is proactively focused on a more cyber-resilient modernization trajectory. Programmers have hardened industry computer systems against cyberattacks and intruders. Extra vigilance is required, as this vulnerability can sometimes be eclipsed by the jet's other more visible and well-known attributes.

Recognizing the importance of flattening the life-cycle cost curve, a substantial part of the early F-35's annual investment went to develop ALIS. The concept made sense. But over time, the sleeping stakeholders, entrenched in service-specific bureaucracies, began reeling its transformational aspects back toward traditional processes. As the aircraft entered operational service, several unanticipated challenges unfolded. These included the maturing of service-specific operational needs and the increased cyber threat. Early assumptions about the quality of maintenance data weren't being met. Untrained military conscripts made mistakes in entering data into a system that was heavily dependent on accuracy. Individual service advocates also began slowly massaging the system to tailor the results to their requirements, and not those of the wider community. And finally, some international clients belatedly realized that the aircraft's software automatically transmitted operational data back to the United States, which might possibly limit or restrict operations that did not align with US interests.[11] Eventually it became clear a sleeker, faster replacement for ALIS was needed, since both the operating environment and the cyber threat had evolved.

The operational data integrated network (ODIN) would be a cloud-based system with a new approach to integrating operational data and a new set of user applications. It was designed to reduce the administrative burden and make it easier for software engineers to push updates to the fleet. This would keep it effective against ever more lethal threats, quickly integrating new technologies without needing to reconstruct the aircraft's computing architecture.

But keeping all this cyber-resilient is a huge challenge.

Russia, China, Iran, and North Korea will only increase their cyber-warfare and cyber-espionage capabilities, particularly on cloud computing technologies in the foreseeable future. All have mobilized very capable personnel who can steal information and attack infrastructure. Their highest-value target is advanced US military hardware.

Daniel Coats, the director of national intelligence in the Trump administration, described it this way:

> Moscow has a highly advanced offensive cyber program, and in recent years, the Kremlin has assumed a more aggressive cyber posture. The threat will only continue to grow as the Kremlin expands its capabilities. We assess that Russian cyber operations will continue to target the United States and its allies to gather intelligence, support Russian decision-making, conduct influence operations to support Russian military and political objectives, and prepare the cyber environment for future contingencies.[12]

Putin's interest in future updates to the Lightning II was underlined recently when the CIA warned Britain that Russian agents may have planted bugs in the UK's "Pentagon" at Abbey Wood in Bristol.[13]

China also remains an active player. "We assess that Beijing will continue actively targeting the US government, its allies, and US companies for cyber espionage," Coats continued. "Private-sector security experts continue to identify ongoing cyber activity from China. Beijing has also selectively used offensive cyber operations against foreign targets that it probably believes threaten Chinese domestic stability or regime legitimacy."

Much of this struggle in cyberspace is still classified. However, despite the numerous assaults, the US government has declared the F-35 to be the most thoroughly tested weapon, ever, for cybersecurity measures.

Steve Over, director of F-35 international business development at Lockheed Martin, said, "To our knowledge we have passed every cyber test that has been applied against the F-35, but it is not an area where any of us, the US, Lockheed Martin, or our customers can afford to be complacent. This is an area where you have to remain vigilant, and we have to remain committed to continuing the evolution of all the IT systems on the airplane so that we stay ahead of the cyber threat that is very real and very existential." Asked whether a cyberattack could be conducted or carried out from an F-35 jet, he stopped short of providing an answer. "I know of nothing there we can talk about," Mr. Over said.[14]

Where is this new dimension of warfare taking us? The only truly existential threats previously developed, in recent history at least, were those of chemical weapons, airpower, and then thermonuclear weaponry. These menaces introduced the sustained study of deterrence as a national strategy. Given its overarching and hybrid nature, since it straddles the divide between military and civilian targets, cyber warfare may well represent another domain where mutual assured destruction is the only credible deterrent. Much of what we think we know about war doesn't apply in this domain. Obviously, we must stay ready to defeat conventional and nuclear threats on the ground, on and under the sea, in the sky, and in space. But now we also must fight aggression, espionage, psychological warfare, and sabotage in a less-familiar realm.[15]

Antonio Prohías published his final *Spy vs. Spy* cartoon in late 1986. But the eternal struggle continues. Cyberwarfare may become the dominant battlefield of the future. Since any battle requires both offensive and defensive strategies, both will be critical to the future of the Lightning II.

Reference

1.   Wiki Leaks on *Spy vs Spy* cartoon series, accessed September 2, 2022.

2.   Filseth, Trevor, "The Crazy Story of How Russia 'Helped' Build the SR-71 Blackbird," *The National Interest*, June 11, 2021.

3.   Turnbull, Grant, *Global Defence Technology*; defence.nridigital.com.

4.   "Multi-Level Security (MSL) Demystified", (Australian) *Defence Connect*, September 10, 2021; https://www.defenceconnect.com.au/key-enablers/8727-multi-level-security-mls-demystified, accessed January 17, 2023.

5.   Bob, Yonah Jeremy, "Is software of Israel's new F-35 fighter jet susceptible to hacking?" *Jerusalem Post*, May 19, 2017. Available online https://www.jpost.com/israel-news/is-software-of-israels-new-f-35-fighter-jets-susceptible-to-hacking-492230. Accessed January 18, 2023.

6.   Minnick, Wendell, "Chinese Businessman Pleads Guilty of Spying on F-22 and F-35," *Defense News*, March 24, 2016. Accessed September 12, 2022.

7.   Minnick, Wendell, "Chinese Businessman Pleads Guilty of Spying on F-22 and F-35," *Defense News*, March 24, 2016. Accessed September 12, 2022.

8.   Tiwari, Sakshi, "Chinese 'Stealth' Espionage!" *The Eurasian Times*, February 3, 2022, Accessed September 12, 2022.

9.   Morris, David, "Hackers Stole Restricted F-35 Data from an Australian Contractor," *Fortune*, October 14, 2017, accessed September 13, 2022.

10. Seligman, Lara, "F-35 Data Smuggler Sentenced to Jail," *Defense News*, November 3, 2015; accessed September 13, 2022.

11. "F-35 Fighters Found Spying of Their Operators," *Military Watch*, November 28, 2017. Accessed September 12, 2022.

12. "How China Stole Top Secret Information on the F-22 and F-35"; *The National Interest*, November 9, 2019.

13. "MOD Sweeps for Russian Spy Bugs after US Intelligence Warning," *Daily Express*, July 3, 2022. Accessed September 12, 2022.

14. Cyber Security Intelligence: "F-35 is the most thoroughly tested Cyber Weapon" 6/13/2018 in NEWS-News Analysis, Government Defence.

15. Ignatius, David, "Will deterrence have a role in the cyberspace 'forever war'?" *Washington Post*, September 15, 2022, accessed September 16, 2022.

Chapter 25

THE LAND DOWN UNDER

Many Americans are surprised to learn Australia is nearly the size of the continental United States. Strategically, it's been a dependable ally in the Indo-Pacific. The country has stood with the United States since 1918: World War I, World War II, Korea, Vietnam, both Iraq conflicts, and Afghanistan. The Australia Defence Force has participated in numerous humanitarian and peace-keeping efforts as well. For example, they aided Japan following the earthquake, tsunami, and Fukushima nuclear meltdown in 2011.

Australia's strategy seeks to balance self-reliance against the need to oper-ate with allies. During World War II, the Japanese attacked. Since the coun-try was a member of the British Commonwealth, one would have expected the UK to come to its defense. However, Britain was facing a dire threat to the home island. The United States stepped up instead. After his escape from Corregidor, General Douglas MacArthur set up his headquarters in Brisbane. The American-Australian Memorial in Canberra stands 240 feet high and is topped by a thirty-three-foot eagle, as a thank-you to the United States for its sacrifices in defending the continent.

By the late 1990s, the Royal Australian Air Force was flying two aging fighter types. One of them was the 1960s-era Grumman/General Dynamics F-111 Aardvark, affectionately called "The Pig." The USAF had retired their last F-111 in 1996, leaving Australia as the sole remaining operator of an "orphaned" design. The second dinosaur was the F-18A/B "classic" Hornet. Australia's had been upgraded over the years, but the airframes were fatiguing. In 1998, the Department of Defence established the new air combat capability (NACC) project to identify a replacement for both planes. The project office set up to manage the NACC was referred to as AIR6000.

Australia's priorities are outlined about every five to seven years in a series of publicly available Defence White Papers. The 2000 edition listed air combat as the single most important capability for Defence. It stated that the Royal

Australian Air Force (RAAF) should buy up to a hundred multi-role aircraft for the future.

The Capability Development area within Defence initially identified nine aircraft options for AIR6000. Air Marshal Mel Hupfeld, Australia's Chief of Air Force from July 2019 to July 2022, described the RAAF strategy.

> We wanted to ensure that we weren't just undertaking a platform-by-platform replacement approach, but were taking a broader view to see what capabilities were out there that could meet our future need. The F-35 wasn't on the books at that stage. We looked at combinations of fighter aircraft such as the Eurofighter Typhoon and the F-18 Super Hornet [a later and larger replacement for the classic Hornet—*Au*]. We were even considering Russian capability to put a broader perspective across what people might think and to shore up better discussion around interoperability needs. And, of course, the F-22 was on the streets at that point. We knew the concept of fifth-generation air combat capability and understood that type of a capability may be realizable.[1]

In Australia, decisions about defense are made after much analysis and deliberation. But when the Lockheed Martin F-22 Raptor promised not only stealth but also to be the finest high-performance fighter ever, defense leadership was interested. In December 2001, as the Raptor was in final testing, the Chief of the RAAF, Air Marshal Angus Houston, approached his US counterpart, General John Jumper. Citing the allies' special relationship, Houston asked if Australia could acquire the new fighter.

In Houston's words, "The answer was a resounding 'no.' The F-22 was for the US only."[2] Some technology leaps just can't be shared if the USAF is to remain dominant.

Although Houston had struck out, he quickly returned to bat. At that point, the F-35 was more of a glossy brochure than an aircraft. Yes, there were the concept demonstrators, but they weren't actual prototypes. They had no stealth capability, no weapons bay, no targeting systems. But it was the only game in town. "Once the F-22 was ruled out, that left us with only one fifth-generation contender. The F-35 was the only genuine multi-role aircraft that would fulfill the requirements laid out in the 2000 Defence White Paper that would meet the RAAF's requirements."

In 2001 Washington was inviting international partners to join the system development and demonstration (SDD) phase of the F-35. By late that year, seven allied nations had decided to join, but Australia had not yet committed.

In Australia, defense priorities and expenditures are governed by several high-level committees that report to parliament. The Defence Capability and Investment Committee met in March 2002 to consider whether the country should participate in the SDD phase. After considerable discussion, they decided not to. They felt they could save the money and buy the airplane later if they needed to.

Houston said, "I was not in support of that decision. I thought we needed to be part of SDD, not only for the benefit we would get out of the industrial terms but also because we needed to be able to fully understand the capability that was on offer since it looked like the most likely contender in the AIR6000 program."

Four months later, the opportunity arose to press his case. The nation's highest-level approval body, the National Security Committee, revisited the issue. As chief of the air force, Houston was invited to express his view.

> I argued very passionately that we had to be involved because that was most likely the aircraft that we would eventually buy. In addition, this would allow Australian industry to compete for work as suppliers to the program.
>
> One of the attendees, Max Moore-Wilton, was a close associate of the prime minister, John Howard. Moore-Wilton told the committee, "You heard it from the Air Marshal. He's the chief of the air force, and I accept his advice completely. Does anybody else have anything to say?"

As Houston recalls, "They all sat there and nobody said a word."

Meeting with the PM, Houston made the same passionate argument. Agreeing, Howard convened a press conference that same day. The minister for defense, Robert Hill, announced that Australia would be joining the F-35 program. In addition, and to everyone's surprise (including Houston's), Hill also announced that the competition among the nine contenders was closed—the F-35 was "it." In October 2002, Australia joined as a Tier 3 partner, the last of the nine international partners to do so.

Hill's announcement kicked over two beehives. One was the potential for Australian companies to become suppliers. (This saga will be sung in the following chapter.) The other was the triggering of vocal and persistent domestic opposition. While the competition had been officially closed, the first NAAC program manager—Air Marshal John Harvey—made sure they kept tabs on alternatives in case the Lightning stumbled. This would prove wise down the track when its development was delayed by the weight issue and subsequent redesign. But Harvey was confident the plane would eventually fly. "We had the U.S. Air Force, Navy, and Marine Corps, and then we had Lockheed Martin, Northrop Grumman, BAE Systems, and Pratt & Whitney on the industry side. I thought if anyone can make this work that arrangement must be able to do it."[3]

Once Australia had partnered up, a team was embedded in the joint program office in the United States. The country was wearing two hats, one as a cheerleader and participant helping the program succeed, and the other as a customer, ensuring Australia was getting what it wanted.

With the selection announcement, antagonism erupted. In the words of Geoff Brown, an ex-F-18 and F-111 pilot who became chief of the air force in 2011, "There was a fair amount of opposition around the original decision because we hadn't done what people thought we should have—tested the airplane against the competitors at the time."[4] Brown had experienced his personal epiphany in the cockpit during the 2002 Red Flag exercises. Red Flag is held periodically at U.S. Air Force bases with the intent to realistically simulate air combat. He describes that simulation:

> At the time, I was flying an F-111, but I also got the privilege to fly in the back of an F-15D, which was an aggressor airplane in the exercise. The F-15 is quite a good fourth-generation fighter. The only trouble was that we were up against eight F-22s. To this day, it's the most frustrating fighter mission I've ever flown in. We got clubbed like a baby seal five times. You can't see or target the other guy. You're at such a disadvantage that it doesn't matter what the rest of the qualities of your machine are.

While Brown and others had faith the F-35 was the right choice, leading the opposition in Australia was Air Power Australia (APA), a nonprofit think tank founded in 2004 by Dr. Carlo Kopp and Peter Goon. APA's charter was to conduct research and analysis. Dr. Kopp had a PhD in airborne networking, and Goon was a career engineer who had attended the U.S. Navy Test Pilot School. As a technical duo, they had street credibility, especially with the general public and politicians. But it was clear from the outset that they had no respect for the F-35.

Arguing that the Lightning could never meet its advertised capabilities, they proposed a reengined and updated version of the F-111. The "Evolved" F-111 would use the Pratt & Whitney F-119 engine that powered the F-22, along with modernized electronics. Additional airframes could be drawn cheaply from American boneyards, since the USAF had phased out the plane many years earlier.

An argument could be made that this was interesting conceptually. The venerable F-111 had been in service with the RAAF since 1973. It was a supersonic strategic bomber, a big airplane with a large payload capacity. In Australia's largely maritime theater of vast distances, combat radius was important, but the F-111 was considered a medium-range bomber at best.[5] Yet the concept took little note of the engineering nightmares such an effort would entail. The much more powerful F-119 power plant would require a complete structural redesign of the older plane. Integrating modern electronics would be difficult and costly as well. Incorporating all that into an elderly and totally non-stealthy airframe made little sense from either a cost-benefit viewpoint or from a long-term survivability perspective.

But Air Power Australia had contacts with major newspapers and a few key politicians. They orchestrated a violent social media assault. Opposition in Australia and the other partner nations egged one another on. Dr. Steve Gumley, the top-level civilian responsible for acquiring systems for the Australian Defence Force, recalled, "I can't remember any other program that I was involved with that has had as much national press as this one. Some people honestly felt the F-35 was the wrong aircraft for Australia."[6]

This storm of abuse required defense leadership to expend considerable time and effort. Houston said, "For the rest of my time as chief of the air force, I rolled from parliamentary hearing to parliamentary hearing having to defend the decisions that had been taken and explain why it was important that we be part of SDD and why the JSF would be the aircraft that will take us into the future. And then when I became chief of the defense force, I had to defend it a number of times."

Perhaps the greatest stumbling block was that the general public had a dated concept of fighter combat, largely based on dogfights portrayed in World War II movies. The F-22 is the ultimate dogfighter, with its killer combination of stealth and thrust vectoring. But, although the F-35 is as capable as any fourth-generation aircraft aerodynamically, its real strength lay less in aerobatics than in its stealth and in its electronic sensors and datalinks. But explaining these capabilities quickly got into classified information, which made it difficult to explain or justify the decision to the press.

While the Frankensteined F-111 gained traction with the media and politicians, it never had any real credibility with the Air Force. Geoff Brown said,

> I didn't mind the argument that they ran. Their argument wasn't that we didn't need a new fighter, it was that the F-35 wasn't good enough. When you think about the possible arguments that you can come against, the Kopp and Goon one wasn't a bad one from the point of view that they just wanted what they perceived to be the best capability for Australia. From my point of view, they were painful because they always had just enough knowledge to be dangerous.

Mark Binskin, whose involvement with the F-35 spanned a twenty-two-year period including as chief of the air force and chief of the defense force, made a similar point:

> We weren't justifying the capability. We were justifying the solution. It was a hard-fought battle to keep people focused on the JSF and not jump on a lesser technology as a solution. Part of that was the delays in the program; that was an issue. The other part was the commentators feeling that they weren't being given a straight answer even though they were being given a straight answer. The fact was that the systems the aircraft bring are highly classified and the fact that it's fighting a war in a different way to what people envisioned for a dogfight was a problem. It doesn't mean that it doesn't need to have good maneuverability and good air combat capabilities but it was a different mindset that we needed to take to the aircraft.[7]

In 2007, the minister for defense, Brendan Nelson, made the decision to retire all the F-111s in 2010. In the meantime, the Defence Science and Technology Organisation was conducting structural analyses to forecast how long the old Hornets could safely fly. As a result, the F-18's retirement was postponed from 2012 to about 2020.

But with the F-35's delays, worries escalated. Houston said, "Brendan Nelson became the defense minister, and he became very concerned about a capability gap and the advice he got was to buy some Super Hornets." And in the words of Mark Binskin, "The F-35 was coming a number of years too late for us to be able to handle the technical risk that was developing around keeping the aged F-111 airframe running."

Nelson made the announcement to buy Super Hornets in 2007. Houston: "I was chief of the defense force at the time. This came in as a surprise from left field."

Meanwhile, the storm of bad press kept on. None of the international partners were immune to the continuing barrage. The delays allowed a vulnerability window and critics and competitors fanned the flames. Dr. Gumley described the concern. "Things got really shaky in 2005. . . . I know in my conversations with other partner countries, we were all concerned about the weight issue and its impacts on capability, cost, and schedule. If reducing weight meant reducing capability so that the aircraft couldn't do certain things, that would be a real issue. A redesign was obviously going to have a schedule effect, and there was always a risk there might be a cost effect."

While the international partner countries may have been worried, Angus Houston was a reassuring presence. Gary North, who spent much of his career with the U.S. Air Force in the Pacific region, eventually rising to a four-star rank as commander of the Pacific Forces, was a keen observer of events in the region. He summed up Houston's influence by saying, "You've got no bigger fan than me of Angus Houston. He really is the dean of all the CHODs [Chiefs of Defense] around the world. In that time frame, he was the most respected, the most appreciated and the most strategically thoughtful leader that everybody would listen to. And so, when Angus talked, the world listened."[8]

This was when the benefits of having each partner country embedded in the JPO became clear. In Gumley's words, "In an international program like this, putting some of your best people as embedded staff into the host country's program is good for Australia, but it's also good for the program as a whole because a lot of the suspicion that might exist goes away. Your people are living it and sending reports back to home base that we've got a problem but here's what we're doing to solve it."

Harvey concurred. "I think the best thing the United States did, to the maximum extent they could, was their openness, their willingness to have us in there as an actual partner and to listen to what we had to say. It wasn't just a token effort."

This period was also marked by intense lobbying by Boeing—the manufacturer of the Super Hornet—for Canberra to take a "less-risky" approach and acquire an additional twenty-four Super Hornets. This would have resulted in a total of forty-eight and cut down the number of F-35s procured.

The first Super Hornets arrived in Australia in March 2010. While this buy wasn't necessarily requested by the RAAF leadership, it was recognized as an opportunity for Australia to be able to transition to the F-35 at a time of Australia's choosing and served as an important stepping stone. Air marshal Mel Hupfeld offered the following explanation:

> The classic Hornet had been upgraded by after-market systems additions. We put good systems on board. . . . But they were all after-market additions so they weren't built as integrated capabilities from the ground up. We began seeing little bits of workaround that we had to do here and there in order to deliver and operate this world-class capability that was represented through its upgrades.
>
> When we started to operate the Super Hornet, we began to see an aircraft that was actually designed and built to the integrating systems—multi-sensor, multisource data, active electronically scanned array radar, some characteristics of signature that we could start to manage. While this very much represented enhanced operational capabilities, the Super Hornet also started to get us at least on a path toward fifth-generation capability as we understood it.

In 2009, the RAAF received government approval to buy fourteen F-35s. Two were to be delivered up front, followed by an option for twelve more. In Brown's words, "When we made the decision to have just two F-35s, that was significant. It was to get ourselves what I termed 'pregnant' at the time because once we got two, it was going to be hard to walk back from there . . . Not only was there external opposition to the F-35 but there was a fair amount of internal opposition as well from Navy and Army, because at the time it was our biggest defense purchase."

Air Vice Marshal Kym Osley began his tenure as Head of the NACC Project Office shortly after the government approved the initial procurement. In 2011, Gumley left his position as CEO of the Defence Materiel Organisation (DMO) and was replaced by Warren King. While Gumley had been a staunch supporter of the F-35, King brought a different perspective, despite the fact that he had been the Deputy CEO for Gumley. He assumed his new post on the heels of defense minister Stephen Smith implementing a series of reforms aimed at reducing DMO program risk across their broad portfolio of some 180 major programs. Not surprisingly, he thought the F-35 represented a high degree of risk. This created a tightrope Osley and Brown had to walk to keep the F-35 moving forward.

Back in Arlington, the JPO had just completed the post-Nunn-McCurdy-breach technical baseline review and replan. This meant an additional three years were added to the development schedule, and more than $4 billion. While that was paid by the United States, as Osley described this period, "The re-plan resulted in a lot of consternation within government and within the media about whether the decision to actually commit to the F-35 in late 2009 was the right one."[9]

Osley noticed a difference in the way the US and Australian governments worked:

> The way you convey information to the government is vastly different in the United States to how it is in Australia. The Australian Government is happy to take bad news and good news, whereas I think that the public relations machine for the F-35—and this is both the JPO and Lockheed Martin—was more attuned to the idea of putting out good information only and trying to downplay any bad information. In Australia I think what was required was a very balanced way of presenting information so that was certainly one of the challenges I had.

2011 was the first of several years of high drama within the Australian defense community, as the plan for a fifth-generation air force came close to being derailed. As noted above, Warren King, whose background was in the navy, wasn't an enthusiastic proponent. Brown was a strong advocate, and found DMO resistance frustrating. But if anyone within the Australian defense community understood the politics of the situation and could move the F-35 forward, that person was Geoff Brown.

Once the first F-35As had been ordered, the next decision point was to buy an additional fifty-eight, which would bring the total to seventy-two. Lobbying from both the pro- and anti F-35 camps reached a crescendo. The anti-camp included Boeing Defence Australia. Binskin and Brown were concerned that a buy of an additional twenty-four Super Hornets would decrease the number of F-35s, leading to a capability split between the fourth-generation Super Hornet and the fifth-generation F-35. Both Binskin and Brown were convinced the country needed an all-fifth-generation force.

Brown came up with a masterful solution to protect the F-35 buys while augmenting the force for the near term. He proposed that the RAAF buy twelve Growlers which are Super Hornets modified to suppress enemy air defenses. Brown also initiated "Project Jericho" to create a fifth-generation air force by extending the interoperability concept. It would no longer be the F-35 with other allied F-35 air forces. It would now encompass the entire Australian Air Force, leveraging the new advanced capabilities of the F-35. Of equal importance, the Growler purchase did not detract from the eventual planned purchase of F-35s. Defense minister Stephen Smith agreed and announced the purchase.

But Smith, with the DMO risk concerns, was still not fully convinced the F-35 was the right choice.

The Avalon Air Show is the largest air show in the southern hemisphere. Lt Gen Chris Bogdan, the new F-35 PEO in 2013, was scheduled to attend. Osley arranged for Bogdan to meet with Smith during the show and to present his personal and candid views on the F-35 and progress on the program. As Brown describes it, "Chris was pretty much an introvert in lots of ways, and so was Smith. And in about ten minutes, they bonded amazingly well. In that one meeting . . . he actually secured in Smith's mind that the F-35 was worth the pain."

The first two Lightning IIs were delivered in 2014. They were based at Luke AFB in Arizona for pilot and maintainer training. The next decision was whether to purchase the additional fifty-eight, completing three of the originally planned four squadrons. There was plenty of opposition, within and outside of the Australian defense community, but most notably from Warren King.

Air Commodore Catherine Roberts had recently joined the program, reporting to Osley. A RAAF engineer for over thirty-five years, "Cath" was the highest-ranking female officer in the DMO and would go on to be the head of air force capability and later the first commander of the Australian Defence Space Command. She said, "Warren wanted what he called a 'field of dreams' approval process which was to obtain government approval for the facilities only first. He viewed approval for actual aircraft as too risky." Cath Roberts, Geoff

Brown, and Kym Osley knew that approval for the entire capability was needed in order to meet IOC in 2020.

In Roberts's words, "I went with Geoff Brown around Canberra and Defence convincing people of the need to do this. We had pictures of corroded F-18s and we had a critical path to reach IOC. We divided the project into eight streams to show the different elements. Essentially, it was eight projects, only one of which was facilities. We showed that we needed to get approval for all eight work streams and the timing required to do that."

The decision to order the final tranche of aircraft came at a meeting attended by the secretary of defence and the chief of the defense force (CDF). While Brown, as chief of the air force, was eager to place the order, King was opposed.

As Brown described it,

Warren had convinced the CDF at the time, David Hurley, that we shouldn't make this commitment for the fifty-eight JSFs. We had an investment committee meeting in the afternoon, and as I tallied up who was going to vote which way, I was particularly worried we were going to go down on this one. The secretary at the time was Dennis Richardson. Dennis and Warren had convinced the CDF that we should delay the order for the fifty-eight. I called up Mark Binskin, the vice chief of the defense force, and I said to him "We're in trouble on this one, because I think CDF is going to side with the Secretary and Warren King." So, we managed to get into David Hurley's office about three hours before the meeting. We spent about half an hour going through why we needed to make the order now for the fifty-eight, and we turned CDF to our side.

That made the vote in the Committee, CDF, VCDF [vice chief of the defense force], and myself. And the other service chiefs and myself had an agreement that if we were passionate about one particular area, we tended to support each other, so I had the other service chiefs on my side. CDF didn't tell the secretary that he'd actually changed his position at that stage so it became a pretty exciting meeting. That's how we ended up with the fifty-eight.

But the pop-up dramas weren't over yet. Roberts was attending a JSF executive steering board meeting in JPO headquarters when it became apparent a number of the partner countries were planning to delay their purchases.

At this point, the program was on a steep price-reduction curve. As a result of increasing efficiency in production, F-35s were getting cheaper each year. This tempted the chintzier partners to delay their buys. Unfortunately, a delay by any one meant an increase in price for the others.

As Roberts listened, she realized Australia was going to have to pay more for their remaining buy. As she recalls,

> I just blurted out, "Oh my goodness! That means that the price of the air-craft is going up." The PEO, General Bogdan was definitely shocked and not happy and then asked "How would you know?" I'm this one female person in a room full of fighter pilots and it is intimidating to speak up. Later, he was very appreciative of my honesty, because his staff hadn't realized that that was going to be the effect and that was going to affect everyone's program. And at the time, I did think about whether I should, at such late notice, advise defense and the government about a potential price increase or say anything, but I was honest and I told Warren. He went a bit crazy. We ended up reaching an agreement that we would explain to the government what had happened and add another 1 percent to the total cost of the program.

In July 2014, Lockheed Martin hosted a ceremony in Fort Worth to mark the rollout of the first two Australian F-35s. The event included a didgeridoo player and a dramatic unveiling of the plane. Geoff Brown was the key speaker for the RAAF and appropriately AVM Kym Osley was in attendance for one of his last official duties before his retirement from the RAAF. Looking back, Roberts sees this as a turning point. "The rollout of the first two aircraft in the United States showed that the F-35 was real, that it existed, that it flew, and it was a fantastic event." But even prepping for the ceremony had its drama. "They painted the tail flash incorrectly, and we got a look at it a couple of days before the ceremony and we said 'You're going to have to repaint it.' So, the paint on the aircraft was actually wet when we had the final ceremony."

Once the aircraft had been ordered, everyone's attention turned to preparing for IOC. Roberts was promoted to head of the aerospace systems division, with air vice marshal Leigh Gordon taking on the F-35 program lead. But Roberts returned to lead the program as the head of air force capability in 2019 to focus on achieving IOC, which was declared in December 2020 despite the COVID-19 pandemic.

At the time of this writing, the F-35 is well received in Australia, especially by the pilot community. Angus Houston said, "The aircraft is delivering a capability that has exceeded the expectations of our fighter pilots and exceeded my expectations. It's also come in at the right cost at this stage of the program and the hope is that in a few years' time, we will be operating the aircraft at a very economical cost per flying hour."

Gumley reflected on the program's achievement. "In any major project, you've got capability, cost, and schedule, and you can never optimize all three simultaneously. You've got to anchor one and let the others float. With the JSF, capability effectively got anchored and that was the right decision."

Harvey summed it up. "The F-35 has changed the whole air force. The constant reference now is we're moving up to a fifth-generation air force and making sure that everything that wraps around the F-35 is up to the mark as well. It really has become the centerpiece of the air force for the future."

The Land Down Under has always been our strongest ally in the faraway reaches of the South Pacific. Their fighting spirit to preserve the democratic freedoms we share and remains enhanced by their fight to preserve the partnership in the F-35 program.

Reference

1. Interview with Air Marshal Mel Hupfeld on August 12, 2020, by Tom Burbage, Betsy Clark and Adrian Pitman. Held in F-35 interview archive.
2. Interview with Air Chief Marshall Sir Angus Houston on June 18, 2020, by Tom Burbage, Betsy Clark and Adrian Pitman. Held in F-35 interview archive.
3. Interview with Air Marshall John Harvey on April 7, 2019, by Tom Burbage, Betsy Clark, and Adrian Pitman. Held in F-35 interview archive.
4. Interview with Air Marshal Geoff Brown on July 9, 2020, by Tom Burbage, Betsy Clark, and Adrian Pitman. Held in F-35 interview archive.
5. http://www.ausairpower.net/TE-F-111-Supercruise-2001.html.
6. Interview with Dr. Stephen Gumley on March 30, 2019, by Tom Burbage, Betsy Clark, and Adrian Pitman. Held in F-35 interview archive.
7. Interview with Air Chief Marshal Mark Binskin on April 4, 2019, by Tom Burbage, Betsy Clark, and Adrian Pitman. Held in F-35 interview archive.
8. Interview with General (Ret.) Gary North on May 14, 2020 by Tom Burbage, Betsy Clark, and Adrian Pitman. Held in F-35 interview archive.
9. Interview with Air Vice Marshal Kym Osley on June 4, 2020, by Tom Burbage, Betsy Clark, and Adrian Pitman. Held in F-35 interview archive.

Chapter 26

G'DAY USA, G'DAY WORLD

Every year, Australia showcases itself to America with a series of black-tie events called G'Day USA. Defense industries are also part of the show, and the F-35 industrial partnerships have generated many invitations to the gala events, especially in Los Angeles and New York.

But underneath the fancy-dress parties, as well as the face-offs in the sky and exciting test flights, lies a more workaday foundation of contracts, business relationships, and manufacturing techniques.

Like the other international partners, Australia's industries were permitted to compete for work on the F-35. This was a major factor in the decision to join and bolstered public support amid the storms of opposition mentioned in a previous chapter.

Much the same might be said of the industries of the other international partners as well. Unfortunately, if each country was covered in the depth they deserve, this book would be too heavy for the reader to lift!

But perhaps a discussion of how one nation's industries managed to rise to the challenge can stand in for the many other engineering and production companies, all around the world, without which the Lightning II could never have sought the clouds.

The F-35 program's timing was especially fortuitous for Australia. A number of domestic companies had supplied the home automotive industry with tooling and parts for many years. Ford, General Motors, Toyota, and Mitsubishi all ran factories. Sadly, early in the century these production lines were closing, faced with withering competition from completed cars shipping in from Japan, Korea, Europe, and America. This downsizing began with Mitsubishi in 2008 and ended with the last Australian-made automobile rolling off the General

Motors production line in 2017. Reading the writing on the wall, suppliers were looking to branch out.

Unfortunately, integrating local industry into an advanced aeronautical supply chain would not be simple. Although their craftspeople had some technical expertise, including precision engineering, manufacturing robotics, advanced carbon composite manufacturing, advanced metal machining capability, and stress engineering, these smaller suppliers weren't exactly famous on the world stage.

Could Australian industries actually become viable aerospace suppliers? Succeed, and they might one day expand to service other countries and aircraft programs. Fail, and thousands of Australians would lose their jobs.

The stakes were immense, and the downside looked forbidding.

Kym Osley, the RAAF F-35 program director from 2010 to 2014, focused on two outcomes during his tenure. In addition to acquiring the new plane and supporting infrastructure, landing work for Aussie companies was an important performance measure. In his words, "It was the first major acquisition where a key part of the responsibility given to the program manager was that they had to come up with good industry outcomes for Australia. . . . I was given the task of actually influencing commercial outcomes in favor of Australia."[1]

While Canberra was dithering over its alternatives for the future fighter, two departments had glimpsed a role for Australian industry. The Department of Defence and the Department of Industry and Tourism formed the JSF Industry Advisory Council to help the country participate. The council consisted of representatives from a number of Australian businesses, large and small. With the help of Osley and the government team, the council would educate prospective participants on the new requirement to compete for contracts on the basis of best value. Lockheed Martin, along with BAE Systems and Northrop Grumman, made several visits to identify candidate companies.

In the beginning, Lockheed Martin had pioneered a concept they called "follow the sun engineering." Australia already had a world-class stress-engineering capability. Two hundred engineers at GKN Australia, under the leadership of Tony Quick, were instrumental in the STOVL Weight Attack

Team (SWAT) redesign. Their counterparts in Fort Worth and El Segundo would punch out about the time those in Brisbane were signing in.

From a manufacturing perspective, two of the most promising companies were Marand Precision Engineering, in Melbourne, and Ferra Engineering, in Brisbane.

★ ★ ★

The Ellul family had founded Marand Precision Engineering in 1969 in Moorabin in greater Melbourne. "Marand" is an amalgamation of the names of the matriarch, Mary Ellul, and the patriarch, Andrew. They served a niche or "boutique" market, equipping the continent's relatively small automobile and aerospace industries with precision tooling.

Tony Ellul, younger son of Mary and Andrew and Marand's managing director, used it to network with members from other companies, including Lockheed Martin and BAE. Equally important, this allowed him to burnish contacts within the defense and industry communities.

Rohan Stocker, Marand's CEO, recalled, "All of a sudden, we had a seat at that table that was planning out the industry enterprise for F-35. And it also enabled us to build very important government and industry networks especially in the first five to ten years of the program out here."[2]

In 2002, teams from Fort Worth and BAE, including Tom Burbage, visited a number of companies to feel out the local supply chain. At Marand, Tony Ellul gave a PowerPoint presentation showcasing that company's experience. One particular job piqued Burbage's interest. The company had fabricated a trailer for Qantas to move engines around a workshop. Tom made a note to himself: Could it be the solution to getting engines in and out of a fighter in carrier hangar decks, at sea?

Up to that visit, Marand had honed its aerospace skills providing precision tooling for Hawker de Haviland-Australia (now part of Boeing). De Haviland had supplied "bolt-on" parts, such as tails, flaps, wings, and doors, to commercial and military companies such as LM, BAE, Boeing, Airbus, and Bombardier. Thus, Marand understood the language and technology and the tooling required.

Rather surprisingly, their automotive experience was also relevant. Stocker recalled,

We were right in the middle of building and designing automotive factories before the decision to stop, so it wasn't just the tooling. We had car companies coming to us saying, "We need a plant to make the floors for a car; there are one hundred parts in that floor, you've got a very constrained amount of space. Can Marand give us a price to build a turn-key solution to build that factory, including the automation and the robotics?" And I believe that Tom saw a connection with the huge ramp-up in production that was ahead of the F-35 program and the need to basically get a plane a day out of the factory.

Marand arranged for the visitors to fly out to a Ford plant in Geelong, Victoria, a fifteen-minute ride in a helicopter versus two and a half hours by road. Expensive, but the executives thought it was more important that the visitors spent their time looking at Marand tooling in action rather than sitting in a car.

Unlike US automotive plants, which usually make only one type of car, Australia's much smaller industry required production lines to build multiple models. The Ford plant made engines for SUVs, sedans, small trucks, and station wagons. In Stocker's words, "The Lockheed team saw that Marand had this ability to have interchangeable tooling and to think about the production line for the F-35 with its three variants. Marand engineers visited Lockheed's Palmdale facility to help the team there think about high-volume production, about the tooling, the automation, and how a plant might be configured."

Sending the engineer to Palmdale was Marand's first contract with the program; a far bigger opportunity was around the corner.

Now Burbage remembered that engine trailer. He sent Stocker a request for quotation to provide engine trailers for the F-35. This was much more capable and complex than the Qantas unit. Actually, calling this piece of equipment a "trailer" is a misnomer. It was arguably the most sophisticated mechanical gizmo in the entire program, aside of course from the plane itself. It let a single person remove and install a STOVL engine aboard a small carrier in rough seas. It was adaptable to any of the three variants, and could even handle either the Pratt & Whitney or the General Electric unit.

Marand's proposal included a technical section describing their approach, a commercial section discussing the company's previous and current work, and a section on costs. To their surprise, LM rejected it. Burbage was flummoxed too, particularly on learning they'd quoted the lowest price. Clearly something had gotten lost in translation.

Reflecting on that rejection, Stocker said,

While we had the right technical solution and we had the right price, what we didn't have was the capability to respond to Lockheed Martin's request for quotation. We hadn't made it easy for Lockheed to understand whether we were compliant or not compliant with their requirements. . . . We just assumed they understood us in the same way our other customers understood us and of course, they didn't. Lockheed assigned different people to independently review the commercial section, the technical section, and the pricing. We hadn't written a proposal that helped each of those people understand us and that's effectively why we lost it.

It also became clear that many of the smaller companies across the supply chain had never responded to a big prime on the military side. This would be a global challenge with the commitment to give these little fish a fair shake. Marand got a second chance to submit, along with some coaching about what information the company needed to provide and how. This time, they won the contract.

The first trailer was only used on aircraft AA-1. It consisted of the wheels, chassis, and a lifting mechanism, plus an adaptor set that fit the two different engines and three variants. The initial adaptor set was designed by Lockheed engineers at Palmdale and then manufactured by Marand. As a result of engineering changes in the early production lots, the trailer had to evolve to match.

In Stocker's words,

We won a contract from Lockheed to design and manufacture the adaptor set to sit on our trailer and we did twelve trailers with that adaptor set on there. Then in the fourth production lot, we designed what we called the "mobility trailer," effectively a completely new trailer that was used on everything from that point onwards. Each of those trailers has about 4,500 parts manufactured by us, plus lots of other commercial off-the-shelf items such as fasteners, seals, and things like that. I'd be very surprised if there's a piece of mechanical equipment made in Australia that's anywhere near the sophistication of the F-35 engine trailer. (**See Figure 29: Marand Precision Engineering engine trailer**)

The lessons from that rejected proposal returned dividends when a few years later, Marand got the chance to compete against other Aussie companies to build new production tooling for the F-35's aft section. This time Stocker had his ducks in a row.

> We made sure that BAE Systems could understand from our proposal, without knowing us, how we're going to do that work, what capabilities we have, how we prove it to them, and how our business was commercially and financially sound. It was, I think, far and away more than what BAE expected. There is no doubt in my mind that came from the education we were given on the trailer program. Based on our proposal, we were selected to lead the production of the majority of BAE's rate tooling.

That set the stage for an even more important assignment.

During that original visit by Lockheed and BAE, aerospace company Hawker De Havilland was one of the stops. At that time, LM thought HDH could be a second source of vertical tails once the F-35 production rate was at a high level. But by 2009, when the rates were ramping up and it became time to identify another supplier, Boeing had acquired the company as an exclusive production source for their commercial aircraft. They were no longer in the military airplane business. Meanwhile, Marand was building the engine trailer for LM and production tooling for BAE. They'd proved themselves.

At the same time, Australia was an attractive location for producing more vertical tails. Quickstep Aerospace Composites in the western territory of Perth was pioneering new technologies that did not require expensive autoclave ovens. They could make the tail skins. BAE Systems in Adelaide were machining the titanium used in the tails from Western Australia. And then there was Marand. Could they all work together to produce a major subassembly?

In 2009, BAE approached Marand about serving as a second source. It was a decision Stocker and others felt they had to think about before they jumped in. "We looked at the business case and weighed up the various risks. We were still a relatively small family business. But we chose to give it a go. And I'd like to add that BAE worked very hard with us to make this a success story."

Stocker estimates that half of Marand's work is currently related to the F-35. Over the past fifteen years, they've expanded to provide tooling to partner countries, including Terma in Denmark, Kongsberg in Norway, and Magellan

Aerospace in Canada. It has grown from a niche company to a global supplier of precision tooling and parts.

Stocker gives much of the credit to the Australian Department of Defence, the F-35 project office in Australia, the Australian team within the JPO, and the Department of Industry. "All those guys have helped us on occasions by opening the right door or by reminding people that we're here and capable to do some more work." He also credits Burbage personally.

> Tom's role in all this cannot be underestimated. He has a remarkable ability to see the big picture but when I look at how he helped us, it was in small steps and in how he connected people. I've never seen anyone else quite operate in the same way. Our success came out of people working together and guys like Tom who were willing to take a phone call from the other side of the world from a little company and make the connection to other people. And anyone he connected us to opened their doors to talk to us and help us.

When Marand delivered its first set of vertical tails in 2014, LM arranged for a full-scale mock-up of the fighter to be brought from the Paris Air Show and displayed in the parking lot. With no nearby airports and a fighter parked out front, curious passersby caused a traffic jam. The Victoria state premier joked that it was a STOVL version that had made a vertical landing there. With all the interest in the demonstrator, Marand put a fence around their parking lot. One night, two police came by and told the security guard on duty that they needed to enter the parking lot. When asked why, they simply said they couldn't say until they were inside. Since they were uniformed police, the guard let them in. Then the secret nature of their visit was revealed. They handed over their cell phones and asked the guard to take their photo standing next to the plane.

★ ★ ★

Mark Scherrer founded Ferra Engineering as a general machining shop in 1992. The company produced engine parts, braking systems, and fuel pumps for the domestic car industry. By 2002, Ferra was building wing ribs for Boeing commercial aircraft and pilot controls for Airbus helicopters. So, when the F-35 team showed up, Scherrer sensed an opportunity: "We had the background of automation, including a significant number of robots in our facility, doing work for the big car companies. Right from the beginning, we started positioning ourselves to Lockheed Martin and other F-35 contractors as a company that really wanted to be on the program to innovate, and to put the best product forward for the war fighter."[3]

As the local car factories shuttered, Ferra began transitioning to other industries, including electronics and medical equipment. Several years after their first F-35 contract, they decided to abandon automobiles altogether.

As Scherrer recalls,

> We divested our large equipment including robots and high-pressure die-casting machines and we invested it into capital equipment for the aerospace industry. We had signed a memorandum of understanding with the F-35 program worth about $30 million over a number of years and that gave us the ability to take the very bold step of moving from one industry to another. . . . Without the F-35 program, a number of engineering companies like Ferra would not have been able to sustain themselves once the automotive industry left Australia.

Mark Scherrer credits Lockheed Martin with encouraging their first-tier contractors—BAE Systems and Northrop Grumman—and their second-tier subcontractors to actively seek out smaller companies that could contribute. One of Ferra's early contracts was with Parker Aerospace, of Irvine, California, to build receptacle housings for actuators. Another early contract was to build weapons adapters, which permit different bombs or missiles to fit the plane's carrier points. They started with two and have so far built eleven different sets. Every plane needs them, so the numbers are significant as production and sustainment repair demands increase.

With its roots in consumer industry, Ferra had a culture of always trying to drive costs down. They experimented with two innovations that promised significant savings. One was a machining process that used a laser to preheat metal an inch ahead of the cutter. This preheating meant hard metals could be cut at the feed rate of softer ones, accelerating throughput and reducing costs. Ferra also experimented with 3D printing of titanium parts, applying thin layers to produce a near-final shape less expensively.

Ferra estimated that these innovations would have resulted in savings of 60 percent to 70 percent but they never made it past the prototype stage for use on aircraft. They did, however, add to manufacturing know-how in other business sectors that didn't require FAA approval. Also, while Ferra was experimenting with saving money, the focus of the program was much more on weight reduction than on penny-pinching.

★ ★ ★

Australians often refer to the "tyranny of distance," a phrase made popular by Geoffrey Blainey. His book of the same title discusses the influence that Australia's remoteness from Mother England has had on its history.[4] Ferra suffered from this tyranny when the company began making parts for the F-35, but with the relevant distance this time being between Australia and the United States.

Certain parts required a number of surfacing steps (veneering and heat treatments) after initial machining. When Ferra came onboard, these techniques were well advanced in the United States, but Australian industry had neither the equipment nor the training to do this in-country; it was unique to aerospace safety requirements. After Ferra completed the initial machining of a part, they would send it to the United States for stress relief. The part then came back around the world for the final machining, and then back again to the States for surface treatment. As a result, components were being flown back and forth across the Pacific as many as six times during production. In Scherrer's words, "We looked at the supply chain, and we quickly realized that it was not sustainable. The raw material came out of the States and most of the time, it had to be flown in because sending it by ship took months." All that to-ing and fro-ing was doubling the cost. So Ferra presented a business case to Lockheed Martin to approve Australian companies to do the surface treatments and quit playing Ping-Pong.

Sherrer adds, "We even managed to get an aluminum supplier in Australia to put standard-size F-35 material into stock so we didn't have to fly everything in. After two years, we went from having all our suppliers and sub-contractors in the United States to having a group of local suppliers. We now have nearly thirty Australian suppliers on F-35."

Ferra also battled distance by relocating people and facilities to the United States. Their first footprint was in California. A company they were using for surface painting allowed Ferra employees to use their facility for the final assembly work. Ferra also acquired a facility outside of Oklahoma City to compete for final assembly.

Lockheed Martin put two programs in place that helped small companies stay competitive. One was a right-to-buy agreement allowing the littler suppliers to buy bulk materials from the United States, at the same discount a competitor ten times their size might pay. The second program was mentoring. Fort Worth sent two female lean-manufacturing experts to Australia. In reference to a popular Hollywood movie, they became affectionately known as Thelma and Louise. As Sherrer recalls, "They walked through our shop making recommendations but always with a great deal of humor. It must have been a significant cost to Lockheed to send these women to Australia, but I think they got that back from having better-performing suppliers in the long run."

As with Marand, Ferra has now grown well beyond its roots. It currently has facilities not only in the United States but also in India and in the UK.

Many other companies deserve mention, but despite everyone's best efforts, not every small participant succeeded. For example, Production Parts was a family-owned and -operated business manufacturing metal components for the F-35. Program changes and delays were just too difficult for them to accommodate, and eventually they went out of business. A bittersweet story, but Marand was able to buy their equipment and rehire their workforce.

By 2021, more than fifty Australian companies had been awarded contracts for development, production, and sustainment worth more than $2.7 billion. And they're typical of the contributions of other companies in all the partner countries.

Such success stories go largely unnoticed outside the industry. But small and medium-sized local companies employing thousands of skilled people around the world contribute mightily to the participating countries' economies. They are a vital if unsung foundation of the F-35 global partnership.

Reference

1. Interview with Air Vice Marshal Kym Osley on June 4, 2020, by Tom Burbage, Betsy Clark, and Adrian Pitman. Held in F-35 interview archive.

2. Interview with Rohan Stocker by Tom Burbage, Betsy Clark, and Adrian Pitman on April 27, 2019. Held in F-35 interview archive.

3. Interview with Mark Sherrer by Tom Burbage, Betsy Clark, and Adrian Pitman on July 26, 2020. Held in F-35 interview archive.

4. Blainey, Geoffrey, *The Tyranny of Distance: How Distance Shaped Australia's History*, Sun Books, 1966.

Chapter 27

THE ARCTIC ALLIANCE: THE RELUCTANT PARTNER—EH, CANADA?

Global warming—a.k.a. climate change—has many implications, from the political, to the economic, to the strategic. As discussed in the High North chapter, the melting of the Arctic Sea and warming of the surrounding land-masses has opened up new sea-lanes and permitted access to new resources. Additionally, the recent modernization and redeployment of Russian military forces into the region calls for countervailing action from the United States and its allies, especially those bordering the Arctic Circle. Northern Europe and the Arctic are quickly emerging as the next possible strategic battleground.

Over the next few years, Norway, Denmark, and the United Kingdom will modernize their air forces. For them, the stealth and interconnectivity of the F-35 provides the ability to react to new, faster weapon delivery systems. Finland and Switzerland have also announced they'll buy the Lightning. Norway has gone even further, recently (2021) concluding an agreement to allow the USAF to deploy bombers, such as the B-1, from its northern bases. Meanwhile, the United States is working with Greenland to expand the base at Thule to host a much larger complement of fighters and bombers.[1]

Altogether, it's clear that Northern European allies and partners sensed a rising threat even before the invasion of Ukraine in 2022. They're responding regardless of how expensive such decisions may be, economically and politically.

So where stands Canada amid this increasingly hotter—in both senses—security environment? That dominion's F-35 journey has been slow and tortu-ous. Ottawa twice decided to buy the fighter. But both times, politics and events colluded to force an abrupt about-face. The first time was in 2010, and the sec-ond in 2015.

★ ★ ★

Let's look at the basic US/Canadian relationship. Ottawa has a long-standing agreement with Washington on the need to defend their North American homeland. Canada's been an integral partner since the North American Aerospace Defense Command's founding in 1957. NORAD's commander is a four-star USAF general. His or her deputy is a three-star Canadian. The Royal Canadian Air Force has an obligation first to their NORAD commitments, and only secondarily to NATO.

Canada had been involved in the JSF program since 1997, and was the very first nation to join the F-35 partnership, in February 2002, under their commitment to interoperability in NORAD.[2] The country signed the production, sustainment, and follow-on development memorandum of understanding in December 2006. At that time, they estimated they would purchase eighty aircraft, procured over an eight-year period, from 2014 to 2021.[3]

Two key players in this saga were Lt. Gen André Deschamps, commander of the Royal Canadian Air Force (RCAF) from 2009 to 2012, and General Tom Lawson, André's deputy from 2009 to 2011. Lawson was also deputy commander of NORAD in Colorado Springs for a portion of 2011 before being promoted to chief of defense in August 2012 by then–prime minister Stephen Harper. Both had started their careers flying the Canadair CF-104, the country's version of the Lockheed F-104 Starfighter, before transitioning to other aircraft. Deschamps flew the C-130 transport and E-3 AWACS while Lawson flew the Canadian version of the F-18 Hornet, known as the CF-18. He also did a stint flying the Canadian version of Air Force One, an Airbus CC-150.

In 2008, the government produced a white paper titled *Canada First Defence Strategy.*[4] As Deschamps recalls, "It was the first time in decades that the government articulated at least a macro strategy for defense, validating the fact that Canada still needs to maintain a fighter fleet. Believe it or not, that was debated, but we now had political cover to replace the F-18s."[5]

The RCAF's requirements for this new fighter included survivability, a high level of interoperability with US and other allied forces, and a high level of sensor fusion. Both Deschamps and Lawson believed that, as the only fifth-generation fighter on the horizon, the F-35 was the sole design that could let the RCAF remain relevant.

As an international partner, though, the steps to be followed in buying F-35s were very different than Canada's normal procurement approach, which is to conduct a competition. As Deschamps explained, "Canada confirmed the procurement by signing the 2006 MOU for production and follow-on support. However, most people in Ottawa were not aware of the MOU or how it was framed. That caused no end of grief and we're still in hot debate over those two approaches."[6] So, the signature "sort of" hinted at Canada's plan to continue as a partner, and to eventually buy, but it wasn't a rock-solid commitment.

While the new plane was a match for their requirements, the Air Force wasn't in a big hurry to start ordering. The plan was to begin replacing the F-18 Hornets around 2020. With the F-35 MOU in place, Canada didn't feel the need to push their chips in until 2012. But another government department was very anxious to start placing orders.

Industry Canada is a government department responsible for industrial policy and for ensuring domestic companies get the benefit of purchases with taxpayer dollars outside the country. Deschamps recalls,

> Industry Canada's knowledge of the F-35 program was well established, given that Canada had been involved in industrial participation since the early 2000's and that work was growing. And they were well aware of the potential should Canada decide to buy the F-35—that there was around $9 billion to $10 billion of industrial participation money available—and that was an attractive proposition.
>
> Understandably, Canadian industry was very pro F-35. So interestingly enough, the impetus to make a downselect on the F-35 in 2010 wasn't the Air Force saying we need to do this now. It was a political analysis based on industrial participation that saw an opportunity for Canada to really leverage the program in a big way. And therefore, that push came from outside Defence.

Along with Industry Canada, Stephen Harper, the prime minister, also decided it was time to formally commit. The air force had a budget and plans in place to buy sixty-five of an eventual eighty-plane purchase. Harper shared Industry Canada's concern that domestic industry would miss out on more lucrative work as production was ramping up and other partner countries were placing their orders. Harper held a series of meetings with his cabinet to discuss the issue and, hopefully, obtain agreement to buy in.

As deputy commander of the RCAF, Lawson was one of the few representatives from the military to attend these meetings. The Air Force's cost estimate for buying the sixty-five jets totaled 9 billion Canadian dollars. Lawson recalls one particularly interesting meeting:

> The leadership really wanted a fully unanimous cabinet so we could go out to Canadians and say, "Look, we all voted thumbs up on this." I gave a briefing on the F-35. A senior minister was very clear about how good this was going to be for Canada, and then the conversation went around the table, asking for comments. And as the conversation got to this one fellow—I can't use real names, but let's call him Chuck—he was asked, "Chuck, how do you feel about this? You haven't spoken." And Chuck said, "Well, nine billion dollars is too much for anything. I don't care what it is." And there was silence around the table and everybody was looking down at their doodle notes and then we heard a loud guffaw of laughter from another minister. Everybody looked at him and he said "Nine billion is too much? For God's sake, we spent nine kajillion dollars on health. So, what do you mean about $9 billion?" and there was general laughter, and at the end of that cabinet meeting, there ended up being unanimous support to commit to the F-35.

The RCAF accelerated their process in preparation for a formal announcement. They put together the necessary paperwork and went through the bureaucratic steps required.[7]

To help prepare the ground, the government sent Lawson on a public relations tour around the country, along with several technical experts, to extol the virtues of the F-35. By and large, they seemed to be well received. He was then posted to NORAD. "I was only down in Colorado Springs for one year but it was in that year when all hell broke loose in Canada."

And break loose it certainly did.

★ ★ ★

While Defence was frantically pushing documents and Industry was enthusiastically on board, a third department wasn't so eager: the Department of Public Works and Government Services.

Lawson describes it as "a 'three men at the helm' process. Defence defined the requirements, Industry Canada did its best to ensure work for Canadian industry, and Public Works did the actual contracting. There had been plenty of discussions in the Air Force about holding a fighter competition but at the end of the day, people felt that a competition was a waste of a lot of time and energy because the plane *had* no real competitor."

As Deschamps described the situation, "You're just going to waste a lot of industry's time and money during the process because they will eventually realize that they cannot achieve many of the high-level mandatory requirements given their level of technologies." In July 2010, Prime Minister Harper announced publicly that Canada had decided to buy sixty-five F-35s.[8]

His pronouncement was immediately followed by a barrage of negative reports from the Canadian media. André Deschamps recalls, "Within hours of the announcement, the media started pulling up US news stories about cost overruns, and they start dragging in all the dirt, and there was plenty of it out there. That started building a lot of negative baggage around the airplane as we got into the fall of 2010."

So that was bad. But things were about to get even worse.

★ ★ ★

In 2011, an independent estimate of costs by the Parliamentary Budget Officer put the government on the defensive. Since none of the analysts had the clearances to access air force data, they were forced to rely on unclassified, publicly available information. Partially as a result, their estimate came in significantly higher than the air force's $9 billion Canadian figure. "Cost escalation" became the rallying cry for anyone opposed to the F-35.

But that was an annoying gnat bite compared to the bombshell that arrived from across the border. A report by the U.S. Government Accountability Office contained a number of negative comments about the F-35, focusing on schedule delays and costs overruns.[9]

Deschamps recalls, "The GAO report of 2011 basically set fire to the F-35. It was a very damning document that pulled no punches about program cost escalation and delays. That became the grenade that was thrown into our process, and it basically took the wind out of our sails. It gutted the Canadian government. They had lost total credibility with the public. And of course, the opposition just ate it up."

The response in the United States was equally vociferous. During one Senate hearing shortly after the release of the GAO report, John McCain said that the program "has been an incredible waste of the taxpayers' dollar."[10] McCain's comments were particularly harmful across the border. Deschamps recalls, "Canadians trusted McCain as much as they trust their own politicians here in Canada, so that was extremely damaging."

The Harper administration felt blindsided. Lawson recalls,

> I called my colleagues in the United States, because I was, to put it mildly, a little flummoxed that we had not been warned about the GAO report coming out in 2011. Unfortunately, they said "We couldn't tell you because we were having our own survival spiral in Washington with this report coming out." From that point on, whatever Defence said had zero credibility. How could we in Canada say that we are confident that this is going to work from a schedule and cost perspective when the United States is having a meltdown over this?

Factions in parliament accused the government of not being transparent. Deschamps said, "Parliament wanted access to classified data and we wouldn't release it because there was no group of folks within parliament that were cleared to look at classified information. It caused a bit of a furor. It was not a good time to be the commander of the air force." This led to a charge that the government was in contempt of parliament and a no-confidence vote which then forced a new election in May 2011.

That March, the government attempted to undo the political damage by reversing their decision. They announced the procurement was off. But there was still more bad news. In April 2012, the auditor general issued a report that was very critical of the government's process in choosing the F-35. The cost estimate in that report was a whopping $25 billion Canadian. This included twenty years of operating costs, as opposed to the Air Force's $9 billion figure, which had covered just the cost to buy the jets, train the pilots, and stand up the infrastructure to start operating.

The Air Force did their best to explain the difference to the public. Lawson said, "Canadians took notice of $25 billion where $9 billion had been the figure.

So, it did an awful amount of damage when not put in the context of the estimate now including life-cycle support costs for twenty years. Even when analo-
gies were made like you can buy a Toyota Corolla for $25,000 Canadian but to
own it for twenty years, you're actually talking $70,000 Canadian. But those
kinds of arguments were way too late."

Liberals called for Harper's resignation.[11] Following the May election, the
Conservatives still held the majority, but many in that party were bitter about
the experience. Deschamps explained. "The government felt they had been lied
to by Defence and by the United States, and now they were paying a very high
political cost for having committed in good faith. In late 2012, the government
froze funding for the future fighter program and removed decisions about the
path forward away from Defence, giving that responsibility to a newly created
National Fighter Procurement Secretariat which was tasked to recommend steps
going forward for the fighter replacement."[12]

★ ★ ★

By late 2012, Lawson had returned from NORAD and was a candidate for
Chief of Defence. He described the auditor general's report as "just awful in
quality. The cost estimate that they came up with was based on some sort of
ridiculous multiplier like the increasing price per pound of fighters since the
Second World War."

The final step of the application process for chief of defense was an interview
with Prime Minister Harper. Lawson describes that meeting:

Interestingly, both of us grew up in the same part of Toronto and we knew a lot
of the same people, and it was a very friendly interview until . . . toward the end,
he asked, "What do you think of the F-35 program?" I said, "I thought it was a
really courageous decision that you and the cabinet made when I was sitting at
the table two years ago. I think you made the right decision, and I'm not sure
there's much more that I can say." And he said, "Well, there's a little bit I can
say. I was lied to about this, and I'm still angry about it. If you're going to be the
chief of defense, I can't be lied to anymore about the F-35."

I coughed and said, "It's not in my character to ever imagine where lying
to the Prime Minister of our nation would be good for me, for the military,
or for our nation, and I find it very hard to believe, knowing the current chief

of defense, that he would have lied either." And he said, "Well, somebody lied to me." We moved on to other things, but it became very clear that our prime minister wasn't feeling the same way about the auditor general's report as the rest of us were.

★ ★ ★

In the next episode of the drama, in 2013 the National Fighter Procurement Secretariat convened a panel of experts to evaluate alternate fighters. They included Boeing's F-18 Super Hornet, the French Rafale, the Eurofighter Typhoon, and the F-35. The panel compared them in terms of a number of different roles, including search and rescue, humanitarian relief, and defense of Canada. The report was released in December 2014.[13]

While the actual findings are classified, Lawson recalled, "The panel asked the right questions and concluded that if we're going to deploy our fighters in a combat zone with air defenses, it's the F-35, but as long as we're never actually going into an armed conflict with these fighters, we could buy almost anything that's out there. But the panel noted that the alternatives are as expensive or more expensive than the F-35 is looking like it will be."

Despite having been burned earlier, Harper was still a supporter of the plane. No other options had the full support of Defence and Canadian industry, plus it was still the bottom-line recommendation from the expert panel. In February 2015, Lawson got a call from the PM. He was ordered to go ahead and try to buy two F-35s. He was hoping the USAF would allow the Canadians to take two of their airplanes that were nearing completion since at this point there were no Canadian aircraft in the production queue. The intent was to be able to test them out. "But just as we were ready to go, the decision got leaked in a briefing somewhere in the United States and the Canadian media got wind of it and the last thing Harper wanted was to have this announced before he was ready. So, the Prime Minister said, 'Absolutely not. We will have a competition.'"

That was Stephen Harper's last attempt to buy the F-35.

★ ★ ★

2015 was an election year. The Liberal candidate, Justin Trudeau, ran on a strong anti-F-35 platform, painting the Conservatives' handling of the issue as an example of incompetence. One of his pledges was that, under his government, Canada would have a competition. It would not buy the F-35, but another, cheaper fighter. Deschamps recalled, "He was talking out of both sides of his mouth because you can't have a competition without having the F-35 as part of it, and the F-35 has won every competition so far. But logic and politics don't necessarily mix."

The Liberals won, victorious to a large extent because of their anti-F-35 message. But then they had to make good on that promise. Deschamps pointed out, "To get into power, to get briefed in, of course, things are not as easy as you necessarily think. Whether he ever even looked at the report from the expert panel that was produced in 2014 is doubtful, since nobody ever formally acknowledged that that report even existed."

With the new government again promising to run a competition, things got strange for Lawson as chief of defense:

> It really looked like we couldn't have much of a competition, and the government didn't like that. Our Public Works and Government Services Deputy Minister was told to find a way to have a competition.
>
> She and I had various lunches together and she said, "Look, we're going to have a competition. And we are going to use criteria from the expert panel where it really doesn't matter which fighter you choose." And I said, "Good God, which criteria are those?" Well, one of them was search and rescue off the coasts, because we have used fighters to track down errant vessels. You just don't really need an F-35 to do that. And I said, "You've got to be kidding me. Our F-18s have been deployed in Iraq. They've been over top of Serbia. They've been over top of Libya. They get deployed all the time." And she said, "Yeah, but the Liberals are in power now, and they're not sure if Canada is ever going to want to deploy fighters again in a hostile sort of sense." And I asked her, "Does that sound reasonable to you?" And she said, "Reasonable or not, it's the only logic that holds together to allow us to have a competition."

As the government prepared for the runoff, a stop-gap had to be found to augment the country's aging F-18s. In 2017, Trudeau signed an agreement to buy twenty-five F-18 Hornets slated for retirement by the Royal Australian Air Force. Eighteen were categorized as "flyable" and seven as "non-flyable for use as spare parts and training aids."[14]

The competition rules required potential vendors to offer what were called "industrial and technological benefits"—in other words, offsets—to guarantee enough cash flowing back into Canada to match the cost of the procurement. Historically, these had been "indirect," meaning they didn't necessarily have to be related to the product being procured. In contrast to this, according to the JSF Government to Government agreements, all the work received so far on the F-35 program had been directly related to the F-35's development and production. As a result, Canadian industry had been able to recapitalize its aerospace industry with new technology. In turn, this helped it compete and win work on other programs.

By late 2018, F-35 industrial participation in Canada had already totaled $1.8 billion (USD) in contracts to Canadian companies.[15] But, in what seemed a very unfair ruling, the benefits already in hand for two decades of subcontracting on the F-35 wouldn't count in the new competition.

These rules caused furor in the United States, not only because it appeared unfair, but it directly violated provisions of the memorandum of understanding Canada had signed in 2006. That MoU *required* that industrial participation dollars be awarded for work related to the F-35 on a best-value basis to benefit the entire international partnership. In late 2018, Ottawa received two letters from the U.S. Department of Defense stating that the F-35 could not participate in the competition under these rules. The letters were from Ellen Lord, undersecretary of defense for acquisition and sustainment, and from Vice-Admiral Matt Winter, PEO of the F-35 joint program office. As a result, the Canadians changed the rules to allow consideration of the industrial benefits already accrued.

The competition officially kicked off in 2019. It began with three competitors: the F-18 Super Hornet, the F-35, and the Saab Gripen. In December 2021, the government downselected to the F-35 and the Gripen. In March 2022, the government of Canada announced that the LM F-35 was selected as the preferred bidder for the competition. As of December 2022, it was reported by the media that $7 billion (USD) had been approved for the initial acquisition of sixteen F-35s along with supporting capability such as munitions, infrastructure, etc. The Canadian government has not denied this media claim but has yet to make a formal announcement. While the battle cry for those opposed to the F-35 in Canada had centered on escalating costs, the air force's original $9 billion estimate appears quite solid.

★ ★ ★

While Deschamps and Lawson were fighting the political battles, another experienced and articulate Canadian came to know the F-35 well. Both Billie Flynn's parents had been in the RCAF. "On Sundays after church," Billie remembered, "my father would take my brother and me into the hangars and I would sit in the cockpit of fighter jets." He too joined the RCAF, after graduating from the Royal Military College of Canada. He was one of the first Canadians to fly the CF-18 in the early 1980s. In 1999, Flynn led NATO's Canadian task force in Aviano, Italy, and commanded the wing of CF-18s that fought in Operation Allied Force over Kosovo and the former Republic of Yugoslavia. He flew twenty-five combat missions, and his unit received battle honors from Queen Elizabeth, the first such designation for a Canadian unit since World War II.

Flynn said, "To walk out to an aircraft and fly a mission when you know you are going to be shot at, and you know your enemy wants desperately to achieve some success in shooting you down, that takes character and nerve that you can never develop or imagine in a peace-time world. It changes you for the rest of your life."

That life lesson stuck as he flew as an engineering test pilot for several modern fighters. He tested the Eurofighter Typhoon and Tornado fighters for the European Aerospace and Defense Company in Germany before joining the Lockheed Martin family, flying the F-16 and then the F-35. "I viewed my job as twofold. First, to dominate combat scenarios and return safely, and second to know where the limits of the airplane truly are."[16]

Flynn retired from LM in 2020 and returned to Canada as a private citizen to urge the need to modernize the country's fighter force. He said,

> The Canadian procurement system is not focused on strategic benefits or capabilities of a weapons system to protect Canada or North America or to project Canadian interests abroad. Instead, this is a hot-potato portfolio that no one has ever wanted to touch, even less so in the middle of the pandemic recovery, where spending billions of dollars on a new fighter will not get broad approval from the electorate. Yet the long-delayed decision needs to be dealt with. The forty-year-old CF-18s are desperately old, tactically irrelevant, and falling apart. The time to buy new jets, build them, train personnel, and prepare the facilities needed will take years, so delaying this decision any longer is not an option.

But getting past Trudeau's election promise *not* to select the F-35 would be tough. One helpful input was the Finnish government's capability assessment, which scored the F-35 higher than Gripen and the other competitors. Flynn said,

> In the case of Finland, the threat of Russia and their shared 1,400-kilometer border, means that operational capability, effectiveness, and survivability are critical issues. The Finns have been invaded twice and are not nearly as complacent as Canada about protecting themselves. Another factor is that there is a very real media bias against the F-35 after all these years. Many Canadians think that Big Brother, south of the border, will save them from the Russians and Chinese, especially in the Arctic.

Canada's participation in what would become the F-35 Lightning II began in 1997. Even before its decision to become the first formal program partner in 2002, Canadian industry was already contributing to the Joint Strike Fighter project. As of 2022, Canadian industry has won more than $2 billion (USD) in nearly two hundred different projects, more than double Canada's current investment to actually purchase the fighter. Over a hundred companies have been awarded these contracts, and every F-35 produced to date contains Canadian-made components. Currently, 100 percent of the F-35 work in Canada is an export. Yet to be measured are the additional opportunities realized by small and medium-sized companies stemming from the manufacturing and engineering expertise they have gained as suppliers.

According to the 2020 independent study done as part of the ongoing Canadian competition, approximately 150,000 jobs will be supported in Canada as a result of choosing the F-35. The economy will benefit by more than $16.9 billion (CAD) over the life of the program. As the F-35 transitions into full-rate production, more opportunities for industry will evolve and endure.[17]

Twenty years after signing the agreement to join the JSF program, the Canadian F-35 saga can best be summed up by André Deschamps: "I think the Canadian chapter should be titled 'Politics, Damn Politics' because it's always about the politics of defense and not about security itself."

But in early 2022, the world changed dramatically when Russia invaded Ukraine. Suddenly the Arctic alliance became a critical part of a new realignment of priorities for the Arctic nations, Northern Europe, and NATO. On 28 May 2022, Canadian Minister of Defense Anita Anand announced that Canada had selected the F-35 as its future fighter. She said the decision to pick the F-35 was done without political interference. "We're living in a new reality," she said, referring to Russia's war in Ukraine.[18] When the threat becomes real, security sometimes trumps politics.

Reference

1. Breum, Martin: "US, Greenland reach agreement on Thule Air Base contract, long a source of dispute." Arctic Today, *Arctic Business Journal*, October 29, 2020.

2. Huebert, Rob: Special Advisor to the *Globe and Mail*, published December 28, 2021

3. Joint Strike Fighter Program Memorandum of Understanding between the United States of America and Other Governments. Department of State, United States of America, Treaties and Other International Acris Series 06-1231, Signed by W. P. D. Elcock, Deputy Minister of National Defence of Canada, December 11, 2006.

4. *Canada First Defence Strategy*, 2008. Available from Government of Canada website (http://www.forces.gc.ca/assets/FORCES_Internet/docs/en/about/CFDS-SDCD-eng.pdf).

5. Interview with Lt Gen Andres Deschamps by Tom Burbage, Betsy Clark, and Adrian Pitman on May 4, 2019. Held in F-35 interview archive.

6. Interview with Lt Gen Andres Deschamps by Tom Burbage, Betsy Clark, and Adrian Pitman on May 4, 2019. Held in F-35 interview archive.

7. Interview with Lt. General Tom Lawson by Tom Burbage, Betsy Clark, and Adrian Pitman on May 11, 2019. Held in F-35 interview archive.

8. BBC News: Row over Canada F-35 fighter jet order, July 16, 2010 (https://www.bbc.com/news/world-us-canada-10667633).

9. US Government Accountability Office Report to Congressional Committees, GAO-11-325, Joint Strike Fighter: Restructuring Places Program on Firmer Footing, but Progress Still Lags, April 2011.

10. *Christian Science Monitor*, "F-35 a waste of taxpayers' dollars says McCain," February 17, 2011.

11. *National Post*, April 12, 2012, "Stephen Harper must resign over bungled F-35 file, say Liberals."

12. National Fighter Procurement Secretariat; Seven-Point Plan: Status Report, December 2012.

13. Government of Canada; Summary Report—The Evaluation of Options for the Replacement of the CF-18 Fighter Fleet; December 2014; (https://www.tpsgc-pwgsc.gc.ca/app-acq/amd-dp/documents/cf18-eval-eng.pdf).

14. Government of Canada website; National Security and Defence, Defence equipment purchases and upgrades, Air defence procurement projects, Fighter Jets, Supplementing the CF-18 Fleet Project Summary.

15. Shimooka, Richard; Macdonald-Laurier Institute, Canada's Future Fighter Replacement, May 2019; The Catastrophe: Assessing the Damage from Canada's Fighter Replacement Fiasco.

16. Interview with Billy Flynn, with Tom Burbage on multiple occasions including January 9, 2022. Held in F-35 interview archive.

17. www.F35.com, Global Enterprise, Canada, accessed March 6, 2022.

18. https://www.defensenews.com/air/2022/03/28/canada-picks-the-f-35-in-fighter-replacement-competition.

Chapter 28

FINAL EXAMS

A final exam can either be aced, or flunked. But how does a teacher, a professor, or an evaluator make that judgment? It's not always as cut and dried as a math test, where the solution's either right or wrong. Often the grade depends on metrics: formal criteria against which the performance can be scored. Sometimes these are subjective. At other times, they may be deeply quantitative.

Regardless, the results can redirect lives and shape subsequent narratives, both positive and negative.

A similar grading process is applied to transformational systems as they progress through their life cycles. In weapon system development, the first important "final exam," once the contractor and program manager think the contractual requirements have been satisfied, is an exhaustive and steely-eyed inquisition carried out by the operational test and evaluation community.

The director of operational test and evaluation is the principal advisor to the secretary of defense on operational test and evaluation. An administrative position, the director provides independent assessments to the secretary of defense and to Congress. They do not have airplanes or pilots but integrate the reports of the individual service operational testing organizations. Service-level operational testing involves taking airplanes away from their developers, inserting them into a near-operational environment, and grading how they perform. (Or don't.) OT&E's job is to formulate and submit unbiased, objective advice to senior decision-makers so they can adjudicate their readiness and value amid the interservice rivalries and various programs and contractors that compete so fiercely for always-finite budgets.

The JSF program managers recognized early on that sequential development and operational testing of three variants would pose a well-nigh endless, complicated time line. It could easily delay acceptance and fleet introduction for several years. To address this, they agreed to integrate operational testing into the development phase, to perhaps speed things up.

Letting OT&E evaluators participate in development testing would have both advantages and risks. The advantage would be in giving them an early understanding of the subtleties of the plane and its transformational properties. A positive outcome might also shorten the traditional OT&E phase.

The major downside would be that (obviously) flying an immature product could have disastrous consequences, for the pilots involved and everyone else. Also, having an outside agency red-flagging the inevitable early weaknesses— issues that would likely already have been fixed before the *usual* OT&E phase— could play a particularly disruptive role for the F-35. Especially, considering its doubting Thomases within Congress and the international partners.

And as a final complication, there were the three variants, similar in flight from a pilot's perspective, but very dissimilar from the perspectives of the various services and partners.

All this made the F-35's final exam different from that of any previous warplane.

There were two major players in the Lightning's OT&E process. The Air Force Operational Test and Evaluation Center is located at Kirtland Air Force Base in Albuquerque, New Mexico. An independent agency, AFOTEC is chartered to evaluate a system's overall capability under operationally realistic conditions.[1] At Kirtland and associated sites, the F-35A endured extensive testing. Participating countries could send observers, too, potentially decreasing any national-level operational testing that might be required of their own jets.

The Navy's Operational Test and Evaluation Force (OPTEVFOR), based in Norfolk, Virginia, also provides independent, objective evaluations, this time of the effectiveness and suitability of naval aviation systems in support of Fleet introduction decisions.[2] The F-35 B and C (both the responsibility of the USN test force) had to complete shipboard trials on the expeditionary USMC aircraft carriers for the B model, and on big-deck nuclear carriers for the C.

The B-model testing was especially critical. It was closely scrutinized by both the UK and Italy. These future operators had staked their political support on successful US testing of the STOVL version.

In 2018 the new British carrier HMS *Queen Elizabeth* conducted initial flight trials. In 2020, she transited to the test range off Pax River to conduct additional tests. In February 2021, the Italian Navy flagship, ITS *Cavour*, arrived at Naval Station Norfolk to attain "Ready for Operations" for their F-35Bs. But perhaps the ultimate carrier suitability final exam occurred when U.S. Marine,

British, and Italian F-35Bs all flew from the *Queen Elizabeth* on the same day in the Mediterranean.

★ ★ ★

OT&E is a pass/fail test in a defined operational scenario. A critical step, yes, but then there's another level of exam.

Exercise Red Flag.

Conceived in November 1975, after studying the air combat losses experienced in the Vietnam War, the most realistic war game was established by the U.S. Air Force Air Combat Command. Named Red Flag–Nellis by the USAF, it is regarded by pilots as the premier aerial combat exercise in the world. It's held in ten to twelve annual events flown out of Nellis Air Force Base, on the outskirts of Las Vegas. A second series is conducted out of Eielson Air Force Base in Alaska, often under much harsher weather conditions. Both involve a three-week simulated exercise. A typical Red Flag includes some seventy-five aircraft and 2,300 participants from various US and allied military branches conducting joint force integration in realistic combat-like situations.[3]

In Red Flags of the past, when different services would fly together in a strike package, communications barriers frustrated cooperation. Squadrons had different airplanes, or different configurations of the same airframe with different electronic systems. This limited everyone's effectiveness in combat, sometimes to a dangerous degree, and offered loopholes an adversary could exploit. When they were brought together back then to operate as a "seamless" force, those seams sometimes tore. Called on to further integrate with allied participants, the rips grew even wider. But the game was about to change.

The F-35's first Red Flag was in 2017, shortly after the USAF declared the fighter had reached initial operational capability. Thirteen F-35 jocks from the 388th Fighter Wing's 4th Fighter Squadron went up against advanced anti-air threats, including simulated near-peer enemy air defenses and air-to-air fighters. The goal of this first trial by fire was to test the Lightning's ability to act as a "quarterback in the sky" for other friendly aircraft.

Situational awareness is the clear perception of a surrounding environment with respect to both time and space. In other words, an accurate understanding of current and projected threats, along with an understanding of where they're heading. Historically, this required the pilot to integrate multiple sensors and displays in his or her head. In the Lightning, that pilot has the luxury of watching the "movie" unfold on his helmet-mounted display.

Red Flag 2017 proved the F-35's ability to act as a force multiplier for older fourth-generation aircraft such as the F-16. Their ability to share sensor fusion information with legacy aircraft provided what one pilot called a "God's-eye view" of the battlefield.

Especially noteworthy, and sort of unexpected, was the ability of pilots who were new to the plane to very quickly exploit its advanced capabilities. One senior pilot commented, "My wingman was a brand-new F-35A pilot, seven or eight flights out of training. He gets on the radio and tells an experienced three-thousand-hour pilot in a very capable fourth-generation aircraft, 'Hey bud, you need to turn around. You're about to die. There's a threat off your nose.'"[4] The F-35s dominated the notional enemy force in every engagement.

The first combat exercise with both Air Force F-35As and Marine Corps F-35Bs operating simultaneously occurred during Red Flag 17-3 a special US-only event. For the first time, the Air Force and Marine Corps validated joint tactics, training, and procedures. The team executed suppression of enemy defenses, attack operations, and defensive counter-air.

But even during that first combined F-35A and B outing in 2017, the data verified that in highly demanding battlefield conditions, the F-35's common systems resulted in a truly unified and interoperable force for the first time. True to the plane's early promise, this connectivity proved a huge force multiplier.

Beyond Red Flags, but still in the training environment, the F-35 also proved itself in region-specific war games. One recent exercise found that, with the Block 4 revision, the F-35 would be one of the few fighters capable of meaningfully contributing to US efforts to counter a full-scale invasion of Taiwan, a scenario recognized as one of the most threatening facing the Pacific alliance.[5]

★ ★ ★

But these were all exercises, tests, evaluations. The ultimate final exam would be when the plane butted heads with an enemy in combat.

History provides a mixed report card and a rich opportunity for lessons learned . . . and one of the lessons is that weapons rarely perform on the battlefield as they do in the lab. The Vietnam War was a case in point. Although North Vietnam was a third-world country, with limited technical savvy, Soviet and

Chinese missile systems backed up the war on the ground. They inflicted significant losses on Air Force, Marine, Army, Navy, and RVN (South Vietnamese) aircraft, and resulted in the capture and imprisonment of many hundreds of American POWs, as well as the deaths in action of hundreds more. This horrifying toll led to a classified program aimed at reducing the vulnerability of US combat aircraft in the surface-to-air threat environment. It launched the initial forays into a radical new concept called *stealth*.

Gulf War 1 validated that innovation. Under the cover of night, and invisible to Soviet-supplied Iraqi radars, F-117s attacked heavily defended strategic targets without incurring a single loss. The science and art of stealth progressed rapidly as new systems like the B-2 evolved. The early requirements of sacrificing aerodynamic stability and maneuverability for low observability were overcome. The technical triumph of designing stealth into a fully combat-capable fighter was first realized in the form of the Lockheed Martin F-22 Raptor.

Since 9/11, recent decades have been dominated by hostilities in Iraq and Afghanistan. These were largely counterinsurgency wars, with little contested airspace. The never-ending war in Syria could have been a greater challenge. However, though Syria employed top-end S-400 surface-to-air defense, this turned out to be much more of a ground war, leading to suffering and displacement of large populations, as the Assad regime brutally employed artillery and barrel bombs on insurgent cities to "save" them.

In early 2022, Putin's unprovoked invasion of Ukraine began a new confrontation, this time with more global implications. The proximity of this war to democratic Europe drove several new nations into the global F-35 partnership, reinforcing the concepts of strength in numbers and shared responsibilities to deter future aggression.

More or less simultaneously, Israeli F-35s have been engaged in a quiet face-off with that country's major regional adversary, Iran. Israel's s air force conducted four large-scale military drills simulating attacks against Iran in a single recent month, with reports of a special bomb being designed for the F-35 to be able to attack hardened nuclear facilities.[6] Its F-35 "Adirs" have also shot down Iranian drones, the first time F-35s have been confirmed as having destroyed airborne threats.[7] This is another hot spot that could erupt into war at very short notice.

While that conflict and Ukraine sort themselves out, the Indo-Pacific region faces a different and perhaps even more sophisticated threat. A tinderbox is heating up as China's aggressive moves in the East and South China Seas threaten Taiwan, Indonesia, and Australia. But the enormous maritime expanse of the Pacific poses an entirely different challenge than the relatively close confines of Europe.

Perhaps the point closest to ignition there is Taiwan, a.k.a. the Republic of China. Ruled by a pseudo-democratically elected government since 1987, it's home to some 23 million people. Taiwan's an economic powerhouse and manufactures most of the advanced computer chips essential to the world economy. Historically, it's never actually been ruled by any mainland dynasty,[8] yet Beijing persists in viewing the island as a renegade province to be reconquered. It continues to threaten to "reunify" China with force if necessary. Today, the United States maintains a strong but unofficial relationship with Taiwan and sells military equipment, including fighter jets, to the island. [9] However, thus far Taiwan has been excluded from the F-35 partnership, mainly to avoid antagonizing China.

Elsewhere in the neighborhood, the U.S. Air Force and Marine Corps maintain a strong strategic relationship and presence in Japan. Lockheed Martin and Mitsubishi Heavy Industries teamed to establish a F-35 FACO in Nagoya. Tokyo will eventually be the plane's largest international customer, with a program of record of 147 F-35s, 105 A variants, and up to 42 F-35Bs.

Between Japan and Taiwan lies a second regional F-35 ally, the Republic of Korea. But South Korea is still nearly a thousand miles from Taiwan. Two thousand miles to the southward lies Singapore, and another 2,400 miles farther, Australia. The sheer expanse of the Indo-Pacific region would make any conflict there very much a maritime war. F-35Cs operating from the US strike carrier fleet and F-35Bs operating off islands as well as US and possibly UK and Italian smaller carriers would be the major players.

Exams are seldom designed to be easy. And the F-35 has been subjected to some tough ones. So far, it's passed them all with excellent grades. But should the Chinese decide to escalate to a fighting war to recapture Taiwan, *that* could be a very hard quiz indeed.

Still, if it happens, the new coalition, and Taiwan's advanced fourth-generation F-16Vs, will be able to operate as a unified force . . . a powerful dynamic never before possible.

Reference

1. AFOTEC; Air Force Operational Test Center; www.afotec.af.mil.

2. OPTEVFOR; Operational Test & Evaluation Force; https://www.cotf.navy.mil.

3. Tisminezky, Ryan, Fox 5 News; Nellis Air Force Base Hosting Red Flag training exercise, issues noise warning, published July 7, 2022. Accessed August 13, 2022.

4. Pickrell, Ryan, "Task & Purpose," *Business Insider*; published February 21, 2019; accessed August 22, 2022.

5. June 18, 2021, *Topic:* F-35 *Blog Brand:* The Buzz *Tags:* F-35, Red Flag Exercise, F-16, U.S. Air Force, War Game, *Military; F-35: How This Stealth Fighter Dominates Every Wargame It 'Fights' In.*

6. "Israel Upgrades F-35 Jets to Facilitate Attack on Iran," *Iran International*, June 8, 2022. Accessed August 26, 2022.

7. Newdick, Thomas, "Israel Shows The F-35's First Aerial Kill in Newly Declassified Video," *The War Zone*, March 8, 2022. Accessed August 26, 2022.

8. Jacobs, Bruce, "Taiwan Was Never Part of China," *Taipei Times*, January 6, 2016, 8.

9. Maizland, Lindsay, Council on Foreign Relations, "Why China-Taiwan Relations Are So Tense," updated August 3, 2022, accessed August 23, 2022.

Chapter 29

THE TYRANNY OF TIME

Time is a mental construct. It defines a span and limit to complete a process, such as growing up or growing old. Or, like delivering a next-generation weapon system by a certain (usually all-too-close) date.

Time is also a tyrant. The world does not stand still while people age or complex undertakings struggle toward completion. Moore's law and advances in materials inexorably alter technology baselines. World political thrusts changes definitions of the threat. Strategic tectonic plates shift, realigning alliances. Rising powers fracture and compress already tight time lines.

Ice hockey great Wayne Gretzky used to say, "Skate to where the puck's going, not where it is." Predicting where that puck will be is always a guessing game. But nowhere is forecasting more important than positioning the very large investments required to keep transformational weapon systems still transformational in the future. Get it wrong, and you'll quickly be labeled obsolete. Or, worse yet, lose a war.

Three dimensions shape any strategy for coping with the tyranny of time. First, how capable and flexible is the system being dealt with? Second, what are the "bad guys" doing to counter any advantages, and how are they reshaping the battlespace? Third, where is technology taking us? The interaction sets up a three-dimensional chess game. Moreover, these separate dimensions can't be dealt with in isolation; a delta (i.e., change) in one ripples through the whole system.

Some experts assert that America's underpinning of military and industrial superiority—and the foundation of its national security and global influence—has eroded to a dangerous degree. At the same time, the world has become more dangerous. The unpredictable and always irritable Russian bear is growling again. China, a rapidly rising power, is flexing its global muscles. Economic dependencies on energy, rare earth elements, food, and water are driving societal vulnerabilities on a global scale.

Unfortunately, the West has naively and (mostly) inadvertently ceded strategic capture of many of those vital resources to our competitors—and our competitors are also our enemies. Strategic dominance, once the unique domain of the United States with its globally deployed Air Force and a U.S. Navy centered on the mighty nuclear carrier battle groups, is now being seriously challenged.

A rapidly modernizing carrier force, eerily similar to ours—right down to the same flight-deck jersey colors (every color designates a critical responsibility) and the same ballet for launching and recovering aircraft—now sails a stormy Indo-Pacific region under a red and yellow flag. Today the United States still has an edge in carrier numbers, as well as in deliverable nuclear weapons. But those advantages are eroding as well.

There's a dark side to the rapid rise of the Peoples' Republic. Following the end of World War II and the Communist victory in 1949, their war-wrecked and agrarian economy lacked the capacity to compete with either the United States or the USSR in technology. Mao's Great Proletarian Cultural Revolution further stifled investment in scientific research, leaving the country lagging even further behind. As a result, the PRC has long supplemented legitimate technology transfers and domestic innovation with an aggressive industrial espionage effort, as a previous chapter documented in detail.

Over the last decade, China's rise has caught the United States between the conflicting objectives of the departments of commerce and defense. The United States continues to send China an array of semiconductors, commercial aerospace components, artificial-intelligence technology, and other items, driven by the corporate need to reduce costs and report quarterly profits, and every administration is sensitive to the needs of American corporations. Critics say such sales, which have been waved through across successive presidencies by both parties, have been taken advantage of by Beijing to further its military interests.

The Department of Commerce claims it's focused on long-term, strategic competition with China and that it makes export-control decisions with its interagency partners in the Departments of Defense, State and Energy. It *says* that, but . . . the lack of awareness on what the real relationships between the two largest economies in the world are and their many complex entanglements at the corporate, governmental, and academic levels only increases the challenge. Recent efforts to dam the flood promise some success going forward. But considering the commercial interdependencies, completely stopping the flow of technology to the People's Republic is virtually impossible . . . and to a large extent, that horse is long gone from the barn anyway.

Also, for export restrictions to be effective, critical allies must impose the same oversight. Although that may seem obvious, some allies have to cope with even more fraught and sensitive relationships. Consider Australia, a nation whose economy is highly dependent on Chinese investors and buyers, especially in the areas of energy, raw materials and ores. China has imposed trade sanctions on Australian exports to China worth billions of dollars due partially to Australia's increasing relationship with the United States on defense cooperation in the South China Sea. Such solutions come at a cost.

Few weapon systems have actually played a role in the realignment of global strategic objectives. F-35 may be an exception to that rule.

Conceptually, resisting Chinese expansionism by means of a common F-35 alliance of Australia, Japan, South Korea, and Singapore, and augmented with the forward-deployed U.S. Navy, Marine Corps, and possibly British forces as well presents a respectable balance of strategic power in the Pacific.

China and Russia are both intent on emulating American airpower. They understand the asymmetric advantages afforded by fifth-generation aircraft such as the F-22 and F-35. Thus, it's probably no accident that eerily similar designs produced by Russia's United Aircraft Corporation and the Chinese Shenyang Aircraft Corporation indicate at least a detailed study, if not a cyber copy, of US designs.

Refer back to the chapter on espionage, and the linkages become striking. The Shenyang FC-31 Gyrfalcon, known as the J-31, is probably the most egregious example of what can only be called outright theft. As noted earlier, Beijing had long been stealing information associated with the F-35. In photographs, the J-31 closely resembles a twin-engine F-35, though it clearly lacks the VSTOL capabilities required for a STOVL variant. (But always bear in mind, physical resemblance and actual combat capability may be quite different.)

The most advanced Chinese fighter at present is the Chengdu J-20 Mighty Dragon, a twin-engine delta wing fighter with a canard to add maneuverability. Advertised as the "third fifth-generation fighter," after the F-22 and F-35, the J-20 combines features of both, at least from a visual perspective. It has a blended fuselage, small internal weapon bays, and low jet engine intakes. *But* true fifth-generation fighters are most sensitive in the front sector (all Lockheed Martin designs avoid movable front control surfaces like canards).

Similarities in design and shaping can be inferred from high-resolution photographs. However, it's far more difficult to speculate about the subtleties of stealth and the relative sophistication of the highly integrated software architectures necessary for all-axis control of the air vehicle and the fusion of the sensor suites. This information can't be derived from visual or photographic observation. And both the United States and China ferociously protect both these essential capabilities from unfriendly eyes.

One of the most significant considerations in an opponent's development of a credible fifth-generation fighter is the ability (or inability) to move from development to high-rate production.[1] In this respect, the Chinese currently seem to lag behind Western capabilities. The J-20 operates four production lines, each capable of producing one aircraft each month, with a total capacity of about fifty airplanes per year. To contrast, the total production capacity of the F-35 on a single production line is about 150 units per year . . . a threefold advantage.

A second example of even more blatant copying exists in the world of unmanned aerial vehicles (UAVs). In 2010, China trailed well behind the United States in that area. According to US intelligence, state-sponsored hackers looted UAV technology from the US government and private companies for the benefit of their home industry. Their newest UAVs closely resemble those fielded by American manufacturers, both visually and in advertised performance. They're also offered at much lower prices.[2]

The Russian Bear has not been hibernating either. The Sukhoi Su-57 Felon started out as an air superiority fighter intended to replace the MiG-29 and Su-27. Designed to compete with the F-22, it also looks a lot like the Raptor.

Some analysts and knowledgeable commentators have suggested that the Su-57 is more like an advanced fourth-generation fighter. At any rate, it's widely viewed as the least stealthy of the currently operational fifth-generation fighters.

As with the Chinese, the Russian inability to attain high production rates will likely limit any export market.[3] Western embargoes on advanced computer chips following the invasion of Ukraine will make this even more difficult.

★ ★ ★

These days, Russia and China aren't our only competitors—at least in the international market. As was true of battleships in an earlier age, developing indigenous modern weapons has long been a major objective of states desiring a front seat on the world stage.

The fifth-generation revolution started with a number of international entrants, but only the United States had the resources to dominate it with the Joint Strike Fighter. The latest race to a sixth generation shows no fewer than ten other nations crouching at the blocks for the starting gun. These include China and Russia, of course, but also the United Kingdom, Italy, Japan, Germany, India, Sweden, France, and Spain. Most of those nations recognize they lack the resources or political will to realize their dream individually. While several are maintaining their own entrants, it appears that some are already joining forces as a risk reduction alternative. The UK, Italy, and Sweden are working on a concept called "Tempest." India and Japan have also been invited to join the effort. France, Germany, and Spain are also jointly working on a separate sixth-generation system.

In the end, building a competitive new twenty-first-century fighter plane is a costly, difficult, and elusive goal, almost as challenging as developing nuclear weapons. In large measure, the desire to become a new player in the game is boosted by a new sense of urgency and a renewed interest.

★ ★ ★

In the longer term, the evolution of warfare will eventually generate startling new capabilities that may make our most advanced current systems laughably obsolete, no matter how capable they seem for the foreseeable future. To take one example, the emerging offensive capabilities of hypersonic flight and hypersonic weapons, once as elusive and unobtainable as stealth, is nearing reality.

The fabled SR-71, the only triple-sonic aircraft ever built, first flew in 1964, nearly sixty years ago. By flying so high and fast, the Blackbird was able to overfly the Soviet Union, evading more than four thousand air-to-air missiles over its operational life. Retired in 1998, (and setting a new speed record in transit on its last flight to the Smithsonian Air and Space Museum just outside Washington, D.C.) the Blackbird marked the pinnacle of America's Cold War dominance in aeronautical engineering. But attempts to create a worthy successor have failed . . . until now.[4]

The trade press is currently speculating about the "Son of Blackbird." The SR-72 is an unmanned hypersonic concept which, like its predecessor, is being developed in the Lockheed Martin Skunk Works. Like most every new high-performance flying machine, its major challenge is propulsion. If the technical stumbling blocks can be overcome, the Blackbird's heir apparent may presage a startling leap ahead.

But such transformational events are uncommon. They're often considered "once in a generation" singularities. Evolution is generally a much more gradual process. Prehistoric fish did not join newly grown hands one fine day and suddenly march out of the water.

Along with being slow, evolution can come in different flavors. *Divergent* evolution, the pattern in which groups within a given species gradually become increasingly different, or "speciate," until they can no longer interbreed, is the most common. It often occurs as organisms diversify to new habitats or discover new ecological niches.

This dynamic operates outside the animal and plant kingdoms as well, and it's working now within the F-35 as the variants gain maturity in their unique operating environments. Combat warriors will always strive to make their limited assets dominant. Recent congressional direction may make the individual services responsible for sustaining their F-35 fleets, a move that could sacrifice economies of scale, interoperability and commonality of parts for the perceived benefits of divergent evolution.

The second form of evolution, referred to as *convergent* evolution, reflects the gaining of analogous traits by different species because of a shared environment or evolutionary challenge. F-35 user communities operating more than one variant, like the U.S. Marine Corps, (the B and the C variants), the Italian Defense

Force (the A and the B variants), and potentially the UK (with the B and the A variants), will likely embrace this strategy eventually. If the US individual services were ever convinced (or forced) to fully accept the economic benefits of joint service, they could also benefit.

A third process, referred to as *parallel* evolution, occurs when two species evolve independently of each other but gradually develop similar structures or capabilities. From an economic perspective, common upgrades could provide economies of scale to all participants, a key feature of the original F-35 concept. The current strategy to update capabilities as a common community of users reflects this thinking.[5]

The F-35 will likely display, or experience, all three forms of evolutionary progress in the decades to come. The basic premise of the Joint Strike Fighter—a tri-service, multi-role allied global fleet that can operate from land or sea but bring an unprecedented fist to the fight needs to operate within these evolution constraints but not lose the real value proposition.

★ ★ ★

But the original problem remains. How does one defeat the tyranny of time and change, and move to the next level of capability, without breaking the bank?

Let's start with the consensus opinion from today's pilots.

LtCol Matt Hayden, 56th Fighter Wing Chief of Safety at Luke Air Force Base, Arizona, was interviewed by Scout Warrior as reported in *The National Interest*. "There is nothing that I have seen from maneuvering an F-35 in a tactical environment that leads me to assume that there is any other airplane I would rather be in. I feel completely comfortable and confident in taking that airplane into any combat environment." The article went on to say, "While Hayden was clear to point out he has not, as of yet, flown simulated missions against the emerging Russian Sukhoi T-50 PAK FA 5th-Generation stealth fighter now in development or the Chinese Shenyang J-31 5th Generation Stealth aircraft . . . he was unambiguous in his assertion regarding confidence in the F-35."[6]

Furthermore, as the US and international pilot communities have grown in numbers and experience, the consensus has solidified that this multi-role fighter can outperform any other platform now in existence.

But how long can that advantage last? That's the real challenge in a budget-constrained environment, constraints that may lie less heavily on a putative enemy.

As of the date of this book, the Block 4 update is planned as the next evolution of the F-35. All three US services plus the original nine-nation partnership established the requirements for the upgrade. But the "wish list" always seems to exceed the available budget, and prioritization gets hard. Couple that with emerging threats, particularly in the cyber domain, and settling on a stable next-generation configuration is problematic, to say the least.

New weapons are a big part of the Block 4 upgrade. And they're not all stickered *Made in USA*. Partner nations also have potent new weapons in development. The Joint Strike Missile, developed over many years by the Norwegian company Kongsberg Defense and Aerospace, will become a key part of the F-35 arsenal. The UK's SPEAR cruise missile will also be part of this upgrade. Other hardware improvements include upgrades to the radar, electro-optical, and electronic warfare systems, to deal with advances in adversarial threat systems. (**See Figure 30: F-35 weapon loadout**)

All these changes drive sophisticated software development, to sustain the highly integrated weapon system (the real secret of the F-35 as a true fifth-generation fighter). Block 4 will be 80 percent software and 20 percent hardware from a cost perspective. The primary goal is to improve the lethality of the system and its effectiveness as an integrated node on the battlefield system of systems.

That said, by far the major hardware upgrade will be to the power plant.

The reference to "power plant" and not "engine" implies there's a lot more involved these days than providing more raw thrust. Every pilot wants more power, sure. But really, it's the delicate interplay of propulsion, electrical power generation, improved combat range, and the never-ending war on weight that drives fighter improvements. Upgrading the engine has huge potential to keep the Lightning II on the leading edge of capability.

The Pratt & Whitney F135 is regarded as the most advanced fighter engine in the world today. But there are significant developments in technology that could portend a big payoff going forward. The basics include the ability to generate more thrust, improve fuel efficiency, increase combat range, and improve engine life.

Sounds logical? Think again. How could one accomplish them all? More thrust usually means higher fuel consumption. More range usually means more weight. And so on. Fighter jocks have always yearned for high-performance and high-thrust engines to win in combat. But a large part of a fighter's time in the air is typically spent on transiting to the combat arena. Fighter engines have traditionally been less efficient in that phase of flight, which reduced effective combat range.

What if you could have an adaptive engine—efficient in the relatively benign transit and return phases, but highly responsive once combat begins? What if it could be automated to switch between modes based on pilot actions with the throttle? In theory, better fuel efficiency, longer range, and perhaps even extended engine life would follow.

As another possibility, what if you could reduce the heat the engine generated? Today that's a limiting factor, involving space and weight-eating cooling hardware. Reducing the cooling requirement could reduce weight and at the same time increase available electrical output to feed hungry new weapons, sensors, and systems. As one example of the latter, futuristic laser weapons are close to attaining operational status. They will demand much more onboard electrical power, making that a must for any future upgrade to the plane.

Another key to a jump in power plant output is new technologies of material modeling and additive manufacturing, better known as 3D printing. AI-driven software is also pointing to new alloys that could improve engine performance, as well as developing them over much shorter time lines. As Dale Hopkins, deputy project manager of NASA's transformational tools and technologies project, had it, "What used to take years through a trial-and-error process now takes a matter of weeks or months to make discoveries, new alloys can now withstand temperatures of over two thousand degrees Fahrenheit and are much more durable at higher temperatures. The alloy can be designed to have much more flexibility and strength to resist fracturing."[7]

Presumably, any future engine would be designed to fit into the same envelope as the F-135 engine inhabits today. In addition, today's complex engine trailers and peripheral maintenance equipment must work, or can be adapted to, such a new engine. That obvious benefit would clearly apply to the USAF and allied F-35A models and the U.S. Navy F-35C variants.

Currently, five companies—Boeing, Pratt & Whitney, General Electric, Lockheed Martin, and Northrop Grumman—are developing prototypes in the Next Generation Adaptive Propulsion program.[8]

Unfortunately, upgrading the F-35B presents additional quandaries. Balancing the STOVL lift-fan system with the main engine and the highly constrained space and weight design parameters of the B-model brings an additional level of complexity. A separate second phase development program to incorporate adaptive engine capabilities in the F-35B will likely be required.

The remaining major piece of the Block 4 update is the Unmanned Teaming initiative. Employing sophisticated UAVs is rapidly becoming a centerpiece of new aerial strategies. The Lightning II will clearly lead in the design of architectures that can exploit the manned/unmanned synergy. A flight of F-35s and UAVs working together in a heavily defended environment is close to a reality. The ability of the program to lead the transformation of the battlespace is just another positive facet of the huge investments made in the plane by the United States and its allies.

★ ★ ★

So that's what could be next for the plane. What's next for its user community?

Can global alliances reshuffle as world dynamics shift? Certainly, but they're based on bureaucratic, economic, diplomatic, and personal relationships built over long periods. They're slow to change. Absent some shocking new development, they don't transition easily or willingly. The Arctic may prove an exception.

The Joint Strike Fighter partnership started as a tight alliance of the three US services and eight close allies that had traditionally flown our aircraft and fought side by side with us. Recognizing that no service and no nation fights alone anymore (unless they are very badly led), the program was meant to replace the aging air forces of our closest allies as well as our own.

The revived specter of a hot war has dramatically reinforced this coalition dynamic of the program. The Northern European countries of Belgium, Finland, Switzerland, Germany, Poland, and the Czech Republic have all recently joined. Even Canada, the "reluctant partner," has finally seen the light.

The scary new reality of imminent war sometimes overwhelms regional and global politics. It opens the door for new relationships that may better define "Western" or "democratic" alliance than the historic post–World War II partners. The rapidly thawing Arctic is solidifying a new layer of allies including Norway, Finland, Denmark, and Canada. The Northern European nations of the Netherlands, Belgium, Germany, Poland, Switzerland, and the Czech

Republic further shield the heart of Europe. Around the periphery, the United Kingdom and Italy offer expeditionary, carrier-based forces that have already demonstrated they can operate as a team. Clearly, they can provide a joint resource maintaining vigilance from the Southern threat. If Ankara could make a clearer decision in favor of the West, rather than flirting with Moscow, Turkey would be more than welcome back in the family.

Pacific allies now include Australia, Japan, the Republic of Korea, and Singapore. Whether or not economic dependencies dominate military strategies is an unfolding story in this region. But the infrastructure to resist Chinese expansionism is becoming militarily significant.

As this global combat and peacekeeping infrastructure continues to develop with the ability to join forces seamlessly, the landscape may well evolve into a more effective chain of solid, mutually reinforcing, unbreakable new alliances.

★ ★ ★

The Block 4 upgrades have been in development for some time. They're well along, but the acquisition system's innate sluggishness almost guarantees their introduction will face additional challenges. Yep, thanks to that tyranny of time.

Looking beyond that horizon, the U.S. Air Force is in the evaluation phase of a conceptual aircraft they have dubbed the NGAD—the Next Generation Air Dominance fighter. The intent is to compete the concept, as was done for the JSF, and move to production on a schedule that should field the new plane circa the early 2030s, replacing the F-22. A prototype has already been flown, but technical and performance details are kept under wraps, of course![9]

Interestingly, the Air Force has already announced that, unlike the one-package deal that won LM the F-35, the NGAD contract will be split into separate contracts, for design, production, and sustainment. Development will be pushed ahead on a tight time frame, and the service will aim at smaller buys at shorter intervals, with upgrades occurring more rapidly and often as threats evolve toward the middle of the century.[10] As the reader will recall, the JSF program originally began with some of the same acquisition reform objectives. Various voices can argue over how well they were met. But going forward, the NGAD, like most new programs, will no doubt face stiff headwinds. Already shock is being expressed in some quarters at the projected per-fighter cost of the new plane.

★ ★ ★

"The word 'impossible,'" Oleksii Reznikov, Ukraine's defense minister, recently said, "Means 'possible in the future.'"[11]

What might the distant future hold? No one really knows, of course. But there are hints and research programs that may guide a bit of speculation.

During World War II, Spitfire pilots described that plane as so responsive it felt like an extension of their limbs. Fighter pilots of the 2030s, however, may have an even closer relationship with their aircraft. The UK's BAE Systems, Rolls-Royce, European Missiles Group, MBDA and Italy's Leonardo are developing a new concept for their sixth-generation Tempest jet that can read brain waves. Artificial intelligence will assist the human pilot when they're overwhelmed or under extreme stress. Sensors in the pilot's helmet will monitor brain signals and other medical data. So, over successive flights AI will amass a huge biometric and psychometric information database.[12]

In the 2022 blockbuster film *Top Gun: Maverick*, Tom Cruise tells his protégé "Rooster": "Don't think, just do!" In the future, the pilot may only need to "think," and the airplane will "just do."

Another possible "blue sky" (almost literally) technology in development extends the concept of radar stealth to wider areas of the electromagnetic spectrum. What if a plane could be made invisible, not just to radar, but to the eye, like the Predator aliens in the movies of the same name, or the "cloaking devices" beloved of other science fiction franchises?

Research during World War II indicated that deceptive lighting could reduce the ranges at which aircraft could be detected visually. More recent work using electroluminescent or "e-ink" panels, as well as totally new metamaterials, could also help blend an aircraft with the backdrop of the sky.[13]

Other advances in exterior coatings could be "mirror" finishes to reduce vulnerability to future laser weapons, or other specialized coatings to lessen visibility to passive infrared targeting systems.[14] Both the F-22 and F-35 are participating in experiments in this domain.

As the dividing line between atmosphere and space continues to blur, the Pentagon is exploring the possibility that F-35s could destroy an attacking nuclear-armed Intercontinental Ballistic Missile targeting the United States.

★ ★ ★

As we end this book, one thing is becoming clear: capable as it is, the F-35 will not be the final evolution of the fighter plane. Until the lion (or the wolf, as the Bible actually has it) lies down with the lamb, there will always be new threats to guard against, and no shortage of challenges in the future. Stay tuned.

And one other aspect needs to be mentioned.

Perhaps no one has seen and experienced the F-35 journey in more roles than Ian Reason. Ian was the original UK Royal Navy deputy in the F-35 Program Office in Washington and then he was the BAE Systems Deputy to the LM Program Office in Fort Worth. He then served as the F-35 contractor lead for the sustainment effort.

"Over time," Reason noted,

> The general population has been conditioned to believe that these big development programs are government behemoths that have no human connection. In fact, the F-35 is a human story and one full of personal sacrifice.
>
> The program changed many lives and had a huge social impact. Northwest England people and Dutch engineers are living in Texas; Australian engineers are living in the high desert of California; weddings and childbirths are creating US citizens; students from Italy, the Netherlands, and Denmark, sharing a house in Fort Worth, are working on a fifth-generation production line and seeing the great expanses of the United States on their free time . . . It fostered collaboration and cooperation across allies that has never been seen before and likely will never be seen again.

The saga of the F-35 Lightning II—its inception as a near-impossible dream, its long and troubled gestation, the building of an international partnership, and its current standing as the West's frontline fighter around the world—is a fascinating and inspiring story. The fondest hope of everyone involved in its development, testing, and fielding has always been that it will never have to engage in combat. That its silhouette against the bright skies of Europe and the Pacific will serve to deter violence and assure peace.

If in the end it does not, though, let any aggressor who dares to take it on beware. For in Carl von Clausewitz's most ominous dictum, "In war more than anywhere else, things never turn out as we expect."

Reference

1. "China's J-20 Stealth Fighter, Military", www.nationalinterest.org; March 7, 2021, accessed August 5, 2022.

2. Farley, Robert, "Industrial Espionage Has Been Key to China's Rise," *The National Interest,* November 6, 2021.

3. Suciu, Peter, "The Sukhoi Su-57," 1945.com, May 29, 2022; accessed August 5, 2022.

4. "Russia's Nightmare: The SR-72 Could Fly at Mach 6 and Bomb Anything," www.nepalikhabar-24hour.com; April 6, 2022, accessed August 8, 2022.

5. www.sparknotes.com/biology/evolution/patternsofevolution; accessed August 2, 2022.

6. Osborne, Kris, "Why the F-35 can't be beaten, according to a pilot that has flown it," *The National Interest*, September 29, 2019; accessed August 9, 2022.

7. Paleja, Ameya, "Material modeling and 3D printing Makes Discoveries Possible in Weeks Now," *Interesting Engineering*, April 20, 2022, accessed August 6, 2022.

8. Losey, Stephen, "US Air Force Picks Five Companies to Prototype Next-Gen Engines," *Defense News*, August 19, 2022. Accessed same day.

9. Losey, Stephen, "Future NGAD Fighter Jets Could Cost 'Hundreds of Millions' Apiece," *Defense News*, April 28, 2022. Accessed August 14, 2022.

10. Hollings, Alex, "Air Force Announces NGAD Fighter Will Be Fast-Tracked into Service," *Sandboxx,* June 2, 2022, accessed August 14, 2022.

11. "What Would Push the West and Russia to Nuclear War?" *The Economist*, August 2, 2022. Accessed August 22, 2022.

12. Dempsey, Michael, BBC News: "A mind reading combat jet for the future," Technology of Business reporter July 26, 2022, accessed August 8, 2022.

13. Tingley, Brett, "Can the US Miliary Make an Airplane Invisible to the Naked Eye?" *The War Zone,* December 19, 2019. Accessed August 14, 2022.

14. Tylor Rogoway, "F-35 And F-117 Spotted Flying with Mysterious Mirror-Like Skin," *The War Zone,* January 24, 2022. Accessed August 14, 2022.

POSTSCRIPT

So, how do we take stock of this program—has it been a success, a debacle, or something in between? Like the human experience, it's not the parental challenges of raising a rambunctious teenager that matter in the end. It's the contribution that teenager makes as an adult. The F-35 has created an asymmetric military advantage for the allied community of F-35 users. It has realigned historical alliances, particularly in the Arctic region and the NATO borders surrounding the Russian-Ukraine conflict. It has transformed the global defense industrial base with the advent of precision machining and complex composite structure to meet the new stealth manufacturing challenges.

A recent press release by the Government of Canada, the last original partner country to commit to procurement of the F-35, stated,

> Canada is confident that the F-35 represents the best fighter jet for our country at the best price for Canadians. During the finalization phase of the procurement process, the US government and Lockheed Martin with Pratt & Whitney successfully demonstrated that an agreement to purchase the F-35 fighter jet meets Canada's requirements and outcomes, including value for money, flexibility, protection against risks, performance and delivery assurances. Today's announcement is also excellent news for Canadian businesses and workers in the Canadian aerospace and defense sector.

This even though the current Canadian administration ran on an anti-F-35 campaign and were absent from the public announcement.

To date, the F-35 operates from twenty-six bases worldwide, with nine nations operating F-35s on their home soil. There are now nearly one thousand F-35s in service with more than two thousand pilots and 14,000 maintainers trained on the aircraft. In December 2022, Germany announced it would procure a fleet of Lightning IIs for its air force. LtGen Michael Schmidt, the F-35 program executive officer, said, "Congratulations to Germany on procuring the F-35A. Germany is the ninth foreign military sales country to join the program." This brings the number of countries (including the US) that are flying or that have committed to buy the F-35 to a total of eighteen.

To economic analysts, the F-35's direct economic impact on the US economy is approximately $34 billion annually. This includes money spent on internal manufacturing and final assembly activities as well as direct spending with multiple tiers of suppliers and a broad range of sustainment activities. These activities in turn spur $38 billion of indirect economic activity, the money that flows out into the broader non-aerospace economy.

Lockheed's cap of 156 aircraft produced per year is driven purely by the supply chain. Should the United States decide to purchase fewer aircraft each year, there seems to be more than enough international demand to make up the difference.

Will the F-35 live to its full potential? It appears to be on that path, but only the great tyranny of time will tell.

EPILOGUE BY TOM BURBAGE: THE BEAUTY OF BUCKET LISTS AND SPECIAL THANKS

As the longtime leader of the F-35 Program and a former naval aviator and test pilot, I had a few "bucket list" items after seeing the movie *Bucket List* with Jack Nicholson and Morgan Freeman. Two of those were connected with the multinational partnership of the F-35.

First, I wanted to fly as many of the airplanes that F-35 was replacing as possible. I may be able to claim an advantage over the current test pilot studs in that I flew the F-111 with the Australian Air Force and the Tornado with the Royal Air Force, which very few of the current crop of test pilots are old enough to claim. My richest experiences as the industry lead on F-35 was to interact with the test pilot community and fly their airplanes with them.

I had the great opportunity to fly the F-18 with the Canadians at Cold Lake, where civilization ends at the end of the runway and the Canadian wilderness presents a special challenge for their defense. I flew the F-16 with the Dutch Air Force over the North Sea, evaluating their embedded training system and the British Tornado on a very low-level route over Wales. It was an E-ticket ride, but when the weather closed to the top of the tail, we both agreed it was time to abort the run. We went vertical in a 6G pull up to a clear sky above.

In a very special and consequential flight, I got to fly the VAAC Harrier at Boscombe Down in the UK and get a close look at the unified control system concept, which later became the foundation for the F-35B STOVL flight control models. It gave me a perspective and opportunity to influence the ultimate decision on this critical piece of the F-35B concept.

I also had the opportunity to fly the 737 Cooperative Avionics Test Bed, better known as the CATBIRD. The BAE Systems program manager, Paul Nafziger, was one of my instructors going through the Navy Test Pilot School nearly fifty years earlier. We flew the initial flight test profile prior to modifying the airplane to become the F-35 virtual wingman.

One of the most interesting and consequential flights was not in an airplane—it was in a simulator where the great NAVAIR engineer Buddy Denham had me fly his very innovative Magic Carpet Ride software designed to simplify the aircraft carrier landing process. It was an eye-opener for me and a number of other decision-makers and changed carrier flight operations dynamics forever. **(See Figure 31: Bucket List Item 1)**

As a former Naval Academy Crew rower, I have kept up a lifelong commitment to the sport. My second bucket list item was to have the opportunity to row in all the F-35 Partner Countries. I rowed with the Dutch Men's Masters Team on a wintry day at the University of Rotterdam. The Dutch are a very hardy group and no strangers to the cold, but the journey was twice as long as I thought. At the end it was a great gathering around a roaring fire with all their girlfriends. All the rowers were wearing their F-35 Ball Caps. **(See Figure 32: My Dutch rowing partner)**

In Australia, I had the opportunity to row with the Men's National team as they prepared for the upcoming Olympics. Like all Aussies, they are driven and to join them I had to run in the dark to the starting point to join up with the team. I left my hotel to jog down to the boat house but was suddenly confronted by a large, angry kangaroo who, after catching my breath, I sidestepped and continued on by. I joined the coach in a double scull as he coached the Men's Eight and then raced them at the end. All of this as the sun was coming up over Lake Burley Griffin in Canberra which was a sight I will always remember.

In the UK, I had the opportunity to row a double scull on the canals leading up to the Henley, site of the famous Oxford-Cambridge crew races. I also got to row on the Tiber River in Rome. Although I have not yet completed this Bucket List item, I will continue to use this excuse to make my life complete since my flying days are over.

SPECIAL THANKS

This book has taken a long time to write and has involved many individuals who contributed immeasurably to the human story of the F-35. A special thanks to Jeff Morris. Jeff was an original participant in this project. He was one of the heroes we often send in to right the ship and he played a key role at a critical time in getting much of the onboard software working. His advice and participation during a number of interviews left an enduring positive mark on this book.

We conducted more than 100 interviews over several years which revealed many of the interesting back stories on this journey. All the interviews contributed to the authors' attempt to chronicle the journey but not all were quoted or referenced in the story. To those that were not, a special thanks for your insight and perspective.

Despite many challenges, both technical and personal, the F-35 story is a human journey and the story of a unique combination of global personalities that somehow came together with a commitment to "make it happen" over a long period of time. Thanks to all of you.

USG leaders
  OSD
        Frank Kenlon, Acting Director, International Cooperation, Office of the Under Secretary of Defense for Acquisition, Technology and Logistics

  USAF
        The Honorable Dr. Donald B. Rice, 17th Secretary of the Air Force
        General Phillip M. Breedlove, Commander U.S. European Command 17th Supreme Allied Commander Europe
        General Gary L. North, Commander, Pacific Air Forces

  USMC
        General James F. Amos, 35th Commandant of the Marine Corps
        Lt Gen Michael Hough, F-35 PEO
        Lt Gen Jon M. Davis, USMC Deputy Commandant for Aviation
        Lt Gen George Trautman, USMC Deputy Commandant for Aviation
        Lt Gen Harold Blot (ret), LM Deputy VP/GM F-35
        Maj Gen David Heinz, F-35 PEO
        Lt Col Dave Berke, Commanding Officer, Marine Fighter Attack Training Squadron 501

  USN
        Vice Admiral Joseph W. Dyer, Commander, Naval Air Systems Command

Vice Admiral David J. Venlet, F-35 PEO
Rear Admiral Steven Enewold, F-35 PEO
Vice Admiral Mathias Winter, F-35 PEO

Joint Program Office Program Executive Officers (JPO PEOs)

USMC Lt Gen Michael Hough	PEO 1999-2001
USAF Lt Gen John L. Hudson	PEO 2001-2002
USN RAdm Steven L. Enewold	PEO 2002-2006
USAF Lt Gen Charles R. Davis	PEO 2006-2009
USMC Maj Gen David Heinz	PEO 2009-2010
USAF Lt Gen C. D. Moore	Deputy PEO 2009-2011/ Acting PEO 2010
USN VAdm David J. Venlet	PEO 2010-2012
USAF Lt Gen Christopher Bogdan	PEO 2012-2017
USN VAdm Mathias W. Winter	PEO 2017-2019

Other Government Joint Program Office Leaders

Matt Mulhern	JPO F-35 Program Manager
Paul Wiedenhafer	JPO Lead Operational Requirements
Doug Ebersole	JPO Director of Engineering/Chief Engineer
Kelly McCool	JPO Deputy Director of Engineering/Chief Engineer
Pam Ansalvish	JPO Test Readiness Review Chair
Will Urshel	JPO Software Director
Buddy Denham	Naval Air Systems Command Flight Controls Director

Lockheed Martin Leaders

Tom Burbage	Executive VP/GM F-35 Program/Program Integration
Harry Blot	Deputy F-35 Program Manager
Orlando Carvalho	Executive VP/GM F-35 Program
Dan Crowley	Executive VP/GM F-35 Program
Larry Lawson	Executive VP/GM F-35 Program
Lorraine Martin	Executive VP/GM F-35 Program
Jeff Babione	Executive VP/GM F-35 Program

Santi Bulnes	Vice President, F-35 Vehicle Systems
Glenn Miller	Vice President, LM Systems Engineering
J.D. McFarlan	Vice President, F-35 Test and Verification
Jeff Peck	Vice President, F-35 Sustainment
Jeff Morris	Vice President, F-35 Mission Systems Software
Norm Malnak	Vice President, F-35 Mission Systems
Bob Hansen	Director, F-35 Mission System Software
Sam Russo	Director, F-35 Sensor Integration/Fusion
Kevin Zummo	Director, F-35 Helmet Mounted Display/Cockpit Displays
Tom Blakely	F-35 Technical Director/LM Vice President Engineering
Art Sheridan	F-35 Director SWAT, Director Affordability
Jude Olsen	LM Manager Organizational Development
Wayne Elbers	F-35 Director, Cooperative Avionics Test Bed
Jim Latham	F-35 Director, Business Development, Europe
Steve Over	F-35 Director, Business Development, Australia
Don Kinard	LM Senior Technical Fellow for Production Operations
Mike Packer	LM Director, Production Strategy

Northrop Grumman Leaders

| Janis Pamiljans | VP F-35 Program/Deputy F-35 GM |
| Mark Tucker | VP F-35 Program/Deputy F-35 GM |

Pratt Whitney Leaders

Bennett Croswell	VP F-119/F-135 Program; President PW Military Engines
Tom Farmer	VP F-135 Program; President PW Military Engines
Bill Gostic	VP F-135 Program
Bob Cea	VP PW Joint Strike Fighter Concept Development Program
Frank Gillette	Chief Engineer, F-119 and JSF F-119 Programs
Ed O'Donnell	VP International Programs and Business Development

BAE Systems leaders
- Martin Taylor — VP F-35/Deputy F-35 GM
- Ian Reason — VP F-35 Sustainment, US Operations/Global Alignment

GE Military Engines leaders
- Jean Lydon-Rogers — President, GE Military Engines
- Rick Kennedy — Director Communications, GE Military Engines

Test Pilots
- Tom Morganfeld — LM X-35 Chief Test Pilot
- Turbo Tomassetti — USMC X-35 Test Pilot
- Simon Hargreaves — BAE Systems X-35B Chief Test Pilot
- Justin Paines — BAE Systems X-35 Test Pilot
- Jon Beesley — F-35 Chief Test Pilot
- Al Norman — F-35 Chief test Pilot
- Jeff "Slim" Knowles — F-35 Test Pilot
- RN Cdr Phil Hayde — RN Lead UK Military Experimental Test Pilot

International Partners
UK
- Admiral Sir George Zambellas-First Sea Lord and Chief of Naval Staff
- Rear Admiral Simon Henley JPO National Deputy/MoD F-35 Director
- Air Vice Marshal Mark Green, JPO National Deputy
- Simon Hargreaves — BAE X-35B Chief Pilot
- Justin Paines — RAF X-35 Test Pilot
- CDR Phil Hayde — RN Lead UK Military Experimental Test Pilot

Netherlands
- Lt Gen Ben Droste — Commander, Royal Dutch Air Force
- Col Bert de Smit — Director, Netherlands F-35 OT&E Flight Test

Italy

General Giovanni Fantuzzi	Commander, Air Force Logistics Command
Admiral Cavo Dragone	Chief of Italian Defense Staff

Turkey

Mr. Murat Bayar	Secretary of Defense Industries
Mr. Osman Okyay	CEO, Kale Aero

Australia

Air Chief Marshall Sir Angus Houston	Chief, Defence Force
Air Chief Marshall Mark Binskin	Chief, Defence Force
Dr. Steven Gumley	CEO Defence Material Organization
Air Marshall John Harvey	Chief, Capability Development
Air Marshall Mel Hupfeld	Air Commander Australia
Air Marshall Geoff Brown	Chief of Air Force
Air Vice Marshall Cath Roberts	Commander, Space Force
Air Vice Marshall Kim Osley	Head, Capability Transition, RAAF
Mr. Rohan Stocker	CEO Marand Precision Engineering
Mr. Mark Sherrer	CEO Ferra Aerospace, Inc

Denmark

Lt Gen Lars Fynbo	Chief, Air Materiel Command
Maj Gen Anders Rex	Chief, Danish Air Force
BGen E.T. Pedersen	Danish National Deputy, F-35 JPO
Kai Paulsen	F-35 Engineering Director, Danish MoD
Lars Knudsen	F-35 Program Director

Norway

General Stein Nodeland	Chief of Staff Norwegian Air Force
Morten Tiller	Deputy Inspector General
Pal Bjorseth	Program Director F-35

Canada

General Andres Deschamps   Chief of Royal Canadian Air Force

General Tom Lawson   Chief of Defense Staff, Canadian Armed Forces

Israel

General Ido Nehustan   Chief, Israeli Air Force

General Emir Eschel   Director General Israeli MoD/ Chief Air Force

ACRONYM LIST

active electronically scanned array (AESA)
advanced short takeoff and vertical landing (ASTOVL)
Advanced Tactical Fighter (ATF)
aircraft intermediate maintenance departments (AIMD)
Air Power Australia (APA)
autonomic logistics global sustainment (ALGS)
autonomic logistics information system (ALIS)

bottom-up review (BUR)

Canadian dollars (CAD)
carrier variant (CV)
ceramic matrix composites (CMC)
chief of the defense force (CDF)
Commanding Officer (CO)
communications, navigation, and identification (CNI)
concept demonstration phase (CDP)
conventional takeoff and landing (CTOL)
Cooperative Avionics Test Bed (CATB)
countermeasures (CM)

Defence Materiel Organisation (DMO)
Defense Advanced Research Projects Agency (DARPA)
diminishing manufacturing sources (DMS)
director of operational test and evaluation (DOT&E)
display aperture system (DAS)

electro-hydrostatic actuation system (EHAS)
electronic warfare (EW)
electro-optical tracking system (EOTS)
European Participating Air Forces (EPAF)

European Union (EU)
executive committee (EC)

final assembly and checkout (FACO)
foreign military sales (FMS)
Future Combat System (FCS)

Government Accountability Office (GAO)

head-up display (HUD)
Her Majesty's Ship (HMS)

Initial Operational Capability (IOC)
integrated power pack (IPP)

Joint Advanced Strike Technologies (JAST)
Joint Executive Steering Board (JESB)
Joint Program Office (JPO)
Joint Strike Fighter (JSF)

landing signal officer (LSO)
Lockheed Martin (LM)
low-rate initial production (LRIP)

Mission Systems and Training (MST)
multifunction advanced data link (MADL)
multilevel security (MLS)
multi-role fighter (MRF)

Naval Advanced Tactical Fighter (NATF)
Naval Air Systems Command (NAVAIR)
North Atlantic Treaty Organization (NATO)

observe-orient-decide-act (OODA)
Office of the Secretary of Defense (OSD)
Operational Concept Document (OCD)
operational data integrated network (ODIN)

operational test and evaluation (OT&E)
Operational Test and Evaluation Force (OPTEVFOR)

production, sustainment, and follow-on development (PSFD)
prognostic health management (PHM)
program executive officer (PEO)

radar cross section (RCS)
Republic of Vietnam (RVN)
Royal Aircraft Establishment (RAE)
Royal Air Force (RAF)
Royal Australian Air Force (RAAF)
Royal Canadian Air Force (RCAF)
Royal Navy (RN)

security cooperative participants (SCP)
short takeoff and landing (STOL)
short takeoff and vertical landing (STOVL)
STOVL Weight Attack Team (SWAT)
System Development and Demonstration (SDD)
system program office (SPO)

thrust vector lever (TVL)
Tomahawk land attack missile (TLAM)
Total System Performance Responsibility (TSPR)
Turkish Aircraft Industries (TAI)

United Kingdom (UK)
United States Air Force (USAF)
United States dollars (USD)
United States Marine Corps (USMC)
United States Navy (USN)
unmanned aerial vehicle (UAV)

vectored-thrust aircraft advanced-flight control (VAAC)
vertical short takeoff and landing (VSTOL)
vertical takeoff and landing (VTOL)

INDEX